"He loves a good deal of rum..."

Military Desertions during the American Revolution, 1775-1783

VOLUME THREE

Joseph Lee Boyle

Copyright © 2022
Joseph Lee Boyle
All Rights Reserved

Published for Clearfield Company by
Genealogical Publishing Company
Baltimore, Maryland

ISBN 9780806359540

Introduction

The first two volumes on deserters were published in 2008 and 2009 respectively by Genealogical Publishing for Clearfield Books. The present volume includes advertisements missed earlier. Most of the names are new, but a few appear in the earlier volumes, though advertised in different papers.

After the initial *rage militaire* died away in 1775, the Patriot cause suffered throughout the war from a chronic shortage of men. Numerous methods of enlistment were tried by the thirteen states and the Continental Congress, but all fell short. While battle casualties, accidents, and especially diseases depleted the ranks, the pernicious problem of desertion continually sapped healthy men from the ranks who were critically needed.

One of the fundamental problems with the Continental Army was that the many Americans were reluctant to establish a European style professional army with long term enlistments, for fear of a strong military leader seizing the government. Short term enlistments were initially the standard, and these continued to some degree throughout the war. Without a professional attitude soldiers were much more likely to be casual about remaining in ranks for the full term of their enlistment period.

At the outset of the war, Washington was reluctant to enlist non-native born men or "Old Countrymen" as he doubted their loyalty. The number of foreign born deserters listed in these volumes would seem to justify his concern, though one wonders whether this was substantially higher than the American born population.

Men were both hesitant to enlist, and deserted for a number of reasons. One of these was the harsh punishments inflicted for relatively minor violations. Civilians refused to enlist as they heard stories from deserters and returning soldiers about the arrogance and severity of the Continental officers. Stories such as a man who received 50 lashes for cutting up his blanket, did nothing to encourage military service.

Untrained officers arrogantly flaunted their authority over, and used it to abuse the enlisted men. In September 1776, General Henry Knox condemned the officer corps as "A parcel of ignorant, stupid men who might make tolerable soldiers, but bad officers." After the mutiny of the Pennsylvania Line in 1781, a Congressional committee commented that "there Seems to be an irreparable breach between the Men and their officers, and a Total want of Confidence." This contrasted to 1775 when officers were often elected by the men themselves and fraternization was entirely too close.

Service in the Continental Army was indeed the stuff of legend for the fortitude and perseverance of those who stayed. Hardships due to poor or non-existent food and clothing, infrequent pay days and those in the face of rampant inflation, fear of combat, homesickness, family problems, crowded unsanitary life in camp, and rampant disease were all contributing factors to soldiers refusing to join, or abruptly leaving military life. Washington wrote happily in June 1777 that "By paying off the Troops and keeping them well supplied with provisions &ca. desertions have become much less frequent." Unfortunately this was the exception not the rule.

Bounties, a cash bonus for enlisting, were offered by both the states and Congress. As early as July 1775 men were leaving one regiment for another on promises of leave or money. The "enlistment bonus" is still in use today, but during the American Revolution they proved to be counterproductive as the states and Congress offered competing and varied bounties of cash, land and clothing. South Carolina went so far as to offer potential recruits "one sound Negro" for each year of military service. At one point Virginia offered 400 dollars and 300 acres of land to men who would enlist for the duration of the war.

The "bounty war" resulted in states bidding against each other for the services of a potential soldier. This motivated some men to enlist, receive a bounty, and then desert and re-enlist in another unit, in order to get another bounty. A soldier who was executed in 1778, had been convicted of deserting seven times. The increasing bounties also caused resentment in the ranks among those who had enlisted for lesser amounts, who envied the bounties of those newly enlisted. This sense of unfairness in turn encouraged some to desert and reenlist in another unit to receive the higher bounty.

Men were also financially tempted to leave for service aboard privateers-privately owned military vessels which had government authority to serve as commerce raiders against enemy shipping. Through rich captures a common seamen could earn far more than a foot soldier, though here too disease, abominable living conditions, fear of capture, and the added perils of the sea, made such service difficult.

In America for most of the war, a skilled workman, could earn far more than a soldier, and even common laborers could make more. This was particularly true during the prime agricultural season when farmhands were in short supply. In July 1777, when private soldiers were paid 6 2/3 dollars a month, David Grier lamented To Anthony Wayne that laborers were being paid a dollar or more per day "which Intirely Prevents any success in Recruiting therefore."

Some deserters went to the enemy, but more often they seem to have gone home. Though the army sent detachments out to get them, but their friends and families sheltered them. In 1780 Washington wrote that in many instances, "Deserters which have been apprehended by Officers, have been rescued by the People." Others moved to Vermont or west of the Alleghenies to avoid capture. In 1783, Washington wrote the "Grants" a mountainous area between New Hampshire and Vermont were "populated by hundreds of Deserters from this Army...."

An accurate measure of the rate of desertion cannot be obtained for a variety of reasons, the lack of accurate records being the foremost. It was unusual, but not unknown for men to be shown dead on a muster roll for a given month, and then appear in a successive month as alive. Fraud also occurred. Some recruiting officers recorded nonexistent enlistments and desertions in order to embezzle the bounty money and obtain the bonus they themselves received for enlisting a soldier.

The most thorough study of the subjects estimates the average desertion rate in the Continental Army at 20 to 25 percent. The desertion rate declined significantly in the latter years of the war, as the army became more professional. In 1777 the New Jersey line had a 42 percent rate of desertion but after 1778, the rate averaged about 10 percent. It is likely that any compiled figures are too low, as the reports of sick absent soldiers contained many who had deserted.

By contrast European armies of the period averaged a 10-12 percent desertion rate. Though the British forces for the duration of the war in North America and the West Indies averaged only slightly over four percent. Perhaps being in enemy territory reduced the likelihood of desertion. But the Hessian mercenaries deserted at a rate of almost 16 percent. In August 1778, civilian Ebenezer Buck considered that there were so many deserters on both sides that he "believed we keep about even with them."

In 1775 Congress adopted Articles of War, specifying military crimes and punishments. The verbiage closely followed the British code, but with milder penalties. Washington and many other officers felt the milder penalties were a large part of the lax discipline in the American army. He asked Congress to establish new rules which they did in September 1776, with tougher penalties, but still not as stringent as the British.

The average number of lashes in 1775 was thirty-nine, whereas British soldiers sometimes received 500 to 1,000. After Congress passed new Articles of War in 1776, the average penalty was 100 lashes, unless there were additional violations such as deserting to the enemy. Then they might be sentenced to serve for the duration of the conflict to service on a Continental man of war, after receiving 100 lashes, or to death.

Washington tried, but was unable to convince Congress to increase the maximum number of lashes to 500, in order to have an interim punishment between 100 lashes and death. He considered confinement at hard labor, but this may have been only slightly worse than standard Continental Army service.

The most severe penalty for desertion was death, usually by hanging. One study found that of 225 sentences of death, only 40 to 75 were actually carried out. Last minute reprieves were common. In May 1780, eleven men were scheduled to be executed, all but one for desertion. Their graves had been dug, eight were on ladders with the ropes around their necks, when a reprieve for ten of the men came from Washington. The one man who was executed, James Coleman, was considered more culpable than the others and was convicted of having forged discharges enabling more than 100 soldiers to leaving the army, including himself.

In another case Joshua Egins of the Third New York was sentenced to be hanged at West Point in October 1780 "for repeated Desertion and leaving his Post when Sentinal at two different times near the Enemy." Despite the seriousness of his crimes, he was given "a full and free pardon" the following month.

A survey of orderly books showed 142 convictions for desertion in 1776 with an all time high of 157 in 1781. But relatively few of the men tried for desertion are found in the advertisements for deserters in these volumes, indicating the ads were not very useful, and may have been part of the reason such ads declined in usage. This, with the increasing professionalism of the Continental Army, likely account for the decreased numbers of deserters after 1777.

In addition to the laws made by Congress, each state had its own law for dealing with deserters from state and militia units. But these do not seem to have been very effective either. And of course the British, Hessians and French all had their codes and punishments.

Occasional mass pardons to deserters were not uncommon in armies of the period. Washington offered general pardons four times, the first on April 6, 1777. In 1782 a pardon was even made to deserters who joined the enemy. Ironically these general amnesties may have acted as such acts often do, encouraged short term violators to remain away. Few deserters took advantage of the pardons, (many may never have heard about them), but the amnesty encouraged others to desert, believing another pardon would issued. Washington "found so little good result from them…desertion is rather encouraged than remedied by a frequent repetition of them."

The British themselves used pardons and rewards for deserters from the Americans. In 1777, deserting revolutionaries would receive a full pardon, purchase of their weapons, and tracts of land for those who enlisted in the British forces for two years.

The Americans tried to entice the Hessian mercenaries to desert from enemy, playing up the frictions between the British and German troops. After the French army arrived in America, they also tried to bolster their ranks from the enemy. In 1780 a proclamation "To GERMAN DESERTERS" promised "proper encouragement" for those who enlisted in the French regiments.

Both sides enlisted prisoners of war and deserters despite repeated bad experiences and various cautions. While the Continental Congress forbad enlistment of prisoners of war in 1778, the continual push to fill the ranks ensured that it still occurred. If a soldier was a prisoner of war, and escaped from the usual lose security where he was being held, was he a still a POW, or a deserter? Recruiters hungry for cannon fodder were unlikely to discriminate.

The various states had their own laws for dealing with deserters, granting rewards for those who captured deserters, and severe penalties for those aiding and abetting the violators. But these did not seem to work any better than those of Congress.

This compilation is from thirty-eight newspapers published from Massachusetts to South Carolina from 1775 to 1783. It should be noted that none of the papers had a complete run for the period, sometimes for business reasons, other times due to the war such as the British occupation of Philadelphia in September 1777. The *Virginia Gazettes* are included in this compilation. Publication of them stopped when the British invaded the state in January 1780, and few notices appear after a new *Virginia Gazette* appeared in 1782. As Virginia permitted her Southern neighbors to recruit in the state, Virginia papers have many advertisements for men deserting from Georgia and Carolina units,

As there were no newspapers published in North Carolina and limited editions from Georgia and South Carolina, few listings will be found for the three southernmost states. All deserter notices in the newspapers have been included. Though most are from the various American units, British, German, and French are also included, as well as naval deserters from both sides.

Advertisements that are largely illegible are not included. Advertisements for the same man or men in successive issues of the same newspaper, or substantially the same in different newspapers are included in the same entry.

Minor differences in the advertisements in different papers are spelling such as trousers/trowsers and 7/seven. When substantial differences between advertisements occur, both versions are included. In some cases verbiage which is considered irrelevant has been eliminated.

A number of Negroes and Indians will be found listed in these advertisements and are listed by race as well as by surname. The American Army was integrated, something that it would not achieve again until the last all Black unit was abolished in 1954. But they faced slavery again if captured as in 1779, British General Clinton issued an order that all Negroes "taken in Arms, or upon any military Duty" were to be purchased for the public service and the money paid to the captors. He also forbad the sale of runaway slaves who sought refuge with the British, and granted all Negroes who "shall desert the Rebel Standard, full Security to follow within these Lines, any occupation he may think proper."

Perhaps the fear of capture led to increased desertions among Black soldiers. Many modern historians have lauded the thousands of Blacks who served in the Continental Army. But in March 1782, Lieutenant Colonel Olney of Rhode Island posted an ad that said, "It has been found, from long and fatal Experience, that Indians, Negroes and Mulattoes, do not (and from a total Want of Perseverance, and Fortitude to bear the various Fatigues incident to any Army) cannot answer the public Service; they will not therefore on any Account be received."

Olney also restated what had been obvious for years that "Experience also confirms how little Reliance we can place on Foreigners, who, not being interested in the Event of the present important Contest, mean only to be Soldiers of Fortune; and no sooner do they riot away their Bounties, or meet with uncommon Fatigues in the Field, than they seek the earliest Opportunity shamefully to desert the Service they solemnly engaged to remain in." Olney ordered that "To avoid future impositions of this Sort, none will be received except those who have served Three Years or upwards in the Continental Army, and can produce an honorable Discharge, or such as are lawfully married, and have resided Three Years or more within this State."

Besides being free with others property, some deserters also brought off other booty. In 1778 South Carolina, John Eymerie advertised for deserter Peter Bourdajau, who eloped with Eymerie's wife and took a horse and hundreds of pounds of property. Two years later Serjeant Bainbridge was another enterprising deserter, who leaving British service he "brought off Captain Steward's wife, two privates, six horses, and a considerable sum of hard money."

For further reading:

Alexander, Arthur J. "Desertion and Its Punishment in Revolutionary Virginia," *William and Mary Quarterly*, 3rd ser. (April 1946), 383-397.

Alexander, Arthur J. "A Footnote on Deserters from the Virginia Forces During the American Revolution," *Virginia Magazine of History and Biography* 55 (1947), 137-146.

Bowman, Allen. "The Morale of the American Revolutionary Army," Washington, D.C.: American Council on Public Affairs, 1943.

Butterfield, Lyman H. "Psychological Warfare in 1776: The Jefferson-Franklin Plan to Cause Hessian Desertions." *Proceedings of the American Philosophical Society* 94 (June 1950).

Chandler, Jonathan. 'To become again our brethren': desertion and community during the American Revolutionary War, 1775-83. *Historical Research,* May 2017, 90 363-380.

Edmonson, James H., "Desertion in the American Army during the Revolutionary War," PhD diss., Louisiana State University, 1971.

Fantina, Robert, *Desertion and the American Soldier, 1776-2006*, (New York: Algora Publishing, 2006.

Neagles, James. *Summer Soldiers: A Survey and Index of Revolutionary War Courts-Martial,* Salt Lake City: Ancestry Inc., 1986.

Neimeyer, Charles Patrick. *America Goes to War: a Social History of the Continental Army,* (New York: New York University Press, 1996.

Royster, Charles, *A Revolutionary People at War: The Continental Army and American Character, 1775-1783*, New York: W. W. Norton & Company, 1981.

Scudieri, James Domenic, "The Continentals: A Comparative Analysis of a Late Eighteenth-Century Standing Army, 1775-1783," PhD diss., City University of New York, 1993,

Tate, Thaddeus W. Jr. "Desertion From the American Revolutionary Army." MA Thesis, University of North Carolina, 1948.

Ward, Harry M. *George Washington's Enforcers: Policing the Continental Army*, Carbondale: Southern Illinois University Press, 2006.

1775

Baltimore, March 29, 1775.
DESERTED
FROM the BALTIMORE INDEPENDENT COMPANY, on the night of the 24th inst. a certain *Thomas Freshwater*, he is an Englishman, about 5 feet 7 inches high, swarthy complexion, long black hair, much given to drink, and when drunk, very impertinent: had on a sute of Drummers clothes. It is suspected that some of the *Tories* of this place, have been assistants in his escape, and forwarded him to Annapolis, where he has been since seen, WHOEVER apprehends said deserter, and will deliver him to me, shall receive
a reward of FORTY SHILLINGS.
MORDECAI GIST.
The Maryland Journal; and Baltimore Advertiser, March 29, 1775.

DESERTED from Capt. Putnam's Company, in Col. Mansfield's Regiment, *George Douglas*, who had on a short blue Coat, with white metal Buttons, long white Trowsers, and round Hat; and *William Gould*, who had on a round Jacket, long white Trowsers, striped linen Shirt, and an old round Hat. It is desired that they may be taken up, and brought to Head-Quarters in Cambridge.
The New England Chronicle: or, The Essex Gazette, From June 15, to June 22, 1775; From June 22, to June 29, 1775; From June 29, to July 6, 1775.

DDSERTED [*sic*] from Capt. Saunders's Company, of Col. Serjeant's Regiment, John Gardner, and Archibald Smith.—If they will return within ten Days from the Date they will be receiv'd; if not 5 Dollars will be paid for each, upon their delivery to
Capt. Saunders, at Cambridge.
The Boston-Gazette, and Country Journal, July 10, 1775; July 31, 1775; August 7, 1775. Later ads correctly spell Deserted.

DESERTED from Roxbury Camp, of Col. John Fellow's Regiment, in Capt. Moses Soul's Company, one Jonathan Hartley, a well-set Fellow, about five Feet nine Inches in Heighth; had on when he went away, a deep blue broad cloth Coat, somewhat worn, with a striped cotton Vest, leather Breeches, white cotton Stockings; and old Country-man, talks with a Brogue, pretends to doctor, professes to have great Skill in curing [Fe]vers. Whoever shall take up said Fellow, and return hm to said Regiment, or confine him in any of the

American Goals, shall have all necessary Charges
paid by   MOSES SOUL, Captain.
July 10, 1775.
The New England Chronicle: Or, The Essex Gazette, From July 6, to July 13, 1775; From July 13, to July 20, 1775.

DESERTED from Roxbury Camp, of Col. John Fellow's Regiment, in Capt. Moses Soul's Company, an old Country Fellow, named James Lee, dark Complexion, black curl'd Hair, about 35 Years of Age; had on when he went away, a brown fustian Coat, a striped linen Vest, black leather Breeches, his Stature five Feet seven Inches. Whoever shall take up said Fellow, and return hm to said Regiment, or confine him in any of the American Goals, shall have all necessary Charges
paid by   MOSES SOUL, Captain.
The New England Chronicle: or, The Essex Gazette, From July 6, to July 13, 1775; From July 13, to July 20, 1775.

RUN away from the subscriber, in *Peytonsburg, Pittsylvania* county, the 24th of *June,* an *English* convict servant man named JOHN WILLIAMS; he carried with him a claret coloured frieze coat, a light coloured *Newmarket* do. either bearskin or beaver coating, two osnabrug and a pair of osnabrug trousers, a pair of leather breeches, and a rackoon hat lined with green persian. He is a thick well set fellow, about 5 feet 9 or 10 inches high, light hair, a brazen look, and is very fond of spirits, has several large warts on his hands, and a very remarkable scar on his upper lip, right under his nose, thus X. He formerly teached a reading school at this place, for about six or eight months past. As he understands the *Prussian* exercise very well, I expect he will endeavour to pass for a deserter from general *Gage,* or some of his majesty's troops. I will give 5 l. reward for him if taken in *Virginia,* and 10 l. if taken in *Carolina, Maryland,* or *Philadelphia,* or secured in any of his majesty's jails, so that I get him.
HENRY WILLIAMS.
The Virginia Gazette, Purdie, August 4, 1775; August 11, 1775; August 18, 1775; September 1, 1775; September 8, 1775; September 15, 1775

DESERTED from the provincial service in the colony of Connecticut, on the 23d day of August, a soldier belonging to the 8th company in the 7th regiment, commanded by Charles Webb, Esq; Colonel, a well-set fellow, about 28 years of age, 5 feet 8 or 9 inches high, understands the manual exercise well, has been a sailor, talks much of

his honesty; he call'd his name when he inlisted Eli Betts, but his proper name is Eliphalet Studavant; had two suits of cloaths, the one short blue, the other striped red, and a white small castor hat, half worn, with a black ribbon and a carv'd silver buckle round the crown. Whoever shall take up said fellow and secure him in any of the provincial goals, or return him to the camp, at Greenwich, in Connecticut, shall have a reward of One Dollars, and all reasonable charges, paid per me,
          WILLIAM G. HUBBELL,
            Captain of said Company.
The New-York Gazette; and the Weekly Mercury, September 11, 1775; September 18, 1775.

          WATERTOWN, September 18.
The following lists of the persons now in Boston goal, and who have died there, for no other crime than that of being friends to their country, was brought out of Boston a few days ago....
Cornelius Tunison, deserted from the American Camp, and confined for attempting to get back.
The Pennsylvania Gazette, September 27, 1775.

D*Eserted from Captain Lemuel Stewart's Company, in Col. Easton's Regiment, Coonrod Dason, Loring Jinks, Jonathan Boid and Benjamin Davis.—Whoever shall take up said Deserters, or either of them; and return them to his or their Company, shall have FIVE DOLLARS Reward for each of them that they return to the Company, and all necessary Charges paid,*
         by me,   LEMUEL STEWART, Capt.
The Boston-Gazette, and Country Journal, October 16, 1775; October 23, 1775; October 30, 1775.

        DESERTED from Colonel Brewer's regiment and Captain Harvey's company, one Simeon Smith of Greenfield, a joiner by trade, a thin spar'd fellow, about 5 feet 4 inches high, had on blue coat and black vest, a metal button on his hat, black long hair, black eyes, his voice in the hermaphrodite fashion, the masculine rather predominant: Likewise one Matthias Smith, a small smart fellow, a sadler by trade, grey headed, has a younger look in his face, is apt to say I swear ! I swear ! and between his words will spit smart; had on a green coat, and an old red great coat; he is a right gamester, although he wears something of a sober look: Likewise one John Daby, a long hump shoulder'd fellow, a shoemaker by trade, drawls his words, and for comfortable says comfable, had a green coat, thick leather breeches, short legs, lost some of his fore teeth. Also one John Guilson, a man well known in Sunderland, wears a watch, midling stature, a cooper by trade, has a black beard, wears a light colour'd coat and jacket, and has a surly look: Likewise his brother in law Gideon Graves, about a midling stature, somewhat stocky, his looks, jestures and words generally crabbed, had on a fad red coat, a pale blue vest, dark brown thickset breeches, and had a large cutlass.—They have been apt to make excuses for their running away, and intimate they took a dislike to one Eliphalet Hastings, who was put in Ensign over them, and found much fault with the continental allowance. Whoever will take up said deserters and secure them or bring them into camp, shall have two dollars reward for each, and all necessary charges paid by me,

MOSES HARVEY, Capt.

Prospect-Hill, Nov. 8, 1775.

P. S. Said deserters have been gone some time, and because I expected they would return, I have omitted advertising them.

The New England Chronicle: or, The Essex Gazette, From November 2, to November 9, 1775; From November 9, to November 16, 1775; From November 16, to November 23, 1775.

WILLIAMSBURG, *November 15, 1775.*

BROKE jail on *Monday* the 13th instant *(November)* a remarkable light mulatto slave, named DICK, the property of mr. *Anthony Lamb* of *Amelia,* about 20 years old, 5 feet 5 or 6 inches high, has a down look, a scar in his upper lip, short dark hair, and dark eyes; had on, a red lappelled sailor's waistcoat, narrow osnabrug trousers and shirt, a cocked hat, and shoes and stockings. He has been run away for 18 months past, and went by water as a freeman, till last summer, when he enlisted as a soldier, in *Princess Anne* county, under capt. *Davis,* by the name of *Will. Thompson,* and came to this city, where he was taken up, and committed to jail. I imagine he will again try to pass for a freeman, and endeavour to get on board some vessel, or return to *Princess Anne,* where I hear he left a crop of corn. Whoever secures him in any jail, so that I get him again, shall have 40s. and if brought home to me 3 l. reward.

JOHN LAMB.

The Virginia Gazette, Purdie, November 17, 1775; November 24, 1775; December 1, 1775.

FIVE GUINEAS REWARD!
BROKE out of the Provost's Custody last Evening, *William Shields*, a private Soldier in the 40th Regt. He is about 21 Years of Age, five Feet three Inches and three Quarters high, brown Complexion, round Vissage, grey Eyes, and brown Hair. He was born in *Glasgow*, in the County of *Lonrick*, and is by Trade a Butcher. As it is by no means likely that the said Person has got out of Town, whoever will secure him so that he may be again restored to the Custody of the Provost, shall have Five Guineas Reward from
    W. CUNNINGHAM, Provost-Martial.
 N. B. All Persons are hereby cautioned against harboring or concealing said *Sheilds*, as they would be answerable for the Consequences; he being committed for robbing a Store when Sentry.
         Boston, November 11, 1775.
The Massachusetts Gazette; And The Boston Weekly Advertiser, November 30, 1775.

RAN-AWAY from the Subscriber, about the latter end of May last, an Apprentice Lad, named JACOB BALDWIN, about twenty Years of Age, short and slim built, with a pale Countenance. He listed in Capt. JAMES CLARKE's Company, in the CONTINENTAL ARMY; but having left that Service, I forbid all Persons harbouring him, as they would avoid the Penalty of the Law in such Case made and provided. Whoever will take up said Apprentice, and bring him to me, shall have FOUR PENCE Reward, and necessary Charges
    paid by ICHABOT BARTLETT.
         Lebanon, December 7, 1775.
The Norwich Packet and the Connecticut, Massachusetts, New-Hampshire, and Rhode-Island Weekly Advertiser, From December 4, to December 11, 1775; From December 11, to December 18, 1775.

1776

         Camp, Prospect-Hill. Jan. 7. 1776.
DEserted on the 3d instant, from Capt. *Nathan Fuller*'s Company, Col. *Bond*'s Regiment, a Soldier named *Benjamin Johnson*, about 25 years of age, five feet ten inches high, of a sandy complexion, had on when he deserted a grey surtuit, a green strait body'd coat, a small brimmed hatt, he is a little pock-broken, speaks good english, he is supposed to have gone to Little Compton in Rhode Island, where he lived the last winter, he served last campaign in Capt. *Willbery*'s Company, in Col. *Church*'s Regiment. Whoever will take up and

return said Deserter, shall have two Dollars reward, and all necessary charges paid

by   *Nathan Fuller* Capt.
The Boston-Gazette, and Country Journal, January 8, 1776.

THIS is to give notice, that *JOHN BUFFEN*, who has been recruiting in the Jerseys, as well as in Philadelphia, whose men were taken from him by Capt. Stewart, Ranaway with a shirt marked G. M. a linen map handkerchief, and a new pair of shoes belonging to the subscriber, at the sign of Hudibras. He had on when he went away, a green coat, red jacket, a pair of ribbed fustian breeches, a pair of spotted worsted stockings, new shoes, and beaver hat; he is about 5 feet 6 inches high, fresh coloured. Whoever takes up said John Buffen, shall receive Two Dollars, paid by me
GEORGE MILLWARD.
The Pennsylvania Ledger; or the Virginia, Maryland, Pennsylvania, & New-Jersey Weekly Advertiser, January 20, 1776.

Whereas Jonathan Silly, Jacob Fowler, and Jacob Blasdel of Brimfield, inlisted under me the subscriber, some time past, and have not joined my company: It is desired they would immediately repair to their quarters at Charlestown camp, No. 3, otherwise they may depend on being published deserters.
THEODORE BLISS, Captain.
The New England Chronicle: Or, The Essex Gazette, From January 18, to January 25, 1776; From January 25, to February 1, 1776; From February 1, to February 8, 1776.

Camp, Dorchester 20th Feb. 1776.
DESERTED from Capt. William King's *Company, Col.* Ward's *Regiment, one* Simeon Woodworth, *he belongs to Norwich, in Connecticut, appears to be about* 23 *years of Age, of hardly midling Stature, but well set, has light Hair, dark Eyes, and is of a dark Complexion; served the last Campaign in Capt. Angel's Company, Colonel David Brewer's Regiment. Since his Desertion, has inlisted by different Names two or three Times, into some of the Regiments raised in Connecticut marched to Cambridge, and (persevering in his Villainous design of ruining himself, and defrauding the Continent) has deserted from thence—He can tell a large Story, and if disbelieved (which is sometimes the Case) can avow the Truth of it, by the most horrid Imprecations. Whoever will take up said Deserter, and return him to the Subscriber, or confine him in Goal, and give due*

Notice of the same, shall receive FIVE DOLLARS Reward, and all necessary Charges.
W. KING, Captain.
The Boston-Gazette, and Country Journal, February 26, 1776; March 11, 1776.

DESERTED on the 16th March, Inst. from the second regiment of New-York colony forces, and Capt. Mill's company, a William Dority, who had on a pale blue coat, turned up with deep blue. Also a William Wilson, in a plain dress of brown. They stole two firelocks, some cloathing such as shirts and shoes, and about 7 l. in cash. Any person that will apprehend and bring them before any Committee, shall receive FOUR POUNDS lawful money,
from me, GOOSE VAN SCHAICK, Colonel.
The New-York Gazette; and the Weekly Mercury, March 25, 1776; April 1, 1776; April 8, 1776; April 11, 1776.

RUN away from the naval service of this province, PETER HIGGINS, about five feet seven inches high, born in the west of Ireland, fair complexion, stout made, broad shouldered, sandy coloured hair, had on when he went away, a brown cloth jacket, white cloth breeches, coarse blue yarn stockings. Whoever will take up said deserter, shall have FOUR DOLLARS reward
paid by JAMES MONTGOMERY.
The Pennsylvania Journal, and the Weekly Advertiser, April 3, 1776; May 1, 1776.

DESERTED from Captain Edward Seagrave's company, in Col. Joseph Read's regiment, Charles White, a native of Ireland, and a noted rogue. Also, Benjamin Rose, who was in the Rhode-Island last year. Also, John Antony, David Long and David Star, all in the service the last campaign. Whoever will take up said deserters, or either of them, and bring them to their company and regiment, shall have Three Dollars reward for each, and all necessary charges
paid by me, EDWARD SEAGRAVE, captain.
The New England Chronicle: Or, The Essex Gazette, From March 28, to April 4, 1776.

DESERTED from Captain Edward Seagrave's company, in Col. Joseph Read's regiment, Elijah Eames, about 23 years old, dark complexion, black hair, pretends to be hard of hearing, about five feet nine or ten inches high, came from Sherburne, supposed to be concealed by some evil-minded people. Also, George Peters, a native of the Jerseys, about five feet three or four inches high, black strait hair, of a pale swarthy countenance, a shoemaker by trade, has received advance pay of two captains. Whoever will take up said deserters, and bring them to their company, shall have FIVE DOLLARS reward for each, and all necessary charges

paid by me, EDWARD SEAGRAVE, captain.

The New England Chronicle: Or, The Essex Gazette, From March 28, to April 4, 1776; April 25, 1776.

John Mitchel, an Irishman, about 5 feet 6 inches, pretty well set, pitted with the small pox, aged about 23 years: Also Thomas Blandfield, an Irishman, about 5 feet 3 inches, middling set, much pitted with the small pox, much of the brogue and an everlasting talker: and Thomas Fuller, about 5 feet 7 inches, says he was born in Jersey, in Europe, but of a dark swarthy complexion, much in appearance like a Portugeeze with a prodigious down look. Whoever will take up all or either of them shall have FIVE DOLLARS a Head, and all necessary charges paid by, *William Mills*, Lieutenant in Capt. Symonds's Company, and Col. Dan. Hitchcock's Regiment.

Prospect Hill, April 1, 1776.

The Boston-Gazette, And Country Journal, April 22, 1776; April 29, 1776.

DESERTED from Col. Edmund Phiney's regiment, and Capt. Hart Williams's company on the 13th of April, STACY BLUSH, belonging to Barnstable; of dark complexion, short black hair, about 5 feet 9 inches high.—And also, JEREMIAH CLARK, said he came from Connecticut; of dark complexion, about 5 feet 8 inches high; he is about 21 years of age; had on when he went away, a cloth coloured regimental coat, turned up with white bright buttons, and a red waistcoat. Whoever shall take up said deserters, or either of them, shall be handsomely rewarded

by me, HART WILLIAMS, Capt.

Boston, *April* 23, 1776.

The New England Chronicle: Or, The Essex Gazette, April 25, 1776; May 2, 1776; May 16, 1776.

THE following Prisoners, lately Officers in the British Navy, who had given their Parole of Honor not to depart from the Bounds of the Town of Northampton without Leave from the Commander in Chief, did, in the Evening of the 27th Instant, abscond and run-away, viz. *Henry Edwin Stanhope*, 24 Years of Age, has lightish Eyes, Hair and Complexion, pitted with the Small-Pox, has a large Nose, and is about

5 Feet 6 Inches in height. Also, *George Gregory*, 24 Years old, with light coloured short hair, light Complexion and thin favoured, about 5 Feet 8 Inches high. They took away a young Stone Horse, almost black, with a white Face and Hog Mane, and an old red roan Gelding, both good horses. It is hoped the greatest Vigilance will be exerted to apprehend the said Prisoners, who, in return for the Indulgence shewdthem, have basely violated their Word of Honor. FIVE DOLLARS, and all necessary Charges will be paid for apprehending and securing either of them.

Per Order of the Committee of Northampton.
     ROBERT BRECK, Chairman.

The Printers in this and the neighbouring Colonies are desired to insert the above in their several Papers.

         Northampton, April 29th, 1776.
The New-York Gazette; and the Weekly Mercury, May 6, 1776.

     Head Quarters, WILLIAMSBURG, *April* 19, 1776.
DESERTED from the *Halifax* regular Company (now in this City) on *Wednesday* the 16th Instant, three Soldiers, *viz.* JOSEPH MITCHELL BLAIR, about 23 Years of Age, 5 Feet 8 or 9 Inches high, has a wide Mouth, blue Eyes, black Hair, and fleckled Face. He carried with him a dark coloured new Hunting Shirt. His inside Clothing I do not remember.— JAMES TROOP, about the Age of *Blair*, about 5 Feet 10 Inches high, has blue Eyes, dark curling Hair, stoops in his Shoulders, but otherwise well made. He carried with him a dark coloured Hunting Shirt. What other Clothes he had I do not know.— WILLIAM HILL, 19 Years of Age, 5 Feet 8 or 9 Inches high, spare made, of a dark Complexion, with black Hair and black Eyes. He had with him a striped *Virginia* Cloth Hunting Shirt, which he has dyed almost black, a Snuff coloured Coat, blue Duffil Waistcoat, and Leather Breeches.—The above Deserters carried away three of the Country's Rifles. They were enlisted in *Halifax* County, to which I expect they will endeavour to return. —Any Person or Persons who will deliver the above Deserters to the Company to which they belong, or secure them so that I may get them, shall be handsomely rewarded by
     NATHANIEL COCKE, Captain.
The Virginia Gazette, Purdie, May 10, 1776.

     HEAD QUARTERS.
   WILLIAMSBURG, *May* 7, 1776.
DESERTED from the *Pittsylvania* regular company now in this city, on *Monday* the 6th instant, four soldiers, *viz. Philip Atkinson*, 30 years

of age, about 5 feet 11 inches high, well made, has black hair and black eyes, and a dark complexion; he carried with him an old hunting shirt died black, a blue duffil *Newmarket* coat, a pair of new shoes, a new blanket, and blue leggings. *Walter Walters,* about 35 years of age, and is 5 feet 11 inches and a half high; he carried with him a black and white mixed *Virginia* cloth coat and waistcoat, new hat and shoes, also a new blanket. *William Freeman,* about 23 years of age, 6 feet high, has light coloured hair, blue eyes, and stoops in his shoulders; he carried with him a copperas striped coat and waistcoat of *Virginia* cloth, new leggings, shoes, and a blanket. *William Davis,* a native of *Great Britain,* has black hair and eyes, is about 5 feet 11 inches high, and spare made; he carried with him a light coloured *Kersey* coat and leather breeches, but his inside clothing I do not remember. The above deserters carried with them four of the country's rifles, and were listed in *Pittsylvania,* to which county I imagine they will endeavour to return. Whoever delivers the above deserters to the company to which they belong, or secures them so that I may get them, shall have 5 l. reward for each.
     THOMAS HUTCHINGS, captain.
 The Virginia Gazette, Purdie, May 10, 1776; May 24, 1776

DESERTED from capt. *Ruffin's* company, *Benjamin Harrison,* about 6 feet high, with light hair, gray eyes, large nose, a thin narrow face, and looks badly. Whoever brings the said *Harrison* to me, in *Williamsburg,* shall have 3 l. for his trouble.
     BILLEY H. AVERY, lieutenant.
 The Virginia Gazette, Purdie, May 10, 1776.

        Albany, 27th of March, 1776.
    TWENTY DOLLARS Reward.
DESERTED, on the 25th inst. in the evening, from the Second New-Jersey regiment, and company of Captain Richard Howell, the two following persons, viz.
 JACOB INGHAM, about twenty-two years of age, 5 feet 8 or 9 inches high, light hair, pale complexion, and grey eyes. The other named JOHN PATTERSON, about the same age, well sett, 5 feet 10 inches high, dark hair and dark complexion, blue eyes. Both of the men are very active and civil, and were little suspected of desertion. Whoever takes up said deserters, and confines them so that they may be sent to join their regiment, shall receive the above reward or ten dollars for each.
     ISRAEL SHREVE, Lieut. Colonel.

The Pennsylvania Journal; and the Weekly Advertiser, May 15, 1776; May 29, 1776.

HEAD QUARTERS,
WILLIAMSBURG, *May* 15, 1776.

DESERTED from my company of continental regulars, now in this city, *Nathaniel Lane,* 5 feet 10 inches high, about 21 years old, is likely, and well formed, has a round face, good features, dark eyes, short curled hair, florid complexion, downcast look, is a sober serious fellow, and talks very little. Whoever delivers the said deserter to me shall have 5l. reward.
THOMAS MASSIE.

The Virginia Gazette, Purdie, May 17, 1776; May 24, 1776; May 31, 1776.

HARTFORD, May 20.

Last Saturday night, the infamous Samuel M'Kay, a Captain in the British service, and well known in this and several of the neighbouring towns, with his servant, nam'd M'Farland who were lately taken prisoners at St. John's, and station'd at this place, made their Escape. M'Kay, is a tall, well set fellow, about 40 years of age, light colour'd hair and eyes, and carried with him several suits of regimental clothes. M'Farland is about 6 feet high, thin and well made, black hair and eyes—It is supposed they are gone off or Canada, where M'Kay has a wife and family; and as he lived many years in that province, and has considerable influence among the Canadians, it is likely he will use his utmost endeavours to spirit them up against the colonies, it is therefore hoped every lover of his country, will keep a good look out for him Ten dollars reward for M'Kay, and Five for M'Farland, and all necessary charges will be paid, to the person who shall take them up, and deliver them to the Committee for the prisoners in this place.

The Connecticut Courant, And Hartford Weekly Intelligencer, May 20, 1776; *The Connecticut Journal,* May 20, 1776; *The Connecticut Gazette; And the Universal Intelligencer,* May 24, 1776. See *The Connecticut Journal,* May 29, 1776, and *The Connecticut Courant, And Hartford Weekly Intelligencer,* September 16, 1776.

FIVE POUNDS REWARD

DESERTED from my Company of the 7th Regiment of *Virginia* Forces, at *Gloucester* Courthouse, on the 15th Day of *April* last, JOSEPH HASKINS about 5 Feet 10 Inches high, stout

robust made, of a swarthy Complexion, and wears his own dark Hair.—Also, EPHRAIM TURPIN, a Lad about 17 or 18 Years old, about 5 Feet 9 Inches high, of a fair Complexion, wears his own Hair, and is very indifferently dressed, without Shoes or Stockings. He was taken up some Time ago, and underwent a trial by a Court-martial at *Williamsburg,* agreeable to whose Sentence he received 15 Lashes for the same Offence, and was ordered to join his Company, which he has failed to do. I will give 5l. Reward for *Haskins,* and 50s. for *Turpin,* to any Person who will deliver them safe at *Gloucester* Courthouse.
                    CHARLES FLEMING.
    The Virginia Gazette, Dixon and Hunter, May 25, 1776; June 1, 1776; June 8, 1776.

                    HARTFORD, May 27.
    The infamous Capt. M'Kay, who is so lost to every principle of honor as to violate his parole, and endeavour to make his escape, as mentioned in our last, was last Monday apprehended and taken by a number of gentlemen at Lainsborough, in Berkshire county, and on Wednesday following was safety brought to this town and lodged in the common goal. His servant, M'Farland, together with a certain John Graves of Pittsfield, were likewise taken with him, and both are committed to prison. Graves is an inhabitant of Pittsfield, in the province of Massachusetts's Bay, where he has considerable property: but, being instigated by the devil and his own wicked heart, he had undertaken to pilot Capt. M'Kay to Albany, and had procured fresh horses on proper stages on the road to expedite his flight.
    The Connecticut Journal, May 29, 1776; *The Continental Journal, And Weekly Advertiser,* May 30, 1776. *The Continental Journal* spells the third man's name as Greaves and Graves. It also ends with: "QUERE, *What does the last mentioned Villain deserve?* See *The Connecticut Courant, And Hartford Weekly Intelligencer,* May 20, 1776, and *The Connecticut Courant, And Hartford Weekly Intelligencer,* September 16, 1776.

                NORTHUMBERLAND county,
                YEOCOMICO, *May* 10, 1776.
DESERTED last night from the *American Congress* sloop of war, the following persons, *viz.*— *Richard Pearl,* born in *Virginia,* 32 years of age, 5 feet 8 inches high, stout, well made, black hair, and swarthy complexion; he is an artful ill looking fellow, and probably may change his name.— *Randolph Biggs,* born in *Fairfax* county, *Virginia,* 19 years of age, 5 feet 7 inches high, brown hair, and is a likely well

made lad.— *John Morgan,* born in *London,* 21 years of age, 5 feet 6 inches high, brown hair, and pitted with the small-pox.— *James Bartlett,* born in *London,* 24 years of age, 5 feet 4 inches high, fair hair, and is a thin spare lad.— *William Wood,* born in *London,* 22 years of age, 5 feet 2 inches high, fair hair, pitted with the small-pox, and plays a little on the fife.—Whoever apprehends the said deserters, and secures them so that they may be returned to their company, or sent to *Alexandria.* shall receive 20s. for each, and reasonable charges,
    paid by
JOHN ALLISON, captain of marines.
The Virginia Gazette, Purdie, June 21, 1776; July 12, 1776; July 19, 1776.

DESERTED from my Company, Col. Shepherd's Regiment, one JAMES LOWD, an old Countryman, 30 years of age, 5 feet 3 Inches high, dark Complexion, and dark Hair, has a Scar on the Head, and was bred to the Sea. Whoever will take up said Deserter, and commit him to any Goal in the United States, so that he may be returned to his Regiment, shall receive TEN DOLLARS reward, and all necessary Charges paid, by MOSES KNAP, Captain.
The Independent Chronicle and the Universal Advertiser, June 26, 1777; July 3, 1777.

RUN away from the Subscriber in *Prince William*, on *Kettle Run*, a Servant Man named JAMES DEVERIX, an *Englishman*, 20 Years of Age, about 5 Feet 6 Inches high, has a round Face, gray Eyes, and crooked Nose, occasioned by a Blow. He had on, when he went away, a Felt Hat, blue Jacket lined with Plaid, on Osnabrug Shirt, coarse Trousers made of Tow, and old Shoes Half soled; he also took with him a light coloured Half worn Jacket. He has some Letters and Marks upon one of his Hands, and upon one of his Thighs, marked with *Indian* Ink. I expect his Design is to enlist under Pretence of being a Friend to the glorious Cause of *America*, but means only to desert when Opportunity serves. Whoever apprehends, and brings Home the said Servant, shall have 5l. Reward,
    paid by WILLIAM WYATT.
The Virginia Gazette, Dixon and Hunter, June 29, 1776.

DESERTED from the *Muskito* armed vessel, *Isaac Younghusband,* esq; commander, on *Saturday* the 8th instant *(June)* JAMES DONOHO, about 5 feet 10 inches high, near 30 years of age, a portly well set man, has a down look, and the remains of an old sore upon one of his legs, which is not yet perfectly cured. He carried with him two brown linen shirts, a pair of old blue breeches, old yarn stockings, new shoes, and a pair of new wrappers of country made linen. I imagine he is gone to *Bedford,* as his parents live in that county, near *New London.* Whoever brings the said deserter to me in *Richmond* town, or to the vessel, lying at *Warwick,* shall have 3 l. reward.   JACOB VALENTINE.

The Virginia Gazette, Purdie, June 28, 1776; July 5, 1776.

DESERTED from capt. *Spencer's* company of regulars, before they left *Orange* county, *JOHN LAMB,* a tall slim man, about 22 years of age, enlisted by lieut. *Garland Burnley.* He was bred in *Orange,* near col. *Burnley's.—* Also *William Bragg,* who deserted from the camp near *Gwyn's* island the 16th of *June.* He is about 5 feet 10 inches high, about 40 years of age, a stout well made man, much addicted to liquor, and when drunk very talkative and impertinent. He was formerly an inhabitant of *Culpeper,* and lived near *Bradley's* ordinary.—Whoever brings the said deserters to head-quarters in *Williamsburg,* or the camp near *Gwyn's* island, shall have 3l. reward for each.
JOSEPH SPENCER.

The Virginia Gazette, Purdie, July 5, 1776; July 12, 1776; July 19, 1776.

WILLIAMSBURG, *July* 5, 1776.
DESERTED last night from the *College* camp, *James Vaughan,* about 23 years of age, about 6 feet 2 inches high, well made, long black hair, of a dark complexion, and long visage; had on, and carried with him, a new suit of gray broadcloth, an old hunting shirt trimmed with red, old leather breeches, and a green broadcloth coat trimmed with silver lace, which he purchased at *Dunmore's* sale. Also *Josiah Cheathum,* about 22 years of age, 6 feet 6 inches high, [sic] well made, of a very dark complexion, has short black hair, and a dejected look; had on, and carried with him, a pair of good leather breeches, a hunting shirt trimmed with red, and a jacket and pair of breeches of light coloured sagathy, almost new. They were enlisted in *Amherst,* where I suppose they will endeavour to get. Whoever delivers them to the 6th *Virginia* regiment shall have 40s. reward for each, and be allowed all reasonable expenses.
SAMUEL CABELL, captain.

The Virginia Gazette, Purdie, July 5, 1776; July 12, 1776; July 19, 1776. See next ad.

WILLIAMSBURG, *July* 5, 1776.
STRAYED or stolen last night, out of mrs. *Camp's* pasture near this city, a dark brown mare near 5 feet high, about 10 years old, with a blaze face, likely and well made, and very fat, shod before, paces well, but trots in rough roads, not branded, that I remember. She is supposed to be rode off by two deserters from capt. *Cabell's* company of regulars, of the names of *Cheatum* and *Vaughan,* who were enlisted in *Amherst,* and may perhaps be gone that way. I will give a reward of 3l. to any person who delivers said mare to capt. *Robert Anderson* in *Williamsburg,* capt. *Abraham Cowley* in *Richmond,* mr. *Richard Woods* in *Albemarle,* capt. *Gabriel Penn* in *Amherst,* mr. *Sampson Matthews* in *Augusta,* or the subscriber in *Botetourt* ; and if stolen, 6l. on conviction of the thief; or if secured in any county not convenient to deliver her to any of the gentlemen above mentioned, the same reward, upon notice being given to
PATRICK LOCKHART.
The Virginia Gazette, Purdie, July 5, 1776; July 12, 1776; July 19, 1776; July 26, 1776. See previous ad.

DEserted from a company under my command the following persons, viz. Nebediah Olney, a man about 6 feet high, dark complection, black hair. Had on when he went away, a dark coloured Surtuit, a striped linnen jacket, and buckskin breeches, something of an artist at playing the slight [*sic*] of hand, belonging to Providence in the colony of Rhode-Island.—Joseph Gooch, a slim man, 6 feet 1 inch high, lightish complection, and may be remarked by having lost two of his upper teeth. Had on when he went away, a light coloured coat, blue jacket and buckskin breeches, belonged to Braintree in the province of the Massachusetts-Bay. Whoever apprehends and deliver up said Deserters, shall receive Five Dollars for each or either of them, and all necessary charges
paid, by   THO's PIERCE, Major.
The Boston Gazette, and Country Journal, July 8, 1776; July 15, 1776; July 22, 1776. The last ad has "*Chamblee, June 2d,* 1776." at the bottom.

DESERTED from my Company in Col. Swift's Battalion for the Continental Service, *Frederick Barene,* an Irishman, about 35 or 40 Years of Age, a thick well set Fellow, wears his own black Hair, is pitted with the Small Pox, says he lately lived in Boston, and formerly lived at Hartford; has left a Wife and Child at Woodbury. 'Tis said he has listed in another Company. Whoever shall take up said Deserter, and confine him in any of the Goals in this or the neighbouring

Colonies, so that he may be dealt with, shall receive Five Dollars Reward, and necessary Charges,
        paid by   STEPHEN MATTHEWS, Captain.
                                        Waterbury, July 4, 1776.
The Connecticut Journal, July 10, 1776; July 24, 1776. See *The Connecticut Journal*, July 24, 1776.

DESERTED from Jamestown, in the colony of Rhode-Island, on the 26th day of June, 1776, BENJAMIN EAGLESTON, an inlisted soldier in Col. Richmond's regiment, belonging to the company under the commanded of Capt. Westcott. Said Eagleston is of a light complexion, brownish coloured hair, about 6 feet and one inch high, and about 23 years of age, and is supposed to be gone to a place called Little Hoosuck:—Whoever will take up said soldier, and return him to said regiment, or secure him in this or any of the United Colonies, so that he may be had by any of his officers, shall have TEN DOLLARS reward, and all necessary charges,
        paid by   ROZZEL SMITH, Lieutenant.
                                        Jamestown, July 3d, 1776.
The Newport Mercury, July 11, 1776; July 15, 1776. A different ad in *The Newport Mercury*, October 21, 1776, in Volume One of this series spells the name as Egelinstone.

                                        Stratford, July 15, 1776.
TAKEN up and committed to Fairfield goal, a man named Frederick Barne, and Irishman 42 years old, a thick set fellow, pitted with the small-pox, good teeth, wears black uncomb'd hair, says he inlisted at Mendon, 35 miles from Boston, at which place his parents lived, has serv'd in the continental army & was at Longville in Canada about four weeks since; has had a wife Molly in Woodbury, & Nabby in Stratford, but each have now got a bill of divorce; has worked at ditching in many places, he pretends to understand 5 languages, and is supposed to be a deserter advertised by Capt. Matthews, in
        this paper.   WOLCOTT HAWLEY.
The Connecticut Journal, And Weekly Advertiser, July 24, 1776; July 31, 1776; August 7, 1776. See *The Connecticut Journal, and Weekly Advertiser,* July 10, 1776.

WHEREAS the House of the Subscriber was Broke open the 23d Instant, and the following Articles Stolen from thence, viz. Two Silver Cups, one mark'd the Gift of PETER HAY, to the Church on *Stoneham*; the other the Church of *Stoneham's* Cup—one large Silver Spoon, mark'd E. B. E.   N. R. B. Two pair of Silver Buckels; two

Gold Rings, one flower'd the other plain—Also about *four Pounds* in Silver Money, a Quantity of Paper Money, with a number of other articles. The House of the Subscriber is supposed to be broke open by one *John Potame*, a large young Negro Man, belonging to Capt. DANFORTH's Company now stationed at Boston.—Whoever will take up said *John Potame*, and bring him to the Subscriber or confine him in any of the Goals in the County of *Middlesex*, shall receive THREE DOLLARS Reward,
    by EDWARD BUCKMAN.
            Stoneham, July 22, 1776.
The Continental Journal, And Weekly Advertiser, July 25, 1776. See *The Continental Journal, And Weekly Advertiser*, August 8, 1776.

      SWAN'S POINT, *July* 7, 1776.
DESERTED from my company of the 6th battalion of continental regulars, JOHN CHAMBLIS, 38 years old, 5 feet 10 inches and a quarter high, is well formed, has a thin face, short brown hair, dark complexion, wants some of his fore teeth, of a downcast look, has dark eyes, which are commonly sore, occasioned by hard drinking, and when drunk has a very simple look; he was but indifferently dressed. Whoever delivers the said deserter to me at *Springfield* camp, in *York* county, shall have 40s. reward.
    JAMES JOHNSON, captain.
The Virginia Gazette, Purdie, July 26, 1776; August 9, 1776.

DESERTED from the *Hero* galley, CHARLES FREEMAN, an *Englishman*, about 25 years of age, 5 feet 6 or 7 inches high, pretty full faced, with short brown hair; had on when he deserted a brown sailor's jacket, with an under jacket of scarlet stuff that had been turned, a check shirt, and a pair of osnabrug trousers. Also JAMES MARTIN, an *Irishman*, about 25 years of age, 5 feet 6 or 7 inches high, dark complexioned, and a little marked with the small-pox; had on when he deserted a brown sailor's jacket, a white linen shirt, osnabrug trousers, and a new hat. Whoever apprehends the said deserters, and secures them so that they may be returned to the said galley, shall receive 20s. for each, and reasonable charges,
    From GEORGE MUTER, capt. of the *Hero*.
The Virginia Gazette, Purdie, July 26, 1776; August 9, 1776.

DESERTED from my company of the 6th regiment of continental regulars, two soldiers, *viz. JOHN PHILLIPS*, a likely young man, of the middle size, well made, has black hair and eyes, a forward

talkative person, and in common dresses tolerably well; he carried off with him a silver watch, the property of lieutenant *Dunn,* also a gun and bayonet, and cartouch box full of cartridges, and a blanket, belonging to the country. He has been seen crossing *Shirley Hundred* with all his clothes. *JOSIAH CREW,* about 24 years of age, 5 feet 8 inches high, has red eyes, of a swarthy complexion, and wears his own light hair tied behind. *EDWARD PARKER,* a stout well made man, wears his own light coloured hair, which curls behind. Whoever apprehends the aforesaid soldiers, and conveys them to their company, shall have a reward of 5 l. for *Phillips,* and 40s. for each of the others.
     NICHOLAS HOBSON.
 The Virginia Gazette, Purdie, July 26, 1776; August 9, 1776.

DESERTED from Capt. Wescott's company in Col. Richmond's regiment at Jamestown, on the 23d. inst. July, one JOSEPH SEARS, about 5 feet 10 inches high, thick set, about 30 years old, full-faced and very talkative, brags much of his being in Bunker hill fight, and of being wounded at that time; is of a dark complexion, with brown hair, had on a beaver hat half worn, a brown surtout, black cloth breeches, a speckled vest, the hind part of a different colour, &c.

 Likewise deserted from said company and regiment, with said Sears, [LE]TIX TOBY, a Mustee fellow, about 5 feet high, having short curled hair slender built, is a considerable [fif]er, took with him a brown-thick cloth jacket, and short breeches of the same, is about 17 years of age:—Whoever will take up said deserters, or either of them, and return them to their officer, or secure both or either in any o the gaols of the United States of America, so that both or either of them may be had again, shall receive TEN DOLLARS reward for each, and all necessary charges
   paid by ROZZEL SMITH, Lieut.
The Newport Mercury, July 29, 1776.

DESERTED from Capt. Westcott's company, in Col. Richmond's regiment, on the 20th of July instant, DAVID RELPH, a Corporal in said company; he is about 5 feet 10 inches high, a pretty thickset saucy fellow, had on a white coat, jacket, and breeches, and a ruffled shirt; he is supposed to be gone towards Providence; whoever takes up said deserter and returns him to the company again, shall have TEN DOLLARS reward, and all necessary charges,
   paid by ROZZEL SMITH, Lieutenant.
          Jamestown, July 27, 1776.
 The Newport Mercury, July 29, 1776.

DESERTED from on Board the armed Schooner LIBERTY, the 20th Instant, while lying in East River, two Seamen, viz. ALEXANDER DAWSON about 6 Feet 7 Inches [sic] high, about 30 Years of Age, well made, has straight Hair, and born in *Britain*—JOHN WILLIAMS 5 Feet 6 or 7 Inches high, slim made, has remarkable light Hair, and born in *New-York*; they both had on Check Shirts, spotted Swan Skin Jackets faced with red, and Check Trousers. Whoever secures them, or contrives them on Board said Schooner lying in Rappahannock River, shall have 20s. Reward for each.
                     RICHARD TAYLOR.
The Virginia Gazette, Dixon and Hunter, July 29, 1776.

                     Jamestown, August 3d, 1776,
DESERTED from Capt. Westcott's company, in Col. Richmond's regiment, of Rhode Island forces, on the 31st of July last, one LOUDEN THOMSON, A mustee fellow, about 5 feet 7 inches high, thick sett, full face, with a scar on one of his cheeks, and a scar on his hand shot with a ball; stole from his messmates when he went away clothing of sundry sorts to the amount of 11 dollars:—Whoever will take up said deserters, and return him to his officers, or secures him in any of the States of the United Colonies, so that he may he had by them, shall have 10 dollars reward, and all necessary charges,
            paid by   ZOROBABLE WESTCOT, Capt.
The Newport Mercury, August 5, 1776.

          AGREEABLE to a Resolve of the
Continental Congress, the Committee of the town of Worcester, having liberated Alexander Gardner, and John Thornhill, two prisoners of war, that they might support themselves by their labour, and on the 28th day of July instant they went from this town together, and have not returned. Gardner had on when he went away a red coat, lappelled with buff, buttons marked 10, he has been a drummer in the 23d regiment of Fuzilleers. Thornhill has been a Sailor, had on a blue sailors jacket, speaks something slow, pretty tall. Whoever will take up and return the said prisoners to the Committee of Safety, &c. for the town of Worcester, shall receive Four Dollars reward, and all reasonable charges, or two dollars for either of them.
            NATHAN BALDWIN, Chairman.
                                Worcester, July 30, 1776.
The Massachusetts Spy Or, American Oracle of Liberty, August 7, 1776; August 14, 1776.

DESERTED from my company last July, on JOHN HUNNIFORD, of North-Yarmouth, in the county of Cumberland, about 5 feet 10 inches high. Whoever will apprehend said deserter, and bring or send him to his company, which is on the march for Ticonderoga, or to join the invalids at Brookline fort, or Boston where proper officers will be left to bring up the rear, shall have Five Dollars reward, and all necessary charges paid, by   JERE. HILL.
Captain in the 18th regiment.
N. B. The Select-men and Committees of any town where a deserter is, are desired to take notice of the Resolve of the General Congress concerning deserters.
The New England Chronicle: Or, The Essex Gazette, August 8, 1776.

Sixty DOLLARS Reward.
IN consequence of my advertisement of *February* last, all my men that returned home from *Gloucester* town on furlough, for the recovery of their health, have joined their company, except the three following persons, viz. *Daniel Musick*, a slender made man, 25 or 26 years old, 5 feet 9 or 10 inches high; enlisted in *Orange* county, but since has gone I understand to *Carolina. Thomas Hill*, 23 or 24 years old, 5 feet 9 or 10 inches high; enlisted in *Culpeper* county, but since, as is supposed, is gone to the back inhabitants. *James Berry*, a mulatto fellow, about 30 years old, 5 feet 8 or 9 inches high; enlisted in *Fredericksburg*, but served his time with mr. *Thomas Bell* of *Orange* county. And as I have the greatest reason to suspect they will not return to the regiment, I will give the above reward to any person that will deliver them to any continental officer on his march to head quarters, or to the commanding officer at *Williamsburg,* or 20 dollars for each of them.
JOSEPH SPENCER, capt. 7th regiment.
The Virginia Gazette, Purdie, August 8, 1777; August 15, 1777.

DESERTED *from my company in the first regiment, under marching orders, WILLIAM WOOD, a soldier, 5 feet 4 and a half or 5 inches high, born in* Elizabeth City *county. I have reason to believe he is now in capt.* Calvert's *galley, as, when she lay off* Hampton, *I sent a serjeant for the* deserter, *but was refused him, although the captain acknowledged his having him on board. I take this method, therefore, to acquaint capt.* Calvert *that the said* William Wood *is a* deserter *from my company, and to desire that he may deliver him up*

immediately to the commandant at Hampton, *or any other place where he may have his trial by a court-martial.*
                    EDMUND B. DICKINSON, *captain.*
The Virginia Gazette, Purdie, August 16, 1776; August 23, 1776; August 30, 1776.

                    WILLIAMSBURG, *August* 16, 1776.
DESERTED from the *College* camp, on *Friday* the 9th of this instant EDWARD MARSHAL, a soldier belonging to the 8th regiment, and a recruiting party of capt. *Knox's* company. He had been about a fortnight recruited, and has gone off with one of the country's rifles, and a blanket. He is below the middle stature, of a brown complexion, very talkative, and given to liquor. He had on when he went away an old hunting shirt, ra[gge]d breeches, stockings with holes in them, an old flapped hat, and was very dirty. He was not long since discharged from on board the *Raleigh* cruiser, by capt. *James Cocke,* which discharge I have now in my possession. Whoever secures the said deserter, and delivers him at the camp, shall have 20s. reward.
                EDWARD MOODY.
The Virginia Gazette, Purdie, August 16, 1776; August 23, 1776.

SOME time in *July* last two men deserted from capt. *Taylor's* minute company of the *Lancaster* battalion, who enlisted with one *Jesse George,* to serve in one of the row-gallies. A serjeant was sent for them, and I understand from him he could not get them. The officer who enlisted them is desired to send them to capt. *Taylor,* in *Lancaster* county.
          PETER PRESLY THORNTON.
                Lieutenant-colonel.
The Virginia Gazette, Purdie, August 16, 1776; August 23, 1776.

                FIVE DOLLARS REWARD.
DESERTED from my company of regulars in the 6th *Virginia* regiment, on the 8th instant, JAMES POORE, fifer. He is about 5 feet 5 inches high, spare made, about 18 years old, short hair, and fond of liquor. I do not know what clothes he had on when he went away, or if he carried any with him. He went off in company with some soldiers of the first regiment who were to rendezvous at *Hanover* courthouse, on their way to *New York.* I make no doubt but he will keep with them, as he was born in some of the northern provinces. The gentlemen officers of the first regiment will please to

confine him (if he should be taken in any of their companies) in some jail, or other secure place; and any person who will deliver the said deserter to the camp at *Deep Spring,* near *Williamsburg,* shall have the above reward, and reasonable charges.
   The Virginia Gazette, Purdie, August 16, 1776; August 23, 1776.

Watertown, August 16, 1776.
D*ESERTED from my Company, in Col. Greaton's Regiment, William Parks, of Newton, about* 24 *Years of Age, about* 5 *feet* 10 *inches high. He carried off with him a gun belonging to the Continent. Whoever will apprehend said Deserter, and return him to the Subscriber shall have* Five Dollars *Reward, and all necessary charges*
         paid by   ABNER CRAFT. Capt.
   The Boston-Gazette, and Country Journal, August 19, 1776; August 26, 1776; September 2, 1776. See *The Boston-Gazette, and Country Journal,* September 16, 1776.

RAN away from on board the Scorpion sloop of war, the following seamen, viz. GEORGE PATTERSON, boatswain, a well set man, about 5 feet 8 inches high, brown complexion, short black hair curl'd round, and snub nose: had on a small round hat bound, a blue jacket and narrow trousers. JAMES PARKS, a likely well made man, about 5 feet 7 inches high, brown complexion and black hair, with a cock'd hat: had on a long blue jacket and short wide trousers. JOHN LOWRY, a stout well made man, with a red face, light hair, about 5 feet 6 inches high: had on an old blue jacket and an old pair of narrow duck trousers. THOMAS DAVIS, a slender made man, about 5 feet 10 inches high, dark complexion, and much pitted with the small-pox, and long black hair: had on, a new felt hat, blue jacket, and new osnabrig trousers. DAVID REES, a short slender man, about 5 feet 5 inches high, dark complexion, short strait black hair, and has a great impediment in his speech: had on an old hat, blue jacket, and very dirty shirt and trousers. Whoever takes up the said seamen, and secures them in any gaol so that I can get them, shall receive eight dollars reward for each.
         WRIGHT WESTCOTT.
   The Maryland Gazette, August 22, 1776.

Watertown, August 23. 1776.
DEserted from captain Joseph Keith's company, in colonel Willard's regiment, on their march to Crown Point, an Indian Fellow, named Isaac Barnabas, about 30 years old, 5 feet high. Whoever will take up

said Indian, and return him to said company, shall have all necessary
cost paid, by me,
Joseph Keith, Captain.
The Boston-Gazette, and Country Journal, August 26, 1776;
September 9, 1776.

DESERTED from Capt. Robinson's company, Col. Mott's regiment, one Joel Johnson, about 40 years of age, 5 feet 10 inches high, dark complection, black eyes, short, black hair, a little [   ] shoulder'd, a stout, well made fellow. Whoever will take up said deserter and confine him in goal, or return him to his company at Skeensborough, shall have four dollars reward, and necessary charges paid by
ALEXANDER KING, [Lieut.]
East-Windsor, August 7, 1776.
The Connecticut Courant, And Hartford Weekly Intelligencer,
August 26, 1776.

DESERTED from my company of marines, JAMES ROBINSON of *Louisa* county, about 20 years of age, 5 feet 5 inches high, well made, stoops a little in his shoulders, is of a dark complexion, and wears short black hair; his dress, when he deserted, was an osnabrug shirt and trousers, and a large felt hat. Whoever secures the said deserter, and delivers him to me on board the *Hero* galley, at *Hampton*, shall have 5 l. reward.
BEN: POLLARD.
The Virginia Gazette, Purdie, August 30, 1776; September 6, 1776; September 13, 1776.

AUGUST 8, 1776.
DESERTED from my company of marines, stationed at *Hobb's Hole*, EDWARD RILEY, an *Irishman*, 5 feet 7 or 8 inches high, has the fourth toe of his right foot higher than the rest, and is a well made man; he was seen a few days ago in *Fredericksburg*, and had been up the country to see a mr. *Ball*, with whom he served his time. Whoever delivers him to me in *Hobb's Hole*, within three weeks, shall have TEN DOLLARS reward.
ALEX: DICK.
The Virginia Gazette, Purdie, August 30, 1776; September 6, 1776.

DEEP SPRING camp, *August* 23, 1776.
JAMES WINN, William Colley, James Butler, Joseph Bohanan, Young Stokes, Charles Hudson, Richard Hooper, James

Jones, *and* Sugar Wright, *soldiers of my company of the* 6th Virginia *regiment, who obtained leave of absence some time past, and have been thoughtless enough to let their furloughs run out, and have not returned to the company, I do hereby inform them, that it they should be so neglectful of their duty as not to join the company without loss of time, I shall be under the disagreeable necessity of considering them as* deserters. *I likewise give notice, to such of my company whose furloughs are not yet out, to return punctual to the time expressed in their different furloughs, as they must know that their staying a longer time is not only prejudicial to the service, but prevents others from obtaining leave of absence, who, from bad state of health, are justly entitled to expect it.*
     JAMES JOHNSON, captain.
 The Virginia Gazette, Purdie, August 30, 1776; September 13, 1776.

DESERTED from Capt. Nathaniel Church's company, in Col. Richmond's regiment, SETH CHURCH, about 22 years old, 5 feet 8 inches high, dark hair, light eyes; whoever will take up said runaway and return him to his company, or confine him in any of the goals of the Thirteen United States, shall receive FIVE DOLLARS reward, and all necessary charges,
    paid by LEMUEL BALEY, Captain.
             Newport, August [ ], 1776.
 The Newport Mercury, September 2, 1776.

     STATE of RHODE ISLAND, &. *Aug.* 24, 1776.
     FIVE DOLLARS REWARD.
DESERTED, the 23d instant, from Capt. James Wallace's company, in Col. William Richmond's regiment, JOHN GARDNER, about 37 years of age, 5 feet 7 inches high, dark hair, light eyes, has been on board a man of war several years, and inclines to drink; any person or person who shall apprehend said GARDNER, and return him to his Captain, or secure him in any jail in the United States of America, so that his Captain may have him again, shall receive the above reward, and reasonable charges,
    paid by JAMES WALLACE, Captain.
N. B. All Captains of vessels and others are desired to be cautious of taking the said Gardner on board, on any pretence whatever, as they will be prosecuted according to law, and all his share or shares, of prize or prized, taken, tis expected will be delivered to the Committee of War of the UNITED STATES, for the benefit of said States.
 The Newport Mercury, September 2, 1776.

Cumberland County, West-New-Jersey,
August 26, 1776.
As committed to Cumberland goal, on the twenty-third of August, the following men: JOEL BENNET and JAMES HENDRICKSON, who appears to be Deserters from Capt. Nathaniel Smith's Company of Artillery of Baltimore, by an advertisement in the Pennsylvania Journal bearing date August 13th, 1776, and he is hereby desired to send for them in a short time, or they will be discharged
with paying cost. JOHN SAULLARD, Goaler.
The Pennsylvania Journal and Weekly Advertiser, September 4, 1776.

TEN DOLLARS REWARD.
DESERTED from Perth Amboy, the 13th ult out of Capt. Jacob Fauns's company, belonging to the Flying Camp, JOHN HIMES, about 5 feet 6 inches high, dark coloured hair, brown complexion, full faced, well set, and round shouldered, this country born, and makes his home in the Northern Liberties of Philadelphia. Likewise, WILLIAM BRYAN, (deserted the 2d of September out of the above company) about 5 feet 6 inches high, dark complexion, well set, lately came from Maryland, and says he is a free man. Had on, a pair of coarse leggings, but no shoes. WHOEVER apprehends the abovementioned Deserters, or either of them, shall receive SIX DOLLARS for John Himes, and Four DOLLARs for William Bryan, or the above Reward for both, if delivered to the Gaoler of this city, or to my quarters in Second Street, above the Barracks, at the sign of the blue ball,
paid by Jacob Fauns, Captain.
The Pennsylvania Journal and Weekly Advertiser, September 4, 1776.

DESERTED from the *College* camp, the 2d instant *(September)* a soldier who says his name is *JOHN BOYD,* born in *New England,* and a shoemaker by trade. He is about 30 years of age, 5 feet 9 or 10 inches high, and has some scars, about his mouth; had on a brown hunting shirt fringed, and trousers of the same colour. He told some persons before he went off, that he was going to *York* town for a rifle, and some clothes that he said he left there. He had taken the place of a soldier in my company the day he went away, and I expect he is either gone towards *York* or *Fredericksburg.* Whoever will deliver the

said *Boyd* to my company of the second regiment shall receive 40s. reward, paid by FRANCIS TAYLOR.
The Virginia Gazette, Purdie, September 6, 1776; September 13, 1776.

DESERTED *from Capt. Dixon's Company, in Col. Sage's Regiment, Peter Hastings, of Warren, about 40 Years of Age. Whoever will deliver said Deserter to the Subscriber, in Plainfield, or secure him in Norwich Goal shall have Four Dollars Reward, and necessary Charges, paid by*
ABRAHAM SHEPARD, *Lieut.*
Plainfield, June 23. 1776.
The Providence Gazette; And Country Journal, September 7, 1776; September 14, 1776; September 21, 1776.

DESERTED from Great Barrington the 18th of August last, two soldiers belonging to Capt. Ezra Hicock's company, Col. Brewer's regiment, (after having received £ 7 bounty each) the one named Thomas Meaughir, is about 5 feet 3 inches high, fair complexion, writes a good hand, says he has been a merchant's clerk, born in Waterford, in Ireland, had on a light colour'd wilton coat and striped trowsers. The other named James Stewart, about 5 feet 8 inches high, dark complexion, somewhat pitted with the small pox, says he came from the west of Ireland, and lived near a year in the north part of the county of Hampshire, had on a brown coat and striped trowsers. Whoever will take up said deserters, and return them to my company, on their march to or at Ticonderoga, or confine them in any of the county goals, so that they may be returned, shall have four dollars reward, and all necessary charges
paid by EZRA HICOCK, Capt.
The Connecticut Courant, And Hartford Weekly Intelligencer, September 9, 1776; September 16, 1776.

DESERTED from Capt. Robinson's company, in Col. Mott's regiment, one Joel Johnson, about 40 years of age, 5 feet 10 inches high, dark complection, black eyes, short, black hair, a little round shoulder'd, a stout, well made Fellow. Whoever will take up said deserter, and confine him in goal, or return him to his company at Skeensborough, shall have four dollars reward, and necessary charges
paid by ALEXANDER KING, Ensign.
East-Windsor, August 7, 1776.
The Connecticut Courant, And Hartford Weekly Intelligencer, September 9, 1776.

Deserted from Col. *Selden*'s Regiment, and Captain *William Belcher*'s Company, a Soldier, when he inlisted he called his Name *William Sherman*, but his right name is *Samuel Sherman*: He is about 40 Years of Ae, well built, about 5 Feet 6 Inches high, his Har Locks [*sic*] something gray. Whoever will take up said Deserter and secure him so that he may be had to join said Regiment, shall have Four Dollars Reward, and all reasonable Charges paid by   *Asa Strong,* Ensign.

Sept. 12, 1776.

The Connecticut Gazette; And The Universal Intelligencer, September 13, 1776; September 20, 1776.

DESERTED from capt. *Crump's* company in the 1st *Virginia* regiment, LEWIS SMITH, about 5 feet 10 inches high, about 20 years of age, born in *Brunswick* county, and enlisted out of capt. *Pelham's* minute company at *York.* Whoever apprehends the said deserter, and delivers him to ensign *Minnis* at *Williamsburg,* shall have TEN DOLLARS reward.

MATTHEW SMITH, lieutenant.

The Virginia Gazette, Purdie, September 13, 1776; September 20, 1776; October 4, 1776.

DEEP SPRING, *Sept.* 11, 1776.

ALL the officers, cadets, and soldiers of the 6th regiment, that are absent with leave, are desired to join their regiment immediately, although their limited time of absence should not be expired. Should any soldiers be so imprudent as to disobey this order, they will be looked on as deserters, and treated accordingly.

∴ Wanted in the 6th regiment, a CHAPLAIN, who is allowed by Congress 33 and one third dollars per month, and 2 rations per day.

MORDECAI BUCKNER,
colonel of the 6th regiment.

The Virginia Gazette, Purdie. September 13, 1776; September 20, 1776

DESERTED from on board the *Muskito* cruiser, lying at *Warwick,* capt. *Isaac Younghusband,* two marines, viz. *JESSE WARDEN,* about 5 feet 6 inches high, noted for his great fondness of liquor, and when intoxicated very troublesome. I have reason to believe he is harboured by his relations in *Henrico* or *Hanover,* as he has been an inhabitant of those counties. He carried with him, at the time of his desertion, one

of the country's muskets. *THOMAS MERRYMAN*, about 5 feet 10 inches high, who has a down inoffensive look; he is an inhabitant of *Caroline* county, where I imagine he is gone. Whoever will deliver the said deserters to me in *Richmond* town, or to the officers on board the *Muskito*, shall have 3 l. reward for each.
JACOB VALENTINE.

The Virginia Gazette, Purdie, September 13, 1776; September 20, 1776; October 4, 1776.

IN your paper of the 19th instant, I observed a malevolent & fallacious advertisement, sign'd by Capt. Abner Craft against me, as a deserter from his company in Col. Greaton's regiment.—Also trying to insinuate into the minds of the public, that I had embezzled, or carried off in a clandestine manner, a gun belonging to the Continent.—But lest he should blind the eyes of the public, and continue to treat me in so scandalous a manner, I would inform the public, (as I informed him, some time before his advertisement.) that being unable at, and after the time the regiment march'd from New-York (by reason of bodily indisposition) to follow the company, was recommended to the honorable General Ward for a discharge from the army by Dr. Morgan, director general of the Continental Hospital, who discharged me accordingly. As to the gun which he says I carried off was one that he left me to march with; but as I could not follow the army, and knew not where to leave it at New-York with safety, I brought it to Watertown, where it has remained ever since, and only waits his reception.

I am the publick's humble servant,
Wm. PARKS, Lieut.

Noddles Island, Aug. 20, 1776.
The Boston-Gazette, and Country Journal, September 16, 1776.
See *The Boston-Gazette, and Country Journal*, August 19, 1776.

PORTSMOUTH, *Sept.* 1, 1776.
DESERTED from on board the *Hero* galley, a certain *JOHN HUDSON,* who some time acted on board the said galley as boatswain's mate. He was born in the north of *England*, is about 35 years of age, about 5 feet 10 inches high, has short hair, and of a sandy colour, which curls a little; had on, when he deserted, a short coat of brown cloth, and a red jacket. There is reason to suppose he will endeavour to get to *West Augusta*, as he has some property of land in the neighbourhood of *Pittsburg*. Whoever apprehends the said deserter, and delivers him on board the galley, shall have 3 l. 10s. reward.

GEORGE MUTER.
The Virginia Gazette, Purdie, September 20, 1776; September 27, 1776.

NINE POUNDS REWARD

DESERTED from my company of the 5th battalion, at *College* camp. *Williamsburg, JOSEPH JOLLEY,* 5 feet 10 or 11 inches high, a stout well made man, stoops in his shoulders, has light brown hair, gray eyes, fair complexion, and large whiskers; he is addicted to strong liquor, and when drunk exceedingly talkative and troublesome. He has a family in the lower end of *Henrico* county, where he may no doubt be apprehended. *JOHN ROBINSON,* 5 feet 8 or 9 inches high, slim made, dark complexion, black hair, black eyes, the whites of which are tinctured yellow with the jaundice, is apt to get drunk, and when so insolent and quarrelsome; he also comes from the lower end of *Henrico* county. *THOMAS ROBINSON,* brother to *John,* 5 feet 7 or 8 inches high, swarthy complexion, gray eyes, brown hair, and is somewhat deaf. He went away with a brother that was down to see him on *Saturday* the 14th instant. *Jolly,* and his brother *John,* absconded the same night. Whoever will secure the said deserters, or either of them, and deliver them to the commanding officer at *Williamsburg,* shall be entitled to a reward of 3 l. for each.
JOHN PLEASANTS.

The Virginia Gazette, Purdie, September 20, 1776; September 27, 1776; October 4, 1776.

DESERTED from my company of regulars in the 4th battalion of *Virginia* forces, the 13th of this instant, from *Portsmouth,* two soldiers, viz. *JOHN LANCASTER,* born in the county of *Isle* of *Wight,* 25 years old, 5 feet 9 inches high, stout made, has brown hair, a reddish beard, dark eyes, and is of a down look. As he is acquainted in *North Carolina,* it is supposed he will go that way until the regiment marches. *KINCHEN TURNER,* born in the same county, about the same age, 5 feet 7 inches high, wears his own short dark hair, of a brown complexion, and stoops when he walks; he wore away a dyed hunting shirt faced with red, a check shirt, and a pair of trousers. Whoever apprehends and delivers the said soldiers to the commanding officer in this state shall receive 3 l. for each, and expenses paid.
ARCHIBALD SMITH, captain.

The Virginia Gazette, Purdie, September 20, 1776; September 27, 1776; October 4, 1776. See *The Virginia Gazette*, Dixon and Hunter, September 21, 1776.

Mount-Washington, 8th Sept. 1776.
DESERTED from Col. Forman's regt. of the Jersey new levies, from Capt. John Webster's company, between the first and seventh of this Inst, viz. John Dennis, Phenias Kent, Peter Augustun, Gersham Dunn, Edward Ridgway, Abraham Smock, Jonathan Allin, Bursun Burcaw, and Nathaniel Hodson. From Capt. Haddin's company, Solomon Tharp. From Capt. Abraham Woolley's company, Jacob Wood, Nathan Lyon, Nathan Sutton, Charles Vandike, and James Tallman. From Capt. Peter Wikoff's company, Isaac Childes. Whoever takes up and returns said deserters, shall receive Forty Shillings New-Jersey money, for each, from the subscriber.
DAVID FORMAN, Col.
The New-York Gazette and Weekly Mercury, September 21, 1776; September 28, 1776; October 5, 1776.

RUN away from the Ship Providence, William Ling, about 5 Feet 8 Inches high, has dark Hair, and dark Eyes: Had on when he went away a light blue Jacket, a Pair of Canvas Trowsers, and an old Felt Hat; says he run away from the Phoenix Man of War. Whoever will apprehend said Runaway, and commit him to any Gaol in the United States of America, shall have Five Dollars Reward, and reasonable Charges, paid by
WILLIAM BARRON, Lieut.
Providence, September 18, 1776.
The Providence Gazette; And Country Journal, September 21, 1776; September 28, 1776; October 12, 1776; October 19, 1776; October 26, 1776.

PORTSMOUTH, *September* 15, 1775.
DESERTED from my Company of Regulars, in the 4th Battalion of *Virginia* Forces, the 13th Instant, from *Portsmouth*, two Soldiers viz. JOHN LANCASTER, born in the County, of *Isle* of *Wight,* 25 Years old, 4 Feet [*sic*] 9 Inches high, stout made, has brown Hair, a redish Beard, dark Eyes, and a down Look. As he is acquainted in *North Carolina,* it is possible he will go that Way till the Regiment marches. —KENCHEN TURNER, born in the same County, about the same Age, 5 Feet 7 Inches high, wears his own short Hair, which is dark, his Complexion is brown, he stoops when he walks, and wore

when he went away a died Hunting-Shirt faced with Red, a checked Cotton Shirt, and a Pair of Trousers. Whoever apprehends, and delivers the said Soldiers to the Commanding Officer in this Colony, shall have THREE POUNDS Reward for each, and Expenses paid.
    ARTHUR SMITH, Captain.
The Virginia Gazette, Dixon and Hunter, September 21, 1776; October 4, 1776. See *The Virginia Gazette*, Purdie, September 20, 1776.

              September 22, 1776.
DESERTED from Jonathan Wallen's company, in Col. Richmond's regiment, WILLIAM BORDEN of New Freetown, about 5 feet 7 inches high, near 20 years of age, dark complexion, dark eyes, brown hair; had on, when he went away, a blueish rifle frock, striped towcloth trowsers, and new shoes:—Whoever will take up said BORDEN, and secure him in any of the gaols in the United States of America, or bring him back to aforesaid company, shall receive a reward of FIVE DOLLARS, and all necessary charges,
   paid by   JONATHAN WALLEN, Captain.
The Newport Mercury, September 23, 1776; September 30, 1776; October 11, 1776.

DESERTED, from the brigantine Liberty, lying at Baltimore, the following seamen, viz. On the 10th inst. WILLIAM PUCKINGHORN, a native of New-England, about five feet six inches high, has ilight [*sic*] coloured hair and yellow at the tops: had on when he went away, a drab coloured jacket with a blue cape; when in liquor is subject to fits. On the 17th, two lads, THOMAS CANE and JESSE CLARKSON; Cane is a native of Ireland: had on a red jacket and osnabrig trousers, is lame by reason of an imposthume [*sic*] rising in one of his thighs. Clarkson is a native of Maryland, about fourteen or fifteen years of age, has light hair, a mild countenance, and engaging address. On the 20th, SAMUEL MERCER, ANDREW BAXTER, and THOMAS TIVY; Mercer is of low stature, a native of Ireland, apparently about forty years of age, halts in walking. Baxter is about five feet seven or eight inches high: had on a red jacket, and is remarkably fond of liquor. Tivy is a native of Ireland, about the size of Baxter, has a bad sore on one of his great toes, if fond of liquor, and when drunk very noisy. Any person who secures them, so that I get them again, shall be paid three pounds reward for each, by
    THOMAS LILLY.
The Maryland Gazette, September 26, 1776. Lilly was captain of the Virginia Navy Brigantine *Liberty*.

Five Pounds Reward.
DESERTED from the Recruits raised for the *Georgia* Service, JOHN CHILDERS of Halifax County, WILLIAM COOPER of *Pittsylvania*, MATTHEW THOMPSON of *Bedford*, CHARLES WILSON of *Halifax*, THOMAS ROGERS of *Charlotte*, NICHOLAS MONEY (alias MOONEY) from *Green Brier* DRURY ALFORD of *Albemarle*, and DANIEL HENDERSON of *Staunton, in Augusta.* We have been informed that several of them are gone on the Indian Expedition with Captain *Bates, Irvine,* and *Arbuckle*, Whoever delivers the said Deserters, or any of them, to the Subscribers at *Prince Edward* Courthouse, or secures them so that we may get them again, shall have the Reward for each, paid by
ROBERT & GEORGE WALTON.
SAMUEL SCOTT.
The Virginia Gazette, Dixon and Hunter, September 27, 1776; October 4, 1776. See *The Virginia Gazette*, Purdie, August 1, 1777, for Alford.

DESERTED from my company of the 5th battalion, on the 14th instant, the following soldiers, *viz.* THOMAS MARTIN, about 25 years of age, of a dark complexion, has black hair, had on red plush breeches, &c. and was listed in *Bedford.* ABRAHAM ROWDEN, about 20 years of age, full 6 high, of a fair complexion, has light hair, and was listed in *Halifax* by capt. *Cocks.* TEN DOLLARS reward will be given for each, if delivered at *Williamsburg.*
HARRY TERRELL, captain.
The Virginia Gazette, Purdie, September 27, 1776; October 4, 1776; October 11, 1776.

DESERTED the 17th instant, from my company of the 5th of battalion, the following soldiers, *viz.* THOMAS HOLLAND, 5 feet 9 or 10 inches high, about 23 years old, of a fair complexion, and has light hair; and on a silver laced hat, and was very well clothed. *JOSEPH PAYNE,* about 5 feet 8 inches high, about 25 years old, has dark hair, and is dressed as soldiers commonly are; he listed in *Bedford. JOHN FRANKLIN,* about 5 feet 10 inches high, has light hair, of a fair complexion, but has a very ugly down look; wore a common soldier's dress, with a white hat, and was listed in *Williamsburg,* though he came from *Hanover.* TEN DOLLARS reward for each, if delivered at *Williamsburg.*
GROSS SCRUGGS.
The Virginia Gazette, Purdie, September 27, 1776; October 4, 1776; October 11, 1776.

DESERTED the 12th of *September,* from my company of the 5th battalion, the following soldiers, viz. *JAMES SELF,* corporal, a lusty well made man, of a ruddy complexion, 5 feet 10 or 11 inches high, short light coloured hair, and about 25 years old; wear a purple linen coat, with the button holes bound with white. *WILLIAM SELF,* a brother of *James*'s, and much like him, but not quite so tall, or of so ruddy a complexion, about 23 years old. *RODHAM KENNER CRALLE,* about 6 feet 1 inch high, slender made, and round shouldered, of a dark complexion, with black hair and eyes, and 21 years old; he wears a purple linen coat, turned up with green. *FRANCIS WADDY,* about 22 years old, 5 feet 11 inches high, and well proportioned, wears short brown hair, and a brown linen coat, turned up with white. These men were concerned in a mutiny the day before they deserted, and being fearful of receiving their deserts, having foolishly taken this method of escaping.

TEN DOLLARS reward will be given for each, if delivered at *Williamsburg.*

THOMAS GASKINS, jun. captain.

The Virginia Gazette, Purdie, September 27, 1776; October 4, 1776.

New-Haven, October 1st, 1776.
DESERTED from the regiment of artillery commanded by Henry Knox, Esq; an indented SERVANT LAD, named THOMAS ELLIOTT, aged nineteen, about 5 feet 6 inches high, slender made, red hair, has a bad look; had on when he went away a blue coat faced with red, a white flannel waistcoat. Whoever will take up said Elliott, and return him to Colonel Knox, or confine him in goal, shall be well rewarded for their trouble.

P. S. it is supposed he is somewhere secreted in New-Haven by some bad designing people.

The Connecticut Journal, October 2, 1776; October 9, 1776; October 16, 1776.

Deserted, on the Evening of the 21st from Capt. Lemuel Baley's Company, in Col. Lippitt's Regiment, *George Rounds*, a private Soldier: He is about six Foot high, has black Hair, dark Complexion; had on a round felt Hat bound with Yellow, and Frock and Trowsers. Also *Joseph Bosworth*, of the same Company, about 5 Feet & Half high, well set, light Complexion, brown curl'd Hair, both belonging to Swansey. Whoever will take up said Deserters and return them to said Company, (which is on a March for New-York, shall receive Ten Dollars for each, and all necessary Charges paid by me   Lemuel Baley, Capt.

Lyme, Sept. 22, 1776.
The Connecticut Gazette; and Universal Intelligencer, October 4, 1776; October 11, 1776.

RUN away from on board the *Scorpion* sloop, two seamen, viz. ADAM LIDDLE, about 5 feet 6 inches high, 18 or 20 years old, born in *Scotland,* and has a down look; had on, when he went away, a coarse blue jacket, osnabrug trousers, and a new felt hat. JOHN CALVERT, about 5 feet 4 inches high, brown complexion, and speaks in the *North Country* dialect; had on, when he went away, a brown jacket without sleeves, long trousers, and round hat. Whoever takes up the said deserters, and secures them in any jail, shall receive EIGHT DOLLARS for each, and if delivered on board TWELVE DOLLARS.
WRIGHT WESTCOTT.
The Virginia Gazette, Purdie, October 4, 1776; October 11, 1776.

DESERTED from Captain WILLIAM GATES's company in Col. JOHN HOLMAN's regiment; ZEBULON and BENJAMIN CUTTING, both belonging to Worcester, in the State of Massachusetts Bay.—ZEBULON, is about 24 years of age, about five feet ten inches high, of light complection, had on when he went away a claret coloured coat, long white trowsers. BENJAMIN is about 16 years of age, of a light complection, had on when he went away a blue coat. Whoever will take up said deserters and return them to the company about five miles below King's-bridge on New-York island, shall receive eight Dollars, and for either four Dollars, reward.
WILLIAM GATES, Captain.

August 29, 1776.
The Massachusetts Spy Or, American Oracle of Liberty, October 9, 1776; October 16, 1776; October 23, 1776; *The New England Chronicle: Or, The Essex Gazette*, October 23, 1776.

DESERTED *from Col. Lippit's Regiment, on its March to New-York, the following Men, viz.*

Capt. Blackmar's Company. Joseph Hackett, *of Freetown;* Zebede Mathewson, *of Johnson;* Thomas Cobb, John Philips, and Daniel Barnes, *of Gloucester;* Charles Hinging Bottom, and John Emmans, *of Cranston;* Oliver Bates, *of Scituate.*

Capt. Dexter's Company. Benjamin Parker, *of Coventry.*

Capt. Carr's Company. Samford Ross, and *Elisha Allen, of Newport.*
Capt. Fenner's Company. Joseph Inman, and *Barziliai Herendeen, of Gloucester.*
Capt. Hoppen's Company. Stephen Barnes, and *Luke Harris, of Gloucester.*
Capt. Dyre's Company. Peter Franklin, of South-Kingstown.
Capt. Bailey's Company. John Brayman, of South-Kingstown; Thomas Fenner, of Richmond; John Walton, of Warwick.
Capt. Jones's Company. Thomas Caswell, of Dartmouth; Samuel Weaver, Simeon Paine, Squire Woodmansee, Jacob Benson, Abraham Fisher, Eliphalet Hoskins, and *Thomas Wood, of Freetown; Benajah Randon, of Stonington.*
Whoever shall take up the above Deserters, or either of them, and deliver them to any of the Committee of Safety in the State of Rhode-island, or secure them in any Gaol within the United States, shall have Five Dollars Reward for each.
                                      Providence, Oct. 4, 1776.
The Providence Gazette; And Country Journal, October 12, 1776; October 19, 1776; October 26, 1776; November 2, 1776

Deserted from the subscriber, a soldier, belonging to the late Col. Fisher Gay's regiment, named John Bissel, belonging to East-Windsor in Connecticut, a well set man, about 40 years of age, dark complexion, black hair, something grey, marked on the hand with powder prick'd in I B, a light brown coat, metal buttons, a blue jacket, long checkt trowsers. Whoever shall take up said deserter, and return him to the regiment, shall have Five Dollars reward, mad necessary charges paid, by
                SIMON WOLCOTT, Capt.
                                              October 4, 1776.
The Connecticut Courant, and Hartford Weekly Intelligencer, October 14, 1776; October 21, 1776.

DESERTED from the sloop *Susannah,* at *Leeds* town, two soldiers of the 6th *Virginia* battalion, belonging to capt. *Hutching's* company, *viz.* WILLIAM FREEMAN, 5 feet 9 or 10 inches high of a pale complexion, and has long yellow hair, which he wore tied behind; had on when he went away a snuff coloured coat and waistcoat, and has a silver button and loop to his hat. *WILLIAM JONES* 5 feet 8 or 9 inches high, of a brown complexion, and has black hair, which curls a little; had on a dark coloured hunting shirt, striped *Virginia* cloth coat and waistcoat under it, and *Russia* drab breeches. Whoever delivers the said deserters to the commanding officer at *Williamsburg* shall have 5l. reward for each.

        HARDEN PERKINS, ensign.

The Virginia Gazette, Purdie, October 18, 1776; October 25, 1776; November 8, 1776.

DEserted from my Company on his march from No. 4 or Charlestown New Hampshire to Ticonderoga, in Sept. 1776; *Edward Norton*, a well built man about 27 years of age, 5 feet 8 inches high, professes to play with a back sword. Whoever shall take up said Deserter, and convey him to his Company shall have Two Dollars Reward, paid by me,

        TIMOTHY EATON, Capt.

The Boston Gazette, and Country Journal, October 21, 1776.

DESERTED from his company, one David Woodruff, is about 5 feet 10 inches high, dark complexion, black, short hair, rather slow of speech, black eyes. Whoever will take up said deserter and return him to Capt. Robinson, Col. Mott's regiment at Mount Independence, shall have three dollars reward and necessary charges

        paid by,   GIDEON MILLS, Lieut.

                                          Oct. 21, 1776.

The Connecticut Courant, And Hartford Weekly Intelligencer, October 21, 1776; October 28, 1776; November 4, 1776.

DESERTED from Capt. Norton's company at Arlington, an Irishman who says his name is Barnet Rine, is about 20 years of age about 5 Feet 4 inches high, had on a hunting shirt, striped trowsers, a red great coat, a new felt hat, is of a pale complexion, short black hair, had a new gun and bayonet. Whoever will take up said deserter, and return him to his company (Col. Mott's regiment) shall have four dollars reward, and necessary charges

        paid, by   JAMES HECOCK. Ensign.

                                          Sept. 30, 1776.

The Connecticut Courant, And Hartford Weekly Intelligencer, October 21, 1776; October 28, 1776; November 4, 1776.

                      Newport, Head-quarters, Oct. 12, 1776.

DESERTED from Major Elliott's train of artillery, the 6th instant, Thomas Peck, Arthur Burket, Samuel Bartlet, and Giles Talman; whoever shall take up said deserters and return them to their company, or secure them in any of the jails in the United States of American, shall receive five dollars reward for each, and all necessary charges,

        paid by   ROBERT ELLIOTT.

The Newport Mercury, October 21, 1776.

HEAD-QUARTERS,
Newport, Oct. 5, 1776.
DESERTED from the Artillery company, in Col. Richmond's regiment, the 29th inst. one ISAAC ROUNDS, 5 feet 8 inches high, light complexion, light hair, light eyes, carpenter by trade, born at Rehoboth, Boston government:—Whoever will take up and secure the above deserter in any of the gaols of the United States of America, or return him back to said company again, shall have a reward of FIVE DOLLARS, and all necessary charges,
paid by ROBERT ELLIOTT,
MAJOR *of the Train.*
The Newport Mercury, October 21, 1776.

DEserted from my company in col. McIntire's regiment, Japher Ellison, an Irishman, 5 feet 8 inches high, a private soldier, and had on light brown clothes. Whoever will take up said deserter and bring him to the said company or regiment in Fairfield, shall have one dollar reward.   *John Boyden*, Capt.

Hartford, Oct. 1, 1776.
The Connecticut Journal, October 23, 1776; October 30, 1776; November 6, 1776.

TEN DOLLARS REWARD.
DESERTED about three weeks ago, from my company of regulars stationed at *York, William Dickerson,* a likely young fellow about 5 feet 10 inches high, with light brown hair and fair complexion. He was born in *Gloucester* county, where I suppose he is still lurking, and I have some reason to believe he was persuaded by some Tory that he could not be compelled to continue in the service longer than pleasure. I will give the above reward for the deserter, and the same on full conviction of the Tory. I hereby forwarn all persons from harbouring or employing the said deserter, as they shall answer at their peril.
CHARLES TOMKIES.
The Virginia Gazette, Purdie, October 25, 1776; November 8, 1776. See *The Virginia Gazette*, Purdie, November 8, 1776.

STOLEN from the subscriber, living on the north fork of *Roanoke,* in *Boteourt* county, on *Wednesday* the 18th of *September,* a light coloured gray horse about 7 years old, 14 hands high, trots and paces, and is branded thus, but I do not remember on which side. Whoever brings said horse to me, or secures him so that I may get him again,

shall have 40s. reward, and 5l. on conviction of the thief. The person who stole the horse calls himself *William Jones,* says he was born in the west of *England,* and that he had followed the sea. He is about 5 feet 8 or 10 inches high, was much troubled with the fever and ague, and looks sickly; had on a copperas coloured cotton coat, coarse linen jacket and trousers, bad shoes, and speaks in the west country dialect. It is believed he was a deserter from some of the regiments belonging to *Virginia.* FREDERICK SMITH.
The Virginia Gazette, Purdie, October 25, 1776; November 8, 1776; November 15, 1776.

BEHOLD a COWARD!
Head Quarters, Ticonderoga Octo. 22, 1776
THE public is desired to take notice, That *Daniel Pittee,* Ensign in Capt. Timothy Stow's company, Col. Wheelock's Regiment, applyed at Head-Quarters for a discharge, upon hearing that the enemy were likely to attack our lines, he was refused, and next day deserted our camp.—This infamous run-away belongs to the south Parish of Dedham, in the county of Suffolk.
Published by order of Brig. Gen. BRICKETT.
ANDREW BROWN Maj. Brigade.
The Boston-Gazette, And Country Journal, October 28, 1776; November 4, 1776.

RAN away from the ship Providence, ABRAHAM WHIPPLE, Esq; Commander, EPHRAIM DAWLEY of Exeter, in this State, 47 years of age, 5 feet 6 inches high, dark hair, eyes, and complexion: Also THOMAS MITCHILL, of North Kingstown, 26 years of age, 5 feet 6 inches high, darkish hair and eyes, both formerly belonging to Capt. Phillips's company in Col. Richmond's regiment:—Whoever will take up said runaways and convey them on board said ship Providence, shall receive FIVE DOLLARS for each, and all necessary charges, paid by JOHN CHANNING, 2d Lieut.
Newport, Oct. 31, 1776.
The Newport Mercury, November 4, 1776; November 11, 1776.

In the night following the 30th
of instant October, five of the continental prisoners broke out of the goal in Windham, and made their escape, viz. David Wardrop, surgeon, a Scotchman, speaks broad, about 5 feet 10 inches high, between 20 and 30 years old, of a sandy complexion, wears his own hair, and walks with his knees wide asunder, had blue clothes and a new beaver hat cock'd up with hooks & eyes; Richard Tillage, a

midshipman between 20 and thirty years old, wears his own hair of a light brown colour and long, wears blue cloth, is an Englishman, he is a well set man, not tall, has white cloth jacket and breeches; also Samuel Gorge, a marine, a lusty well set man, had a red jacket and metal buttons with an anchor on each button, about 30 years old; also James Bussel, has a bushy head of hair, long foretop, small legs and thighs, and is a worsted comber; also one Joseph Reed, a short thick-set fellow about 22 years old, walks quick and nimble, wears his own hair, of a light brown colour, has a red cloth jacket, pewter buttons with an anchor on each, he has tow-cloth cloths, a wire drawer by trade. Whoever will take up said prisoners, or any one or more of them, and safety commit them to goal in Windham county goal in the State of Connecticut, and give me notice thereof, shall be paid all his necessary expence and Trouble,

By me NATHANIEL HEBBARD, Goal-keeper.

Windham, October 31, 1776.

The Connecticut Gazette; And The Universal Intelligencer, November 8, 1776; November 15, 1776; November 22, 1776.

GLOUCESTER, *Nov.* 1, 1776.

WHEREAS capt. *Charles Tomkies* has advertised *William Dickerson* in this Gazette as a deserter, and supposes him to be persuaded so to do by some Tory, I beg leave to relate the truth of that matter. The said *William Dickerson,* who is my son, was enlisted by capt. *Tomkies* when under age, and without my consent; and in some short time after I applied to capt. *Tomkies,* and put him in mind, that as I had not given my consent I would endeavour to get my son home again. However, as there was soon a call for every man in the county capable of bearing arms, to oppose lord *Dunmore's* invasion of *Gwyn's* island, I made no farther application for him, till necessity compelled me, by the illness of my wife. He accordingly came to see his mother; and as I had never consented to his enlisting, and the family was in great need of his presence, I thought I had a right to keep him. But I am not a Tory, and as warm a friend to my country as any man in it; and if ever there should be a call, no one will be more ready than

DAVID DICKERSON.

N. B. I can prove that my son *William Dickerson* will be but 16 years of age the 5th day of next month.

The Virginia Gazette, Purdie, November 8, 1776; November 29, 1776. See *The Virginia Gazette*, Purdie, October 25, 1776.

DEEP SPRING camp, *Sept.* 17, 1776.
DESERTED last night from my company of riflemen, the following soldiers, *viz.* JOSIAH JONES, about 22 years old, 6 feet 2 inches high, well made, has short black hair, a very lively countenance, and when intoxicated very talkative, and desirous of raising disputes; he carried away with him a hunting shirt trimmed with red, a pair of leather breeches, several new shirts, and other things which I cannot recollect at present. DAVID BARNETT, aged 21 years, 6 feet 4 inches high, well made, has short black hair, a thin visage, occasioned by the ague and fever, which he had when he deserted, is very serious, and speaks but seldom; he carried with him a hunting shirt trimmed with red, a pair of leather breeches, a pair of new shoes, and several yards of linen, which I had delivered to him about two days before he deserted. JOSEPH CANTERBURY, aged 28 years, 5 feet 10 inches high, well made, has short red hair, a reddish complexion, and a dejected look; he carried along with him a hunting shirt trimmed with red, a gray coloured broadcloth waistcoat and breeches, a pair of black stockings, two pair of shoes, and several yards of linen, which I delivered to him a few days before he deserted. They went off indebted to the publick store, and were raised and enlisted in *Amherst,* where I expect they will endeavour to get. Whoever will deliver the said deserters to the commanding officer in *Williamsburg,* or safely contrive them to the 6th *Virginia* regiment at *New York,* shall have 4 l. 10s. for each, and all reasonable expenses paid.
      SAMUEL JORDAN CABELL, captain
       in the 6th *Virginia* regiment.
  The Virginia Gazette, Purdie, November 8, 1776.

ALL marines out upon furlough, belonging to my quota, are desired immediately to repair on board the brig *Muskito,* capt. *Harris.*— Deserted, *Jesse Harden, Joseph Hairlow,* and *Thomas Meriman,* for apprehending each of whom I will give 3 l. reward.
          JACOB VALENTINE.
  The Virginia Gazette, Purdie, November 8, 1776; November 22, 1776.

       Ticonderoga, October 17th, 1776.
DESERTED my Company, Col. Ruggles Woodbridge's Regiment, one *Noah Gold* of the Town of Amherst, aged 30 Years; five feet eight inches high: had on when he went away, a pale blue and white mix'd coloured Coat, lightish colour'd Vest, a caster Hat, wore a Wig or green Cap, light complexion. Likewise one *Benjamin Hubbard,* an Indian Fellow, about five feet seven inches high, thick set, about forty-

five years old: had on when he went away a Frock and Trowsers, belonging to the Town of Granby—Whosoever will take up said Deserters and return one or both before the last day of November next shall have Five Dollar each of Ten Dollars or both,
   by me, REUBEN DICKENSEN, Capt.
The Boston-Gazette, and Country Journal, November 11, 1776; November 18, 1776; November 25, 1776.

Escaped from the Goal in Northampton, Robert Arnold and Henry E. Stanhope two Prisoners, lately Midshipmen in the British Navy, the former a short, well-set, smart-looking, fresh complexioned Man, about thirty five years old, wore a Coat of a London brown colour. The latter absconded heretofore when on Parole, and was retaken at Middletown; he also is a short Man with light Hair and pale Complexion, and has large Eyes, Lips and Nose. Whoever will apprehend and secure either of said Persons, shall receive Twenty Dollars and necessary Charges
   from AARON WRIGHT, Goaler.
           Northampton, Nov. 7th. 1776.
The Boston-Gazette, And Country Journal, November 11, 1776; November 18, 1776; November 25, 1776; *The Connecticut Courant, And Hartford Weekly Intelligencer*, November 11, 1776; November 18, 1776; Minor differences between the papers. The *Courant* does not show Stanhope's middle initial.

ESCAPED from the Goal in Springfield, in the county of Hampshire, the night after the 16th instant, John Johnson, Joshua Ferris, Thomas Gleason, Samuel Wilson, Henry Chace, Ryner Van Rosen, six persons who were sent by the committee of the State of New-York to the goal in said Springfield, for aiding, assisting and abetting in treasonable practices against the liberties of America; also Robert Patterson and John Hamilton, both Highlanders, and Allen Soper and Bryan Cullen, marines, which were prisoners of war, confined in goal by orders from his Excellency General Washington, and by the council of the State of Massachusetts-Bay.—All persons are requested to assist in pursuing and taking up said prisoners.—Whoever shall take up and return either of the above-persons sent by the committee of the State of New-York to said goal, shall be entitled to a premium of FIVE DOLLARS; and for each of said prisoners or war, the thanks of the committee of the town of Springfield, and all necessary charges
     paid by THO'S STEBBINS,
       Chairman of the Committee of Springfield,
           Springfield, Nov. 17, 1776.

The Connecticut Courant, And Hartford Weekly Intelligencer, November 18, 1776.

Fifty Dollars Reward.

WHEREAS Major Christopher French, Ensign Joseph Moyland, and John Bickle, belonging to the British Army, Peter Herron, a Tory, and Capt. Jacob Smith, who was taken lately on Long Island in Arms, all escaped from Goal last Night to join the British Army; said French is little in Stature, said Moyland and Herron are tall and slim, said Bickle is middling sized and of a ruddy Countenance.—All Persons, and especially all Officers, Civil and Military, are requested to assist in pursuing and taking said Prisoners.—Whoever shall take up and return either of said Prisoners to Harford Goal shall be entitled to a premium of TEN DOLLARS, and all necessary Charges,
        paid by   EZEKIEL WILLIAMS, sheriff.
                                      Hartford, Nov, 16, 1776.
The Connecticut Courant, and Hartford Weekly Intelligencer, November 18, 1776; November 25, 1776. See *The Connecticut Courant, And Hartford Weekly Intelligencer,* December 30, 1776, for French and Moyland. See *The Connecticut Journal,* February 12, 1777, for French.

TEN DOLLARS REWARD.

DESERTED from my company of regulars, stationed at *York,* THOMAS MAY, a likely young fellow about 5 feet 10 inches high, of a fair complexion, has short sandy hair, and was born in the upper end of *King & Queen,* where I have reason to believe he is now harboured.   GREGORY SMITH.

The Virginia Gazette, Purdie, November 22, 1776; November 29, 1776.

NEW-LONDON, Nov. 29.

Tuesday night last, one John Coggin, late Boatswain of the Bomb Brig, (who with three other Prisoners lately broke out of Windham Goal) was found on board a Brig in this Harbour: He gives the following Account of said Prisoners, viz. That the Night after breaking out of Goal, they, with the help of one Lewis, who was taken in a Prize Vessel, stole a Canoe near Norwich Landing, with which they attempted to cross the Sound to Long-Island, but at the Entrance of the Race, near Gull-Islands, the Canoe overset, and all of them except Goggin, were drowned. Their Names are Edward Sneyd, (late Commander of the Bomb Brig) William Cook, John Russel, and — Lewis.

The Connecticut Gazette; And The Universal Intelligencer, November 29, 1776; *The Connecticut Courant, And Hartford Weekly Intelligencer*, December 2, 1776; *The Connecticut Journal*, December 4, 1776. Minor differences between the papers. The *Courant* shows the name of the survivor as Goggin. See *The Connecticut Gazette; And The Universal Intelligencer*, November 15, 1776. Coggins

TWENTY DOLLARS REWARD.

DESERTED from my company of the 2d *Georgia* battalion, the following soldiers, viz. PATRICK DUFFY, an *Irishman*, about 5 feet 8 inches high, well made, full faced, wore a short blue jacket with sleeves half worn, and it is supposed was in the marine service. EMANUEL KELLY, country born, about 5 feet 8 inches high, a wheelwright by trade, is very fond of liquor, and wore an old hat, with clothes much worn. Whoever secures said deserters shall have the above reward, or 3 l. for each.
   WILLIAM SMITH, captain.

The Virginia Gazette, Purdie, December 6, 1776; December 20, 1776; December 27, 1776. See *The Virginia Gazette*, Purdie, March 7, 1777, for Duffy.

        PRINCE GEORGE, *Nov.* 23, 1776.

CONTRARY to my desire, and express order, my servant man JAMES BULLOCK enlisted with mr. *Robert Poythress*, an officer, he says, under captain *Scott* of the *Georgia* service; upon which I demanded my servant of the said *Poythress*, without effect. This is therefore to request of capt. *Scott* to have my said servant returned to me without delay or farther expense, or I shall certainly prosecute him according to law.
   JAMES ANDERSON.

The Virginia Gazette, Purdie, December 6, 1776; December 20, 1776.

TEN DOLLARS REWARD.

FOR *securing WILLIAM FRAZER, a soldier in my company, enlisted for the defence of the state of* Georgia. *He is a slender made man, about* 19 *years of age, has short light coloured hair, and said he lived in* Hampton, *but was born in* Chesterfield, *at or near Osborne's warehouse. The said* Frazer *enlisted with me in* Williamsburg *the* 27th *of last* August, *and at his request I granted him a furlough for* 30 *days, at the end of which time he was to join my company at* Newgate, *in* Loudoun *county, but has not as yet appeared. I will give*

the above reward to any person that secures the said Frazer *in any publick jail, and advertises the same in this paper, or TWENTY DOLLARS if delivered to me at the above mentioned place.*
    WILLIAM LANE, jun. capt.
The Virginia Gazette, Purdie, December 6, 1776; December 20, 1776; December 27, 1776. See *The Virginia Gazette*, Purdie, April 25, 1777.

            State of New-York, Rye, December 3d, 1776.
WHEREAS Josiah Turrel, Ze[ ] Beebe, Ebenezer Hoadley, Abraham Osborn, Ebenezer Scott, and Joseph Beebe, soldiers in the 10th regiment if militia, from the state of Connecticut, inhabitants of the town of Waterbury, did shamefully desert the service of their country, in the hour of danger, and sneekingly returned home; intending to create a mutiny in the camp; thereby violating all order and regulation given to these United States. These are therefore to request all officers, civil and military, magistrates and committees, to take every method to apprehend said deserters, and return them to their respective corps, at this place, that they may be dealt with as the martial law directs for such offences. Given at the Saw Pits in Rye.
            THADDEUS COOK, Colonel.
    The Connecticut Journal, December 11, 1776.

DESERTED from capt. *Croghan's* company in the 8th battalion, *HIGH GREEN,* about 5 feet 7 inches high, well built, has a full face, fair hair, thick and short; had on when he went away an old blue coat, black silk waistcoat, and country linen shirts; and from capt. *Westfall's* company, in the said battalion, *THOMAS M'DANIEL,* 5 feet 7 or 8 inches high, who had on a pale blue coat, a macaroni hat with gold button and loop, and plenty of other cloths. They are both tailors, and enlisted for the continuance of the war. They also enlisted in capt. *Richard K. Meade's* company, and took the bounty about two hours before they deserted. It is supposed they have entered on board some of the row-gallies. Whoever apprehends the said deserter, and delivers them at head quarters in *Williamsburg,* shall have 5 l. reward for each. JAMES HIGGIN.
    The Virginia Gazette, Purdie, December 13, 1776; December 20, 1776; December 27, 1776.

            Bristol Head Quarters, Dec. 17, 1776.
DESERTED on the 13th Inst. from Ensign Springer's Company, commanded by Col. Sayles, a private Soldier named William Middleton, says he was born in Ireland; he is of a light Complexion,

pitted with the Small-pox; had on when he went away a short light coloured Sailor's Jacket, Leather Breeches, and white woollen Hose. Whoever takes up said Deserter, so that he may be returned to his Regiment or Company, shall receive Five Dollars Reward, and all reasonable Charges,
     paid by me, JOSEPH SPRINGER, Ensign.
The Providence Gazette; And Country Journal, December 21, 1776; January 11, 1777; January 18, 1777.

MADE their escape from Litchfield, the 11th instant, at night, serjeant Roderic M'Cleod of the 71st. or Fraser's regiment of highlanders, and corporal William Bradshaw, of the 7th regiment; both prisoners of war, M'Cloud is about 6 feet high, slim built, short brown hair, and blue eyes; had on the highland dress; Bradshaw is about five feet 8 inches high, pretty slim built, carried with him his regimentals, and a brown short coat of American manufacture. 'Tis probable they will attempt to get to New-York. Whoever will take up, and return said runaways, shall have five dollars reward for each, and all necessary charges paid by
     Lynde Lord, Reuben Smith,
      Committee to take care of prisoners.
        Litchfield, December 12, 1776.
The Connecticut Journal, December 25, 1776; January 8, 1777; January 15, 1777.

       Princeton, N. Jersey, Dec. 5, 1776.
     STOP THE ROBBERS!
    One Hundred DOLLARS Reward.
LAST Tuesday three villains came to the house of Mr. Nowel Furman, near Princeton, and, after abusing the family in a barbarous manner, took with them goods to the amount of between one and two hundred pounds, consisting chiefly of Germantown woollen stockings milled, of several colours, large pocket handkerchiefs of several kinds of red and blue stripes, kenting ditto, pins of the small kind, four dozen razors, one pair of four thread fine black worsted hose, black leather pocket books, pocket almanacks, a few pieces of childrens garters, and many other goods unknown.
 One of the above rogues is an Irishman, a middle sized man, well set, has bushy sandy hair, and supposed to be marked with the small pox; had on a blue coat, his name is said to be WATSON, and have been informed he belongs to Capt. Brown's company of Pennsylvania Riflemen, under Col. Brodhead. The second person I cannot describe. The third is a tall slim man, with light colored clothes. It is said they

have already changed their clothes. They put the goods into bags or knapsacks. There were seen near the Baptist meeting-house at Hopewell on Wednesday evening, but could not be taken for want of men of resolution, and it is supposed they are bound for Delaware, and so on to Shamokin. Whoever secures said goods and the men, so that they be convicted, shall have the above reward, of Fifty Dollars for the men, or in proportion for any of the men or part of the goods, by applying to Mr. STACY POTTS, *at Trenton, or Mr.* WILLIAM WOODHOUSE, *in Philadelphia, or the subscriber in Princeton,*
          JOHN DENTON.
    The Pennsylvania Packet; and the General Advertiser, December 27, 1776.

WHEREAS the following soldiers, enlisted by mr. *Moses Hawkins* in my company, failed to meet me at *Prince Edward* courthouse according to appointment, I give them this notice to be at the said courthouse by the 25th instant, as those who fail will be deemed deserters, and treated accordingly. Their names are, *James Parker, William M'Clure, Edward Cantwell, Simon Savage, James Kemp, Elijah Ellis, Daniel Bailey, James Fleming, Joseph Sampson, Cornelius Fitzgerald, William Grant, John Ray,* and *John M'Connelly,* of the counties of *Augusta, Frederick,* and *Dunmore.*—I also give notice to all the gentlemen soldiers that have been enlisted by myself or lieutenants *Ward* and *Hancock,* ensign *Morrison,* or any serjeant or soldier in my company, being the first company of the 2d battalion for the state of *Georgia,* to meet me at *Prince Edward* courthouse on the said 25th instant, without fail.
          JOSEPH PANNILL.
    The Virginia Gazette, Purdie, December 27, 1776

DESERTED *from* Alexandria, *on the* 15*th of this instant* (December) *JOHN BRITT, a marine in my company, who is an Irishman, about* 26 *years old,* 5 *feet* 8 *or* 9 *inches high, a stout well made fellow, much pitted with the smallpox, has a blemish in one of his eyes (I think the right) and when he went off was labouring under the venereal disease. Also EDWARD LEE, an* Irishman, 5 *feet* 10 *or* 11 *inches high,* 27 *or* 28 *years old, a thin spare fellow, occasioned by his being sick some time. They served their time in* Loudoun *county, and I am informed have enlisted at* Newgate, *with capt.* Smith *or capt.* Lane. *They were seen two or three days ago near* Fredericksburg *with guns, &c. in search, as they said, of* deserters. *Whoever apprehends them, and delivers them to me in* Alexandria, *shall have* 40 *s. reward for each. Any officer who may have enlisted them, I hope, will return*

them to their company immediately, and thereby discourage desertion a practice so pernicious to the general goods and which ought to be discountenanced by all who are friends to America.
    SAMUEL ARELL.
I gave them a furlough till the 12th of December.
  The Virginia Gazette, Purdie, December 27, 1776; January 3, 1777.

MADE their Escape out of the Main Guard-House at Bristol on Thursday Evening, the 26th Instant, Zebulon Weathers, and Francis Marvill: They were confined for abusing sundry Persons in the Camp, &c. Any Person that will apprehend and secure them, so that they may be dealt with according to their Deserts, shall have Ten Dollars Reward, and all necessary Charges,
    paid by WILLIAM WEST, Brig. General.
                Bristol, Dec. 27. 1776.
  The Providence Gazette; and Country Journal, December 28, 1776; January 4, 1777; January 11, 1777.

Stolen from the subscriber on the night following the 23d instant, out of a hogshead of goods, which was broke open, sundry striped cotton shirts, several pair of shoes, one pair of pale blue yarn stockings, and two cheeses. The thief is one James M'Lean, a prisoner belonging to the 51st regiment in the British service, is of a middling stature, a well sett man, red complexion, has light hair something pitted with the small pox, slow of speech, wears his regimental coat and Scotch bonnet, and long plaid trowsers. Whoever will apprehend and secure the said thief, and give information to the subscriber, shall have TWO DOLLARS reward and all necessary charges.
    MOSES ROOT.   Westfield, Dec. 25th, 1776.
  The Connecticut Courant, And Hartford Weekly Intelligencer, December 30, 1776; January 6, 1777; January 13, 1777; January 20, 1777.

        120 Dollars Reward.
MAJOR Christopher French, Ens. Joseph Moyland, and the infamous Gurdon Whitmore, broke goal and escaped this evening. Said French and Moyland are Continental Prisoners.—Said French is about 50 years of age, wears his hair, is small of stature, and hard favoured. Said Moyland is about 25 years of age, tall, walks erect, wears his hair, light complexion. Said Whitmore is short and well made, has black eyes, wears his hair.—It's expected they will change their dress as they did when they run away before. Any person that shall take up

the aforesaid prisoners, or either of them, and return them to the goal at Hartford, shall receive as a premium, Forty Dollars for each, and all necessary charges, by
>> BARZ. HUDSON, Goaler.

Hartford, Dec. 27th, 1776.

The Connecticut Courant, And Hartford Weekly Intelligencer, December 30, 1776; January 6, 1777; *The Continental Journal, And Weekly Advertiser*, January 2, 1777; January 9, 1777; *The Independent Chronicle and the Universal Advertiser*, January 2, 1777; January 9, 1777. Minor differences between the papers. The *Journal* and *Chronicle* spell the second man's name as Moland. The *Chronicle* spells the third man's name as both Whitmore and Whitemore. See *The Connecticut Courant, and Hartford Weekly Intelligencer*, November 18, 1776, for French and Moyland. See *The Connecticut Journal*, February 12, 1777, for French.

1777

DESERTED from the *Hero* Galley, a certain *John Brown* born in *England,* but sometimes pretends to pass for a *Virginian.* He is about 5 feet 7 inches high, of a fair complexion, with almost white hair, which is short and curling. He has been for some time troubled with a rupture, which occasions him to walk badly. Any person apprehending and delivering the said deserter on board the *Hero* galley, lying at *Hampton,* shall have 3 l.
>> GEORGE MUTER, captain of the *Hero.*

The Virginia Gazette, Purdie, January 3, 1777; January 17, 1777.

CHESTERFIELD, *Jan.* 6, 1777.

THE following soldiers, enlisted by me for the 2d *Georgia* battalion, are desired to meet me on the 20th instant at *Cumberland* courthouse, with their blankets and muskets (if any) and they shall be paid for them should they disobey this notice, they will be considered as *deserters*, and treated accordingly. Their names are, *John Lee* and *John Stith* of *Bedford, John Vest* of *Buckingham, Robert Wilkins* of *Henrico, John Dorton, John Williams, William Strange,* and *Anthony Hooper,* enlisted in *Williamsburg* —The officers of the 7th company of the said regiment are desired by the colonel to attend with their men likewise, at the above time and place.
>> ALEX: BAUGH, lieut.

The Virginia Gazette, Purdie, January 10, 1777; January 17, 1777.

YORK town, *Jan.* 13, 1777.
ALL those men that are out upon furlough, belonging to the party or artillery stationed at *York* town, are desired to return by the 28th instant, in order that their accounts may be adjusted.—*Austin Lawless, Jesse Dillon,* and *Nicholas Ware,* whose furloughs have been out for some time, are hereby ordered to return home, or send immediately a certificate from some gentleman of the county to which they belong of their impotency. A neglect of this will be attended with the consequence of punishment as *deserters.*
                      WILLIAM PIERCE, jun.
                      Capt. of artillery.
   N. B. Edward Valentine, of *King William,* is desired to make a return of what men he has enlisted for my company.
   The Virginia Gazette, Purdie, January 17, 1777; January 24, 1777.

DESERTED from on board the sloop Betsey *and* Polly, *lying in* York *river the mate and three seamen, viz* Zorobabel Kellam, *mate, about* 23 *years old* 5 *feet* 9 *inches high, well made,* Virginia *born, has a sore leg, short hair, and wears a white or blue jacket and trouser.* Abel Willis *seaman, about* 23 *years old, 5 feet 10 inches high, is much pitted with the smallpox. Lame in one of his hands, and wears a blue jacket and trousers.* Francis Moore, *seaman, about* 21 *years old, 5 feet 6 inches high, slender made,* New England *born, has long dark hair, and wears a blue jacket and trousers.* Hugh Harris, *seaman, about* 28 *years old,* 5 *feet* 4 *inches high, has short dark hair, and wears a blue jacket and trousers. Whoever delivers the said* deserters *to me at* Blackwater *up* North *river, in* Mobjack *bay, or confines them in any of the jails within this commonwealth, so as I get them again, shall have* 20 *1. reward,* 10 *1. for the mate alone, or 5 l. for each seaman.*
                    ROBERT LENNIS.
   The Virginia Gazette, Purdie. January 17, 1777; January 24, 1777.

                                      Philad. Jan 7, 1777.
WAS committed to my custody yesterday, a certain JAMES PITT, a soldier belonging to Capt. Vansant's company, in the American army. The said Captain is desired to apply to the subscriber, that the soldier may be taken to his respective company.
   Two Negroes are also in my custody, one is a man, and says he belongs to William Bailey, near George town, Maryland; the other is a

wench, and says she belongs to Thomas Senick in Salem, New-Jersey, Their masters, &c. are desired to come, pay the charges, and take them away, or they will be sold for their fees, in one month from this date.
THOMAS DEWEES jailor.
The Pennsylvania Evening Post, January 14, 1777.

WILLIAMSBURG, *Jan.* 15, 1777.
DESERTED from capt. *William Sanford's* company of the 2d regiment, *WILLIAM TURNER,* about 5 feet 9 or 10 inches high, well made, with short light coloured hair, and was enlisted in *Amelia* county by lieut. *Joseph Archer.* Whoever will deliver the said deserter to the commanding office at this place shall have TEN DOLLARS reward.
ALEXANDER PARKER, lieut.
The Virginia Gazette, Purdie, January 17, 1777; January 24, 1777.

DESERTED *from* Trenton, New Jersey, December 4, 1776, *JOHN WAGSTAFF, a soldier belonging to capt.* Thomas Nelson's *company of regulars of the first* Virginia *regiment; he is a stout young lad, about* 20 *years of age, had light hair, his uniform was blue, turned up with red. The said* Wagstaff *was enlisted near* York *town, in* Virginia. *Whoever takes up the said* deserter, *and delivers him to capt.* Nelson *in* York *town, or the subscriber now with the company in* Pennsylvania, *shall receive TWELVE DOLLARS reward.*
JOHN MOSS, *lieutenant.*
The Virginia Gazette, Purdie, January 17, 1777.

SIX POUNDS REWARD
DESERTED from my recruits enlisted for capt. *William Lane,* jun. his company of regulars, raised for the defence of the state of *Georgia, John Graham* (commonly called *Grimes*) about 23 years of age, 5 feet 9 or 10 inches high, slender made, thin visage, a pleasing countenance, slow in speech, long black hair, which he generally wears in a club. The said *Graham* was a resident of *Albemarle,* deserted last *November,* and I am apprehensive is gone to *Pittsylvania* county. I will give the above reward to any person who will deliver the said *deserter* at *Prince Edward* courthouse.
ELISHA MILLER, lieut.
The Virginia Gazette, Purdie, January 17, 1777; January 24, 1777.

Providence, Jan. 9. 1777.

DESERTED from the Rhode-Island State Train of Artillery, George Newmash Stanley, born in Marblehead, about 18 Years of Age, five Feet nine Inches high, has light short Hair, light Eyes, and small Legs: Also, Thomas Snoke, born in Marblehead, about 22 Years of Age, five Feet six Inches high, has dark Eyes, and dark brown Hair. Whoever will secure said Deserters in any of the Gaols of the United States, shall receive Five Dollars Reward for each, and all necessary Charges, paid by
     GID. WESTCOTT, Capt. in the Train, or
     NATH. LINDSEY, Capt. of the Battalion.
The Providence Gazette; And Country Journal, January 18, 1777.

DESERTED from Col. Robert Elliot's Regiment of Artillery, at Providence, John Robinson, a Seaman, a Native of Ireland, 27 Years of Age, five Feet eight Inches high; has dark grey Eyes, and dark Hair. Whoever will apprehend said Deserter, and return him to said Regiment, shall have Five Dollars Reward, and all necessary Charges, paid by JOHN WARNER, Capt. Lieut.
Providence, Jan. 16, 1777.
The Providence Gazette; And Country Journal, January 18, 1777; February 8, 1777.

DESERTED from my Company, Benjamin Bussol, about five Feet seven Inches high, has dark Hair, blue Eyes, and is near 27 Years of Age: Had on a long red Coat, faced with Buff, also a brown Broadcloth Waistcoat. Whoever will take up and confine said Bussol in any of the Gaols of the United States and give Notice to me at Providence, shall have Six Dollars Reward, and all necessary Charges, paid by JONATHAN WALLEN, Captain.
Providence, Jan. 13, 1777.
The Providence Gazette; And Country Journal, January 18, 1777; February 8, 1777.

DESERTED from Capt. Roswell Smith's Company, at Quidneset, James Bolden, about 5 Feet 8 or 9 inches high, very talkative; had of a blue Surtout, Claret coloured Waistcoat or Coatee, and Half Boots; he took with him some Cloaths, such as Jackets without Sleeves, and 2 new Holland Shirts; he has a Scar on his Cheek, and others on his Legs; has had some of his Ribs broke, and wears a Plaister. Whoever will take up said Deserter, and confine him so that he may join his

Company again, shall have Five Dollars Reward, and all Charges,
paid by   THOMAS POTTER, jun. Major.
The Providence Gazette; And Country Journal, January 18, 1777; February 8, 1777.

DESERTED from the Rhode-Island Train of Artillery, Colonel Elliot's Regiment, Gilbert Rathbone, a Seaman, born in Cork, in Ireland, five Feet nine Inches and a Half high, of a light Complexion, has blue Eyes, light Hair, about 29 Years of Age, Has a Scar in his Face: Had on a short blue Jacket, and Duffil Trowsers. Whoever will secure said Deserter in any of the Gaols of the United States, shall receive Five Dollars Reward, and necessary Charges,
paid by JOSHUA SAGER, Captain.
Providence, Jan. 7, 1777.
The Providence Gazette; And Country Journal, January 18, 1777.

OBSERVE.
AN Advertisement appearing in the Boston Paper, dated at Ticonderoga, Nov. 13, 1776, and sign'd by Charles Miller, offering a Reward of One Dollar for apprehending Samuel Danforth, of Weston, as a Deserter from Col. Reed's Regiment. I would just inform the Public, that it is a malicious and false Insinuation designedly to asperse the Character of Mr. Danforth, who was appointed a Lieutenant in Col. Alden's Regiment, and Furlough'd by me
per Order of Major General Gates.
Wm. STACY, Col. Boston, Jan. 2, 1777.
The Boston-Gazette, And Country Journal, January 20, 1777; January 27, 1777. See *The Boston Gazette, and Country Journal*, December 23, 1776.

FIVE POUNDS REWARD.
DESERTED from my company, of the 2d *Virginia* regiment, JOHN JONES, of a dark complexion, and has black hair and eyes; had on when he deserted a blue coat, a pair of brown linen trousers, and a large flapped hat. I gave him a furlough for ten days. Whoever will deliver said deserter at head quarters in *Williamsburg* shall receive the above reward.   JOHN WILLIS.
The Virginia Gazette, Purdie, January 24, 1777.

One hundred and sixty dollars reward.
DESERTED from the company formerly commanded by capt. *Charles Tomkies,* of the 7th regiment, the following soldiers. Viz

Simon Green, Thomas Peed, George Weston, James White, Zachariah Pryor, Lewis Belvin, Aaron Belvin, George Belvin, Thomas Ransone, Augustine Ransone, Thomas Blacknall, William Anderson, John Willis, Robert Graves, Richard Anderson, and *Matthew Hundley.* I will give the above reward for apprehending said deserters, or *TEN DOLLARS* for each, to be delivered to lieut. *James Baytop* at *Williamsburg.* I expect they are in *Gloucester,* where the company was raised, and are all natives of that county.—Such soldiers of the said company as have been indulged with furloughs are desired to join lieut. *Baytop* on or before the 5th of next month at *Williamsburg,* or they will be treated as deserters.
     REUBEN LIPSCOMB.
 The Virginia Gazette, Purdie, January 24, 1777; January 31, 1777; February 7, 1777; See *The Virginia Gazette*, Dixon and Hunter, January 24, 1777, and *The Virginia Gazette*, Dixon and Hunter, March 28, 1777, for Anderson and Hundley.

     WILLIAMSBURG, *January* 23, 1777.
    DESERTED, RICHARD PARKER,
an *Irishman* between 35 and 40 Years of Age, and about 5 Feet 6 or 7 Inches high. He is a slovenly Fellow, and much addicted to Liquor; had on, and took with him, an old Hat, a new brown Coat, purchased from the Country Store, a Pair of Leather Breeches, and other Clothes, which I do not remember. If he returns to me in *Williamsburg* by the 5th of next Month, it shall operate much in his Favour; if not, he may expect the utmost Rigour of the Martial-Law; and I will give four Dollars to any Person who will secure him so that I get him again. As Desertion is become but too common, it is to be hoped that every Friend and well wisher to the Cause will exert himself in bringing such Offenders to Justice, and thereby timely suppress an Evil, which, if not discouraged, must be attended with the worst of Consequences.
    JOHN R. DAVIES, Lieutenant.
 The Virginia Gazette, Dixon and Hunter, January 24, 1777; January 31, 1777; February 7, 1777

    TWENTY FIVE POUNDS REWARD.
DESERTED *from capt.* Alexander's *company, of the 2d regiment, the following soldiers, viz. JOHN LICHENS, about 5 feet 10 inches high, and of a dark complexion. WILLIAM OWENS, about 5 feet 6 inches high. THOMAS LOVE, about 6 feet high. WILLIAM HARDY, about 5 feet 11 inches high, had on a brown coat, buckskin breeches, and a macaroni hat with a black band and silver buckle in it. HUGH NELSON, about 5 feet 5 inches high, a very well set fellow, and pretty*

well dressed. All of them enlisted in Frederick *county,* Virginia. *The dress of the other soldiers, except* Hardy *and* Nelson, *I cannot describe. Whoever will deliver the said* deserters *at head quarters in* Williamsburg *shall receive the above reward, or 5 l. for each.*
                    MARQUIS CALMES, lieutenant.
         The Virginia Gazette, Purdie, January 24, 1777.

                     SIXTY DOLLARS REWARD.
DESERTED from my Company, in the 2d *Georgia* Battalion, the following Soldiers, who enlisted with me in *Williamsburg,* viz.— HUGH GREEN, MICAJAH DEFOOS, JAMES STEPHENS, JOHN WILSON, JOHN CAINE, and BENJAMIN DELK. Whoever delivers them to me at *Prince Edward* Courthouse shall receive the above Reward, or TEN DOLLARS for each.
                      ROBERT WARD, Lieut.
     The Virginia Gazette, Dixon and Hunter, January 24, 1777; January 31, 1777; February 7, 1777.

                One Hundred and Sixty Dollars Reward.
DESERTED from the Company formerly commanded by Captain *Charles Tomkies,* of the 7th Regiment, the following Soldiers, viz. *Simon Green, Thomas Peed, George Weston, James White, Zachariah Pryor, Lewis Belvin, Aaron Belvin, George Belvin, Thomas Ransone, Augustine Ransone, Thomas Blacknall, William Anderson, John Willis, Robert Graves, Richard Anderson,* and *Matthew Hunley.* I will give the above Reward for apprehending the above Deserters, or ten Dollars for each, to be delivered to Lieutenant *James Baytop,* at *Williamsburg* . The Whole of them I expect are in *Gloucester* County, as the Company Was raised there, and are Natives of that Place.
                      REUBEN LIPSCOMB.
    ∴ Those soldiers of the said Company who have been indulged with Furlough, are desired to join Lieutenant *Baytop,* on or before the 5th Day of *February* , at *Williamsburg* , or they will be treated as Deserters.
     The Virginia Gazette, Dixon and Hunter, January 24, 1777; February 7, 1777; February 21, 1777. See *The Virginia Gazette,* Purdie, January 24, 1777, and *The Virginia Gazette,* Dixon and Hunter, March 28, 1777, for Anderson and Hundley.

DESERTED *from my company, at Providence, William Gipson, about forty-five years of age, five feet seven or eight inches high, has yellow hair, pitted with the small-pox, blue eyes, of a light complexion, has*

on when he went away, a light brown coat and vest, felt hat, and leather breeches. Whoever will apprehend said deserter, and return him to said company, shall have Three Dollars reward, and all necessary charges,
            paid by   SANFORD KINGSBERRY, Captain.
Providence, Jan. 18, 1777.
The Providence Gazette; And Country Journal, January 25, 1777; February 8, 1777.

DESERTED from Capt. Gazee's Company of Colonel Elliott's Regiment of Artillery, in the State of Rhode-Island, James Brown, a Native of Scotland, 22 Years of Age, a Seaman; has light grey Eyes, and red Hair; had on a Sailor's Habit. Whoever will apprehend said Deserter, and confine him in any Gaol in the United States, giving his Officers Notice, or convey him to his Regiment, shall have 5 Dollars Reward, and all necessary Charges,
            paid by   JOHN GAZEE, Capt.
Providence, Jan. 31, 1777.
The Providence Gazette; And Country Journal, February 1, 1777; February 8, 1777; February 15, 1777. The last ad shows the captain's surname as Garzia.

DESERTED from Capt. Abimeleck Riggs's Company, in Colonel Talman's Regiment, Benjamain Wood, belonging to Norton, about 5 Feet 9 Inches high, somewhat slim built, of a dark Complexion, has short brown Hair; had on when he went away a round Felt Har, short grey Coat, Jacket and Breeches. Whoever will take up said Deserter, and secure him in any Gaol, or return him to this Company, shall have Five Dollars Reward, and all necessary Charges,
            paid by   ABIMELECK RIGGS, Capt.
The Providence Gazette; And Country Journal, February 1, 1777; February 8, 1777; February 15, 1777.

DESERTED from Capt. Reuben Ballou's Company, in Col. Talman's Regiment, Reuben Fisk, a private Soldier, about 5 Feet 8 or 9 inches high, of a dark Complexion, has black Hair, thin favoured, said he belonged to Scituate. Arthur Rodgers, about 5 Feet 9 or 10 Inches high, an Irishman, a Weaver by Trade, of a light Complexion, a large fat Fellow, very much pitted with the Small-Pox, about 40 Years of Age, has short dark Hair. And John Rankin, about 5 Feet 7 Inches high, of a dark Complexion, appears to be about 20 Years of Age, formerly belonged to Scituate. Whoever will take up said Deserters, and bring them, or either of them, to me in Providence, shall have 5

Dollars Reward for each, and all necessary Charges,
        paid by   REUBEN BALLOU.
The Providence Gazette; And Country Journal, February 8, 1777; February 15, 1777.

DESERTED from Capt. Asaph Hall's company in Col. Cook's regiment, Richard Dale, and Bryan Hamblin; Said Dale is a tall slim fellow, and Hamblin is of middling size. Whoever shall take up and return to their regiment both or either of the above deserters, shall have Five Dollars reward for each, and all charges
        paid, by   DANIEL KINGSBURY, Ensign.
                                      Hartland, January 30. 1777.
The Connecticut Courant, And Hartford Weekly Intelligencer, February 10, 1777; February 17, 1777; February 24, 1777.

DESERTED 29th of January, from Capt. Hawkins's company, in Col. Stanton's regiment, an inlisted soldier of the new raised troops of the state of Rhode Island, one THOMAS WALCH, a native of Ireland, about 22 years of age, a well built fellow, had on when he went away a blue sailor jacket, round hatt, and leather breeches, speaks very hoarse and broad. Whoever will take up said deserter, and return him to said company at Quidnesit, in North Kingston, or secure him in any of the goals of the United States, and give notice to the commanded of said company so that he may have him again, shall have five Dollars reward and all necessary charges
        paid by   JOHN PEARSE, Lieut.
The Connecticut Gazette; And The Universal Intelligencer, February 14, 1777.

DESERTED from Capt. *Jonathan Calkins* Company, in Col. *Ely's* Regiment, two Soldiers, viz *Simeon Woodworth*, a short well-set Fellow of light Complexion, belongs to Norwich, has inlisted 3 several Times in said Regiment; had on a brown coat faced with buff, about 24 years old: Also *James Jonson* of the State of Massachusetts Bay, of light complexion, a well-set Fellow about 5 feet 6 inches high, about 30 years old. Whoever will apprehend and return either of the said Deserters to me the subscriber at the Camp in Providence, shall receive five Dollars Reward,
        paid by JONA. CALKINS,
                                      Providence, Feb. 3, 1777.
The Connecticut Gazette; And The Universal Intelligencer, February 14, 1777.

DESERTED from Capt. Jeremiah Halsey's company, in Col. Ely's regiment, three soldiers, viz. *Simeon Woodworth,* a short well set fellow of a light complexion, belongs to Norwich, had on a brown coat faced with buff, about 24 years old; also *James Aaelsworth,* of the state of Rhode-Island, of a light complexion, about five feet nine inches high, about 35 years old; and *John Wompey,* an Indian, belonging to Groton, about 25 years old, about five feet eight inches high. Whoever will apprehend and secure either of said deserters to me the subscriber, at the camp in Providence, shall receive Five DOLLARS reward,
                paid by   JEREMIAH HALSEY, Capt.
                                    Providence, February 3, 1777.
The Connecticut Gazette; And The Universal Intelligencer, February 14, 1777; February 21, 1777.

JOHN WEBSTER, of *Prince Edward,* who enlisted under me that first of last month, and obtained a furlough, which has been expired for some time is desired to repair to the place of rendezvous, in *New Kent* county, immediately, otherwise he will be treated as a deserter.
                ABNER CRUMP, capt.
*The Virginia Gazette,*Purdie. February 14, 1777; February 21, 1777. See *The Virginia Gazette,* March 14, 1777.

                          KING WILLIAM *Feb.* 10, 1777.
WHEREAS mr. *Thomas Armistead,* in my absence did enlist my apprentice *Charles Palmer,* I do hereby inform the said *Armistead* that I have got the *bounty* money which my apprentice received, and am ready to pay the same to him or his order, and at the same time forewarn the said *Armistead,* or any other person, from taking the said *Charles Palmer* from my service.
                NATHANIEL FOX.
The Virginia Gazette, Dixon and Hunter, February 14, 1777

JEREMIAH BRADSHAW, CHARLES IRBY, and JESSE HARPER, soldiers in the 4th troop of horse, having refused to send a certificate of their inability to join the regiment to which they belong, as was directed by major Theodorick Bland, are deemed deserters. Bradshaw lives in Amelia county, is about 5 feet 10 inches high, has sandy coloured hair, a little, and about 22 years of age. Irby also in Amelia, has light hair, is 5 feet 9 or 10 inches high, and about 19 years of age. Harper lives in Prince Edward, is about 10 or 11 inches high, has light brown hair, and about 21 years of age. A reward of 3 l.

will be given for each of the above deserters, upon their being delivered to capt. Benjamin Temple at Fredericksburg.

    ALEX: S. DANDRIDGE. lieut.

The Virginia Gazette, Purdie, February 14, 1777; February 21, 1777. See *The Virginia Gazette*, Purdie, March 21, 1777, for Irby.

THIS may inform the following persons, viz.—*Joseph Foster, John Smith, John Strong, Thomas Hopkins, William Cutler, Zachariah Willis, William Edwards, Arnold Darby, John Pickett, John Disko, Jacob Wherton* and *William Hilton*,—that were inlisted by John G. Frazer, at Ticonderoga, are returned over to my company at Boston or Springfield, by the 10th of March next, otherwise they will be advertised as deserters.

    NATHANIEL CUSHING, Captain.

The Continental Journal, and Weekly Advertiser, February 20, 1777; February 27, 1777; March 6, 1777.

    TEN DOLLARS REWARD.

JOHN Adams, *of Sussex County, in the State of New-Jersey,* 5 *feet* 8 *inches high, light hair, and black eyes, dressed in blue faced with red, white jacket and breeches; and John White, of the aforesaid County and State,* 5 *feet* 8 *inches high, dark hair, blue eyes, dressed in blue faced with yellow, white jacket and breeches, having inlisted in Col. Durkee's regiment during the present war, and received the bounty allowed by the Continent; deserted the service at Newtown, in Pennsylvania, on the 5th day of January,* 1777. *Whoever will apprehend either of said deserters and return him to the regiment, shall receive* 10 *dollars reward*

   by JOHN ALDEN, Ensign.

    Morris-Town, New-Jersey, January 20, 1777.

The Connecticut Gazette; And The Universal Intelligencer, February 21, 1777; February 28, 1777; March 7, 1777.

ADAM JONES and *Dudley Ballard,* late of capt. *Ballard's* company of minute men from *Mecklenburg, William Winston* and *Zachariah King,* late of capt. *Winston's* company of minute-men from *Hanover,* who enlisted in the company lately commanded by capt. *Nicholas,* are ordered to wait on the commanding officer at *Williamsburg* immediately. On failure, they will be treated as deserters.

    SAMUEL COBBS, lieut.

The Virginia Gazette, Purdie, February 21, 1777; February 28, 1777; March 7, 1777.

FREDERICKSBURG, *Jan.* 6, 1777.
DESERTED from my troop of light horse, about the 1st of *November* last, *GEORGE WEST,* 5 feet 11 inches high, very slender made, born in *Hanover,* has dark hair, and is 18 years old. *James M'CALLION,* upwards of 6 feet high, born in *Newcastle, Pennsylvania,* has dark hair and blue eyes, stoops in his shoulders, and is 24 years old. The said *M'Callion,* I am informed, has enlisted under one *Robert Poythress,* who was recruiting for the *Georgia* service under capt. *Scott.* I therefore forewarn the said *Scott* or *Poythress* from carrying him out of this colony, and will give *TWENTY DOLLARS* reward to any person who will secure the said deserter and deliver him to general *Lewis,* or his Excellency the Governour in *Williamsburg,* and *TEN DOLLARS* reward for securing *West,* on delivering him to either of the above mentioned gentlemen.
RICHARD CALL.
The Virginia Gazette, Purdie, February 21, 1777.

DESERTED from my company, in Colonel Talman's regiment on the 26th of January last, one Michael Briant, an Irishman, about 5 feet 8 inches high, of a light complexion, has light eyes, short brown hair, somewhat round shouldered, about 22 years of age. Whoever will secure the said deserter, so that he may be returned to his company at Tivertown, or to me the subscriber in Providence, shall have Five Dollars reward, and all necessary charges.
ABIMELECK RIGGS, Capt.
The Providence Gazette; And Country Journal, February 22, 1777; March 1, 1777.

DEserted from my Company, in Col. Greaton's Regiment, the following Persons, viz. John Lewis Welsh, aged 25, an Irishman, 5 Feet 10 Inches high, belong'd to New-York, light Complexion, short Hair, much Pock broken.—John Butler, of Palmer, 5 feet 8, dark Complexion, short black Hair, pock broken, aged 22.—John Burn, said he belong'd to Roxbury, aged about 29, about 5 Feet 8 Inches high, short brown Hair, pock broken. Whoever will take up said Deserters, and bring them to me in Roxbury-Street, shall have TEN DOLLARS Reward for each of them, and all necessary Charges paid, by JOSEPH WILLIAMS, *Captain.*
The Boston-Gazette and Country Journal, February 24, 1777; March 3, 1777; March 10. 1777.

INLISTED with me the subscriber, and then absconded, one John Graham, had on blue regimentals turned up with white, he is 32 years of age, about 5 feet 6 inches high, brown complexion, blue eyes, black hair, one leg shorter than the other by reason of its being broke. Whoever shall take up said Graham, and return him to me, shall have FIVE DOLLARS reward and all necessary charges
paid, by   JOHN CHIPMAN, Lieut.
Salisbury, Feb. 13, 1777.
The Connecticut Courant, And Hartford Weekly Intelligencer, February 24, 1777; March 3, 1777.

D*ESERTED from Capt. Ely's company, in Colonel Huntington's regiment, a soldier who calls himself by the name of* John Smith, *of Coventry, in the state of Rhode-Island, 5 feet* 6 inches and ½ *high, black eyes, short black hair, dark complexion, a pretty well sett comely man; he inlisted Jan.* 20. 1777, *and went toward Coventry or Providence. Whoever will apprehend said deserter and secure him in any goal in the United States, and notify the subscriber at Lyme, shall receive five Dollars and charges.*
ENOCH REED, Lieut.
The Connecticut Gazette; And The Universal Intelligencer, February 28, 1777; March 7, 1777.

140 *DOLLARS reward.*
D**ESERTED** from capt *Francis Moore's* company in the 2d *Georgia* battalion, the 16th of this instant (*February*) the following soldiers, *viz. Nathaniel Hall,* and *Thomas Ellis* (who I understand are gone to the Northward) *Littleton Williamson, Beverley Shelton, John Jordan, William Adams,* and *Elisha Heathcock.* The above reward will be given delivering the said deserters to capt Moore's company, on their way to Georgia, or ten dollars for each, upon their being delivered to capt. Andrew Geter, or any other commissioned officer, or if secured in Brunswick jail, till I can get them. The five last mentioned deserters I imagine are in *Brunswick,* being natives of the county, and where the company was chiefly raised.
ABRAHAM JONES, ensign.
The Virginia Gazette, Purdie, February 28, 1777; March 7, 1777; March 14, 1777.

One Hundred and Sixty Dollars Reward,
FOR securing the undermentioned Deserters, enlisted under me for Captain *Smith's* Company of the 2d *Georgia* Battalion, *viz.* WILLIAM

DORTON of *Williamsburg,* of a pale Complexion, served 12 Months in the 2d *Virginia* Regiment, under Captain *R. K. Meade,* and I have been informed has since enlisted under one Lieutenant *Mason*; WILLIAM STRANGE of *Brunswick,* who served in the same Regiment; JOHN WILLIAMS, who served under Capt. *Morgan Alexander,* but what County he came from I do not remember; ROBERT WILKINS of *Henrico*; JOHN LEE and JOHN STITH of *Bedford*; JOHN VEST of *Buckingham*; and THOMAS KELLY, who informed me he had been a Prisoner with the *Indians.* I will give the above Reward for the above Deserters, or TWENTY DOLLARS where they may join their Company.
     ALEX: BAUGH, Lieut.

The Virginia Gazette, Purdie, February 28, 1777; March 7, 1777; March 14, 1777; March 21, 1777. Dorton is not listed in the last two ads. *Virginia Gazette*, Dixon and Hunter, March 7, 1777; March 14, 1777.Dorton is not in the March 14 ad.

         FEBRUARY 25, 1777.
JAMES DAVIS, a drummer in my company of continental regulars, who was left *August* at *King & Queen* court-house, has notice to repair to *Williamsburg* by the 15th of *March*; otherwise he will be considered as a deserter, and a reward of TEN DOLLARS will be paid to any person who delivers him to any continental officer in *Williamsburg* after that time.
     GOODRICH CRUMP.

The Virginia Gazette, Purdie, February 28, 1777; March 7, 1777.

         ALEXANDRIA, *Feb.* 9, 1777.
ON the 9th of *January* last I enlisted one JOHN BULMAN for the service of the commonwealth of *Virginia,* and granted him a furlough until the 16th, since which time he has not made his appearance; he informed me his name was *Bulman,* and lived in the lower part of *Prince George's* county, *Maryland.* He had in his pocket a certificate of service done by one *John Hesley* (whom he said was his brother in law) at the time the house of *William Brent,* esq; was destroyed by *Dunmore* and crew. He is about 21 or 22 years of age, 5 feet 5 or 6 inches high, well made, has light hair, and a fair complexion; had on a new fashionable hunting shirt, and was otherwise well dressed. Whoever will apprehend the said deserter, so that I get him again, shall have 3 l. reward, and reasonable charges if brought home.
     SAMUEL ARELL.

The Virginia Gazette, Purdie, February 28, 1777; March 7, 1777. See *The Virginia Gazette*, May 2, 1777.

DESERTED from Capt. Thomas Waters' company, who was in the carting business, the 12th of this instant from Peeks-Kill, Simon Deane, an apprentice to the subscriber, in the 17th year of his age, 5 feet 3 inches high. Whoever will return said Deserter to his duty at Peek's Kill, or to his master in Salisbury, shall have One Shilling reward, paid by   OLIVER JEWELL.
N. B. All people are forbid harbouring or trusting him on my account.
February 28, 1777.
The Connecticut Courant, and Hartford Weekly Intelligencer, March 3, 1777; March 24, 1777.

Philadelphia, Feb. 26, 1777.
RAN AWAY last night, a servant lad named JACOB BROOKS, a short lad, about 17 or 18 years of age, and squints. Had on a whitish country made cloth coat, and yellow leggings. He is the property of Frederick Kemp, of Maryland, and was in the subscriber's company, in Col. Beatty's battalion of Maryland Militia. Whoever apprehends and secures said servant in any goal of the United States, so that his said Captain or Master may get him again, shall have Three Pounds Reward from   JOHN STONER, Captain.
Dunlap's Pennsylvania Packet or, the General Advertiser, March 4, 1777; March 25, 1777.

CUMBERLAND, *March* 7, 1777.
DESERTED from the third Company of the 2d continental Battalion recruited in this State for the Defence of *Georgia,* the following Soldiers, *viz.* ROBERT TATE, about 26 or 27 Years old, 5 Feet 8 or 9 Inches high, a thin visage, much addicted to Liquor, and when intoxicated very talkative and impertinent. ANDREW HARDY, recruited by Lieutenant *Winfrey* in *Albemarle,* about the same Age and Height. BARTLETT ANDERSON, very tall, and well made, who was a Waggoner and marched as far as *Prince Edward,* where the company was stationed for some Time, from whence he rode off a large Sorrel Horse belonging to the Country, about 5 Feet 2 Inches high, and paces and gallops exceedingly well.—Whoever apprehends the said scoundrels, and brings them to *Cumberland* Courthouse, or secures them in any Gaol, shall have six Pounds Reward for each.

I flatter myself with the greatest Hopes that all Friends to *America* will spare no Pains in apprehending the said Deserters, if

they should hear of them, as they have received their full Bounty, and near four Months Pay.
    JOHN CLARKE, Lieut.
The Virginia Gazette, Dixon and Hunter, March 7, 1777; March 14, 1777.

WHEREAS *mr.* William Fleming Gaines, *an officer of the artillery, hath enlisted CHARLS* [sic] *ERSKINE, who is bound to me as an apprentice under the laws of this commonwealth, without my consent, I do hereby inform mr.* Gaines, *that I shall not consent that the said apprentice may serve under him in that service, and on his applying, either personally or by order, he may receive twenty dollars, which I am informed by Erskine is the* bounty *he received.*
    RICHARD JONES, jun.
The Virginia Gazette, Purdie, March 7, 1777; March 14, 1777.

TWENTY DOLLARS REWARD.
DESERTED *from any company, JESSE JOHNS about* 19 *years old, about* 5 *feet* 10 *inches high, has a fair complexion, light hair and has* [resi]ded *in* Amherst *county for three years past I will give the above reward to any person who delivers the said* deserter *to the commander of the continental forces at Williamsburg, or to me or secures him in any in this state, besides all reasonable charges that attend securing the said* deserter.   JAMES FRANKLIN.
The Virginia Gazette, Purdie, March 7, 1777; March 14, 1777.

Ten DOLLARS reward.
DESERTED *from my company of regulars in the service of the commonwealth of* Virginia, *HEZEKIAH GOODHUE, an* American, *about* 5 *feet* 11 *inches high, had on a sailor's blue jacket, a pair of green cloth breeches patched with blue cloth between the legs. He enlisted lately with lieut.* John Shield *at* York. *Whoever apprehends the* said *deserter, and returns him to the company in* Williamsburg, *shall have the above reward.*
    THOMAS MERIWETHER, capt.
The Virginia Gazette, Purdie, March 7, 1777; March 14, 1777; March 21, 1777.

DESERTED, JEREMIAH HARLEY, who enlisted under me in the Service of this State the 3d of *January,* at which Time I gave him a Furlough for 20 Days; but has since, I am informed, enlisted with one Mr. *Hawkins,* a Lieutenant in the *Georgia* Service. Whoever apprehends the said *Harley,* and secures him so that he may be returned to his Company, or sent to the commanding Officers in *Williamsburg,* shall have TEN DOLLARS Reward.

GEORGE TRIPLETT, Lieut.

The Virginia Gazette, Dixon and Hunter, March 7, 1777; March 14, 1777.

NEWGATE, *Loudoun* county, *Feb.* 20, 1777.
DESERTED from my company in the 2d *Georgia* battalion, *Patrick Duffy,* an *Irishman,* who is fond of liquor, and has been in the marine service. *William Hardy,* born in or near *Frederick* town, *Maryland,* about 6 feet high, well made, about 25 years old, wore a cocked hat, and buckskin breeches. *Owen Cawfield* an *Irishman,* by trade a weaver, well dressed, and is a likely fellow; he sometimes works at brick making, and has lived in *Alexandria. Charles Melton,* born in *Loudoun* county, near col. *Russell's,* and is supposed to be lurking about that neighbourhood. *Charles Phillis* (but sometimes calls himself *John Ferr*) 5 feet 6 or 7 inches high, very well made, seems to be religious at times, though I believe him to be a great villain, and lived near the *Short Hills* in *Loudoun* county.

WILLIAM SMITH, Captain.

∴ Mr. *John Hawkins,* formerly commissary in the 5th *Virginia* regiment, and afterwards accepted of the first lieutenancy in my company, says he is listed 33 men, but afterwards took the liberty to discharge them, and resigned himself. I desire the said men to repair immediately to *Prince Edward* or *Cumberland* court-houses, otherwise they will be treated as deserters.

The Virginia Gazette, Purdie, March 7, 1777; March 21, 1777.

See *The Virginia Gazette,* Purdie, December 6, 1776, for Duffy.

SIX DOLLARS Reward,

RAN away, on Saturday the 22d of February, 1777, an apprentice lad, named SAMUEL WHITE, about 18 years of age, 5 feet 8 inches high, wears his own short black hair; took with him the following clothes, viz. a new light blue coat, made of French cloth, a pair of leather breeches, a good wool hat, yarn stockings, good shoes, two oznaburg shirts, one hunting shirt, and sundry other old clothes. He had been in the Flying Camp, under Captain Tillard, of Maryland, and has since re-inlisted with the same Captain, and received half his bounty money; it is expected that he intends to inlist in some other company in Maryland, or Virginia.—Whoever takes up said lad and secures him in any gaol, shall have the above reward, including what the law allow,

and if brought home, all reasonable charges paid, by me living in Alexandria, Virginia.
> JOHN SAUNDERS.

The Maryland Journal And Baltimore Advertiser, March 11, 1777; March 18, 1777.

DESERTED from the Continental Ship of War the BOSTON, Elkanah Elmes, John Hanes, Jonathan Stearns, Daniel Bain, Elijah Burnam, Andrew Smith, Michael Flanagan, Gideon Washburn, John Laden, William Williamson, William Crow, Samuel Averill, John Cumstock, William Shiels, John Cowling, Richard Sweetland.
EIGHT DOLLARS Reward and necessary Charges will be paid for each of the
> above Deserters, by *Hector McNeil*,
> on board the Ship at BOSTON.

The Continental Journal, And Weekly Advertiser, March 13, 1777; March 20, 1777; March 27, 1777.

> THIS is to give Notice to *Aaron Harris*

a Melatto Fellow, that belonged, of late, to *Edmund Chandler*, of North-Yarmouth, but inlisted with the Subscriber, before he left that Place; this is to inform him, that if he repairs immediately to Boston, he may have his Freedom on honourable Terms,
> by SAMUEL STUBBS, Lieutenant.

The Independent Chronicle and the Universal Advertiser, March 13, 1777.

DESERTED from company, [sic] JOHN WEBSTER, of *Prince Edward*, about 22 years old, 5 feet 9 or 10 inches high, has blue eyes and light hair, his dress, I cannot describe. I will give TWENTY DOLLARS for delivering him to me, or the commanding officer at *Williamsburg*.
> ABNER CRUMP, capt

The Virginia Gazette, Purdie, March 14, 1777; March 21, 1777.
See *The Virginia Gazette*, Purdie. February 14, 1777.

> *Ten DOLLARS reward.*

DESERTED from col. *Charles Harrison's* regiment of artillery, DUNCAN COWAN, a short well made man, with red hair and eyes, by trade a ditcher. He has taken bounty money from three or four recruiting officers, and will no doubt endeavour to deceive more. I have reason to think he is lurking about the town of *Richmond*, where I enlisted him.

WILLIAM F. GAINES, lieut. of artillery.
The Virginia Gazette, Purdie, March 14, 1777.

MARCH 4, 1777.
RALPH COBBS, Edward Cook, Richard Worsham, John M'Carter, John Thompson, Matthew Durham, Jonathan Terrel, John M'Neal, *and* Gideon Patteson, *of my company, who enlisted as privates in the continental service last* August, *had a furlough given them of ten days, after which time they were to join my company, then on their march for general* Washington's *army. And as I have not heard from either of the above mentioned persons since their enlistments, I deem them* deserters, *and will give a reward of TEN DOLLARS for each, upon their being delivered to any continental officer after the* 20*th instant, unless they, or all of them, will deliver themselves up to me in* Mecklenburg, *or to any officers of the first* Virginia *regiment before the* 20*th instant, in which case I promise them a farther bounty of TEN DOLLARS.* ROBERT BALLARD.
The Virginia Gazette, Purdie, March 14, 1777; March 21, 1777.
See *The Virginia Gazette*, Purdie, April 18, 1777, for Worsham.
See *The Virginia Gazette*, Purdie, May 23, 1777, for Terrel/ Terrell.

GEORGE COX, of my company, who has been some time absent on furlough, is hereby ordered to repair immediately to *Williamsburg,* to join his company, otherwise he will be treated as a deserter. Those persons who are properly authorised to receive the wages of *John Taylor, William Hamlet,* and *Frederick Hix,* deceased, are desired to apply to me in *Williamsburg* for what is in my hands.
BEN: POLLARD.
The Virginia Gazette, Purdie, March 14, 1777; March 21, 1777.

DEserted from Col. Talman's Regiment, Capt. James Parker's Company, Benjamin Verry, five Feet ten Inches high, of a light Complexion, a little Pock-broken, and somewhat round shouldered; had on a light Surtout. Daniel Cook, 5 Feet 9 or 19 Inches high, of a dark Complexion; had on a dark great Coat. Isaac Kendel, 6 Feet high, of a light Complexion, stoops a little forward. Ishmael Harris, 5 Feet high, of a dark Complexion; had on a ragged blue Coat. Whoever secures either of the above Deserters, so that they may be returned to their Regiment, shall receive Five Dollars for each,
paid by HENRY ALEXANDER, Lieut.
The Providence Gazette; And Country Journal, March 15, 1777; March 22, 1777.

DESERTED from Capt. Thomas Cole's Company, in Col. Crary's Battalion, John Collins, a Seaman, 5 Feet 5 Inches high, brought up at Marblehead, has red Hair and blue Eyes, 19 Years of Age; had on a red Jacket, a striped Flannel under Jacket, a Check Shirt, and striped Trowsers. Whoever will secure said Deserter in any of the Goals of the United States, and give Notice to me at East-Greenwich, shall have Six Dollars Reward, and all necessary Charges,
    paid by   ROBERT ROGERS, 2d *Lieut.*
The Providence Gazette; And Country Journal, March 15, 1777; March 22, 1777; March 29, 1777.

D*Eserted from my Company, in Col. Patterson's Regiment, the following Persons, viz. Joseph Plaisted of Kittery, aged 23, 5 feet 4, light complexion, served last in Col. Phinney's Regiment, and Capt. Hill's company, bow legged. Stephen Caswell, of Marblehead, a Seafaring Man, aged 25, 5 feet 5, dark complexion. Matthews Teamey, of Marblehead, aged 42, 5 feet 9, light complexion, served last in Col. Stark's Regiment, and Captain Reed's Company. Dennis Cosgrieff, of Stoughton, aged 42, 5 feet 6 light complexion, served last in Colonel Greaton's Regiment, and Captain Bent's Company. Whoever apprehends the above mentioned Deserters, and shall convey them to me at this Place, or shall confine them, and send Intelligence thereat to me, so that they may be taken up, shall receive a Reward of* FIVE DOLLARS *for each of them.*
    ABRAHAM TUCKERMAN, *Captain.*
              Boston, *March* 13. 1777.
The Boston Gazette, And Country Journal, March 17, 1777; March 24, 1777; March 31, 1777.

DESERTED from Capt. John Lewis Venjoul's company, Col. Sheldon's regiment of Cavalry, Nathaniel Stanly, who is so well known that he required no discription. Also, Joseph Harvey, is 23 years of age, well proportioned, light coloured hair, and about 5 feet 6 inches high; it is supposed said Deserters have gone to Massachusetts State. Whoever shall secure the said Stanley and Harvey, and return them to Hartford, shall have Five Dollars for each, and necessary charges paid, by
    THOMAS Y. SEYMOUR, L. L. D.
                 March 17th, 1777.
The Connecticut Courant, And Hartford Weekly Intelligencer, March 17, 1777; March 24, 1777.

DESERTED from his Majesty's ship Brune, James Hurd, belonging to the detachment of marines on that ship; he was servant to the lieut. of marines, and was about the age of 23, five feet eight inches in stature, or thereabouts, of a fresh complexion, wears his hair short, with a Tyburn top: Had on when he deserted a thickset frock and waistcoat, with a red collar; red drilling breeches, with a leather cap such as the light infantry wear. Whoever apprehends the said deserter shall have what is customary on those occasions.
The New-York Gazette; and the Weekly Mercury, March 17, 1777; March 24, 1777.

FOUR POUNDS REWARD.

Annapolis, March 12, 1777.
RAN away from the subscriber, on Tuesday the 11th inst. in the morning, an indented servant man, named THOMAS HARRISON, about 5 feet 5 inches high, fair complexion, and about 26 years of age; by trade a barber and peruke-maker: had on an old blue coat with a red cape, and red flannel jacket. He is fond of strong liquor, and when drunk extremely talkative. Whoever takes up said servant, and secures him so that his master gets him again, shall receive the above reward, if taken ten miles from home, including what the law allows.

SAMUEL HARVEY HOWARD.

P. S. I understand he inlisted in the 2d Virginia regiment, in order to desert to the enemy.
The Maryland Gazette, March 20, 1777.

Twenty DOLLARS reward.
DESERTED from my company of regulars, *THOMAS CHEWNING,* a soldier upwards of 6 feet high, with short black hair, and is well made. He left *Caroline* county, with *John Chewning,* his brother, of capt. *Francis Taylor's* company, also *Thomas Cross,* who enlisted with capt. *Henry Garnett,* and *Samuel Cross* of the train, and it is suspected that the said *Thomas Chewning* has enlisted in the train. whoever delivers the said soldier to the commanding officer at *Williamsburg,* or to me, shall have the above reward.

SAMUEL HAWS, jun.

capt. of the 2d *Virginia* regiment.
The Virginia Gazette, Purdie, March 21, 1777; March 28, 1777; April 4, 1777.

WILLIAMSBURG, *March* 21, 1777.
THE soldiers who deserted from the battalions raised in this state for continental service, who have not yet returned to their duty, it is feared

are concealed, or at least countenanced, by those who falsely call or think themselves their friends though they are in reality not only enemies to the deserters, but to themselves and country in general, by weakening the hands of those who are struggling in the glorious cause of liberty. It is hoped, therefore, that those infatuated people with whom they reside will no longer give them countenance or protection, but on the contrary exert themselves in apprehending and safely delivering them to the officer or officers to whom they belong, or at this place. A reward of FIVE POUNDS for each deserter so apprehended, and safely delivered, if all be paid, Those who return to their respective companies immediately, of their own accord, shall be received with impunity.
    ANDREW LEWIS, Brig. Gen.
The Virginia Gazette, Purdie, March 21, 1777; March 28, 1777.

DESERTED from the *Hero* galley, *JOHN CURLE,* who was enlisted by mr. *Henry Stratton as a marine in Chesterfield* county(of which I believe he is a native) and afterwards enlisted with the subscriber as a seaman. He is about 5 feet 7 inches high, and of a dark complexion. I have been informed that he is lurking some where in *Amelia* county. Whoever will apprehend the said deserter, and deliver him to the subscriber at *Hampton* or (in case of absence) to the commanding officer at *Hampton,* shall receive 8 l. reward
    GEORGE MUTER,
∴ *George Thomson* and *Samuel Ragland,* who had furloughs from me a considerable time ago, to go to *Charles City,* are desired immediately to return to their duty, otherwise they will be considered as deserters.
The Virginia Gazette, Purdie, March 21, 1777; March 28, 1777. 1777.

    KING GEORGE, *March* 10, 1777.
DESERTED from me, about the first of *February* last, *RICHARD MOTT* and *WILLIAM THACKER,* who enlisted with me in the regular service, have taken the bounty money, and got certificates for them; which two men, I am informed, have since enlisted under mr. *Edward Waller,* who is, I understand, to march immediately to *Williamsburg.* Whoever delivers the said two men at *Fredericksburg,* or to me at *King George* courthouse, shall have TEN DOLLARS reward, or FIVE DOLLARS for each.
    JOHN TANKERSLEY, lieut.
The Virginia Gazette, Purdie, March 21, 1777; March 28, 1777.

Mr. PURDIE,

FINDING myself, by an advertisement in your Gazette of the 14th instant, set forth as a deserter from the service of my country, which of all other characters I (at this time particularly) most heartily despise, and which I conceive must have been occasioned by some misunderstanding, thinking it necessary as well to rectify the same as to relieve myself from the odium which would otherwise justly belong to me, I must beg leave to trouble the publick, through your means, with the following narrative of facts.

Some time towards the latter end of August 1776, I enlisted under capt. Lewelling Jones as a trooper in the 4th troop of horse, and until the 24th day of December, in the same year, as far as my indisposition (contracted by the hardships of the service) would permit, continued to act in that capacity; but as my ill state of health would, I found, disable me from going through it with the alacrity and closeness of attention I could wish, I thought proper to apply to the captain for a discharge, which demand was consistent with his promise to me at the time of my enlistment. I therefore provided myself with a man (though under no obligation) to serve in my room, he being first approved of by the captain; and having afterwards qualified, as appears by the following certificate, viz.—AMELIA *sc. This day* Isaac Chapman *qualified before me as a trooper in capt.* Lewelling Jones's *company of light horse, in the place of* Charles Irby, *who is discharged from the service. Given under my hand this* 24*th day of* December, 1776. JOHN WINN—I received from the captain the following discharge, viz.—*Dec.* 24, 1776. *This is to certify, that* Charles Irby *is discharged from the service of my troop of light horse, having got a good man in his room.* LEWELLING JONES—And in consequence of this I promised to send the said Chapman to Fredricksburg, pursuant to which I prepared horses to attend him, but being desirous of informing capt. Jones before I sent him up, directed him in his way to call on the captain, then in the county, who forbid his proceeding any farther, as he would wish he might attend him when he went himself, and for that purpose appointed a day when he should be ready. The man was accordingly provided with horses as before, but was again directed to meet another time, and then at the courthouse, when being upon his way, and informed that the captain as not there, nor likely to be so, he returned as before. Tired out with this delay, the trouble and expense, and anxious to get the said Chapman to the general rendezvous, I furnished him with money and necessaries to set out on foot, who, joining the captain at the courthouse, proceeded to Fredericksburg;

since which, satisfied with having complied with my undertaking, I have not made any inquiry.

Injured reputation compels me to make the above recital. The impartial publick will be able to determine whether the charge of desertion is justly attributed to, sir, your and the
>publick's very humble servant.
>>CHARLES IRBY.

The Virginia Gazette, Purdie, March 21, 1777. See *The Virginia Gazette*, Purdie, February 14, 1777.

DESERTED from my Company, in Col. Marshall's Regiment, *Martin Brinnon*, a Native of Ireland, 21 Years of age, 5 Feet 10 Inches high, dark Complexion, brown Hair, has a meaching [sic] Look, pitted with the Small Pox.— *Philip Fitzpatrick*, about 21 Years old, 5 Feet 8 Inches high, dark Complexion, black Hair, Pock marked, a Native of Ireland, is an ignorant Fellow. Any Person that will take up said Deserters and bring them to Boston, shall have *Ten Dollars*
>Reward, by   CHRIST'r MARSALL. Capt.

The Boston Gazette, And Country Journal, March 24, 1777; March 31, 1777; April 7, 1777.

DESERTED from Capt. Beebe's Company, stationed at Fort Trumbull, on the 24 th Instant, one LEE PECK, of Lyme, a Soldier belonging to said Company; he is about 6 Feet 10 Inches [sic] high, about 28 Years old, light Complexion, sandy Hair. Whoever will return him to said Company, by the 15th of next month, shall receive three Dollars Reward,
>paid by   JABEZ BEEBE, Capt.
>>New London, March 27, 1777.

The Connecticut Gazette; And The Universal Intelligencer, March 28, 1777; April 4, 1777.

SIXTY DOLLARS REWARD

FOR securing the under-mentioned Deserters, enlisted under me for the 15th continental Battalion, NEHEMIAH FENTRESS of *Norfolk* County, RICHARD PHILLIPS of *Louisa* County, LEVI WHITEHURST of *Princes Anne* County, and EMANUEL KELLY, of what County I do not remember. The said *Kelly,* when enlisted, called himself *E. Kemble,* and is thought to be on *Potowmack* River. I will give the above Reward for said Deserters, or twenty Dollars for each, if brought to *Williamsburg,* and delivered to the commanding Officer of that Place.
>WILLIAM GRIMES, Captain.

The Virginia Gazette, Dixon and Hunter, March 28, 1777; April 4, 1777; April 11, 1777.

SOUTHAMPTON county, *March* 27, 1777.
DESERTED, *Daniel Christian* and *John Bescott,* who enlisted with me in the continental service. Any person that will deliver the above deserters to the commanding officer in *Williamsburg* shall receive *TWENTY DOLLARS* reward for each.
JAMES GRAY, capt.
The Virginia Gazette, Purdie, March 28, 1777; April 4, 1777; April 11, 1777.

TWENTY FIVE POUNDS REWARD.
DESERTED from the Company formerly commanded by Captain *Nathaniel Cocke* of the 7th *Virginia* Regiment, the following Soldiers, *viz.* JULIAS DEAN, WILLIAM DEAN, WILLIAM LUCAS, and two of Captain *Reuben Lipscomb*'s Company, that deserted from me in *Amelia* County, *viz.* RICHARD ANDERSON and MATTHEW HUNDLEY. I will give the above Reward for apprehending said Deserters, or five Pounds for each.
TARPLEY WHITE, Lieut.
The Virginia Gazette, Dixon and Hunter, March 28, 1777; April 11, 1777; April 18, 1777. See *The Virginia Gazette*, Purdie, January 24, 1777, for Anderson and Hundley.

ROBERT TATE WHITE, who formerly lived with *David White* near *Richmond,* is desired to repair to *York* Town immediately to do Duty as a Matross, agreeable to his Enlistment with *John Hughes,* to serve in my Company of Artillery; also JOHN WILLIAMS, of *Prince George,* who enlisted the 9th of *January* with Bombardier *Jones* at *Jamestown.* If the said *White* and *Williams* neglect this Summons, they may expect to be treated as Deserters. I will give a Reward of ten Dollars each for JOHN and CORKER HOWARD of *Gloucester* County, who deserted from my Company the 11th of this Month. I have some Reason to believe they are in *Robins's Neck,* harboured by some disaffected Persons.
WILLIAM PIERCE, Junior.
The Virginia Gazette, Dixon and Hunter, March 28, 1777; April 4, 1777. See *The Virginia Gazette*, June 6, 1777, for White and Williams.

DESERTED from my company the 7th *Virginia* regiment, on their march from *Williamsburg* to *Fredericksburg*, the following soldiers viz. *Reuben Cox,* a stout young fellow, about 6 feet high, 22 years old, has dark hair and complexion, but his dress I cannot describe. *Carter Fletcher,* about 20 years old, 5 feet 8 inches high, has dark hair and complexion, and his uniform was pale blue, turned up with red calimanco. *Benjamin Dean,* about 23 years old, and *Curtis Hardy,* about 20 years old, their dress I cannot describe. *Cox* and *Fletcher* were enlisted in *Essex, Dean* in *King and Queen,* and *Hardy* in *Middlesex.* Whoever apprehends the said deserters, and deliver them at head quarters in *Williamsburg,* shall have *TEN DOLLARS* reward for each.
     JOHN WEBB, capt.
The Virginia Gazette, Purdie, March 28, 1777; April 4, 1777.

DEserted from Capt. Potter's Company, in Col. Angell's Regiment, David Starr, about 5 Feet 9 Inches high, of a dark Complexion, has dark brown Hair, and dark Eyes, says he was born in Middleborough. Whoever will take up said Deserter, and return him to the Subscriber in Providence, shall have Five Dollars Reward, and all reasonable Charges, paid by
     ABEL CARPENTER, Lieut.
The Providence Gazette; And Country Journal, March 29, 1777.

THIS is to give Notice to Lewis Sylli[a], inlisted by me at Ticonderoga, in Capt. Abraham Hunt's Company—To John Stover, inlisted at Albany in said Company—And to Thomas Chilman, inlisted likewise at Albany in said Company, to repair to their Companies at Boston or Springfield by the first of April, otherwise they will be deemed and treated as Deserters.
     PHILIP ULMER, Lieut. of said Comp'y.
The Boston-Gazette, and Country Journal, March 31, 1777; April 7, 1777.

D*Eserted from Captain Webb's Company, and Colonel Shepard's Regiment, the following Persons, viz. John Thomas, aged 19, 5 Feet 6, light Complexion, light short Hair, and blue Eyes; John Gilbert Smith, aged 17, 5 Feet 5, dark short Hair, grey Eyes: They have both received the Continental Bounty. Whoever will take up said Deserters, and bring them to me at Westfield, or confine them in Goal and give Intelligence, shall have* Ten Dollars *Reward each, and all necessary Charges paid by*
     LEVI LINDLEY, Lieut.

N. B. *Said Thomas has a Mark under his Left Ear, about a big as a Copper, of a bright Claret Colour—said Smith belongs to Boston. It is hoped that every Friend to his Country will take Care to detect all such Persons, that they may be dealt with according to the Nature of their Crimes.*
The Boston-Gazette, and Country Journal, March 31, 1777; April 7, 1777; April 14, 1777.

DESERTED from Captain Champion's company, in Col. Wyllys's regiment, on the 5th inst. one *James Alexander Johnson*, he is about 40 years of age, 5 feet 6 inches high, light coloured hair, grey eyes, middling size, walks upright, slow in speech, had on a light coloured broad cloth coat, a jacket of the same, and an old pair of leather breeches. Whoever will take up said deserter and confine him, or return him to the subscriber at Hartford, shall have FIVE DOLLARS reward and all necessary charges
          paid by   PRENTICE HOSMER, *Ensign.*
                                            March 15, 1777.
The Connecticut Courant, And Hartford Weekly Intelligencer, March 31, 1777.

ON Sunday evening last, Serjeants James Aitkin and Uriah Rowland, and Robert Simpson, a Matross, all of Captain Samuel Mansfield's company, in Colonel John Lamb's battalion of Continental artillery, absented themselves. They are hereby ordered to return immediately to their company in New-Haven, or join any of the recruiting officers in that State, belonging to Col. Lamb's battalion, on pain of being punished as deserters.
          ELEAZER OSWALD, Lt. Col.
          (Continental Artillery.
It is supposed they have absconded in order to avoid being thrown into the common jail, (and confined with persons committed for his treason against the United American States) by the civil authority, for being charges with having committed a riot, sequently a *"capital crime,"* terminated to the satisfaction of the major part of the inhabitants, and the party most injured.
The Connecticut Journal, April 2, 1777.

DESERTED from my Company in Col. BRADFORD's Regiment, *John Johnson*, belonging to *Martha's-Vineyard.*—Whoever will take up said *Jonson*, and secure him in *Barnstable* or *Plymouth* Goal, shall have TWENTY DOLLARS Reward, and all necessary Charges paid,
          by   THOMAS TURNER, Capt.

Pembroke, March 30, 1777.
The Continental Journal, And Weekly Advertiser, April 3, 1777;
April 10, 1777.

DESERTED from Capt. *Abraham Hunt's* Company, Colonel *Patterson's* Regiment, *William Jackson*, aged 21, 5 Feet 10 Inches, light Complexion, dark Hair and Eyes, Pock marked, a very stout, well set Fellow: *Daniel Patterson*, aged 27, 5 Feet 10, dark Complexion, grey Eyes, dark Hair, a little Pock marked: *John Welsh*, aged 22, 5 Feet 7, dark Complexion, grey Eyes, dark Hair. Whoever will take up and return one or all of said Deserters, shall receive *Five Dollars*
        for each, by   A. HUNT, Capt.
The Independent Chronicle and the Universal Advertiser, April 3, 1777.

DESERTED from the 15th *Virginia* regiment, WILLIAM LYAL, country born, about 28 years, old, 5 feet 10 or 11 inches high, has a very thin visage, black hair, and commonly wears a blue coat turned up with white. Also WILLIAM CATTON, about 6 feet high, 23 or 24 years old, of a fresh complexion, has a cast in one of his eyes, and short light hair. They both deserted from *King William* county. Whoever brings the said deserters to head quarters in Williamsburg shall have *TWENTY DOLLARS* reward for each.
        GILES RAINES, lieut.
The Virginia Gazette, Purdie, April 4, 1777; April 11, 1777; April 18, 1777. See *The Virginia Gazette*, April 18, 1777.

WHEREAS a certain *HENRY PEAY* enlisted as a soldier with lieut. *Raines* of *King William* county, and was qualified by mr. *Francis West* of said county on the first of *January* 1777. (a certificate of which I have now got in my possession) at which time he received part of his bounty money, but since hath enlisted in the *Georgia* service under capt. *Porter,* and the said lieut. *Raines* having made over to me his right to the said *Peay*. I do hereby require that he repair to *Williamsburg* by the 10th of *April* and join the troops raised for the defence of this state, when I will pay him what part of his bounty money is still due.
        EDWARD WALLER, lieut. in the colonial service.
    N. B. Should the said *Peay* neglect complying with the above advertisement, he may depend on being treated as a deserter, and I will give TEN DOLLARS reward to whoever delivers him to me after this time.

The Virginia Gazette, Purdie, April 4, 1777; April 11, 1777; April 18, 1777.

NOTICE is hereby given to the soldiers that are absent from my company on furlough, or that were sick when I marched from *Culpeper,* that if they do not come to head quarters in *Williamsburg* within 12 days after the publication of this advertisement they will be treated as *deserters* —Deserted from my company of regulars, *JOSEPH WARWICK,* about 5 feet 10 inches high, a well looking man, stout made, was formerly skipper of a vessel, and is commonly about *Hobbs's Hole.* Also *DAVID VAUTERS,* who is about the heighth of *Warwick,* has black hair and eyes, and was formerly a deputy commissary to col. Barber. Whoever delivers the said deserters to me, or mr. *Peter Stubblefield,* my first lieutenant, in *Williamsburg,* shall have 5 l. reward for each.— *John Alexander* is requested to come to the camp immediately, that I may give him up as a marine to the Hon. the Board of Admiralty, or otherwise I shall treat him as a deserter.
    JOHN CAMP, capt.
The Virginia Gazette, Purdie, April 4, 1777.

Twenty DOLLARS reward.

DESERTED from *Elk Ridge* landing, *Maryland,* the 5th of February last, four soldiers belonging to capt. *Charles Fleming's* company of the 7th *Virginia* regiment. *PLEASANT LOCKETT,* 5 feet 9 or 10 inches high, rather spare made, smooth faced, has dark brown hair, wore a light coloured coarse cloth coat, a red waistcoat, and a pair of brown frieze leggins, and had with him a bundle in a blanket. *RICHARD COX,* a stout well set man, about 6 feet high, round shouldered, wears his own dark hair, had on a hunting shirt, died with a dark colour, a pair of brown frieze leggings, his other dress I do not recollect; had with him a bundle in a blanket, a small red trunk, and a rifle. *ABRAHAM LEAR,* very near the height of *Richard Cox* in much the same dress, has with him a bundle in a blanket, and a rifle. *JOEL JOHNSON,* a low well set man, about 5 feet 5 or 6 inches high, wears his own hair and very large whiskers, full faced; had on a hunting shirt dyed black, fringed round the capes, ruffles, tail, and down the breast, belted with the skin of a rattle snake, and had with him a bundle in a blanket. The above reward, or *FIVE DOLLARS* for each, will be given on their being apprehended and delivered to the commanding officer at *Williamsburg,* or to the commanding officer of the 7th *Virginia* regiment at the continental camp, and all reasonable expenses paid.

M. CARRINGTON, lieut.
The Virginia Gazette, Purdie, April 4, 1777. See *The Virginia Gazette*, Purdie, May 2, 1777. for Lear.

DESERTED *from Hartford, on the night after the* 21*st of March last, from Capt. Bernard's company, in Col. Wylly's regiment, two soldiers: James Jefferys, a native of Ireland about 5 feet 10 inches high, dark short strait hair, a scar over each eye on his forehead and right cheek, wears or carried with him, a grey Surtout, one brown short coat, three waistcoats, a light brown, a red, and one striped, green breeches, and a light brown regimental coat without faceings. William Davidson, a Scotchman, about 5 feet 6 inches high, dark complexion, brown hair them club'd, carried off a light brown regimental coat, with red faceings, one blue coat, buff coloured waistcoat, buck-skin breeches.—Whoever will apprehend either of said deserters and return him to the regiment, shall have five dollars reward for each, and all expences*
    paid, by CHARLES MILLER, Lieut.
               Hartford, April 1, 1777.
The Connecticut Courant, And Hartford Weekly Intelligencer, April 7, 1777; April 14, 1777.

DESERTED from Capt. Ball's company, in Col. Shepard's regiment, one Azariah Sweet, about 22 years of age, 5 feet 6 inches high, dark complexion, had on a brown homemade coat and jacket, a pair of old leather breeches. Whoever will take up said deserter, and return him to Westfield, or confine him and give information to the subscriber, shall have FIVE DOLLARS reward and necessary charges
    paid, by MARTIN SMITH, Lieut.
               Westfield, April 4, 1777.
The Connecticut Courant, And Hartford Weekly Intelligencer, April 7, 1777; April 14, 1777; April 21, 1777.

       Ten Dollars reward.
FOR *John Taylor,* who enlisted under me as lieutenant of the 15th battalion, and deserted from *King William* county. He is an inhabitant of *Gloucester,* about 5 feet 10 inches high, his clothing I do not recollect. The above reward will be thankfully given to any person who delivers the said *Taylor* to his commanding officer in *Williamsburg.*
    HENRY QUARLES, lieut.
The Virginia Gazette, Purdie, April 11, 1777; April 18, 1777.

Fifty DOLLARS REWARD.

DESERTED from me, out of my quota of regulars, *Thomas Gratton,* who is supposed to have since enlisted with capt. *John Willis* of the 2d regiment; *Randolph Thornton,* and *Ishmael Lawrence* who have since enlisted with ensign *Hopson* in the service of this state; *Joseph Benjamin,* who has gone in capt. *Lee's* company of light horse; and *Luke Hazlewood.* Those officers in whose companies they are in are requested to send the above deserters to *Williamsburg* without delay, and I hereby offer a reward of *TEN DOLLARS* each for the deserters above mentioned.
          JOHN TOWNS, ensign.
The Virginia Gazette, Purdie, April 11, 1777; April 18, 1777; April 25, 1777.

140 *DOLLARS reward*

FOR securing the under mentioned deserters enlisted under me for capt. *Smith*'s company of the 2d *Georgia* battalion, *viz. John Williams,* who served under capt. *Morgan Alexander* but what county he came from I do not remember. *Robert Wilkins,* of *Henrico* (who I have been informed has since enlisted with one lieut. *Valentine,* and therefore forewarn the said *Valentine* from keeping him) *John Lee,* and *John Stiff,* of *Bedford, John Vest* of *Buckingham,* and *Thomas Kelly,* who informed me he had been a prisoner with the *Indians.* I will give the above reward for the said deserters, or *TWENTY DOLLARS* for each, if brought to *Cumberland* or *Prince Edward* courthouses, where they may join their company.
          ALEX: BAUGH, lieut.
The Virginia Gazette, Purdie, April 11, 1777; April 18, 1777.

WHEREAS *James Richey,* an inhabitant of *Lunenburg,* enlisted under me as a soldier, agreeable to act of Assembly, and has since enlisted under mr. *Edward Ragsdale,* and refuses to serve under me, I therefore deem him a deserter, and offer a reward of FIFTY DOLLARS to any person or persons that will apprehend the said *James Richey,* and deliver him to me, or the commanding officer in *Williamsburg.*
          EPAPHRODITUS RUDDER. lieut.
The Virginia Gazette, Purdie, April 11, 1777.

Ten *DOLLARS reward.*

DESERTED from my company, enlisted in *Westmoreland* county, a certain *John Lefavour, Virginia,* born, about 5 feet 8 or 9 inches high,

remarkably knock-kneed, his countenance long, very hard features, and his looks very surly (but not more so than his disposition and speech) his hair long, straight, and lightish, and his speech slow. He is supposed to be lurking either in the upper parts of *Northumberland* or the lower parts of *Westmoreland.* I have heard that he went to *Maryland,* but should rather think that he will not leave this neighbourhood, as he is a very ignorant person. Whoever will take up the said deserter, and convey him to me now in *Fredericksburg,* or hereafter to the place where the 15th *Virginia* regiment will be stationed, or will secure him where I may get him again, shall receive the reward aforesaid, together with the expenses they may be at
     for him. GEO: LEE TURBERVILLE, capt.
The Virginia Gazette, Purdie, April 11, 1777.

Ten POUNDS reward.

DESERTED from my recruits belonging to capt *James Mason*'s company of the 15th *Virginia* battalion, *William Fog,* a native of *Great Britain,* about 6 feet high, with black hair; also *Benjamin Seward* a *Virginian,* about 5 feet 10 inches high, stout made. The above reward will be paid to the person that delivers the said deserters to the commanding officer of the continental troops at *Williamsburg,* or 5 l. for either.
     BINNS JONES lieut.
The Virginia Gazette, Purdie, April 11, 1777; April 18, 1777.

Forty DOLLARS reward.

FOR delivering to the commanding officer in *Williamsburg* the following deserters belonging to capt. *Anderson*'s company 5th of the regiment, or TEN DOLLARS for each *Henry Dickerson, William Archer, Cluverious Duke,* and *Jesse Meeks. Dickerson and Archer* deserted from *Williamsburg* a few days before the regiment marched for *New York; Duke* and *Meeks* deserted from *Trenton, New Jersey.* They are now lurking in *Hanover* county where they were enlisted, and where they are so well known that any description is needless. W. BENTLEY, lieut.
The Virginia Gazette, Purdie, April 11, 1777; April 18, 1777.

Eighty DOLLARS reward.

DESERTED from my company of the 15th battalion of continental troops, ROBERT PEALE, about 25 years old, 5 feet 10 inches high, and I am informed was seen crossing *Fishing* creek in *North Carolina. SAMUEL HOSCA,* about 35 years old, 5 feet 9 or 10 inches high, of a ruddy healthy complexion, and drinks hard. *MARTIN REDMAN,*

about 22 years old, 5 feet 6 inches high, has light coloured hair, and is very impertinent; he is by trade a shoemaker. *GEORGE RATCLIFF,* about 30 years of age, 5 feet 10 inches high, a native of *England,* and slightly marked with the smallpox. I will give the above reward for the said deserters, or TWENTY DOLLARS for each that shall be delivered to me in *Williamsburg,* or confined in jail so that I get them again. JOHN GREGORY.
The Virginia Gazette, Purdie, April 11, 1777; April 18, 1777; April 25, 1777; May 2, 1777; May 9, 1777.

DESERTED from my company of regulars in the 6th *Virginia* regiment, WILLIAM MANGUM, about 4 feet [*sic*] 10 inches high, has a light complexion, blue eyes, and is well proportioned. Also CHARLES COCKRAM, about 4 feet [*sic*] 11 inches high, round shouldered, knock-kneed, and of a dark complexion. I suspect some of *Mangum*'s relations in *Sussex* have concealed him, and that *Cockram* is near the fork of *Roanoake,*. If either of the above soldiers will deliver themselves up within 15 days after the publication of this advertisement to the commanding officer in *Williamsburg,* they shall receive pardon; but if taken, and safely conveyed to the commanding officer, I will give a reward of TEN DOLLARS for each.
 SAMUEL HOPKINS, capt.
The Virginia Gazette, Purdie, April 11, 1777; April 18, 1777.

DESERTED from capt. *Richard Steven's* company, of Caroline county, the following soldiers, viz. *George Holloway,* a young man, who was seen to pass to the upper end of *Hanover. Thomas Chandler,* who lived in the lower end of *Caroline. John Melone,* much noted for his shrill speech. *Henry Webster, William Stevens, James Grigsby, Joshua Dunn* (of *Essex* county) and *John Taylor.* As I am unacquainted with these men, it is out of my power to give a particular description of them, but I expect every man who wishes well to his country will examine all suspected persons; and if any of them are taken and conveyed to me, or to any officer in *Fredericksburg,* I will give FIVE DOLLARS reward for each.
 DANIEL TOMPKINS, 2d. lieut.
The Virginia Gazette, Purdie, April 11, 1777; April 18, 1777. See *The Virginia Gazette*, Purdie, May 16, 1777, for Melone/Malone.

DESERTED from head quarters, at or near *Princeton,* the following soldiers belonging to my company in the 4th *Virginia* regiment, viz. *Aaron Brown,* serjeant, about 21 years old, 5 feet 9 or 10 inches, high freckle faced, with short curled hair. *John Edmunds,* a carpenter by trade, stoops and well made, with short curled hair, of a brown cast. *James Blick,* about 20 years old, 5 feet 8 or 9 inches high, with black curled hair, *Robert Jones,* a close well set man, about 5 feet the 6 or 7 inches high. They lately got into the county of *Brunswick,* where all, or most of them, were horn, and are well known. Whoever secures the said deserters, so as I get them before I return to the Northward, which will be in a few weeks, shall receive for *Brown* 40 *DOLLARS,* and for each of the others 30 *DOLLARS,* if delivered to me in *Brunswick* county, or to the commanding officer at *Williamsburg.*

JAMES LUCAS, captain.

The Virginia Gazette, Purdie, April 11, 1777; April 18, 1777; May 2, 1777.

LEWIS CHARES, [*sic*] jun, of *Brunswick,* belonging to the 15th battalion, having stayed beyond the time prescribed by his furlough, I will give a reward of *FORTY DOLLARS* for him, if brought to *Fredericksburg,.* He is upwards of 6 feet high, has a light complexion, with red curled hair, and has lost one eye.

PHILIP MALLORY. lieut.

The Virginia Gazette, Purdie, April 11, 1777.

RICHARD HOOPER, about 20 years of age, about 6 feet high, of dark complexion, dark eyes and hair, had a furlough on account of sickness some time last summer, since which he has failed to return to my company in the 6th *Virginia* regiment, and is still lurking about his father's in *Lunenburg* county. I will therefore give a reward of 10 l. *Virginia* currency to any person that will deliver him to the commanding officer in *Williamsburg,* or to the above regiment.

JAMES JOHNSON, capt.

The Virginia Gazette, Purdie, April 11, 1777

DESERTED from capt. *John Willis* company, on their march to the Northward, a soldier by the name of *Jos Bryant,* who lives in the upper end of *Westmoreland,* and frequently to be seen at mr. *Benjamin Johnston*'s ordinary, where he was enlisted. He is a well made man, with a dark skin, and black hair, about 5 feet 9 or 10 inches high; had on when he deserted a dark hunting shirt. Whoever will bring the said *Bryant* to *Fredericksburg,* and deliver him to capt. *Willis* shall receive TEN DOLLARS reward.

BEN HOOMES. lieut.

The Virginia Gazette, Purdie, April 11, 1777; April 18, 1777.

DESERTED from Capt. Lee's Company in Col. Durkee's Regiment, some Time past, one John Gills, is 27 Years old, 5 Feet 7 Inches high, grey Eyes, short black Hair, much Pock-broken; said Gills serv'd last Campaign in Col. Tyler's Regiment, 'tis suppos'd he is gone to the State of Rhode Island, or some Part of Hartford where he formerly lived. Whoever will secure in Goal, or return him to his Duty in said Regiment, shall receive a Reward of EIGHT DOLLARS, and all necessary Charges.   DANIEL WAIT, Lieut.
The Connecticut Gazette; and Universal Intelligencer, April 18, 1777; May 2, 1777.

Ten DOLLARS reward.
DESERTED from capt. *Winstin*'s company of continental infantry, *JOHN SOREL,* about 5 feet 8 or 9 inches high, light hair, and is subject to drink. He will, I expect, try to get to *North Carolina.* Whoever delivers the said deserter to the commanding officer at *Williamsburg,* or to the subscriber in *Fredericksburg,* shall have the above reward.   J. OVERTON, jun. lieut.
The Virginia Gazette, Purdie, April 18, 1777.

WHEREAS lieut. *Giles Raines* has advertised *William Lyall* as a deserter, I wish he had done it before he left this state, as I might have mentioned some circumstances relative to this affair which I should be glad to avoid in his absence. However, I think it my duty to inform the publick, or at least those whom it may concern, that mr. *Lyall* has regularly enlisted with me in col. *Charles Harrison*'s regiment of artillery, and may be found in *York* garrison at any time, and in my opinion will be able to acquit himself from that heinous crime with which mr. *Raines* has been pleased to charge him.
   DRURY RAGSDALE.
The Virginia Gazette, April 18, 1777; April 25, 1777; May 2, 1777. See *The Virginia Gazette,* April 4, 1777.

CHARLOTTE, *April* 3, 1777.
WHEREAS capt. *Ballard* has advertised me as a deserter, I beg leave to acquaint that gentleman, and the publick, with the whole truth of the case. On account of my ill state of health, I obtained a furlough for ten days, at the expiration of which I repaired to *Hanover* courthouse, which was appointed the place of rendezvous; but as my ill state of health continued, and not being able to march, lieut. *John Clayton* gave me leave to return home till the men he was to recruit

should march, during which time the recruiting officers of *Charlotte* were chosen, and I was appointed an ensign, have enlisted my quota of men, obtained my commission, and shall march in a few days. RICHARD WORSHAM, ensign.
The Virginia Gazette, Purdie, April 18, 1777. See *The Virginia Gazette*, Purdie, March 14, 1777.

JOSEPH WILSON and *Joseph Smith*, soldiers, whom I enlisted in *Prince Edward*, are ordered to repair to *Dumfries* by the 15th of *April*. Those who fail will be considered as deserters, and treated as such. GRANVILLE SMITH.
The Virginia Gazette, Purdie, April 18, 1777.

DESERTED from my company of continental regulars, *John Bently, Charles Hansley, Josiah Blankenship,* and *James Watts*. I will give a reward of 15 *DOLLARS* for apprehending each of the above deserters, on their being delivered at head quarters in *Williamsburg.*
HENRY CONWAY, capt.
The Virginia Gazette, Purdie, April 18, 1777; May 2, 1777.

DESERTED from my company of continental regulars, from *Pittsylvania* county, the following soldiers, viz. *Peter Monro, William Harrison, Walter Walters, Peter Hutchison, Archibald Williams, John Tomlin, William Still, Isaac Ferris, William Lawson, Terry McDaniel, John Tamborough,* and *David [Free]man*. I will give 10 DOLLARS reward for each of the above deserters, upon their being sent to head quarters in *Williamsburg,* and for the said *Peter Monro* 5 l.
PETER DUNN, capt.
The Virginia Gazette Purdie, April 18, 1777.

DESERTED from capt. *Nathaniel Fox* 's company in the 6th Virginia, regiment, *Benjamin Watt* of *Southampton,* for apprehending of whom, and bringing him to head quarters in *Williamsburg,* I will give 20 DOLLARS reward. BILLY H. AVERY.
The Virginia Gazette, Purdie, April 18, 1777; May 2, 1777.

DESERTED from capt. *Samuel Hopkins's* company of the 6th Virginia 6th *Virginia* regiment, *BERRY HUNT,* and *JOHN CORDILL. Hunt* is a small man, with black hair and eyes. *Cordill* is a low man, and well made, with black hair and eyes. The above soldiers are from *Mecklenburg* county, in this state. Whoever will apprehend and bring the above mentioned soldiers to head quarters in *Williamsburg* shall have *TEN DOLLARS* reward.

PHILEMON HOCKADAY. ensign.
The Virginia Gazette, Purdie, April 18, 1777.

CUMBERLAND TOWN, *April* 9, 1777.
DESERTED from on board the ship JANE, last night, three *Spaniards,* sailors, viz. *Anthony Samator,* a tall fellow, about 23 years old, much pitted with the smallpox, about 5 feet 10 or 11 inches high. *Lewis Morrel,* a short well set fellow, of a very dark complexion, almost black. The other a short well set fellow, with three of his fingers on his right hand much wounded. The above mentioned men were shipped on board the *Defiance* at *Curacoa,* to serve this state 12 months as seamen according to the rules and regulations of Congress, and cannot speak *English.* I will give ten dollars reward for each man, if secured in any jail so that I get them again.
WILLIAM GREEN, capt.
The Virginia Gazette, Purdie, April 18, 1777.

DESERTED *Claiborne Hall,* a stout well set young man, about 5 feet 7 or 8 inches high, with a downish look, and brown hair cut short in the neck. He is supposed to be in the upper end of *Hanover,* and I am told offered to enlist with capt. *Thompson.* Also deserted, *Jury Smith,* a stout young man, about the same height of *Hall* has red hair, and many warts on his hands; he was born in *King Williams,* and am informed enlisted with mr. *James Quarles.* The aforesaid men were enlisted by me for the service of this commonwealth. Whoever will deliver them to me in *Hanover,* or the commanding officer in *Williamsburg,* shall receive TWENTY DOLLARS reward; but if the said men will return to their duty, I promise that no farther notice shall be taken of the affair.
THOMAS SMITH.
The Virginia Gazette, Purdie, April 18, 1777; May 2, 1777.

DEserted, last Week, from Capt. Rigg's Company, in Col. Smith's Regiment, Nicholas Shippey, 28 Years of Age, about 5 Feet 10 Inches high, has a down Look, black Hair, is somewhat given to Liquor: Had on when he went away, a lightish outside jacket, a blue Waistcoat, white Tow and Linen Trowsers, much wore, and an old bound Hat. Whoever takes up said Deserter, and confines him in any Gaol, or returns him to his Company again, shall have Five Dollars Reward, and all necessary Charges paid by SQUIRE FISK, Lieut.
The Providence Gazette; And Country Journal, April 19, 1777; April 26, 1777; May 3, 1777; May 10, 1777.

THIS is to give Notice to Benjamin Stephens and William Smith of Old York, Samuel Fall, of Berwick; John Hutchings, of Casco-Bay; John Blachford, of Cape-Ann; and Jacob Lankerster, of Woolwich; to Repair to Springfield, and join Col. Alden's Regiment, to which you belong, being the Place of Rendezvous for said Regiment, you being Inlisted into my Company.
     LUKE DAY, Capt.
             Springfield, April 10th, 1777.
The Boston-Gazette, And Country Journal, April 21, 1777; April 28, 1777; May 5, 1777; *The Continental Journal, And Weekly Advertiser*, April 24, 1777; May 2, 1777.

IN the *Connecticut Courant,* March 17th, 1777, James Taylor was so ungenerous, unhumane and abusive as to advertise Deborah his wife as a deserter from his bed and board, which is so abusive to the unfortunate Deborah as to oblige her to declare to the public, that James Taylor never did provide neither bed or board for his wife or family, but was for most part of his time absent, but for what purpose I cannot say; he brought nothing home but abusive language for my comfort and the support of his children; and since this unhappy war, he has been inlisted as a soldier, and went to Canada, from whence he deserted, and his unusual return, on account the unusual season of the year, he was suspected for a deserter, was the reason I would not find him any longer bed or board, and am now under the necessity of applying to my friends for necessary subsistence for myself
    and children. DEBORAH TAYLOR.
The Connecticut Courant, and Hartford Weekly Intelligencer, April 21, 1777; April 28, 1777; May 5, 1777; May 12, 1777. See *The Connecticut Courant, and Hartford Weekly Intelligencer,* March 17, 1777.

INLISTED with me the subscriber and then absconded, one John Lloyd had on blue regimentals turned up with red, he is about 30 years of age, 5 feet 10 inches high, light complexion, has a white film over his right eye. Whoever takes up said deserter, and returns him to me in Capt. Jeremiah Miller's company, in Col. Patterson's regiment, shall receive five dollars and all necessary charges
     paid, by JONAH FRISBIE, Capt.
            Lai[e]sbourough, March 20, 1777.
The Connecticut Courant, and Hartford Weekly Intelligencer, April 21, 1777; April 28, 1777

DESERTED on the 11th instant, from Capt. Samuel Mansfield's company, in Col. John Lamb's battalion, a matross, named Thomas Mory, a native of Ireland, is about 5 feet 7 inches high, light complexion, pitted with the small-pox, had on a light colour'd coat, pair of leather breeches, and a pair of white threat stockings. Whoever takes him up, and delivers him to any officer belonging to the above battalion, or secures him in any continental goal, shall receive Eight Dollars reward, and all necessary charges
            paid by   JOHN MILES, (*the third*) Lieut.
                              New-Haven, April 23, 1777.
The Connecticut Journal, April 23, 1777; April 30, 1777; May 7, 1777.

THIS is to give Notice to *Zachariah Gatchel*, of Wells, *Samuel Lancaster*, of Newbury, and *William*, alias *Solomon Jordon*, of Cape-Elizabeth, all of Capt. Donnel's Company, in Col. Brewer's Battalion, who have kept themselves concealed from said Company; that if they will voluntarily surrender themselves to any Office, [*sic*] in the Continental Army, or join any Corps (bound to Ticonderoga) before the 15th Day of May next, they shall be intitled to, and receive the Pardon offered in General Washington's Proclamation, otherwise they will be dealt with, in every respect, as Deserters.
            HENRY SEWALL, Lieutenant.
                              Boston, April 23, 1777.
The Independent Chronicle and the Universal Advertiser, April 24, 1777; May 2, 1777.

THE Committee of Correspondence &c. of Rutland, hereby inform the Public, that on the night of the 17th instant SAMUEL MURRAY, Prisoner of war, escaped from his confinement in Rutland. Any person that shall take up and confine the said Prisoner in any Goal in this State, shall have ONE DOLLAR reward and necessary Charges paid.
                              Rutland, April 21, 1777.
The Massachusetts Spy: Or, American Oracle of Liberty, April 24, 1777.

DESERTED from Capt. James Eldridge's Company, in Col. Huntington's Regiment, a soldier who calls himself Robert Patterson, of Ashford, in the State of Connecticut, is about 5 Feet 6 or 7 Inches high, light Eyes, light Complexion, and sandy Hair, a pretty well set Man, he went towards Boston. Whoever will apprehend said Deserter, and secure him in any Goal in the United States, and notify the

Subscriber at Middletown, shall receive Eight Dollars Reward and all necessary Charges. ELISHA BREWSTER, Lieut.
The Connecticut Gazette; and Universal Intelligencer, April 25, 1777; May 2, 1777.

DESERTED from Col. John Durkee's Regiment of Continental Troops, an inlisted Soldier, whose Name is AMOS GREEN, is about 26 Years old, and about 5 Feet and 11 Inches high, well-set, short black Hair, a brown Eye, down look, something round shouldered, well dressed and a Suit of Regimentals, the Coat brown faced with red, one strip'd Shirt, one white Holland Ditto, one Pair of long Breeches, one Pair of gray Stockings, two Pair of Shoes, one Pair of brown cloth Breeches, a Castor Hatt, bound with a yellow Tinsey Lace, and some other Things besides, has a sore Toe on his right Foot. Whoever will take up said Deserter, and confine him in any of the Goals in this State shall have TEN DOLLARS Reward, or the same Reward to return him to said Regiment.
NATH'l BISHOP, Lieut.
The Connecticut Gazette; and Universal Intelligencer, April 25, 1777; May 2, 1777.

DESERTED from *Williamsburg,* the 19th of *January* 1777, *Edward Hammond,* a man about 45 years old, 5 feet 9 or 10 inches high, wears short hair, speaks very fast, and is very brisk and active to his age. *John Adams* (whose proper name is *Grigg*) who deserted the 1st of *March* ; he is a stout well set man, 30 years of age, 5 feet 8 or 9 inches high, has short black curly hair, large whiskers, black eyes, a round full face, writes a good hand, and is a pretty good scholar. Also *James Linney,* a young man, has a boyish look, a long visage, wears short bushy lightish coloured hair, and is tolerably slim made. A reward of 20 DOLLARS will be given on their being apprehended and delivered to the commanding officer at *York,* and all reasonable charges paid.
RICHARD HILL, lieut. in the artillery.
N. B. The above men have been accustomed to the sea.
The Virginia Gazette, Purdie, April 25, 1777; May 2, 1777.

Fifteen Pounds Reward
For taking up and securing *John Foster, Francis Kenley,* and *Joel Melton,* who *deserted* from my company of continental regulars of the 7th regiment. *Foster* was born in *Louisa,* and I hear is lurking thereabouts and in *Amelia.* The other two are natives of *Albemarle.*

The above reward will be paid by lieutenant *Fox* now at *Williamsburg,* or the subscriber at *Albemarle* courthouse.
M. JOUETT.
The Virginia Gazette, Purdie, April 25, 1777.

HANOVER, *April* 9, 1777.
WILLIAM FRASER, who was advertised as a deserter by capt. *William Lane,* jun. of *Georgia,* is a ward of mine. He is at very unhappy young gentleman, and returned lately to me in a most wretched situation. I have now got him in order to join his company, which he shall forthwith do, unless I can come upon other terms. I could at any time get a letter from the post office in *Newcastle,* where I wish one to be sent as soon as possible.
RICHARD CHAPMAN.
The Virginia Gazette, Purdie, April 25, 1777; May 2, 1777. See *The Virginia Gazette*, Purdie, December 6, 1776.

WILLIAM CROXTON, and *James Davis,* of my company, are ordered to repair immediately to *Williamsburg,* and to join the detachment of the 1st *Virginia* regiment now on their march to the continental army in the *Jerseys. Croxton* is desired to pay the money lodged with him for the purpose of recruiting men to capt. *Charles Pelham* at *Williamsburg* ; and if either of them should sail to comply with this advertisement, they will be considered as deserters, and treated accordingly. GOODRICH CRUMP.
The Virginia Gazette, Purdie, April 25, 1777; May 2, 1777; May 9, 1777.

DESERTED from my company of regulars, *John Kersey,* about 30 years old, between 5 feet 8 and 10 inches high, well proportioned, and it is supposed has gone to *Carolina,* as he married the daughter of one *George Brown* of *Gilford* county. William Harris Taliaferro, about 21 years old, 5 feet 11 inches high, remarkable for his genteelity of shape, very much pock marked, a cabinet maker by trade; his place of residence, he said, was with his uncle, *Peter Taliaferro* in *Culpeper,* near mr. *Henry Fry*'s. Sixty dollars will be given for the above deserters, if delivered at *Williamsburg,* by
JOHN NICHOLAS, captain.
The Virginia Gazette, Purdie, April 25, 1777; May 2, 1777.

DESERTED from capt. *Dickinson*'s company of the 1st *Virginia* regiment, at head quarters in the *Jerseys,* JOHN PHILIPS, an *Irishman,* about 5 feet 8 inches high, with short dark hair, and is

supposed to be lurking about *Hampton,* as he lately made his escape from a guard conveying him to *Williamsburg* from *Hampton.* A reward of 10 *DOLLARS* will be given on delivering him to the commanding officer at *Williamsburg* —JOHN CAMPBELL, who took the place of *William Wood* to serve till the 10th of *April* next, is ordered to come immediately to *Williamsburg,* in order to join the recruits of said regiments, otherwise he will be considered as a deserter, and treated accordingly.
    CHARLES PELHAM.
The Virginia Gazette, Purdie, April 25, 1777; May 2, 1777; May 9, 1777.

DESERTED from my recruits of the 1st Virginia *regiment,* John Johnson, *about* 5 *feet* 10 *inches high, dark complexion, round shouldered, short black hair, and has lost one of his upper fore teeth; he is by trade a carpenter, and was an inhabitant of* Amelia *county.* John Smith, 5 *feet* 10 *inches high, of a ruddy complexion, has short black hair, and a great impediment in his speech; he was recruited in* Chesterfield, *where it is probable he may be now lurking. Whoever will deliver the above* deserters *to the officers who marches the recruits of the* 1st Virginia *regiment to the Northward, or to the commanding officer at* Williamsburg, *shall receive for each* 20 *dollars.*   JOSEPH SCOTT, *adjutant* 1st Virginia *regiment.*
The Virginia Gazette, Purdie, April 25, 1777; May 2, 1777; May 9, 1777.

           Philadelphia, April 24, 1777.
 ABSCONDED from the subscriber's house on Wednesday morning last, a certain JOHN GROOME, by trade a cutler, indented for four years, and has about two to serve. He went into the militia in November last under Capt. Ming, but left him without his leave, and inlisted under Capt. Gib Jones of the train, received twenty dollars bounty, and spent it. Some time after he came to town from headquarters, without leave, with some others, and I got permission from said Capt. Jones to take him to work again, but have not paid Capt. Jones any consideration for his bounty, nor some clothes he has drawn, for which he must be accountable for. I have several times requested Capt. Jones to know what demand he had on me for him, but never could get any satisfaction from him, otherwise than he once told me he would have him again. Now said Groome has endeavoured to impose on Capt. Robinson, having offered himself as an armourer on board this vessel, and has receive an order for the bounty given him, and will probably try to impose on some others in like manner, as

him, and will probably try to impose on some others in like manner, as he at present secrets himself from me, therefore this is to caution all officers not to engage him, as he now lies under these circumstances. Any person giving information to me so that I get him again, shall have Three Dollars reward.
JOHN FOX, cutler.
The Pennsylvania Evening Post, April 26, 1777.

DEserted the 20th of February last, from Capt. Samuel Phillips's Company, one John Airs, about 40 Years of Age, formerly lived on Block-Island. Also deserted from said Company, two Indians, viz. John Daniels, about 20 Years of Age, 5 Feet 7 Inches high, long Hair, belongs to Charlestown. Toby Coy, about 17 Years of Age, 5 Feet 6 Inches high, belongs to Charlestown. Whoever will take up said Deserters, and confine them in any Gaol of the United States, shall have Five Dollars Reward, for each, and all necessary Charges,
paid by   SAMUEL PHILLIPS, Capt.
The Providence Gazette; And Country Journal, April 26, 1777; May 3, 1777; May 10, 1777.

DEserted from Capt. Thomas Cole's Company, in the Ninth Regiment of Foot, commanded by Col. Crary, William Horton, 20 Years of Age, 5 Feet 6 Inches high, a slim active Fellow, says he was born at Rehoboth, in Massachusetts State, has dark Hair, dark Eyes: Had on a blue out-side Jacket, striped Trowsers, and a round Hat. Whoever will take up said Deserter, and return him at East-Greenwich, or secure him in any Gaol in the United States, shall receive Ten Dollars Reward, and all reasonable Charges, paid by
JOHN COOKE, Ensign.
The Providence Gazette; And Country Journal, April 26, 1777; May 3, 1777.

JAMES HISKETT, who had leave of absence for 20 days from the 8th of March, is ordered to join his regiment immediately, on failure of which he will be returned as a deserter.
ELISHA HOPKINS, Adj.
Col. S. B. WEBB's Regt.
Hartford, April 26, 1777.
The Connecticut Courant, and Hartford Weekly Intelligencer, April 28, 1777; May 12, 1777.

DESERTED from my company, in Colonel Ebenezer Francis's regiment, the following recruits, viz.—*Samuel Bentley*, aged 24 years,

5 feet, 8 inches high, dark complexion—*John Snow*, 18 years old, 5 feet 6, light complexion—*John Ryan*, of Marblehead, about 30 years old, a stout, well built fellow, light complexion, and pockbroken—*James Maher, James Turner*, and *James Downe*, light complexion and sore eyes—*John Mull[ins]*, light complexion, and light short curl'd hair—*William Fitzpatrick*, a tall, slim fellow, of a light complexion—*William Davis*, light complexion, short light hair, and reddish eyes—*James Welsh*, a short fellow, has lost his right eye—*Thomas Ryan, John Brown, Michael Hogan, James Carson, John Brown*, and *Thomas Green*, a dark complexion fellow—*Matthew Doyle*, 28 years old, 5 feet 7 inches high, light complexion—*Patrick Horon*, 34 years old, 4 and a half inches high, [sic] dark complexion, black hair—*John Martin*, 29 years old, 5 feet, 11 inches, light complexion, a thick sett, well built fellow—*Thomas Jones*, 21 years old, 5 feet, 6 inches, light complexion—*Thomas Allen*, 24 years old, 5 feet, 7 inches, light complexion—And *Patrick Sullivan*, 24 years old, light complexion, brown hair.

The above named deserters, would have been more particularly described, but the paper on which their descriptions were taken down upon, is lost. WHOEVER will take up any or all of said deserters, and secure them in goal, or give information so that they can be brought to justice, shall have a REWARD of five dollars for each, and all necessary charges paid,

by me   SAMUEL PAGE, Captain.

N. B. The above deserters are chiefly transient persons, and it is hoped that all friends to America, will take up all persons they may suspect, and deal with them as directed by a late resolve of the Great and General Court of this State, that such villains may be brought to justice.

The Independent Chronicle and the Universal Advertiser, May 2, 1777.

JAMES PRATT, a soldier in capt. *Charles Fleming's* company of the 7th *Virginia* regiment, who was some time past indulged with a furlough, is required to repair to *Cumberland* courthouse by the first day of *May* next, or to *Fredericksburg* by the 10th, otherwise he will be considered as a deserter, and treated as such accordingly.

M. CARRINGTON, lieut.

∴ Among some deserters I lately advertised, there was one called, through mistakes, *Abraham Lear* whereas his right name is *Abraham Cox*.

The Virginia Gazette, Purdie, May 2, 1777. See *The Virginia Gazette*, Purdie, April 4, 1777, for Lear/Cox.

Sixty DOLLARS Reward.

DESERTED the 20th instant (*April*) from *Fredericksburg*, the following soldiers, viz. *Peter Barham,* about 34 years old, stout made, about 5 feet 10 inches high, red complexion, with red whiskers, his upper fore teeth broke off to his gums, and when laughing shews them much; he is very artful, and will when taken up make his escape if not properly secured. *Jesse New*, a slender made fellow, about 20 years old, about 5 feet 9 inches high, of a fair complexion, with sandy coloured hair, and a freckled face. I paid him 20 dollars for taking him on his march to *Fredericksburg. Thomas Roach*, about 24 years old, 5 feet 4 inches high, dark complexion, and wears his own hair, which is often tied behind. They are all natives of *Charles City* county. I will give the above reward, or twenty dollars for either of them that are delivered to the commanding officer at *Williamsburg* or any commanding officer marching to the Northward.

JOHN BELL, lieut. in the 6th *Virginia* regiment

The Virginia Gazette, Purdie, May 2, 1777; May 9, 1777; May 16, 1777.

Five POUNDS Reward

FOR delivering to the commanding officer, at *Williamsburg, William Hollins,* a soldier who enlisted under me in the service of this state, and deserted while on his march to that place. He is about 5 feet 11 inches high, rather slender made, dark complexion, and has a down look; he is, I expect, lurking in the upper end of *New Kent* county, where I enlisted him, It is hoped that all good people, who really prefer the true interest of the publick to any private connection with individuals, or who would wish not to see their cruel enemies triumphantly accomplish the ruin of their country, now awfully suspended in the balance of a doubtful event, will, before is be too late, employ every exertion in their power to prevent the only circumstance which can cause in to preponderate against us, and to detect all such who, having no true sense of the impending and the bad consequences of their conduct, can idly sport, at the publick expense, with their own calamity, and, instead of being a defence, not only become themselves a pest to their honest neighbours, but contribute to influence others into the same infatuation.

JOHN CLOPTON.

The Virginia Gazette, Purdie, May 2, 1777; May 9, 1777.

WHEREAS lieut. *John Mercer*, of the 3d *Virginia* regiment, delivered me a list of four soldiers recruited by him for the service of the United States, and left orders with me to carry them to camp, which recruits, after a most diligent search and inquiry, I can neither find nor hear of; and as it is inconvenient for me to stay any longer, they are hereby ordered to repair to camp immediately. Their names are, *William Alsop, James Givion, Archibald Macbane, and Daniel Macneil.*
     JAMES HANSBROUGH.
 The Virginia Gazette, Purdie, May 9, 1777.

DESERTED from my company in the 7th regiment of *North Carolina* continental troops, *Michael Henry,* who said he was a *Frenchman,* and has lost off his left hand the thumb and two fingers. Since his desertion I am informed he enlisted with capt. *James Mason* of the *Virginia* regiment, who exchanged him with capt. *Edward Travis* of the *Raleigh* armed brig. Whoever delivers the said deserter to me in *Halifax* town, *N. Carolina,* shall have 20 *DOLLARS* reward; and I hereby Forewarn all officers from detaining the said deserter.
     JAMES VAUGHAN, capt. 7th reg.
 The Virginia Gazette, Purdie, May 2, 1777; May 9, 1777; May 16, 1777; May 23, 1776.

DESERTED the 6th instant (*April*) from my company of regulars, *John Munro,* an *Englishman,* 5 feet 6 inches high, who was enlisted by lieut. *John Shield* in *York.* Whoever apprehends and delivers the said deserter to the commanding officer at *Williamsburg,* or to me at *Hampton,* shall have 10 *DOLLARS* reward.
     JOHN LEE, capt.
 The Virginia Gazette, Purdie, May 2, 1777; May 9, 1777.

WHEREAS a certain *Christopher Butler* and *Robert Saunders* were duly enlisted by me for the service of this commonwealth, and have failed to attend agreeable to orders, they are therefore considered as deserters, and I will give a reward of ten dollars for each to any person who will deliver them to the commanding officer in *Williamsburg. Saunders* is a resident of *Louisa,* about 5 feet 10 inches high, 35 or 40 years of age, and has red hair. *Butler* is about the same age, a small man, has dark hair, and a pert look; he was an inhabitant of *Hanover,* where his family still resides, but am informed he has connections in *Charlotte* county, where he is supposed
   to be lurking. THOMAS SMITH.

The Virginia Gazette, Purdie, May 2, 1777; May 9, 1777; May 16, 1777.

Twelve POUNDS Reward.

DESERTED from *Alexandria,* belonging to my company of *Virginia* troops, the following soldiers, *viz. JOHN BULMAN,* on the 23d of *February* last. When I enlisted him he informed me he lived in *Prince George's* county, *Maryland.* He is about 21 or 22 years old age, 5 feet 5 or 6 inches high, well made, has fair hair, and fair complexion. *SAMUEL WARNER,* on the 4th ult, born in Charles county, *Maryland,* 34 or 35 years of age, 5 feet 9 or 10 inches high; he is a stout well made man, talks sensibly, and writes well. *EDWARD WELLMAN,* born in *England,* a lusty well made man, 5 feet 7 or 8 inches high, about 24 or 25 years old, and lived some time in *Charles* county, *Maryland,* where I enlisted him. *JAMES FRAZER,* from this place, on the 20th instant, born in *Ireland* 5 feet 6 or 7 inches high, about 25 years of age, had on a striped *Virginia* cloth coat, drill breeches, new white stockings, and new shoes. I have some reason to believe that he followed the 15th regiment, now on their march to the Northward, Whoever apprehends said deserters, and returns them to their company, or secures them in any publick jail, shall have the above reward, or 3 l. for each, and reasonable charges
         paid by   THOMAS HAMILTON.

The Virginia Gazette, Purdie, May 2, 1777; May 9, 1777; May 16, 1777. See *The Virginia Gazette*, February 28, 1777, for Bulman.

DEserted from Capt. Sergant's Company in Col. John Crane's Battalion of Artillery, William Candull, late of New-York, aged 23, 5 feet 10 inches, dark Complexion, and black short Hair, somewhat Pock broken. William Thompson, formerly of Newport, aged 22 years, 5 feet 3 inches, dark complexion, and black long Hair. Whoever shall take up said Deserters and confine them in any of the Continental Goals, or bring them to the North Rendezvous in Boston, shall receive Six Dollars for each and all necessary Charges
         paid by   SAMUEL BASS, Lieut. (Artillery.
                                              Boston May 4, 1777.

The Boston-Gazette, And Country Journal, May 5, 1777; May 12, 1777; May 19, 1777.

                                    Boston, April 29th, 1777.
THIS is to give Notice to John Durham, belonging to Old York, in this State, and William Doyle, belonging to Boston, to repair and join

Capt. Eute's [sic] Company, in Col. Crane's Battalion, at Boston, in order to pass Master, or they will be reported as Deserters.
WILLIAM STEVENS.   (Capt. Lieut. of Artillery.
The Boston-Gazette, And Country Journal, May 5, 1777; May 12, 1777; May 19, 1777.

This to give notice to all whom it may concern, to Lieut. John Buell, in Col. Durkey's regiment, in particular, that on Sunday the 13th instant I took up a fellow advertised in the Connecticut Courant of the 7th of April; he appears to be undoubtedly the same man, has every mark and all the cloaths by which he is described, the scar in the forehead; I put him under the care of two men, but he escaped in the night and fled; but for fear he wou'd escape I took all his money and cloaths from him, he had 30 l. 16s. and 8d. Any officer that has receipts for bounty against said fellow, may have the money, to the value of what I have got, except my own cost, by applying to BENJAMIN READ, 1st. Lieutenant of Capt. Luke Day's company, in Col. Aldens regiment, destined to Peeks-Kills.
Williamsburgh, Massachusetts-Bay, county of Hampshire,
April 24, 1777.
The Connecticut Courant, and Hartford Weekly Intelligencer, May 5, 1777; May 12, 1777. The deserter was William Angel. Ads describing him appear in volume one of this series.

THESE are to notify Alexander Graham, a Soldier inlisted into the Continental Service by me the Subscriber, and belonging to Col. Chandler's Regiment, forthwith to repair to Hebron, in order to receive the Remainder of his Bounty, and be in Readiness to march.
ORLANDER MACK, Ensign.
Hebron, April 12, 1777.
The Norwich Packet and the Connecticut, Massachusetts, New-Hampshire, and Rhode-Island Weekly Advertiser, May 5, 1777; May 12, 1777; May 19, 1777.

INLISTED with Capt. Lewis of Col. Webb's regiment, about 1st of January, 1777, four Men, viz. John Turner, Enos Blackslee, Asa Brunson and Norman Newel, supposed to belong to the County of New-London; are ordered to march and join their respective regiments without delay, to rendezvous at Danbury, by order of Brig. Gen. *Parsons*,
John Mills, Captain,
(in the room of Captain *Lewis*, deceased.

DESERTED from Capt. *Rob. Lewis*, of Stratford, in Col. Webb's Regiment, about 10 Weeks past, one John Wright, any Persons apprehending him shall have Twenty Dollars Reward,
JOHN MILLS, Capt.
The Connecticut Gazette; and Universal Intelligencer, May 9, 1777; May 16, 1777; June 2, 1777. *The Connecticut Courant, and Hartford Weekly Intelligencer*, May 12, 1777, for Blackslee.

HANOVER, *April* 29, 1777.
WILLIAM FUGLER, a soldier enlisted by me at *Williamsburg* in the service of this commonwealth, is hereby desired to repair, without loss of time, to the commanding officer at that place. Should he fail to comply with this direction, he will be considered as a deserter, and treated accordingly.
JOHN CLOPTON.
The Virginia Gazette, Purdie, May 9, 1777.

DUMFRIES, *April* 26, 1777.
TEN dollars reward for *Samuel Hamilton*, who enlisted in my company of guards on the 11th of *February* last, his county unknown. He is a slim made lad, about 20 years of age, 5 feet 9 or 10 inches high, is freckled, and wears his own red hair. Upon his enlistment he had a furlough for ten days, and has since failed to appear agreeable thereto.   CLEON MOORE.
The Virginia Gazette, Purdie, May 9, 1777; May 16, 1777.

DESERTED from *Williamsburg,* the 2d instant, *Jesse Galden,* a soldier in capt. *John Pope's* company of regulars in the service of this state; he is an impudent fellow, subject to drink, shakes his head frequently when conversed with, about 5 feet 8 or 9 inches high, and about 25 years of age, dark complexion. Ten dollars reward will be paid for delivering him to the commanding officer at *Williamsburg.* —
William Clarke, of *Louisa* county, is desired to repair to *Williamsburg* immediately, to join said company, or he will be deemed a deserter.
WILLIAM PETTIT.
The Virginia Gazette, Purdie, May 9, 1777.

THIS is to give notice to the following soldiers, enlisted by lieut. *Bowker* and ensign *Baskerville,* that they are to meet at *Cumberland* courthouse on or before the 15th day of *May,* in order to follow their company to the Northward, viz. *Josiah Clark Clark* of *Buckingham, William Goalman* of *Henrico, Eake Brown,*

Thomas Watkins, John Day, and *Samuel Vawter,* of *Cumberland,* and *Anderson Green* of *Buckingham.* The above soldiers are requested to pay due regard to this advertisement, and if not obeyed they will be considered as deserters, and treated accordingly.
                HUGHES WOODSON, 1st lieut.
The Virginia Gazette, Purdie, May 9, 1777; May 16, 1777. See *The Virginia Gazette,* June 13, 1777.

DESERTED from Capt. *Turner's* Company of the 3d Regiment of *North Carolina* continental Troops, DARLING MADREY, a tall young Man, about 21 Years of Age, of a dark Complexion; WILLIAM MADREY, a short well made Man, of a dark Complexion; RICHARD JONES, short, well made, of a dark Complexion; DUGLESS CARHELL, a slender young Man, with reddish Hair, and blue Eyes; THEOPHILUS DINKINS, about 40 Years of Age, a tall Man, with lightish coloured Hair. The above Soldiers were enlisted in *Bute* County, *North Carolina,* and it is expected they will be harboured in said County. Whoever will apprehend the said Deserters, and deliver them to any continental Officer, shall receive TWENTY DOLLARS Reward for each.
               &␣WILLIAM LINTON, Lieut.
The Virginia Gazette, Dixon and Hunter, May 9, 1777; May 16, 1777.

          PITTSYLVANIA, HALIFAX OLD TOWN,
                  March 17, 1777.
DESERTED from capt. *William Lane's* company of the 2d *Georgia* battalion, the following soldiers, *viz. Stephen Rice,* an *Englishman,* 30 years of age, about 5 feet 2 inches high, has short red hair, a fair complexion, pitted with the smallpox, and deformed in the right shoulder. *John Miller,* an *Englishman,* 32 years of age, 5 feet 5 or 6 inches high, has dark coloured hair, a fair complexion, and is well made, *Sylvester Cary,* an *Irishman,* 25 years of age, 5 feet 6 or 7 inches high, well made, has a dark complexion, with black curled hair. They were enlisted in *Loudoun* county, and I am apprehensive they will return to the said county. Any person who will apprehend the said deserters, and secure them in any publick jail, shall have 60 DOLLARS reward, or 20 DOLLARS for either of them.
                ELISHA MILLER, Lieut. 2d.
                  Georgia battalion.
The Virginia Gazette, Purdie, May 9, 1777; May 16, 1777; May 23, 1777.

DESERTED from the 3d Regiment of *North Carolina* continental Troops, the following Soldiers, *viz.* NATHANIEL BILBERY, JACOB FORT, HENRY HOWELL, HENRY SPEAR, and MATTHEW JOINER, all of *Edgecombe* County; also WILLIAM GLOVER of *Northampton*. *Bilberry* is about 20 Years of Age, 5 Feet 9 Inches high; and of a light Complexion. Fort, about 6 Feet 2 Inches high, 21 Years old, dark Complexion. *Howell*, about 20 Years of Age, 5 Feet 7 Inches high, Complexion ruddy. Joiner is a stout well set Man, bow legged, about 10 Years old, 5 Feet 8 Inches high, complexion dark. *Glover*, about 6 Feet 4 Inches high, of a dark Complexion, and wears his Hair tied.—Whoever delivers them to their Company shall have TWENTY DOLLASR [*sic*] Reward.
    JAMES BRADBY, Capt.
 The Virginia Gazette, Dixon and Hunter, May 9, 1777

    80 DOLLARS *Reward.*
DESERTED from the 4th company of the 2d battalion for the state of *Georgia,* the following soldiers, *viz. Thomas Sack* an *Englishman,* about 47 years old, of the middle size, dark complexion, and by trade a weaver. *John Sack,* and by trade a weaver. I suspect they will endeavour to get to the *English* army. *Robert Yates,* an *Irishman* of the middle size, very confident, and by trade a wood cutter. The above soldiers were enlisted in *Henry* country, and deserted from lieutenant *Mosby* on their march to *Georgia. James Arnold,* of *Halifax* county, *Virginia,* about 25 years old, of a dark complexion, tall of stature, and very insinuating in his discourse, he was ordered to march, but failed to appear. I will give the above reward, of 20 dollars for each, to any person that delivers them to any officer marching to *Georgia,* or confines them in *Halifax, Pittsylvania,* or *Henry* jails, in *Virginia,* or the borough of *Salisbury* in *North Carolina.*
    SHEM COOK
 The Virginia Gazette, Purdie, May 9, 1777.

THIS *is to inform George Walker, who inlisted with me some time past, into Capt. Cushing's Company, of Col. Patterson's Regiment, (and has since absented himself under a pretence of Deserting as it is supposed;) that unless he returns and joins his Company at Boston immediately, he may expect the treatment due to his Crimes, and in Case of Non-compliance with these Orders the Public are hereby informed that the said George Walker is a Native of Ireland, about* 27 *years of age, dark complexion, black hair, five feet ten inches high, round shoulder'd. Whoever will take up and secure said Deserter,*

shall have a Reward of FIVE DOLLARS, and all necessary Charges paid by me BELCHER HANCOCK, Lieut.
N. B. The above described Persons last Place of Residence was at Kennebeck. Boston, May 19th, 1777.
The Boston-Gazette, And Country Journal, May 12, 1777; May 19, 1777; May 26, 1777.

DESERTED *from Stockbridge December and January, David Purdie, belonging to the Nine Partners, 23 years of age, 5 feet 10, light complection, light hair and eyes. Peter Patterson, a High Dutchman, speaks broken English, has a down look 5 feet 10, 50 years of age. Edward White of Beckit, 5 feet 4, dark complection, dark hair and eyes. Silas Fay, of Beckit, 5 feet 7, dark hair and eyes, 21 years of all, all of capt Chadwick's company, col. Brewer's regiment, at Ticonderoga. Whoever shall take up one or all of the above deserters, and return them to their regiment, or confine them in goal in any of the United States, shall receive 10 dollars reward for each, and all necessary charges paid by*
THEOPHILUS MANSFIELD, Lieut.
May 10, 1777.
The Connecticut Courant, and Hartford Weekly Intelligencer, May 12, 1777; May 19, 1777.

DESERTED from Captain Abby's company, in Colonel Wylly's regiment, on the 5th instant, a soldier who called himself John Delany, is a native of Ireland, twenty-four years of age, five feet ten inches high, black hair, light coloured eyes, and red complexion, [mark]ed with the small pox. Had on when he went away a linnen frock, a brown outside vest, with a red [one] under it, new dark brown woollen breeches, brown woollen stockings. Whoever will take up said deserter and return him to his regiment shall have five dollars reward and all necessary charges paid,
by me THOMAS ABBY, Captain.
Enfield, May 7, 1777.
The Connecticut Courant, and Hartford Weekly Intelligencer, May 12, 1777; May 19, 1777.

DESERTED from the subscriber on the 10th of March last, two soldiers belonging to Capt. Hall's Company, in Col. Swift's Regiment, viz. John Rano, aged 25 Years, says he belongs to New-Britain, New-Hampshire, 5 feet 10 inches high, light eyes, brown hair, has a scar across the right side of his lips; Ebenezer Williams, says he belongs near Boston, has a natural mark on his face of a redish colour, and has

redish hair; Samuel Orell, formerly of Boston, but now of North-Haven, where he has a family, about 5 feet 11 inches high, long nose, light complexion, 23 years of age, light eyes, black hair; they had all received their bounties, and it is likely have since inlisted in some other companies. Whoever shall take up either or all the above deserters, and secure them, shall receive Eight Dollars for each, and all necessary charges paid, by
    EPHRAIM CHAMBERLAIN, Lieut.
              Wallingford, April 9, 1777.
The Connecticut Courant, and Hartford Weekly Intelligencer, May 12, 1777; May 19, 1777.

WILLIAM BENTLEY, of Little Hoosuck, soldier in my company, Col. Greaton's regiment, Massachusetts State, is directed forthwith to join his company at West-Springfield, or he will be deemed a deserter and must suffer accordingly.
    SAMUEL FLOWER, Capt.
           West-Springfield, April 22, 1777.
The Connecticut Courant, and Hartford Weekly Intelligencer, May 12, 1777.

We hear that at a General Court Martial, held the 9th instant, one Peter Pickman Frye, a soldier of Capt. King's company, in Col. Marshall's regiment, being found guilty of deserting from his regiment, with a design to have gone to the enemy, was sentenced to be shot; which is to be put in execution on Thursday the 22d instant, at eleven o'clock.
The Norwich Packet and the Connecticut, Massachusetts, New-Hampshire, and Rhode-Island Weekly Advertiser, May 12, 1777; *The Continental Journal, And Weekly Advertiser,* May 15, 1777; *The Connecticut Gazette; And The Universal Intelligencer,* May 23, 1777. Minor differences between the papers

On Tuesday last, three soldiers, belonging to the Continental Army, viz. Robert Key, Peter Nagle, and Richard Querry, under sentence of death for attempting to desert to the enemy, were conducted from here, under guard, to Coventry, where, on Wednesday, the first mentioned person, was shot. He behaved, in his last moments, as became a man in his unhappy position; appeared to be truly sensible of the enormity of his crime, and hoped that the ignominious death, he was about to suffer, would be serviceable to prevent others from deserting. Nagle and Querry were repreived.

The Independent Chronicle and the Universal Advertiser, May 15, 1777.

I hereby desire ASA PORTER, of Ipswich, an enlisted Soldier, under me, immediately to join the Regiment at Roxbury, or I shall deem him as a Deserter.
JUDAH ALLEN, Captain
The Independent Chronicle and the Universal Advertiser, May 15, 1777.

To capt. RICHARD STEVENS.
SIR,
AS you have been induced, by necessary, to punish me in the *Virginia* Gazette as a deserter, I now am obliged to take a publick notice of you, sir, in consequence of this attack, as unwarrantable in its nature, as liberal in its manner, which you have been pleased to make upon my character. Liberality, indeed. I had no right to expect justice. This language, sir, may be considered as very free, but it cannot be considered as very improper. Elevated as your situation is, and humble as mine may be, the eye of unprejudiced reason does not behold us in a light of disparity. Now, sir, I will not hesitate a moment to justify the liberty I now take, and do most humbly request of you to give attention to what I am going to relate. Are you not sensible of the engagements that were made between me and mr. *Vivion,* whom I was only to serve one year as a waggoner? Mr. *Vivion* was then lieutenant in your company, but has now resigned, in consequence whereof you have violated that contract, by endeavouring to make me a common soldier, to serve three years. You have published me as a deserter undeservedly, but I am ready and willing to follow the calling in which I engaged. As a common soldier, I did not enlist, nor will I ever submit to be one. I hope, sir, you will let these circumstances teach you to avoid the meanness of injuring so inconsiderable an object as myself. I could say much more. sir, and aggravate the impropriety of your procedure to me, but I shall conclude here, and save you from the shame of doing me an additional wrong, even while I despair of your retraction to do me a common act of justice. I am, sir, your sincere well wisher, though not your much obliged,
JOHN MALONE.
Mr. VIVION'*s Certificate.*
This is to certify, that *John Malone* entered into the service with me only for one year, and in that time to serve as a waggoner. Given under my hand.
CHARLES VIVION.

The Virginia Gazette, Purdie, May 16, 1777. See *The Virginia Gazette*, Purdie, April 11, 1777.

Twenty DOLLARS Reward

DESERTED from my company, *Jadock Dailey,* a very lusty man, who is supposed to be lurking about *Pasquowtank North Carolina.* I will give the above reward to any person that will apprehend the said deserter, and deliver him to me in *Portsmouth.*
THOMAS BRESSIE, capt.
May 5, 1777.
The Virginia Gazette, Purdie, May 16, 1777; May 23, 1777.

STEPHEN BOOKER, a seaman belonging to the *Hero* galley, who went to *Williamsburg* some time ago as a witness on the trial of *Hugh Cassedy,* is ordered immediately to return to his duty on board the said galley, otherwise he will be considered as a deserter, and treated accordingly.
GEORGE MUTER, capt. of the *Hero.*
The Virginia Gazette, Purdie, May 16, 1777.

WILLIAM CLARKE, of *Louisa* county (who enlisted with capt. *John Pope at Goochland* courthouse) is hereby required to join the said company now at *Williamsburg,* or in a few days he will be deemed a deserter, and a reward bid for securing him. Also *Thomas Gaskins,* who went down York river on board an armed vessel without permission.   WILLIAM PETTIT.
The Virginia Gazette, Purdie, May 16, 1777.

PRINCE WILLIAM county, *March* 27 1777.
DESERTED, *Lawrence Keenan* (who enlisted with me in col. *Grayson*'s regiment) born in *Ireland,* about 23 years of age, 6 feet 1 or 2 inches high, had on a white hunting shirt and red waistcoat, buckskin breeches, yarn stockings, good shoes, and brass buckles his other clothes not known. Whoever apprehends the above deserter, and delivers him to the commanding officer in *Dumfries,* or to me, shall receive 10 *DOLLARS,* exclusive of what is allowed in such cases.
JOHN WILKINSON, ensign.
The Virginia Gazette, Purdie, May 16, 1777

DESERTED from the MANLY Galley, three Men, *viz.* FRANCIS ARBADO, a black *Frenchman,* about 30 Years of Age, 5 Feet 7 or 8 Inches high, the other two belonging to Mr. *Peters* at *Hood's,* one a

thick stout made Fellow, about 30 Years of Age, 5 Feet 9 or 10 Inches high, the other a short thick Fellow, about 25 Years of Age, 5 Feet 6 or 7 Inches high. Whoever apprehends the said Deserters shall have TEN DOLLARS Reward for each.
WILLIAM SAUNDERS.
The Virginia Gazette, Dixon and Hunter, May 16, 1777; May 23, 1777; May 30, 1777.

Forty DOLLARS Reward.
DESERTED from my recruits, *Thomas Longest,* who has since enlisted under lieut. *Page* of the troop of horse. The said *Longest* has received the full bounty; and *Isaac Hudgin* who has been carried off by one *Crockett* of Maryland. The said *Hudgin* has also enlisted, and passed a receipt for the full bounty. I hope mr. *Page* will take care to leave *Longest* in this state, so that he joins my recruits. The said *Crockett* is hereby forewarned from carrying the said *Hudgin* to sea, as he shall suffer accordingly. The above reward I will give to any one that will deliver the above deserters to the commanding officer in *Williamsburg.*
The Virginia Gazette, Purdie, May 16, 1777.

VIRGINIA, *Prince William* county, *May* 5, 1777.
180 DOLLARS Reward.
DESERTED from my company of the 15th *Virginia* regiment, the following soldiers, *viz John Thomas,* enlisted in *Amelia,* but late from *Prince William* county, where he is well known, by trade a carpenter, about 5 feet 11 inches high, between 30 and 40 years of age, has yellow hair, and is thick of hearing. *William Pratt,* of *Charlotte* county, enlisted in *Amelia,* about 5 feet 11 inches high, 25 years of age, has dark brown hair. *Joseph Holland, of Amelia* county, upwards of 6 feet high about 30 years of age, brown complexion, with dark hair, and stoops in his shoulders when he walks. *John Quesenburg,* enlisted in *Amelia,* about 5 feet 10 inches high, well made, between 30 and 40 years of age, with dark coloured hair. *Benjamin Jones,* of *Amelia,* about 5 feet 4 inches high 25 years of age, well made, of a yellowish complexion much freckled, with dark hair. *Edmund Massey,* of *Amelia,* about 6 feet high, 20 years of age, fair complexion, light hair, and has some little impediment in his speech. *George Lovell,* enlisted in *Amelia,* where he is well known, but lately came from *North Carolina,* about 5 feet 11 inches high, 25 years of age, thin visage, dark complexion, with dark hair, and at the time he deserted complained much of one of his eyes. *Asa Cawley,* of *Cumberland* county, about 5 feet 10 inches high, 18 or 19 years of

age, brown hair, and slender made. *John Quinn,* of Amelia about 5 feet 6 or 7 inches high, well made, 24 years of age and black hair; who, as he has always bore the character of an orderly good soldier, and had not notice of the time of marching, if he will repair immediately to the continental camp, he shall escape with impurity. Whoever takes up the said deserters, and delivers them to some officer in the continental service, that they may be conveyed to their regiment, shall have 20 *DOLLARS* reward for each
    JAMES FOSTER, captain.
The Virginia Gazette, Purdie, May 16, 1777; May 23, 1777.

THE following Persons inlisted under Nathaniel Hill, in Capt. Ward's Company, in Col. Weston's Regiment, viz. Joseph Bowers, Abijah Adams, and Nathaniel Showels, are ordered immediately to repair to Cambridge, the Place of Rendezvous.
The Boston-Gazette, and Country Journal, May 19, 1777; May 26, 1777; June 2, 1777.

DESERTED from Capt. Sanford's company, Col. Bradley's regiment, William Fleet, about 32 years of age, 5 feet 8 inches high, full face, blue eyes, red complexion, dark brown short hair.—Henry Williams, an Irish lad about 5 feet 6 inches high, 35 years of age, dark complection, black eyes, short curled hair, is very much given to drink. Whoever will take up said soldiers and return them to their regiment, or confine them in any goal in any of the United States shall receive Five Dollars for each,
   by EZEKIEL SANFORD, Capt.
                May 16, 1777,
The Connecticut Courant, and Hartford Weekly Intelligencer, May 19, 1777; May 26, 1777; June 2, 1777.

RUN-away from Farmington, in the State of Connecticut, (where he was stationed) on the 10th day of May instant, one John Manning, a prisoner of war, belonging to the 40th regiment in the British forces:—He is about 30 years of age, 5 feet 5 inches high, well set, short black hair, hat a large scar on his upper lip: Had on when he went away a soldiers red coat, the lappels and cuffs taken off, a white waistcoat, woolen shirt, a pair of long trowsers made of fulled cloth; took with his some other articles of cloathing tied up in a shirt. Whoever shall take up said prisoner and bring him to the committed of prisoners in Hartford, or shall secure him in any of the goals in the State and give notice to said committee, shall have Five Dollars reward, paid by

BENJA. PAYNE, Chairman of said Committee.
Hartford, May 13 1777.
The Connecticut Courant, And Hartford Weekly Intelligencer,
May 19, 1777; May 26, 1777; June 2, 1777.

ISAAC AMOS, of my company, in Col. Rufus Putnam's regiment, is once more ordered to join the regiment, at Worcester, or will be looked upon as a deserter and treated as such.
NATHAN GOODWELL, Captain.
May 10, 1777.
The Connecticut Courant, and Hartford Weekly Intelligencer,
May 19, 1777; May 26, 1777.

GILL Belcher of Hebron, Ambrose Tyler of Torrington, Amasa Scott of Harwinton, Abiel Canfield and John Gardner, are hereby directed to repair to Litchfield immediately, in order to join the continental army.   JAMES MORRIS, Lieut.
Litchfield, May 15, 1777.
The Connecticut Courant, and Hartford Weekly Intelligencer,
May 19, 1777; May 26, 1777.

WHEREAS Jedidiah Hall of North-Fairfield, is inlisted with me as a Matross, in the Battalion commanded by Col. John Lamb, had Leave of Absence from the 11th Instant, and should have returned to his Duty on the 13th. The said Hall is commanded to return forthwith and join his Company, otherwise will be deemed a Deserter and treated accordingly.   JONATHAN BROWN, Capt.
New-Haven, May 20, 1777.
The Connecticut Journal, May 21, 1777; May 28, 1777.

DEserted from Capt. Ezekiel Sanford's company, in Col. P. B. Bradley's regiment, about the first of this instant, May, Thomas Chilman, near six feet high, well-made, short hair, large gray eyes, red complexion, about 30 years old, had on a blue coat, red jacket, leather breeches, has belong'd to the northern artillery, and is very smart in the exercise. Also, Abraham DeVoice of said company and regiment, about 25 years of age, is a Dutchman, and talks very broken English, has short black hair, and black eyes, and is well made. Whoever shall take up said deserters, and convey them to the above regiment, shall have twenty dollars for both, or ten dollars for either of them, and all charges paid by me.
John St. John, Lieut.

The Connecticut Journal, May 21, 1777; May 28, 1777; June 3, 1777.

DESERTED from Capt. Parsons Company, in Col. Webb's regiment, one NATHANIEL ROSE, 32 Years old, 5 feet 10 inches high, brown Hair, grey Eyes, light Complexion, deserted about the 10th instant. Whoever will secure said Deserter or return him to the Subscriber, shall have FIVE DOLLARS Reward, and necessary Charges paid by
DAVID PARSONS, Capt.
May 17, 1777.
The Connecticut Gazette; and Universal Intelligencer, May 23, 1777; May 30, 1777.

DEserted from Col. Wylly's Regiment of Continental Troops, one Jedidiah Green, a Soldier, about 5 Feet 11 Inches high, black Hair, dark Eyes and Complexion, about 24 Years old, a smart well built Fellow, slow of Speech, belongs to Canterbury, has left a Family there. Whoever will bring said Deserter to the Subscriber, or secure him, so that I may have him again, shall have Ten Dollars Reward, and all necessary Charges paid per
WILLS CLIFT, Capt.
The Connecticut Gazette; and Universal Intelligencer, May 23, 1777; May 30, 1777.

MR. PURDIE,
FINDING myself advertised in favour Gazette to the 21st of *March* as a deserter from my country's service, which of all other characters I at this time in particular most heartily despise, I hereby beg leave to reliever myself from the odium that would otherwise justly belong to me, and shall therefore trouble the publick, through your means, with the following narrative of facts. Some time about the 6th of *August* 1776 I enlisted as a private soldier in the continental service under capt. *Ballard*, when I got a for ten days at the expiration thereof to meet at *Hanover* courthouse in order to march to the *Northward*. I accordingly did so; but not being able to travel, I procured another *furlough* from mr. *Clayton*, Lieutenant of the company which directed me to meet *Williamsburg*. I repaired to that place on the 7th of *December*, when I was ordered by general *Lewis* to join the regiments the on their march to general *Washington*, which I immediately complied with and marched within 49 miles of *Philadelphia*; but being there taken sick, I hired *John James* in my room, who was well approved of by the commanding officer, and got my discharge on the 15th.

JONATHAN TERRELL.
The Virginia Gazette, Purdie, May 23, 1777. See *The Virginia Gazette*, March 14, 1777.

THIS is to certify, that I some Time ago enlisted under *William Black* of *Chesterfield* County, in the Service of this State, for one Year, at which Time of my Enlistment the said *William Black* agreed to appoint me Serjeant, and my Wages to go on from last *Christmas.* His failing to fulfill this Agreement, which I have from under his Hand, was my Reason for leaving the Company, but am ready and willing to return into the Service with *Black,* or any other Person, as soon as said Agreement is complied with.
JOHN RAGLAND.
The Virginia Gazette, Dixon and Hunter, May 23, 1777; May 30, 1777.

Twenty DOLLARS Reward
FOR apprehending *John O'Neal,* who deserted from *Winchester* the 3d instant. He is about 5 feet 9 inches high, stout made, and wears a yellow hunting suit. He was enlisted by col. *Neaville,* and served some time at fort *Pitt.* Since his desertion I have been informed he enlisted with capt. *Craghorn* of the 8th regiment, and was left sick at *Williamsburg* when that company marched to *New York,* and that he has received the bounty of several recruiting officers besides myself.
MATTHEW SMITH, 1st *Virginia* regiment.
Winchester, *April* 15, 1777.
The Virginia Gazette, Purdie, May 23, 1777; June 6, 1777.

Eighty DOLLARS Reward.
ENLISTED in my company from *Halifax* county, and have deserted, the following soldiers. viz. *John Read, William Black,* jun. *William Land, Jeremy Stevens, John Whitlow, Richard Mullins, John Willard, William Warren, Thomas Dulaney,* and *William Dearen,* whose proper name I have since been informed is *William Dear.* The above reward, or 8 *DOLLARS* for each will be paid upon their being delivered to the commanding officer in *Williamsburg.*
THOMAS THWEATT, capt. 14th *Virginia* regiment.
The Virginia Gazette, Purdie, May 23, 1777.

DESERTED from *Charlestown* in *October* last, *Jesse Meeks,* about 5 feet 8 or 9 inches high 28 or 29 years of age, well made, and has short dark hair. *Cleviers Duke* 5 feet 10 or 11 inches high, 22 or 23 years of

age, well made, and has short black hair. I will give 20 DOLLARS reward for each.
    RICHARD C. ANDERSON. capt.
 The Virginia Gazette, Purdie, May 23, 1777; June 6, 1777; May 23, 1777.

    Forty DOLLARS Reward,
DESERTED from my company of continental regulars, *John S[orrel]* of *Henrico* county, of middling stature, and *Joseph Fre[etsell]* of *Cumberland* county, about 5 feet 10 inches high, and at a pale come who, whoever delivers the said deserters me, or the commanding officer at *Williamsburg,* shall be paid the above reward, or 20 dollars for either of them.
    JOHN HOLCOMB, capt. 4th. *Virginia.*
 The Virginia Gazette, Purdie, May 23, 1777.

 TWENTY DOLLARS Reward for one RICHARD FOXWELL, who deserted from *Williamsburg* the 10th of April last. He is about 5 Feet 10 Inches high, of a ruddy Complexion, very talkative, snuffles in his Speech, and had on, when he went away, a dark Coat and Jacket. I understand he has since enlisted with one Perkins, and again deserted. His first Push was to the *Eastern Shore,* where he lived some Time after leaving the Northward, of which he said he was a Native.
    CHARLES COLLIER, 1st Lieut
 The Virginia Gazette, Dixon and Hunter, 1777; May 23, 1777; May 30, 1777.

DESERTED from my quota, fortnight ago *James Hopkins Arnold,* above 6 feet high, is remarkably bald headed, occasioned by a scald, and affects to be very virtuous, though he is a very lying dissembling fellow. Enlisted him in *Lunenburg* County. Whoever delivers him to me, or the commanding officer at *Williamsburg,* shall have 20 DOLLARS reward.
    EPAPH. RUDINER, lieut
 The Virginia Gazette, Purdie, May 23, 1777; June 6, 1777.

ALL the inlisted Soldiers in the continental Army, under Capt. James Carr in Col. Hale's Battalion, are hereby ordered immediately to repair to Exeter, in order to march to join their corps, otherwise they will be returned Deserters; particularly, Nathaniel Chaney, below Casco Bay, of a dark complexion, about 5 Feet 5 Inches high, not muster'd; David Morgan, of Brintwood, Robert Marshal, a transient Person 5 Feet 8 Inches high, pock mark'd in the nose, light

Complexion, light Hair & Eyes; as my Orders is to march immediately.
                    GEORGE PEPPERREL FROST, Ensign.
The Freeman's Journal, Or New-Hampshire Gazette, May 24, 1777.

DESERTED from Greenwich, the beginning of May, SOLOMON BROWN, of Col. Charles Webb's regiment, about 19 years of age, 5 feet 8 inches high, light short hair, light complexion; had on when he went away a good felt hat, a light short jacket, and buckskin breeches, about half worn.—WILLIAM GAULDIN, belonging to said regiment about 40 years of age, 5 feet 6 inches high, short grey hair, a thick sett well built fellow; had on when he went off an old castor hat, a good broad cloth coat, which was a mixture of blue and white, and buckskin breeches much worn. Whoever will take up said deserters and secure them till notice may be given to the subscriber, or return them to said regiment, shall receive ten dollars reward for each, and all reasonable charges paid, by
                    STEPHEN BETTS, Lieut.
The Connecticut Courant, and Hartford Weekly Intelligencer, May 26, 1777; June 2, 1777.

WHEREAS on the night of the 30th of April last, we the Subscribers having the care of one Joseph Moors, a prisoner, supposed to be one of those cursed persons who have been trying to destroy the country by counterfeiting bills of this and other States, who belongs to Lancaster, in the county of Worcester, about 10 o'clock in this evening, there came in a man into said Moore's house, who called his name Benjamin Criss, though his name is Jacob Criss; he wanted to have some private discourse with the said prisoner, and as he thought proper to take said Chriss with us to some justice to be examined concerning this affair, in the first asking him if he was willing to go; it being very dark and his horse was tired, he said he would go a foot with us; as soon as he had got from door he made his escape, leaving his horse, saddle and bridle. As we thought proper to take said Horse, &c. into our care, the owner may have them again by paying charges. The beast is a black roan mare; any person that is the right owner, may have said mare again, by applying to either of the persons undermentioned in Lancaster aforesaid.
            JONAS WYMAN.   ANDREW HASKALL.
                Dated the 8th day of May, 1777.

N. B. The said Chriss has enlisted under me the subscriber, therefore a reward of THREE DOLLARS to any person who will secure him and give me intelligence thereof.
    HENRY ERVING, *Lieutenant, of Lancaster, aforesaid.*
  The said Chriss is about 20 *years old, and about* 5 *feet* 7 *or* 8 *inches high, light complexion, a blacksmith by trade.*
  The Independent Chronicle and the Universal Advertiser, May 29, 1777; June 5, 1777.

DESERTED from Capt. Parsons Company, in Col. Webb's Regiment, one NATHANIEL ROSE, 32 Years old, 5 Feet 10 Inches high, brown Hair, grey Eyes, light Complexion, deserted about the 10th Instant. Whoever will secure said Deserter or return him to the Subscriber, shall have FIVE DOLLARS Reward, and necessary Charges paid by
      DAVID PARSONS, Capt.
                May 17, 1777.
  The Connecticut Gazette; and Universal Intelligencer, May 30, 1777.

DESERTED from Capt. Champion's company, Col. Wyllys's regiment, one Charles Wiempey, born in Farmington, in Connecticut, 6 feet high, strait and well proportioned, black long hair, black eyes and dark complexion, wore away a homespun coat and vest, leather breeches and a new felt hat.—Whoever secures said deserter, in any goal in this State and gives information thereof or returns him to Hartford shall have 5 dollars reward and all necessary charges paid, by
      SAMUEL RICHARDS, Lieut.
  The Connecticut Gazette; and Universal Intelligencer, May 30, 1777.

DEserted from Capt. James Webb's Company, in Col. Sherburne's Regiment, Ephraim Cole, about 5 Feet 7 Inches high, black Hair and black Eyes, his fore Teeth gone. Samuel Handley, about the same Height, of a light Complexion; both of Swansey. Whoever will take up said Deserters, and secure them in any Gaol in the United States, or return them to their Officers in Warren, shall have Five Dollars for each, and all reasonable Charges, paid by me
      JAMES WEBB, Capt.
             Warren, May 16, 1777.
  The Providence Gazette; And Country Journal, May 31, 1777.

WHEREAS Edward Watkins, John Blatchford, Josiah Woodworth, William Toomlinson, Elijah Parks and William Bennet, Dragoons,

belonging Col. Sheldon's regiment, some time since obtained a furlough from Capt. Vernejoul, and the period of their joining their corps long since has elapsed. This may notify them that unless they immediately repair to Wethersfield the place of their rendezvous, or in case of sickness, forthwith transmit their Captain a certificate from under the hand of a respectable physician and a magistrate of the town to which they respectively belong, they shall be deemed and treated as DESERTERS.   JOHN LEWIS DE VERNEJOUL,
                  Capt. of American Light Dragoons.
                              Wethersfield, May 29, 1777.
The Connecticut Courant, and Hartford Weekly Intelligencer, June 2, 1777; June 9, 1777; June 16, 1777; June 23, 1777.

DEserted from Capt. Ely's company, Col. Douglas's regiment, some time since, one Garret Degrout, of Long Island, 5 feet 10 inches high, pock broken, about 30 years old. Four dollars reward, and all necessary charges will be paid for taking him up, and returning him to any officer in the regiment.
        Asa Lay, Lieut.   May 30 1777.
The Connecticut Journal, June 3, 1777; June 11, 1777; June 18, 1777.

DEserted from Capt. Goodwin's company, in Col. Charles Webb's regiment, one *Nedebiah Aldrich,* about 22 years of age, a well built fellow, about 5 feet 7 inches high, light eyes, short hair, an American born. Whoever shall secure the said Aldrich in any gaol in this or the neighbouring States, or return him to the regiment, shall receive Five Dollars reward, and all necessary charges paid,
        by   *Silas Benham*, Ensign.
                                          New-Haven, April 2, 1777.
The Connecticut Journal, June 3, 1777; June 11, 1777; June 18, 1777.

                    TEN-SILVER DOLLARS REWARD.
RODE away on the 29th of May, a chestnut coloured Horse, thick set, a star in the forehead, off hind foot white, paces chiefly; had on a bridle with a strap just below the eyes, a strap for a throat latch; an old saddle with leather house, a patch set on the fore part of the saddle, a pair of saddle-bags—Said Horse was rode away by one Jeremiah Hutchinson, darkish complexion, had on when he went away, a blue sagathee coat, white waistcoat and breeches, a feather and a black ribbon in his hat is about 30 years old, about 5 feet 7 inches high, was inlisted by Mr. Barber of Torrington for three years. Whoever will

take up said man and horse and secure them shall have the above reward, and necessary charges, or five dollars for the horse only,
    by NOAH STONE.
Litchfield, June 3, 1777.
The Connecticut Courant, and Hartford Weekly Intelligencer, June 5, 1777; June 12, 1777.

Thomas Manning, and John Brown, are called upon to join their Regiment immediately, either at Cambridge or Pecks-Kill, unless they would be published as Deserters.
    JOHN COTTON, Lieut.
Boston, *May* 30th, 1777.
The Continental Journal, And Weekly Advertiser, June 5, 1777.

DEserted from Capt. Elderkin's company in Col. Swift's regiment, Ebenezer Wescot, of Scituate, in the state of Rhode Island 5 feet 7 inches high, 21 years old, dark complexion, black hair and eyes; also, John West, of Plainfield, in this state, 5 feet 3 inches high, 23 years old, light complexion, light coloured hair and dark eyes; also, one James Wood, of Marblehead, in the state of Massachusetts Bay, 5 feet 4 inches high, between twenty and thirty years of age, light coloured hair and eyes, has a very remarkable long chin. Whoever will return said Deserters to me the subscriber, or secure them so that I may have them again, shall have ten Dollars reward for each, and necessary charges paid per
    VINE ELDERKIN. Capt.
Windham, May 26, 1777.
The Connecticut Gazette; and Universal Intelligencer, June 6, 1777.

TWENTY DOLLARS REWARD

DESERTED from Captain *de Clovay's* Company, a young Man about 20 Years of Age, named MINGOVINTJOLE, about 5 Feet high, a round pale Face, short black Hair, is an *Irishman,* speaks bad *English,* bad *French,* and bad *Spanish.* Whoever apprehends the said Deserter, and delivers him to his Captain, in the *French* Regiment, at *Williamsburg,* shall have the above Reward.

 The Virginia Gazette, Dixon and Hunter, June 6, 1777; June 13, 1777.

WILLIAMSBURG, *May* 23, 1777.

BROKE out of the publick jail, last *Monday* night, the following prisoners, *viz. Adam Bell* and *Robert Lamb,* two Tories. *Bell* is well

set, has a florid complexion is of the middle stature, speaks bold, and is pretty talkative. *Lamb* is a tall slender fellow, appears to be strong and hardy. Both may be known as *Scotchmen* by their dialect. Whoever apprehends them will be entitled to a reward of 40s. for each of them. At the same time made their escape four deserters, *viz. Robert Jackson,* in the colonial service, under sentence of death; *John Smith, John Johnson,* and *John Foster,* of the continental army. Whoever apprehends and delivers the said deserters to the keeper of the publick jail shall receive 5l. for each.
    PETER PELHAM.
 The Virginia Gazette, Purdie, June 6, 1777.

           WILLIAMSBURG, *June* 6, 1777.
DESERTED from the troops of this state now in this city, on the 2d instant, *Joshua Perkins,* a mulatto, about 5 feet 6 or 7 inches high, 24 or 25 years old, and is a straight well made fellow; had on a short striped jacket, a felt hat bound round with *French* lace, the remainder of his dress not remembered. Whoever apprehends the said deserter, and returns him to his company, shall have 5 *DOLLARS* reward.
    WINDSOR BROWN, capt.
 The Virginia Gazette, Purdie, June 6, 1777; June 20, 1777.

     Five DOLLARS Reward.
DESERTED last night from this city, *Michael Eversage* a drummer, 5 feet 6 inches high, about 30 years of age, has brown hair, and dark complexion; he was enlisted in *Westmoreland* by lieut. *Lovell,* and probably he may make that way, as he has a wife with him. Whoever secures said deserter, and delivers him to any officer is the service of this state, so that he may be returned to his regiment, shall be entitled to the above reward, paid by
    JOHN ALLISON, capt.
            Williamsburg, *May* 22, 1777.
 The Virginia Gazette, Purdie, June 6, 1777.

     Ten DOLLARS Reward.
DESERTED from col. *Grayson's* regiment of guards, a certain *John Goodwin,* a native of *America,* about 5 feet 10 inches high, well made, pitted with the smallpox, his dress uncertain, but I believe it is indifferent. He has resided for some time in *Loudoun* county, near mr. *Farling Ball's* at which place he was recruited. I expect he has made for the western frontiers of this state, as he was seen traveling that way. Whoever will secure the said deserter, and give information

to me, so that he may be brought to join the said regiment, shall receive the above reward.

    CHRIST. GREENUP, lieut.

          LEESBURG, May 13, 1777.

The Virginia Gazette, Purdie, June 6, 1777; June 13, 1777; June 20, 1777.

DESERTED from the *Henry* galley, *Robert Bernard*, born in *Gloucester* county, who is a tall fellow, very talkative, and speaks much in the blackguard strain. *John Cluverius,* about 5 feet 11 inches high, has an old and homely look, and is as much of a blackguard as the other. They are but indifferent landsmen. Whoever delivers the above deserters to me shall have 10 *DOLLARS* reward for each.

    ROBERT TOMPKINS, capt.

     of the *Henry galley.*

The Virginia Gazette, June 6, 1777; June 13, 1777; June 20, 1777. See *The Virginia Gazette*, March 28, 1777.

I WILL give 5 l. reward, besides reasonable travelling expenses, for apprehending and bringing to *Williamsburg JAMES ORANGE,* who deserted from my company last week. He is an *Englishman* about 6 feet and an inch high, and was lately a grenadier of the 17th *British* regiment, from which he deserted 6 or 8 weeks ago. He has a pass signed by several gentlemen on his way from *Philadelphia* here.

    THOMAS MERIWETHER, capt.

The Virginia Gazette, Purdie, June 6, 1777. See *The Virginia Gazette,* June 20, 1777, and *The Virginia Gazette*, Purdie, June 27, 1777.

IF ROBERT TATE WHITE and JOHN WILLIAMS, who I advertised some little Time since as Deserters, will, agreeable to their Enlistment, join my Company of Artillery at *York* Town immediately, I will with Pleasure forgive them; if not, they may expect the worst of Consequences. The Martial Law inflicts Death, and I should be sorry they should experience the Necessity of it.

    WILLIAM PIERCE, Junior.

The Virginia Gazette, Dixon and White, June 6, 1777; June 13, 1777. See *The Virginia Gazette*, Dixon and Hunter, March 28, 1777.

DESERTED from my company in Col. Greaton's regiment and State of Massachusetts Bay, one Solomon Farley, about 22 years of age 5

feet 7 or 8 inches high, born in Hollis in Grafton county, State of New-Hampshire; fair complexion, light brown hair, grey eyes; had on when he went away a light colored coat, striped jacket and linnen breeches. Also, one David Clark, jun. 19 years of age, 5 feet 9 inches high, born in Ashburnham, Massachusetts State; fair complexion, light brown hair, grey eyes, and is very [ ] and walks upright. Said Farley and Clark deserted about the 10th of March. Also, one William Angell, 25 years of age, 5 feet 8 inches high, short black hair, a scar in his forehead, pitted with the small-pox, speaks quick and broken; had on a brown mixed colour'd coat and vest, striped velvet breeches, is the same person advertised by Lieut. Beuell, in this paper, and since taken up by Lieut. Reed of Williamsburg, and made his escape. Said Angell deserted about the 22d of March. Also, one Alexander Smith who absconded about the 27th of March, 45 years of age, 5 feet 7 inches high, sandy complexion, hair clubbed behind; had on a brown coat and vest, long trowsers striped with black. Whoever will take up said William Angell and return him to his company at West-Springfield, shall be entitled to thirty dollars reward, and for either of the others twenty dollars and all necessary charges
   paid, by SAMUEL FLOWER, Capt.
 N. B. Abijah Edcon is ordered to join his company at West-Springfield, or he will be returned as a deserter.
                 June 4, 1777.
The Connecticut Courant, and Hartford Weekly Intelligencer, June 9, 1777; June 16, 1777.

DESERTED from Capt. John Chadwick's company in Col. Brewer's regiment at Ticonderoga, one William Steward, a soldier belonging to the army from Great Barrington the 26th of May last; he is an old countryman, about 5 feet 6 inches high, about 21 years of age, short brown hair, brown eyes, dark complexion, somewhat pitted with the small-pox; had on when he went away a grey home-made coat, and a pair of trowsers, and took with him his arms and accoutrements. Whoever will take up said deserter and sent him to the regiment or secure him, shall have ten dollars reward and all charges paid by
      THEOPHILUS MANSFIELD.
                 June 6, 1777.
The Connecticut Courant, and Hartford Weekly Intelligencer, June 9, 1777; June 16, 1777.

      Mount Independence, May 13, 1777.
INLISTED in my company last November, at this place, one Jeremiah Eldridge, who had at the same time a furlough for thirty days, and has

not yet return'd; he is about 33 years of age, 5 feet 10 inches high, thick set, dark complexion, gray eyes, black hair, a wheel wright by trade; says he was born in the State of Rhode Island. Also, Enos Lin[e], an Irishman, inlisted at the same time and place, and had a furlough to go to Saratoga last February, not yet returned; he is about 21 years old, 5 feet 8 inches high, thick set, dark complexion, gray eyes, black hair—a farmer. Whoever will take up said deserters and send them to their company, or secure them and give notice to me that I may get them again shall have fourteen dollars reward for each, by
                 STEPHEN BUCKLAND, Capt. Artillery.
The Connecticut Courant, and Hartford Weekly Intelligencer, June 9, 1777.

THIS may certify that ENOS BLAKESLEE, (by mistake) was fully advertised in the [   ] page of this paper for desertion; and that he joined the regiment to which he belongs agreeable to the said order.
                                             June 6th, 1777.
The Connecticut Courant, and Hartford Weekly Intelligencer, June 9, 1777; June 16, 1777. Under the name of Blackslee he was advertised as a deserter in *The Connecticut Gazette; and Universal Intelligencer*, May 9, 1777.

WHEREAS *Tone Lyon*, a Molatto Fellow, of North-Fairfield, is inlisted with me in the late Colonel Douglas's Regiment, had Leave of Absence from the 21st of May, and should have returned to his Duty on the 27th: The said Tone is commanded to return forthwith and join his Company, otherwise he will be deemed a Deserter, and treated accordingly.
                 JONAS PRENTICE, Capt.
                                 New-Haven, June 10. 1777.
The Connecticut Journal, June 11, 1777; June 18, 1777; June 25, 1777.

                     Eighty DOLLARS Reward.
DESERTED from the 10th *Virginia* regiment, the following soldiers, viz. *Eake Brown* of *Cumberland* county, and *Josiah Clark, Anderson Green*, and *James Hopkins*, of *Buckingham*, I will give 20 dollars for each, if delivered to me or any continental officer so as they may be conveyed to their regiment; but if they will meet me at *Cumberland* courthouse on the 16th instant, in order to march, they shall be received with impunity. All the men enlisted by me, who have not yet marched, are desired to meet me at that time without fail.
                 HUGHES WOODSON.

The Virginia Gazette, June 13, 1777; June 20, 1777. See *The Virginia Gazette*, May 9, 1777.

DESERTED *from my company, some time in* February *last* John Webster *of* Prince Edward, *about 22 years old, 5 feet 10 inches high, with height hair and eyes; his dress I cannot describe. I am lately informed he has enlisted with a capt. Baird in the* Georgia *service, who is hereby forewarned from carrying him out of this state; and I will give* 40 DOLLARS *reward for delivering him to the commanding officer at Williamsburg. David Ross, and* John Slaughter, *whom I enlisted in* New Kent *country, are hereby desired to repair to* Williamsburg *immediately, or they will be considered as* deserters *and treated accordingly.*
                ABNER CRUMP, capt.
The Virginia Gazette, Purdie. June 13, 1777.

DESERTED from my company of the 3d *Georgia* battalion, the following soldiers, viz. *Benjamin Seaward,* 24 or 25 years old, 5 feet 9 or 10 inches high, well set. Has a fresh look, and straight black hair. *Thomas Williams,* 22 or 23 years old, 5 feet 8 or 9 inches high, dark hair and dark complexion, looks well, and is well sec. Whoever delivers them to the commanding officer in *Williamsburg* shall have 30 dollars for each.
                ISAAC HICKS.
The Virginia Gazette, Purdie, June 13, 1777; June 20, 1777.

DESERTED from my company of colonial regulars, now raising, *William Clark,* and *Charles Sprouse,* both of *Louisa* County. Clark is a likely stout young man, about 5 feet 8 or 9 inches high, dark complexion, and about 20 years of age, by trade a carpenter. *Sprouse* may be about 30 years old, much of same size of *Clark,* fair complexion, sandy hair, and is a planter. Ten DOLLARS reward for each will be paid to any person who discovers them to the commanding officer at *Williamsburg.*
                JOHN POPE.
The Virginia Gazette, Purdie, June 13, 1777.

DESERTED from capt. *John Webb's* company of the 7th *Virginia* regiment of continental forces, the following soldiers, *viz Reuben Cox,* about 6 feet 1 inch high, black hair, dark complexion, and about 22 years old. *Carter Fletcher,* about 5 feet 8 inches, remarkable black hair, dark complexion, and about 19 years old. *Rice Graves,* 5 feet 10 inches high, black hair, dark complexion, very stout, about 24 years of

age. *Vincent Hudson,* a lad about 5 feet 5 inches high, spare made, and very much freckled; he sounds the fife well, for which he was enlisted. *William Jones,* about 5 feet 8 inches high, dark hair, fair complexion, is a very modest man, and about 21 years old. The above soldiers enlisted in Essex county. *Benjamin Deane,* light hair, fair complexion, about 5 feet 8 inches high, and about 21 years old; enlisted in *King & Queen. Curtis Hardy,* about the height of *Deane,* dark hair and skin, very stout, and about 21 years old; enlisted in *Middlesex.* It is hoped the reward offered by general *Lewis* in his proclamation will be a sufficient inducement to the well wishers of their country to apprehend the above deserters.
HENRY YOUNG, lieut.
The Virginia Gazette, Purdie, June 13, 1777; June 20, 1777. See *The Virginia Gazette*, Purdie, March 28, 1777.

DESERTED from the 5th *Virginia* regiment, at *Wilmington* in *Pennsylvania,* last *October* the following soldiers, viz. *Job Martin,* about 25 years old, and about 5 feet 6 inches high. *Edmund Fair,* about 22 years old, and about 5 feet 8 inches high. *William Taller,* about 24 years old, and about 5 feet 7 inches high. *Joel Doss,* about 25 years old, and about 5 feet 8 inches high. *John Shearman,* about 23 years old, and 5 feet 9 or 10 inches high. *Zachariah Kennett,* about 25 years old, and about 5 feet 7 inches high. Also deserted from *Williamsburg,* last *September, Thomas Marlin,* about 25 years old, and about 5 feet 10 or 11 inches high, *Samuel Saunders,* a new recruit for 3 years, about 24 years old, and 5 feet 8 or 9 inches high, who deserted from *Bedford* county in *February* last. The following soldiers got furloughs at *Williamsburg* last fall to go home, *viz. George Burt,* about 23 years old, and about 5 feet 10 inches high, *Joseph Stith,* son of mr. *Richard Stith* of *Bedford,* about 6 feet high, and about 18 or 19 years old, and 5 feet 9 or 10 inches high. *TEN DOLLARS* reward will be paid for each of the above deserters, on their being delivered at head quarters, or to any officer of the 5th regiment on his march to the Northward. HARRY TERRELL, captain.
The Virginia Gazette, Purdie, June 13, 1777. See *The Virginia Gazette*, Purdie, June 20, 1777.

DESERTED *John Jackson,* enlisted by me in *Fauquier* county, who had leave of absence till the middle of *May.* He is of a dark complexion, about 22 years old, 5 feet 11 or 12 inches high, is much pitted with the smallpox, and has short yellow hair. Whoever deliver him to the commanding officer at *Williamsburg* shall have 10 DOLLARS reward.

JAMES WITHERS, ensign.
The Virginia Gazette, Purdie, June 13, 1777; June 20, 1777.

DEserted from Capt. Granger's company, about the 2nd day of this Month, Andrew Blackman an inlisted soldier under me, about 22 years of age, dark complexion, something short of six feet high, black hair and eyes, has lately had the small pox; also; William Crawford, about 20 years of age, about 5 feet 5 inches high, thick set and well made, light hair and eyes, large lips, has an impediment in his speech, and a scar on one cheek, and has lately had the small pox, they were both from New-Town, and 'tis supposed they are in company with one another. Whoever shall take up said deserters, and confine them in any of the goals in the United States, or brings them to me, or to any officer in Col. Charles Webb's regiment, so that they may be returned to their duty in the army of the United States, shall have Eight Dollars reward for each, and all necessary charges paid by me,
James Beebee, Lieut.
The Connecticut Journal, June 18, 1777; June 25, 1777; July 2, 1777.

DEserted from Capt. Allen's company, Col. Wyllys's regiment, about the 1st instant William Hall, a shoemaker, is a native of Ireland, 5 feet 9 inches high, light complexion, dark coloured hair, blue eyes and about 25 years old. Whoever shall apprehend said deserter and return him to said regiment, or secure him so he may be brought to his duty, shall receive five Dollars reward, and all necessary charges paid, by
DUDLEY WRIGHT, Lieut.
The Connecticut Gazette; And The Universal Intelligencer, June 20, 1777; June 27, 1777.

200 DOLLARS *Reward.*
DESERTED out of capt. *Benjamin Porter*'s company in the 2d *Georgia* battalion, *Gabriel Wilkinson,* about 5 feet 7 or 8 inches high, with fair hair; lived in *Frederick* county, on *Back* creek, and enlisted in *Winchester. Timothy Gerard,* about 5 feet 8 or 9 inches high, who also enlisted in *Frederick,* about 12 miles from *Winchester. Aaron Dilley,* about 5 feet 7 or 8 inches high, dark hair, on *Mill* creek, near capt. *Handshaw*'s. *William Jenkins* of *Berkeley,* about 5 feet 5 or 6 inches high. *Randolph Fugate,* of *Culpeper,* near *Chester*'s *Gap,* about 5 feet 5 inches high, well made. *Nathaniel Berry* (Alias *Smith*) 5 feet 4 inches high, dark hair and eyes. *Joseph Price,* an *Englishman,* fair hair, well made. *Berry* enlisted with me in *Culpeper,* but has enlisted with lieut. *Rucker* since, by whom he is concealed. *Price* has since

enlisted in col. troop of horse. *Jeremiah Hurley* of *King William*, a short, thick, well set man enlisted by *James Hawkins*. *William Darton* and *William Hood* both young men, enlisted in *Williamsburg* by the captain. *John Phillips* of *Dunmore*, and *Thomas Robertson* of *Frederick*, both middle sized dark skinned men. *Benjamin James* of *Spotsylvania*, a small man. The three latter were enlisted by lieut. *Strother*. Whoever so as they may be brought to the company, shall have the above reward, or 20 dollars for each of them, and reasonable charges, paid by

                JOHN CUNNINGHAM 1st. lieut.
The Virginia Gazette, Purdie, June 20, 1777.

                                        JUNE 20, 1777.
I WILL give great Wages, as well as agreeable Accommodations, by the Year, to any Person well skilled in managing Hemp, Flax, Cotton, and Wool for the Spinning Wheel, for the Growth; one who is also capable to instruct others, and conduct the Business of Weaving, and direct the making proper Looms, &c. for manufacturing such Materials into useful and decent Wear. Note, my Son on or about Saturday *May* 24, did, as he imagined, agree with a certain Orangeman, as he then stiled himself, a professed Manchester Weaver, at Hobb's Hole, in his Way to *Williamsburg*, to see a Half Brother by the Name of Atwell, living in or near that City. But it is now to be concluded he was the same *James Orange*, who is advertised as a Deserter in Purdie's Paper of June 6; for he owned himself to have been a Serjeant who came over with the 34th picket Guard from the British army, to General *Washington's* Camp about 5 Weeks before; and he had Letters of Passport from Gentlemen to the Northward. But it wants some explanation, how such a Deserter could be enlisted, consistent with what is deemed our General's Instructions, which seem to be issued with a View to remove a strong Impression prevailing among the Soldiers in our Enemy's Army, that, all the Deserters from thence would be made to take up Arms against their Country *Britain*. However, Mr. Orangeman, or Mr. Orange, seems to pay as little Regard to his private Engagements as he is advertised to have done for his public contract under Captain *Thomas Meriwether*. Nevertheless the unhappy Creature deserves to have his rare Virtue recorded; for he absolutely refused to receive Money from my Son to bear his Expences to and from *Williamsburg* for 5 or 6 Days, in which Time he was to come to *Sabine Hall*.
                LANDON CARTER.

The Virginia Gazette, June 20, 1777; June 27, 1777. See *The Virginia Gazette,* Purdie, June 6, 1777, *The Virginia Gazette,* Purdie, June 27, 1777.

220 DOLLARS Reward

DESERTED from capt. *William Grimes*'s company, the following deserters, viz. *Caleb M'Fession, Wilson Pinginton, Solomon Smith, Caleb Woodward, William Barber, Anthony Payne, Jesse Tooley, William Nickerson, Thomas Banks, Abraham Hill,* and *Lewis Charles.* The above reward, or 20 dollars for each deserter, will be paid upon their being delivered at head quarters in *Williamsburg,* and 40 dollars for each if delivered at head quarters in *New Jersey,* and all reasonable charges allowed for *Lewis Charles,* who is about 6 feet high, has lost one of his eyes, and has reddish coloured hair.

PHILIP MALLORY, lieut. 15th battal.

The Virginia Gazette, Purdie, June 20, 1777; July 4, 1777; July 11, 1777. See *The Virginia Gazette,* Dixon and Hunter, August 8, 1777.

Mr. PURDIE,
OBSERVING by capt. *Henry Terell* 's publication in your last paper that I am included with the number of deserters from the 5th *Virginia* regiment, as that publication is unjust, and as I detest the character of a deserter, and do not deserve that appellation, must beg leave to trouble the publick with a true narration of my conduct as a soldier in that service. At the age of 15 years, I, with the approbation of my father, entered into the service of my country, and after some time serving as a minute soldier, enlisted with this captain *Terrell,* came down to *Williamsburg,* and faithfully did my duty till the latter end of last summer, when I was taken ill, and languished under sickness and disorders till about the month of *January* last; and being in a low state of health, and not able to render my country the service required of me, with the advice of my friends I applied to general *Lewis* for a furlough of 30 days, in order to recover my health, which was obtained, and at the same time obtained leave to provide another man in my stead, in case I found myself unable to return to the service. When my furlough was nearly out, finding myself to continue in a low situation, I procured, at the expense of 40 dollars, one *James Weaver,* an able bodied man, to enter the service in my room, who was approved of by capt. *Terrell,* as will appear by the annexed certificates. Having thus conducted myself, the publick are left to determine as to the justice of captain *Terrell* 's publication in regard to me, more especially when he knows I am still in a situation not able to

render any service to my country as a soldier. As the above facts are well known to several gentlemen of character, I hope I shall be acquitted by my country, and stand fair in the opinion of all who will judge impartially. JOSEPH STITH.

The Virginia Gazette, Purdie, June 20, 1777. See *The Virginia Gazette*, Purdie, June 13, 1777. See below.

I JAMES WEAVER, of *Beaford* county (now a soldier in capt. *Terrell*'s company of the 5th *Virginia* regiment) about the 10th day of *February* last went to *Joseph* Stith, then a soldier in the said company, and did offer to him that I would serve in his place and stead for 40 dollars reward, which he agreed to. We then went from mr. *Richard* Stith's house to capt. *Terrell*'s, where he accepted of me instead of the said Joseph Stith, and I took the oath appointed to be taken by soldiers, and received the above reward the same day. *William M'Cord,* a soldier in the said company, was present through all the above circumstances.

Witness my hand, this 26th day of March 1777.
JAMES WEAVER.
Test,
W. CLARK. JOHN M'CORD.

BEDFORD, sc. The above named *William M'Cord* made oath before me this 26th day of *March* 1777, that capt. *Terrell* did, as above, accept of *James Weaver* in the stead of *Joseph* Stith, if the superiour officers do not object to the change.
CHARLES TALBOT.
The Virginia Gazette, Purdie, June 20, 1777. See above.

Thirty five POUNDS *Reward*

DESERTED from my company of state troops, the following soldiers, *viz. Elijah Bigby,* by trade a saddler, living in and about *Dumfries,* where he was enlisted; he is about 5 feet 4 inches high, well made, of fair complexion, wears his hair, which is long, and tied behind. *Thomas Cole,* a dark mulatto, about 5 feet 7 inches high; living in *Prince William* county. *Archibald Cash,* about 6 feet high, fair complexion, wears his hair, which is reddish coloured; living in *King George* county. *John Chaple,* about 5 feet 10 inches high, fair complexion, black hair, has a scar on his right check, by a blow from a bottle; living in *Fairfax* county. *William Johnson,* by trade a tailor, about 5 feet 5 inches high, slender made; was enlisted to *Colchester,* and got leave of absence to before the company to *Williamsburg,* as he said his friends lived near the city. *John Farley,* about 6 feet high, fair complexion, much freckled, wears his own hair, which is red; when enlisted lived near *Dumfries,* but since I have been informed he has removed for fear of being apprehended. *John Haden,* about 5 feet 10 inches high, well made, living near *Colchester,* dark complexion and hair; enlisted at *Dumfries.* Whoever apprehends the said deserters, and delivers them to the commanding officer at *Williamsburg,* shall receive the above reward, and so in proportion for each man.

∴ Those on furlough to repair to *Williamsburg.*

THOMAS W. EWELL.

The Virginia Gazette, Purdie, June 20, 1777. See *The Virginia Gazette,* Purdie, July 18, 1777, for Cash.

AGREABLE to my orders from the hon. Major General HEATH, to march with all my Men, and likewise to forward on without delay, all inlisted soldiers in the Continental army, and also all stragling soldiers that are loitering behind & idling away their time, let them belong to who they will, to their places of destination—this therefore to desire the committees & selectmen of the several towns in the old Province of Main, [*sic*] to collect them together, & send them along by the 24th & 26th instant. Lieut. Remick will march on with the first party—likewise advertize here, Stephen Nason of Kittery, a deserter; he did voluntarily inlist with me on the 17th day of march last, into the continental army, for during the war—but has refused to pass muster, and receive the publick's bounty, tho' offer'd to him, & is still ready for him, but has since deserted & gone up late into the country to make a farm for one Capt. Whipple behind the White Hills. Whoever will take up said deserter, & send him to his company to his duty, Capt. Silas Burbank, in Colo. Samuel Brewer's Battalion, shall have

FIVE DOLLARS reward
paid by William Frost, Lieut.

Kittery, June 19th, 1777.

The Freeman's Journal, Or New-Hampshire Gazette, June 21, 1777.

DESERTED from Capt. Talbert's Company, in Col. Greene's regiment, the following persons; William Raymend, 26 years of age, 6 feet 2 inches high, of a light complexion, light hair, light eyes, somewhat freckled: Benoni Taylor, 30 years of age, 5 feet 9 inches high, of a dark complexion, dark hair, light eyes, has a blemish in his right eye: Stephen Fones Hazard, about 30 years of age, 6 feet high, of a dark complexion, of a slender make. Whoever will apprehend the aforesaid deserters, and secure them in any of the gaols of the United States, and give notice to me the subscriber, or return them to the aforesaid regiment, shall have a reward for the first mentioned twenty-

five dollars, for the second fifteen, for the third five.
EDWARD SLOCUM, Lieut.
The Providence Gazette; And Country Journal, June 21, 1777; June 28, 1777.

D*Eserted from my Company in Col. Greaton's Regiment, John Linnen,* 22 *Years of age,* 5 *Feet* 6 *Inches high, light Complexion. John Gordon,* 34 *Years of age,* 6 *Feet* 3 *Inches high, dark Complexion. John Barter, aged* 21, 5 *feet* 6, *dark Complexion. Stephen Laskin, aged* 22, 5 *feet* 8, *dark Complexion. Zoath Henderson, aged* 29, 5 *feet* 10, *dark Complexion. Benjamin Cleveland, aged* 25, 5 *feet* 8, *dark Complexion. Whoever shall take up said Deserters, or either of them, and bring them to the Barracks at Roxbury, or to the Regiment at York, or elsewhere, shall have TEN DOLLARS Reward for each of them.* ABIJAH CHILD, *Captain.*
Waltham, June 12, 1777.
The Boston-Gazette, and Country Journal, June 23, 1777; June 30, 1777; July 7, 1777.

Ticonderoga, June 9, 1777.
A Return of Deserters belonging to Captain John Chadwick's Company, in Colonel Samuel Brewer's Regiment, viz.

Ichabod Sheffield of South-Kingston, aged 32, 5 feet 6 inches, dark complexion, dark eyes, dark hair. Nathaniel Ring, or Worthington, aged 18, 5 feet 4, dark complexion, dark eyes, dark hair. William Phillips, an Irishman, aged 30, 5 feet 8, dark complexion, dark eyes, black hair, Nathaniel Day, of Wells, aged 21, 5 feet 8, the same description. Gershom Boston, of Wells, aged 19, 5 feet 4, dark complexion, black eyes, black hair. William Grady, of Boston, aged 20, 5 feet 9, light complexion, dark eyes, dark hair. Joseph Arter, of Truro, aged 17, 5 feet 4, dark complexion, dark hair. Israel Newport, of Sandwich, a Mulatto, aged 21, 5 Feet 8, William Thompson, of Sandwich, an Indian, aged 28, 5 feet 10, Samuel Wampee, of ditto, an Indian, aged 30, 5 feet 8. James Robbins, of ditto, an Indian, aged 27, 5 feet 6. Daniel Brown, of ditto, an Indian, aged 35, 5 feet 6. Moses Akins of Great Barrington, a Dutchman, aged 22, 5 feet 10, dark complexion, dark eyes, dark hair. David Parday, of Nine Partners, aged 23, 5 feet 10, dark complexion, grey eyes, brown hair. Peter Patterson, of Stockbridge, aged 48, 5 feet 8, light complexion, grey eyes, dark brown hair. Edward Whigh, of Becket. Aged 25, 5 feet 4, dark complexion, dark eyes, dark hair. Silas Fay, of Becket, aged 22, 5 feet 7, dark complexion, dark eyes, dark hair. Benjamin Johnson, of

Pomfret, aged 34, 5 feet 10, dark complexion, grey eyes, brown hair. Moses Brown, of Oblong, aged 24, 5 feet 7, light complexion, light eyes, light hair. Aaron Wright, of Brookfield, aged 22, 5 feet 9, dark complexion, dark eyes, dark hair. John Smith, of Hoosuck, aged 23, 5 feet 6, light complexion, light eyes, grey hair.

Capt. JAMES DONNELL's Company.

Samuel Lancaster, of Newbury, aged 37, 5 feet 10, dark. William ailas [sic] Solomon Jordon, of Cape-Elizabeth, aged 23, 5 feet 6, dark.

Capt. ELISHA BREWER's Company.

Benja. Robinson, of Pomfret, an Irishman, aged 26, 5 feet 11, dark complexion, black eyes, brown hair. John Privart, of Stilwater, aged 22, 4 feet [sic] 8, light complexion, dark eyes, brown hair. John Troubridge, of Littlefield, aged 28, 5 feet 6, dark complexion, brown eyes, brown hair. Edward Fuller, of Northfield, aged 22, 5 feet 3, dark complexion, brown eyes, brown hair. David Horn, of Casco-Bay, aged 21, 5 feet 3, light complexion, dark eyes, dark hair. John Fullerton, of Westfield, aged 23, 5 feet 4, light complexion, dark eyes, black hair. Francis Sulfa, of Pownalboro, a Frenchman, aged 18, 4 feet 9, dark complexion, black eyes, black hair. James Mecaffatee, of Casco-Bay, an Irishman, aged 33, 6 feet, dark complexion, black eyes, black hair. John Mechuet, of Natick, aged 27, 5 feet 10, black complexion, white eyes, black hair. Moses Starr, of Danbury, aged 23, 5 feet 7, black complexion, white eyes, black hair, James Wood, of Boston, aged 34, 4 feet 8, dark complexion, black eyes, brown hair. John English, of Lancaster, aged 15, 5 feet 8, black complexion, white eyes, black hair. Nathan Johnston, of Worcester, aged 19, 5 feet, light complexion, sandy eyes, brown hair. John Cook, of Lunenburg, Irish, aged 25, 5 feet 8, dark complexion, grey eyes, dark hair. Samuel Pool, of Lunenburgh, Irish, aged 23, 5 feet 4, light complexion, brown eyes, blue hair. [sic] Azel Goodridge, of Douglass, aged 19, 4 feet 4, light complexion, brown eyes, blue hair.

Capt. ENOS STONE's Company.

Edward Edwards, of Stockbridge, aged 30, 5 feet 8, dark complexion, black hair, a scar on his arm, James Johnson, of Canaan, aged 15, 5 feet 7, dark complexion, brown hair, a blemish in one eye. James Sufield, a transient person aged 23, 5 feet 7, dark complexion, brown hair. John Huffman, a transient person, aged 20, 5 feet 5, light complexion, brown hair. David Williams, aged 19, 5 feet 6, light brown complexion, brown hair. Richard Mitchell, aged 21, 5 feet 7, brown complexion, brown hair. Hugh Ames, of New-Concord, in New-York Government, aged 45, 5 feet 6 light complexion, dark hair. Nathan James, a transient person, aged 35, 5 feet 7, dark complexion.

Capt. DANIEL MARRIL's Company.

James Ellison, of Boston, aged 40, 5 feet 3, light complexion, grey hair, light eyes.
> Captain JOSIAH JENKINS's Company.

David Kilby, of Boston, aged 19, 5 feet 6, light.
> Captain NATHAN WATKINS's Company.

Right Allen, of Scarboro', aged 24, 5 feet 8, dark complexion, dark hair, dark eyes. James Coolbuth, of Boxford, aged 22, 5 feet 10, light complexion, blue eyes, brown hair. Samuel Blood, of Concord, aged 21, 6 Feet, black complexion, black hair, black eyes. John Patten, of Bodoinham, aged 26, 5 feet 8, dark complexion, dark hair, dark eyes. John Smith, of Kingston, aged 24, 5 feet 7, black hair, blue eyes, light complexion. Bigford Diah, of Gorham, aged 26, 5 feet 10, light complexion, dark eyes, dark hair. Rufus Hemingway, of Framingham, aged 18, 5 feet 7, light complexion, brown hair, blue eyes. Jacob Adams, of Boston, aged 21, 5 feet 8, light complexion, light hair, light eyes. Daniel Pribble, of Old-York, aged 24, 5 feet 8, light complexion, light hair, light eyes. E[l]emuel W[a]lsh, of North-Yarmouth, aged 21, 5 feet 9, dark complexion, dark hair, dark eyes. Eli Hubbert, of Ware, aged 22, 5 feet 11, light complexion, light eyes, light hair. Samuel March, of Falmouth, aged 19, 5 feet 6, light complexion, light eyes, light hair. James Whittam, aged 18, 5 feet 5, dark complexion, black hair, dark eyes. Edward Pakis.

Whoever shall apprehend the aforementioned Deserters, or either of them, and shall bring and confine them under the Main Guard at Boston, upon Certificate thereof, shall receive FIVE DOLLARS Reward, and all reasonable Charges paid, by the Deputy Pay Master General, agreeable to the Resolve of the honorable the Continental Congress.

The Boston-Gazette, And Country Journal, June 23, 1777; June 30, 1777; July 7, 1777.

DEserted *from my Company, in Col. Alden's Regiment, the following Persons, viz. David Littlefield, of Wells 18 Years old, 5 feet 9 inches high, light complexion, Mas[ ]s Treadwell, of Wells, aged 23, 5 feet 11 inches, light complexion, James Moody, of Buxton, aged 26, 5 feet 9 Inches, light complexion. William Phillips, of Mendon, aged 15. John McLaughlin, of Boston, aged 19, 5 feet 6, light complexion. Samuel Belcher, of Dartmouth, aged 17, 5 feet 8. John Armstrong, of Boston, aged 56, 5 feet 10, dark complexion. Abraham Buzwell, aged 22, 5 feet 9, light complexion. Samuel Reed of Boston, aged 22, 5 feet 4, dark complexion. Thomas Ramor. Any Person that will take up and secure said Deserters, or either of them, in any Goal, or Return them, or either of them, in any Goal, or Return them, or either of them to*

their respective Corps, shall have Three Dollars Reward, and all necessary Charges
paid by me,   DANIEL LANE.
The Boston-Gazette, and Country Journal, June 23, 1777; June 30, 1777; July 7, 1777.

DESERTED from Captain Enos Stone's company, in Col. Samuel Brewer's regiment, about the first of April, one Richard Mitchel of Arundel, thirty-five years of age, sandy complection, brownish hair, grey eyes, five feet eight inches high, is an Old Country man, much pitted with the small-pox. Also one David Williams, of old Groton, twenty years of age, light complection, light coloured hair, grey eyes, 5 feet 7 inches high, thick set, well built. Also one James Scolfield of Leicester, in Worcester county, is 28 years of age, 5 feet 10 inches high, black hair, black eyes, dark complection, well built thick set fellow, is an old country man, speaks good English. Also one John Haftman, is a transient fellow, but lived at Great-Barrington last winter where he inlisted, he is 30 years of age, light complection, grey eyes, dark hair, is a sadler by trade, very quarelsome, much given to talk, is a great gamester at cards, has lately been heard of at Susquehannah, bound up the river. Whoever will take said deserters and secure them until notice can be given to the subscriber, or return them to the Regiment at Tyconderoga, shall have eight dollars for each, and all necessary charges
    paid, by   JOSEPH FOOT, Lieut.
N. B. Said deserters have all been residents in the Massachusetts State, at the above named towns, last winter.
The Connecticut Courant, and Hartford Weekly Intelligencer, June 23, 1777; June 30, 1777; July 7, 1777.

THIRTY DOLLARS REWARD.
Annapolis, June 17, 1777.
DESERTED last night from the subscriber's recruiting party, belonging to Col. THOMAS PRICE's regiment, WILSON JACKSON, born in England, about 40 years of age, 5 feet 10 or 11 inches high, swarthy complexion, and has some grey hairs on the top of his head, his clothes unknown.

ALEXANDER SMART, deserted the 14th of May last, born in Ireland, about 20 years of age, 5 feet 9 or 10 inches high much pitted with the small-pox: Had on when he went away a coarse linen hunting shirt, buckskin breeches, old [blue] stockings; says he came from the Jersies, and has a pass signed by Colonel Hartly, late of York-Town, Pennsylvania. Whoever apprehends said deserters and secures them,

so that they may be brought to join said regiment now in camp, or to any of the recruiting officers belonging to the regiment, shall have the above reward, or FIFTEEN DOLLARS for either,
   paid by JAMES WINCHESTER, Lieut.

Dunlap's Maryland Gazette, or, the Baltimore General Advertiser, June 24, 1777; July 1, 1777; July 8, 1777. See *The Pennsylvania Gazette*, June 11, 1777, in the second volume of this series, for Smart, and *The Maryland Gazette*, August 7, 1777, for both men.

      EIGHT DOLLARS Reward.
DEserted from Capt. Jeremiah Parmele's company, in Col. Moses Hazen's regiment, in the continental service, Walter Butler, lately residing at Branford, in Connecticut, of a light complexion, grey eyes, brown hair, about five feet and a half high, thick set. Whoever shall take up said deserter and return him to his regiment, or secure him in any of the goals on the continent, and give information to any of the officers of said company or regiment, shall have the above reward, and all reasonable charges
   paid by Mark Mazuzen.
             New Haven, June 17, 1777.

The Connecticut Journal, June 25, 1777; July 2, 1777; July 9, 1777.

DESERTED from my Band, in Colonel Crane's Regiment of Artillery, John Mewse, a Drummer, about 14 Years old, a likely Lad, of light Complexion, and short dark Hair. Whoever takes up said Deserter, and conveys him to my Band, or to the Regiment above-mentioned, shall receive TEN DOLLARS, and all reasonable Charges, from me, JOHN HIWILL, Musician of Artillery.
             Boston, June 23, 1777.

The Independent Chronicle and the Universal Advertiser, June 26, 1777; July 3, 1777.

DESERTED from me the Subscriber, one Jacob Clark, about 19 years old, well set, light complexion, about 5 feet 5 inches high, a blacksmith by trade. Whoever will take up said person shall receive FOUR DOLLARS reward. HENRY ERVING, Lieut.
             Worcester, June 18, 1777.

The Massachusetts Spy Or, American Oracle of Liberty, June 26, 1777.

100 DOLLARS *Reward.*
DESERTED from the 15th battalion of *Virginia* continental regulars, the following soldiers, viz. *Joseph Norwood, William Thomas, Joseph Philips, Joseph Davis, Lazarus Williams, Thomas France, Joshua Boing,* and *John Robertson.* Whoever apprehends the said deserters, and delivers them to any continental or militia officer, shall have the above reward, or 20 dollars for each.
     GEORGE ESKRIDGE, lieut.
The Virginia Gazette, Purdie, June 27, 1777.

DESERTED from my recruits, *James Orange* and *Larking Rogers,* both of which enlisted with me in *Caroline. Orange* is 6 feet 2 inches high, very lusty, well made, and has dark eyes and hair; had on when he went away a light cloth coat and breeches with pewter buttons numbered 17 Rogers, I understand, has enlisted with capt. *Samuel Scott* of the *Georgia* battalion; he is about 5 feet 10 inches high, and has a down lock. Whoever apprehends the said deserters, and delivers them to the commanding officer at *Williamsburg,*
  shall have 20 dollars reward for each.
     CHA: YARBOROUGH, lieut.
The Virginia Gazette, Purdie, June 27, 1777. See *The Virginia Gazette*, Purdie, June 6, 1777. See *The Virginia Gazette*, June 20, 1777.

Essex, §. IN the Evening of the 26th Day of June, 1777, the following Persons made their Escape from the Goal in *Newbury-Port*, in the County of *Essex.*—Collin Mackenzie, a Lieutenant in the 71st (British) Regiment of Foot, 19 Years of Age, short thick sett, 5 Feet 5 Inches high, fair Complexion. Had on when he went away, a short Linnen Coat, Trowsers, and a Highland Bonnet.—Also, John Gilroy, a Corporal in the 10th Regiment, 25 Years of Age, sandy hair, 5 feet 8 inches high, strong, well made, thin Vissage, fair Complexion. Had on when he went away a Regimental Coat of the 10th Regiment, faced with yellow, Buttons No. 10, both Prisoners of War.—Whoever shall take up and secure either of the above Prisoners in any Goal in the State of the Massachusetts Bay, shall have TWENTY DOLLARS Reward for the Lieutenant, and TEN DOLLARS Reward for the Corporal, and all necessary Charges paid.
     MICHAEL FARLEY, Sheriff.
The Boston-Gazette, And Country Journal, June 30, 1777; July 14, 1777; July 21, 1777.

DESERTED from Col. SAMUEL WYLLY's regiment, in the continental army at King's Ferry, on the fourteenth instant, JOHN DAVIS, a soldier, who is five feet four or five inches high, light eyes, hair and complection; thirty-nine years old, an Irishman. Whoever will take up said deserter and return him to said regiment shall receive eight DOLLARS reward and all necessary charges paid, by   HENRY CHAMPION, Capt.
June 16, 1777.
The Connecticut Courant, and Hartford Weekly Intelligencer, June 30, 1777; July 7, 1777.

THIS is to notify that *Calvan Gardiner,* of *Hanover, James Harden Dyer,* of *Truro, Asael Potter,* of *Beverly, James Snow,* of *Rochester, Gideon Rose,* of *Sandwich,* and *Samuel Cotley,* of *Norwich,* in Capt. POPE'S company, in Col. WILLIAM SHEPPARD'S regiment, at *Pitts-Kill,* or where they shall be as soon as possible, or they will be deemed as deserters.

THIS is to notify Joseph Losmer, of Partridgefield, and James Matthews, of *Casco-Bay,* in Capt. KEEP'S company, in Col. SHEPPARD'S regiment, to join their regiment at Pitts-Kill, or where it shall be, as soon as possible, or they will be deemed as deserters.

The Continental Journal, And Weekly Advertiser, July 3, 1777; July 10, 1777; July 17, 1777.

FREDERICKSBURG, *June* 23, 1777.
JOHN MOORE, a soldier in my troop of light dragoons, who was indulged with a furlough for 8 days, in ordered to join the regiment by the 15th of *July,* or he will be considered as a deserter, and a reward of dollars given to any person who will convey him to this place after the time limited for his joining the regiment. The said deserter was born in *Maryland,* and is now a resident in *Halifax* county; he is about 5 feet 8 inches high, about 24 years old, has dark hair and gray eyes, and is much pitted with the smallpox.
CADWALLADER JONES.
The Virginia Gazette, Purdie, July 4, 1777; July 11, 1777; July 18, 1777.

*D*ANIEL AMONETT, *a soldier in capt.* Meriwether's *company of the troops of this state, who enlisted under me in* Cumberland *county, is desired to join the company at* Fredericksburg *by the 17th instant, or he will be considered as a* deserter.
RO. HYDE SAUNDERS, *ensign.*
The Virginia Gazette, Purdie, July 4, 1777.

DESERTED from *Williamsburg* last week, *WILLIAM ALLEN,* about 5 feet 9 inches high, his dress, I forget. This ungrateful wretch was lately pardoned by his Excellency the Governour for a like offence, and enlisted with me by his order. I will give 20 dollars to any person who will bring him to *Williamsburg,* and the same sum him for *Lunsford Jones* of *Albemarle,* whom I formerly advertised to repair hither, which he neglected.
    JAMES MERIWETHER.
The Virginia Gazette, Purdie, July 4, 1777. See *The Virginia Gazette,* Purdie, August 8, 1777.

BENJAMIN PEARCE, who was enlisted by me in *King & Queen* county, is desired to repair to *Williamsburg* immediately, to join the first battalion of the troops of this state, or he will be deemed a deserter, and treated accordingly.
    THOMAS GAINES, ensign 1st *Virginia* regiment.
The Virginia Gazette, Purdie, July 4, 1777.

DESERTED from on board the brig *Greyhound,* capt. *Edward Wonycott,* lying at *Minge* 's on *James* river, the following men, *viz. William Johnson* 35 years old, 5 feet 6 or 7 inches high, well set, has a fresh look, and straight sandy coloured hair; also *John Stephens* 23, years old, 5 feet 3 inches high, has a fair complexion and straight black hair. I will give ten dollars reward for apprehending and confining each of the said deserters.
    EDWARD WONYCOTT, capt.
The Virginia Gazette, Purdie, July 4, 1777.

Twenty DOLLARS Reward.
DESERTED from capt. *Thomas Thweatt*'s company of regulars, *Benjamin Turner,* about 20 years of age, about 5 feet 10 or 11 inches high, and stout made; also *Roderick Carmichael,* about 22 years of age, near 6 feet high, slender made, and of a fresh complexion. They were both enlisted in the county of *Halifax.* Whoever apprehends the said deserters, and delivers them to me in the aforesaid county, or to any continental officer, so as they may be conveyed to their regiment, shall have the above reward, or 10 dollars for each.
    WILLIAM SHACKELFORD, lieut.
The Virginia Gazette, Purdie, July 4, 1777; July 11, 1777.

Forty DOLLARS Reward.
DESERTED from capt. *Thomas Bressie* 's company, of this state, *John Lee* and *Ennell Tooley. Lee* is near 6 feet high, about 25

years old, well made, has a very red complexion, and came from near *Halifax* in *N. Carolina,* where it may be supposed he will make for again; he carried off with him a rifle gun belonging to the country, and also furnished himself with a pair of pistols. Since his desertion I am informed his right name is *Daniel Young,* therefore it is likely he will pass by some forged one again. *Tooley* is about 19 or 20 years old, 5 feet 5 or 6 inches high, has a very hardy complexion, having followed the sea, and came from *Hartford* county in *N. Carolina.* The night on which they deserted there were two horses missing. Whoever delivers the said deserters to me at *Portsmouth,* or secures them so that I get them again, shall have the above reward, or 20 dollars for each.
     JOHN HUDSON, lieut.
 The Virginia Gazette, Purdie, July 4, 1777; July 11, 1777; July 18, 1777.

Twenty five POUNDS *Reward*
FOR apprehending the following deserters belonging to my company of the 14th *Virginia* regiment, *viz. Richard Wright,* a native, about 19 years of age, 5 feet 4 or 5 inches high, with very black hair, which he wears short, remarkably bow-legged, and strong made. *Joseph Clarke,* a native, about 38 years of age, 5 feet 8 or 9 inches high, with light hair, and is a well looking healthy man. *Williamson Plant,* about 40 years of age, 5 feet 7 or 8 inches high of a dark complexion, and wears his hair short. *Phillip McDonald,* an *Irishman,* about 25 years of age, 5 feet 8 or 9 inches high; he denies his being an *Irishman,* though it may be plainly discovered by conversing with him. *John Sorrell,* a native, about 25 years of age, 5 feet 9 or 10 inches high, slender made, has a thin visage, a down look, and is fond of drink. The above soldiers were enlisted in *Hanover,* in which county I suspect they are now lurking, except *Sorrel* and *McDonald,* the former of whom I have reason to believe is in *Amelia,* and the other in *Fauquier* or *Culpeper,* Whoever secures the above deserters, and delivers them to the subscriber, or, in his absence, to capt. *Nathan Reid* or to any continental officer under marching orders to the Northward, to the commanding officer in *Williamsburg,* shall receive the above reward, or 5 l. for each.   JOHN WINSTON.
 The Virginia Gazette, Purdie, July 4, 1777; July 11, 1777.

Forty POUNDS Reward.
DESERTED from my company of continental regulars raised in *Washington* county, *Virginia,* the following soldiers, *viz. Thomas Price,* of a fair complexion, about 5 feet 10 inches high, had on when he went away a striped cotton fly coat and waistcoat, linen drawers

and leggings; he was born in *South Carolina,* on the waters of *Broad* river. *John Chambers,* born in *England,* has lost one of his great toes, and has a large scar on the back of his neck, occasioned by the wound of a ball; he is about 5 feet 9 inches high, and had on when he went away a white hunting shirt and leather leggings and mockasons. *Charles Sinclair,* about 5 feet 10 inches high, *Virginia* born, about 20 years of age, of a fair complexion, and has a blemish in one of his eyes. *William Wakefield,* alias *Price,* born in the west of *England,* about 5 feet 8 inches high, of a down look, has short brown hair, and has lately had sore legs; he winks quick with his eyes when he talks. *William King, Virginia* born, about 20 years of age, of a fair complexion, has short brown hair, about 5 feet 7 inches high. He left my company at *New* river, in *Montgomery* county, and I imagine he is still in that part of the country, as he has a brother living there. *Prichard Stone, Virginia* born, about 35 years of age, of a dark complexion, 6 feet and an inch high. He left the company in *Montgomery* county and I imagine he returned to *Washington* county, as he has children living there. *Robert Hambleton,* 22 or 23 years of age, of a fair complexion, and has short brown hair. I have understood he went with capt. *Eliot,* from *Augusta. Robert Gray,* about 20 years of age, of a dark complexion, with dark coloured hair. He left my company on *Rockfish* gap, and I imagine he has gone to one *John Montgomery*'s, in *Amherst* county. *Thomas Price, John Chambers, Charles Sinclair,* and *William Wakefield,* have gone towards the *Moravian* town in *North Carolina.* Whoever secures the above deserters, so as I may have them again, or delivers them to any of the officers of col. *Charles Lewis's* battalion, shall have the above reward, or five pounds for each.

NATHAN REID, capt.

The Virginia Gazette, Purdie, July 4, 1777; July 11, 1777.

DEserted *from Captain Thomas Seward's Company, in Col. John Crane's Regiment of Artillery—James Brown, aged 25 years, 5 feet 6 inches high, fair complexion, red curl'd hair, grey eyes, born in Ireland. Joseph Gardner, aged 23, 5 feet 4, fair complexion, dark curl'd hair, blue eyes, born in Salem. John Summer, aged 27, 5 feet 4, fair complexion, light curl'd hair, grey eyes, born in Old England. James Watson, aged 31, fair complexion, black curl'd hair, dark eyes, born in Scotland. Morris White, aged 27, 6 feet, fair complexion, dark short hair, grey eyes, born in Casco-Bay. John Bush, aged 25, 5 feet 4, dark complexion, dark curl'd hair, dark eyes, born in Old England. Florra [sic] Ellis, aged 23, 5 feet 6, dark complexion, dark short hair, black eyes, born in Italy. Adam Miller, aged 24, 5 feet 6, light*

complexion, dark short hair, dark eyes. Jeremiah Brigs, born in Dighton, aged 21, 5 feet 6, dark short hair, much pock-mark'd, dark eyes.—Whoever shall take up said Deserters, and secure them in any of the States Goals, shall receive SIX DOLLARS Reward for each, and all necessary Charges paid, by me
    THOMAS JACKSON, Captain Lieut. of Artillery.
The Boston-Gazette, and Country Journal, July 7, 1777; July 14, 1777; July 21, 1777.

DEserted from my Company, in Col. Sherburn's Regiment, James Hill of Kennebeck, 5 feet 6 inches high, dark hair, brown complexion. Whoever will take up said Hill, and send him to Cambridge, or secure him in any Goal, shall have FIVE DOLLARS Reward, and all Charges paid by me, BENJA. BURTON, Capt.
             Boston, *July* 1, 1777.
The Boston-Gazette, and Country Journal, July 7, 1777; July 14, 1777; July 21, 1777.

DEserted from Captain Paul Ellis's Company, in Col. Bigelow's Regiment, James Babb, belonging to Newbury-Port, about 5 feet 6 inches high, dark complexion, black hair, light coloured eyes. Whoever will take up said Deserter, shall have FIVE DOLLARS Reward by me, and all necessary Charges paid.
    ABNER DOW, Lieut.
             Boston, *July* 1, 1777.
The Boston-Gazette, and Country Journal, July 7, 1777; July 14, 1777; July 21, 1777.

DEserted from Capt. Megriegier's company in Col. Durkee's regiment, John Clark, said he belong'd to Say-Brook, he inlisted in Plainfield the 10th of June, said had been privateering the year past, and was taken & set at liberty at Providence, and was then on his return home, he appear'd to be a very honest fellow, is about 20 years old, 5 feet & 10 inches high, light colour'd hair and eyes, dark complexion, had on an old brown coat, coarse linen shirt & duffil trowsers, carried an old tar'd frock in his hand. Whoever will apprehend said deserter and secure him in any goal or return him to his regiment so that he may be bro't to justice, shall have ten Dollars reward, and all necessary charges
    paid by Lemuel Clift, Lieu.
            Peck's-Kill, July 5, 1777.
The Connecticut Gazette; And the Universal Intelligencer, July 11, 1777.

Three POUNDS Reward.
DESERTED from my quota of state troops, *Lewis Brown*, about 6 feet high, of a dark complexion is much addicted to drink, and lives on *Deep* run in *Henrico* county. Whoever delivers the said deserter to me, or to the commanding officer in *Williamsburg* shall receive the above reward. JOSEPH SELDEN. lieut.
The Virginia Gazette, Purdie, 11, 1777.

DESERTED from Captain *John Blair*'s Company in the 9th *Virginia* Regiment, when under marching Orders in *December* last, the following Soldiers, *viz.* LEVIN SMITH, WILLIAM CHANCE, JOHN CAMPBELL, MAJOR JONES, and THOMAS PETTIT. I will give TEN DOLLARS Reward for apprehending either of the above Deserters, or FIFTY DOLLARS for the Whole.
THOMAS OVERTON, Lieut.
The Virginia Gazette, Dixon and Hunter, July 11, 1777.

FORTY DOLLARS REWARD
FOR delivering to the Gaoler in *Williamsburg,* JAMES PATTERSON, a Deserter from my Company, of the 6th *Virginia* Regiment. *Patterson* is a *Virginian,* about 5 Feet 6 Inches high, 20 Years of Age, light coloured Hair and Eyes. He was decoyed off by his Father, and carried either to *Louisa* or *Albemarle* County.
TAOMAS [*sic*] MASSIE, Captain 6th Virg. Regt.
The Virginia Gazette, Dixon and Hunter, July 11, 1777; July 18, 1777; July 25, 1777.

DEserted from the Galley SPITFIRE, commanded by Capt. Joseph Crandall, Thomas Barker, 30 Years of Age, about 5 Feet 10 Inches high, short curled black Hair: Had on when he went away, a blue Coatee, new Ravens Duck Trowsers, and white Yarn Stockings. Whoever will take up said Deserter, and secure him in any Gaol in this State, or deliver him to the Subscriber, shall have Five Dollars Reward, and all necessary Charges,
paid by me, JOSEPH CRANDALL.
The Providence Gazette; And Country Journal, July 12, 1777; July 19, 1777.

July 10.
Stolen from the Plantation of Samuel Hill, near Orangeburgh, last Friday se'nnight,
A bright bay Stallion,

about 13 hands high, 5 years old, has a bald face, four white legs, a wall eye on the mounting side, and a bay spot near it; a natural pacer:—By information he was stolen by one Charles Wood, a recruit who deserted from the regiment of artillery, as he was seen riding him on the road to Charles-Town.

Twenty Pounds reward will be given for taking up the said Wood, over and above the State allowance for apprehending deserters, and Ten Pounds on the recovery of the Horse,
                by   SAMUEL HILL.
The Gazette Of The State of South-Carolina, July 14, 1777; July 21, 1777.

JOHN SMITH, a transient person about 26 years old, somewhat pock-broken, 5 feet 9 inches high, well built, blue eyes, light hair, almost bald, dress'd in a dark regimental coat fac'd with red, flower'd flannel vest, and linen over-haulls, but had other cloaths with him, deserted from Capt. Andrew Fitch's company in Col. Durkee's regiment on the road from Colchester to Danbury, from a party of Col. Huntington's regiment on the 26th of April, supposed the Cromwell, [sic] or gone into the country in company with a large fat woman, light hair & complexion, whom he call'd his wife. Whoever will return said deserter to the Regiment, or confine him and give information to the subscriber, so that he may be brought to the regiment, shall receive Ten Dollars reward, and all necessary charges,
           from Pownall Deming, Lieut.
                                            Peek's-Kill, June 25, 1777.
The Connecticut Gazette; And The Universal Intelligencer, July 18, 1777.

Mr. PURDIE,
OBSERVING in your paper of *June* 20th the name of *Archibald Cash* advertised as a deserter, by capt. *Thomas Ewell,* you will please to inform the publick, that I borrowed 20 dollars of him, and sent soon after, by a friend, 7 l. 4s. to repay him. The money was tendered, but capt. *Ewell* would not receive it; therefore, I submit to the publick what right he has to publish me in the publick papers. Notwithstanding, I am willing, and ready, upon any pressing emergency, to serve my country without being advertised or taken up at a deserter; and ready, able, and willing, to pay capt. *Ewell* the money when demanded.
                ARCHDELL CASH,
The Virginia Gazette, Purdie, July 18, 1777; July 25, 1777. See *The Virginia Gazette,* Purdie, June 20, 1777.

YORK GARRISON, *July,* 9, 1777.

WILLIAM BROWN, belonging to the 7th company of artillery, who has been absent on furlough for some time, is desired to repair immediately to *York* and join his company, or he will be deemed a deserter, and treated accordingly.

JOHN C. CARTER, lieut.

The Virginia Gazette, Purdie, July 18, 1777.

DESERTED from *Williamsburg,* the 1st instant, *John Kennedy,* a soldier in my company of artillery. He is well made, about 5 feet 8 inches high, of a dark complexion, had on a brown coat and breeches, and a half worn hat. The other articles of his dress are unknown. Twenty dollars will be given for the above deserter, if delivered to the commanding; officer of artillery at *York* or *Portsmouth.*

WILLIAM WATERS, capt. artillery.

The Virginia Gazette, Purdie, July 18, 1777; July 25, 1777; August 1, 1777.

DESERTED from the *Manly* galley, *Thomas Glen,* a marine, who, formerly enlisted under capt. *John Catesby Cocke,* and was put on board by the commodore. He is tall, and slim made; had on when he went away, a yellow *Virginia* cloth coat, and yellow striped cotton trousers. Whoever delivers the said deserter on board the *Manly* galley or secures him so that I get him again, shall have

TEN DOLLARS reward. WILLIAM SAUNDERS.

The Virginia Gazette, Purdie, July 18, 1777; July 25, 1777; August 1, 1777.

DESERTED from capt. *Hoffler's* company of the 1st regiment of the troops of this state, the following soldiers, who all lived in *Norfolk* and *Princess Anne* counties, and stole a number of horses when they went off, *viz. William Hewlett, Maximilian Steward, James Woodward, John Tart, Thomas Thorington, Samuel Hattan, Solomon Hattan, George Townsing, John Townsing, Thomas Willie, Thomas Stafford, Thomas Taylor, James Tumberlen, John Brown, John Damore, John Brinston, Charles Woodward, John Hardy, William Josea, and Thomas Esdale.* Whoever delivers the said deserters to the commanding officer in *Williamsburg* shall have 10 dollars reward for each.

The Virginia Gazette, Purdie, July 18, 1777; July 25, 1777.

Deserted from the first New-
Hampshire battalion, John Reemer, 27 years of age, 5 feet 11 inches high, dark complexion, dark brown hair, belonging to Landaff, in the county of Cheshire. Whoever will apprehend said deserter and send him to his regiment, or secure him in any of the goals in this State, shall have five dollars reward and all necessary charges
    paid by Samuel Sweet, Ensign.
              Ticonderoga, June 28, 1777.
The Freeman's Journal, Or New-Hampshire Gazette, July 19, 1777; July 26, 1777.

Deserted April 20th, 1777,
from Number Four, Joseph Frost, belonging to the town of Unity in Cheshire County, about 23 years of age, and about five feet six inches high, dark complexion, had on when he went away, a blanket coat, and blanket overhalls. Seth Rice of Paramount, about 26 years of age, dark complexion, five feet, ten inches high. Whoever will take up said deserters & secures them in any goal or send them to Ticonderoga to Capt. Nathaniel Hutchin's company in Co. Cilly's regiment belonging to this State, shall have five dollars reward for each, and all necessary
    charges paid by SIMON SARTWELL, Lieut
The Freeman's Journal, Or New-Hampshire Gazette, July 19, 1777; July 26, 1777.

DEserted from the Galley SPITFIRE, commanded by Capt. Joseph Crandall, Thomas Barker, 30 Years of Age, about 5 Feet 10 Inches high, short curled black Hair: Had on when he went away, a blue Coatee, new Ravens Duck Trowsers, and white Yarn Stockings. Whoever will take up said Deserter, and secure him in any Gaol in this State, or deliver him to the Subscriber, shall have Five Dollars Reward, and all necessary Charges, paid by me,
  JOSEPH CRANDALL.
The Providence Gazette; And Country Journal, July 19, 1777.

DESERTED from Capt. Daniel Barnes Company, in Col. Bigelow's regiment, viz. Elisha Astins, about 5 feet 5 inches high, dark complexion, Black hair about 2[2] years old, and James Crosman about 5 feet 7 inches high, a Stockey, well built fellow, about 35 years old. Whoever will take up said deserters and bring them to Worcester, or give information where they are, shall receive 5 Dollars and necessary charges paid by
    DANIEL BARNES Capt.   July, 8th. 1777.

The Massachusetts Spy: Or, American Oracle of Liberty, July 24, 1777.

WILLIAMSBURG, *July* 15, 1777.
JERIDAM LEHEW, *Daniel Warner, Philip Crume, Benjamin Pierceall, Abraham Kirkendall, Francis Wright, James Russell, William Holloway, James Turner, Thomas Tutt, Thomas Morris,* and *John Peyton,* having been returned to me by the late captain *William Field* (then in the service of this compant) as soldiers enlisted by him, and on command, but does not account on what command, or where they are, as also *Caleb Ramsay, Francis Brown, John Conner, William Hill, Thomas Hand, William Hopkins, Henry Hand,* and *John Grigby,* returned to me on furlough, which limited time to each of them is long since expired, it is therefore ordered, that each and every of the above named soldiers repair to *Williamsburg* and join their company immediately, otherwise they will be deemed deserters, and treated accordingly.
HAYNES MORGAN, col.
∴ Deserted also, *William Wright,* James Rice, Lancelot Sutherland, Thomas Sutherland, John Steele, Hezekiah Roberts, Nehemiah Roberts, and John Corder, FIVE POUNDS reward for each.
The Virginia Gazette, Purdie, July 25, 1777.

DESERTED the 5th of June last, from the Regiment commanded by Lieut. Colonel Prentice, David McDuel, a Soldier about 5 Feet 5 Inches high, 20 Years old light Complexion, light coloured Eyes, dark Hair, something pitted with the Small Pox, had on a red regimental Coat. Whoever will take up said Deserter and return him to said Regiment, or secure him and give Notice to the Subscriber, shall have Eight Dollars Reward, and all necessary Charges paid by
RICHARD DOUGLAS, Lieut.
The Connecticut Gazette; And The Universal Intelligencer, August 1, 1777; *The Connecticut Journal*, August 6, 1777; August 13, 1777; August 20, 1777.

WHEREAS some persons have made themselves so mean as to say they saw me advertised as having received the bounty of one of the *Georgia* officers, and failed to appear, from which report it has become a general talk that I was a deserter: Now, if it can be made appear that I ever received such bounty, I am willing to serve as ordinance directs, and shall be in the county of *Amherst* till this dispute is ended.
DRURY ALFORD.

The Virginia Gazette, Purdie, August 1, 1777. See *The Virginia Gazette*, Dixon and Hunter, September 27, 1776.

DESERTED from my company formerly commanded by Capt. *Patteson,* of the 6th *Virginia* regiment, *John Childress,* about 20 years of age, 5 feet 8 or 9 inches high, of a red complexion, has yellow hair, and gray eyes. Whoever apprehends the said deserter, and delivers him to me in *Lunenburg* county, or to any continental officer, shall receive TEN DOLLARS reward. *Henry Still,* who was sick in *Buckingham* county when the regiment marched to *New Jersey,* and *John Williams,* who was left sick at *Tawny* town in *Maryland,* are hereby expressly ordered forth with to repair to some continental officer marching to the grand camp, in order to join their regiment; otherwise they must expect to be considered as deserters, and treated accordingly.
      JOHN STOKES, lieut. 6th *Virginia* regiment.
The Virginia Gazette, Purdie, August 1, 1777; August 8, 1777.

THOMAS VAUGHAN NANCE, who enlisted with me in col. *Harrison's* train of artillery, is ordered to repair to *York* immediately, or he will be deemed a deserter.
      H. PRYOR, lieut.
The Virginia Gazette, Purdie, August 1, 1777

      WILLIAMSBURG, *August* 1, 1777.
      TWENTY DOLLARS REWARD
FOR apprehending and delivering to the Commandant of this Place CHARLES SMITH of *Henrico* County, a stout well formed Mulatto, about 5 Feet 10 Inches high, who *deserted* from me on my March hither about 10 Days ago. The Thumb and fore Finger of his left Hand are somewhat contracted.
      JOHN SHARPE, Serj. to Capt. *Pope.*
The Virginia Gazette, Dixon and Hunter, August 1, 1777; August 8, 1777; August 15, 1777.

DESERTED from me at Springfield, Aaron Sampson, belonging to Capt. Hunts company, Col. Vose' regiment. Said Sampson is about 30 years of age, 6 feet 1 inches high, sandy hair, looks very down, is very slim; had on when he went away, a green coat and jacket, white tow shirt, white long trowsers. Whoever will take up said Sampson and bring him to me in Springfield, or secure him in any goal so that he may be sent to his regiment at Peck's Kill, shall have six dollars

reward and necessary charges paid,
                    by   JOHN MARCH, Lieut.
    The Connecticut Courant, and Hartford Weekly Intelligencer,
August 4, 1777, August 11, 1777; August 18, 1777.

DESERTED from my company one Ebenezer Dam, of Haverhill, in the State of New Hampshire. Whoever will return said deserter to his company at Kingstown on North river, shall have five dollars reward and all necessary charges paid,
                    by me   SAMUEL PAINE, Capt.
    N. B. If said Dam will return to his duty like an honest soldier, he will save the reward to himself.
    The Connecticut Courant, and Hartford Weekly Intelligencer, August 4, 1777; August 11, 1777; August 18, 1777.

DESERTED from Capt. Elijah Blakman's company, in Col. Sherburn's regiment, on the 20th of July last, a soldier, inlisted by the name of John Williams, about 5 feet 7 inches high, thick set, dark complexion, short dark brown hair, wears a large blue outside jacket, tow cloth trowsers, or white drilling breeches, receiv'd a regimental hat, but it's not likely he will wear it, upwards of 40 years of age, great talker, sometimes carries a red eye by hard drinking; properly inlisted and sworn, and received his bounty. Whoever will secure, or return said deserter to the company he belongs, shall receive ten dollars reward, and all necessary charges paid by me.
                    ELIJAH BLAKMAN, Capt.
                                        Middletown, Aug. 1, 1777.
    The Connecticut Courant, and Hartford Weekly Intelligencer, August 4, 1777; August 11, 1777; August 18, 1777.

COMMITTED to Queen-Anne's county gaol, on the 20th of June, as a deserter, one Rowland Harris, who says he belongs to capt. William Sandford's company of the second Virginia regiment, commanded by colonel Spotswood, who hereby is requested to send his order for him.
                    W. Wright, Sheriff.
    The Maryland Gazette, August 7, 1777.

To Lieutenant JAMES MERIWETHER.
    SIR
IN *Purdie's* paper of *July* the 4th you offer a reward of 20 dollars to any person who will deliver to you my son, *Lunsford Jones*, whom you seem to consider as enlisted by you into the colonial service. I have too much confidence in the wisdom of those who have formed

our new constitution to suppose they have left it in the power of every recruiting officer, by declaring a man enlisted, to subject him to the penalties of desertion. That those who might be allured by your offer to lay violent hands on my son may know that the point will be contested at least, I shall, through the channel of the same paper, state some facts to the public. My son is a youth of 17 years of age only. I some time ago sent him from home on the business of our plantation. On his return, I was informed he had met with you, had undertaken to enlist with you, and had received the bounty, but had not gone through the other ceremonies required by the act of Assembly, to wit, hearing the articles of war read to him, subscribing them, and taking the oath of fidelity and obedience; and I knew you had not attended to a circumstance I thought still more important, of obtaining my consent to the enlistment of my infant son. I immediately forbad his following you, took from him the money, delivered it to a gentleman going to *Williamsburg,* who, on my behalf, tendered it to you, and notified my withholding my son by virtue of my paternal power. You chose to reject the money. It is returned to my hands, and shall be faithfully preserved for you till you shall please to call for it. Not trusting to my own judgment, I applied to counsel at law for on two points: I. Whether an enlistment, deficient in the legal circumstances before stated, would have transferred a citizen, even of full age, from the civil into the military body? 2. Whether the paternal power, so absolute in all other cases, has, in this particular, been encroached by any law, so as to emancipate a child from his natural subjection to his parents? I shall pass over his reasonings, and only say, he answered both questions negatively. My dissent did not proceed from any want of zeal for the *American* cause, but from in attention to some circumstances of the service in which my son had engaged. There need not be mentioned here. My son continuing in the disposition to serve his country in the military way, I attended him to an officer, saw him regularly enlisted in the continental service, by taking the bounty and oath, subscribing the articles, and hearing them read, and confirmed the whole by my consent in writing. Had I deferred this step a few longer, the act for draughting the militia, which I had before understood would certainly pass, would have been the means of his receiving a much higher bounty; but I chose to preclude the imputation of acting on mercenary principles. I have endeavoured, in this, to unite the duties of a father and a friend to my country. Whether I have so far missed my aim as thereby to work out the death of my son, as for a desertion of the publick cause, not your advertisement, I trust, nor yet any military usages, but the laws of my country, will decide, if it should be rendered necessary to appeal to them.

JAMES JONES.
The Virginia Gazette, Purdie, August 8, 1777. See *The Virginia Gazette*, Purdie, July 4, 1777.

DESERTED *from the ship* Tartar, *lying at* Frazer's *ferry, on* Mattapony, Joseph Martin, *about* 30 *years old, about* 5 *feet* 6 *inches high, of a dark complexion, and has black hair. Also John Bass, near* 50 *years old, about* 5 *feet* 8 *inches high, of a dark complexion, and has short black hair. They came both from* Middlesex. *Whoever brings them to the shop at* Frazier's, *or secures them so as they may be had again, shall have* 10 *dollars for each, and reasonable charges,*
    paid by   RICHARD TAYLOR, *capt.*
The Virginia Gazette, Purdie, August 8, 1777; August 15, 1777.

DESERTED from capt. *Pierce's* company of artillery, *John Griffith* (alias *Wells*) who is about 5 feet 10 inches high, has a family on the *Eastern Shore,* and is very well acquainted about *Back* river and *Hampton.* He was a sailor on board the *Virginia* frigate, and has taken several unlawful bounties. Whoever delivers the said deserter to his company, at *Portsmouth* shall have 20 dollars reward.
    WILLIAM POYTHRESS. lieut.
The Virginia Gazette, Purdie, August 8, 1777; August 15, 1777.

            BRUNSWICK, *July* 9, 1777.
WHEREAS a certain *Philip Mallory,* second Lieutenant in the 15th *Virginia* Regiment, has thought proper to cause me to be advertised in the *Virginia* Gazette, as a deserted Person, I hereby certify the Grounds upon which the said *Mallory* claims me as a Soldier, and leave the Judgment of my Cause to the impartial Public.

After I had served as a Soldier 3 Months in the regular Service, and 3 Months more as Serjeant in the Minute Service, having obtained a Discharge from my Captain, returned Home, not long after meeting with *Philip Mallory,* he solicited me to enlist, telling me at the same Time, he did not expect me to enlist as a Soldier, but if I would enter the Service he would have the Serjeant Major's Place procured for me, I told him that I was undetermined in that Respect, therefore we made a Contract conditionally. He gave me from *Christmas* until the Spring to consider of it, at which Time it should lie to my Choice whether or not I would comply with his Offer, when, provided I should, was to have the Serjeant Major's Place; but upon the Contrary, if I should choose to decline he promised not to make a Return of me; and also at the same Time proffered me Money, which I refused, telling him it was Time enough to receive Money when I should enlist. He may here

object, and say "that I subscribed the list," to which I answer, if I did he well knew the Motive, which was to encourage others to enlist who were then present. Accordingly in the Spring I told him that I had declined to enlist, and that he might decline returning my Name, and give the Serjeant Major's Place to some other Person; since he still claims me a Soldier. I offered to meet him with Witnesses to our Agreement, and appointed a Day for the Purpose, and accordingly appeared with Persons, who were Witnesses, more than once; but *Mallory* never met to have our Agreement determined, therefore, I hereby inform the Public, as well as *Mallory,* that I am determined not to be obligated to serve by Reason of the aforesaid Agreement.
    LEWIS CHARLES, Jun.

This is to certify, that Thomas Charles *made Oath before me, that at the Time of* Lewis Charles's *enlisting into the Service of the Commonwealth, under Lieutenant* Mallory, *it was on Condition that he should be a Serjeant Major in the said Service.* Francis Stanback *also made Oath before me, that be heard Lieutenant* Mallory *say that* Lewis Charles *had entered into the Service as a Serjeant, or Serjeant Major, he does not recollect which.*
    W. STARK.   MARCH 11, 1777.

 The Virginia Gazette, Dixon and Hunter, August 8, 1777. See *The Virginia Gazette,* Purdie, June 20, 1777.

DESERTED from my company in the 15th *Virginia* regiment, the following soldiers, viz. *John Saunders, Richard Haydon, Peter Kaeeve, John Cottrell,* and *John Watts.* Whoever delivers the said deserters to a continental officer shall have 20 dollars for each.
    EDWIN HALL, capt.

 The Virginia Gazette, Purdie, August 8, 1777; August 15, 1777.

DESERTED from capt. *Halcomb's* company in the 4th *Virginia* regiment, *Levi Cooper,* serjeant, *Charles Jordin, John White, Jesse Brown, and Charles Key,* privates. The two first deserted from *Christiana* bridge, in the *Delaware* state; the other three were left sick in *Virginia* when the regiment marched to the Northward, and have since refused to joint it. A reward of 25 dollars will be paid for *Cooper,* and 20 dollars for each of the privates, upon their being brought to *Williamsburg,* and delivered to any officer of the continental troops.
    WILLIAM ROGERS, lieut. 4th reg.

 The Virginia Gazette, Purdie, August 8, 1777.

DESERTED from Westfield the night after the 7th inst. three Highland prisoners, viz. Alexander Adams, James Terry and Robert Smith, all short men, speak broken English; Terry and Smith had brown coats and brown hair, Adams's hair almost red. Whoever will take up said prisoners and confine them, or return them to the committee of correspondence and safety of Westfield, shall have five dollars reward and charges paid,
    by   DAVID MOSELEY, *Chairman.*
                Westfield, Aug. 9, 1777,
The Connecticut Courant, And Weekly Intelligencer, August 11, 1777; August 18, 1777. See *The Connecticut Courant, and Hartford Weekly Intelligencer,* September 29, 1777, for Adams.

ELIJAH HILL, Timothy Case, and Samuel Thomas of Simsbury, regularly drafted and returned in May last to serve as soldiers in Col. Wyllys's regiment having absconded after refusing to join. Whoever will secure said delinquents or either of them, in any goal in this State, or return them to said regiment, shall have eight dollars reward, and all necessary charges paid.
    per order of Col. Wyllys.
    SAMUEL RICHARDS, Lieut.
The Connecticut Courant, And Weekly Intelligencer, August 11, 1777; August 18, 1777.

DESERTED from my company, in the 10th *Virginia* regiment, the following soldiers, *viz. Joseph Philips,* about 6 feet high, 22 or 23 years old, well made, has short brown hair, and formerly lived in *Augusta. James Hamilton,* about 40 years old, about 5 feet 8 inches high, has a thin visage, and it is said is gone to *Carolina. Jeremiah Christie,* a young man about 5 feet 7 inches high, well made, full faced, has gray eyes, and brown hair. *John Nelson,* 25 years old, 5 feet 9 inches high, stout made, has dark hair and eyes, and formerly followed the water business. *William Bettesworth,* 23 years old, 5 feet 11 inches high, well made, and has light hair. *James Jones,* 30 years old, 5 feet 10 inches high, well made, has black hair and eyes, and is a planter. All but the first mentioned deserter came out of *Stafford* and *King George.* Whoever delivers the above deserters to any officer of the 10th regiment shall have 20 dollars for each.
    J. MOUNTJOY, capt.
The Virginia Gazette, Purdie, August 15, 1777.

WHEREAS a certain *John Howerton,* a resident of *Essex* county, was properly enlisted by me for the service of this state, and hath failed to attend agreeable to orders, this is therefore to give the said *Howerton* public notice to repair to *York* garrison within ten days from the publication hereof, other wise he, will be deemed a deserter, and treated accordingly.

    J. RENNOLDS, jun, lieut.

 The Virginia Gazette, Purdie, August 15, 1777; September 5, 1777.

DESERTED from on board the *Hero* galley, the 7th of *June* last, the following men, *viz. John Baker,* a middling sized man, has short black hair, is very talkative, and formerly belonged to the brig *Liberty. Barnaby Carrigan,* a short thick man, very much marked with the smallpox, and formerly belonged to capt. *Bell's* company of the 4th regiment. *James Dunn,* who deserted the 15th of *July,* from on board the said vessel, a middle sized man, has light short hair, and formerly belonged to capt. *Stevenson's* company of the 8th regiment. They are all *Irishmen.* Whoever apprehends said deserters, and secures them in any jail, or on board any armed vessel belonging to this state, shall receive 10 dollars reward for each. I flatter myself that all friends to *America* will spare no pains in apprehending the said deserters, if they should hear of them, as they have received their full bounty, and are enlisted for three years.

    PHILIP CHAMBERLAIN, capt.

 The Virginia Gazette, Purdie, August 15, 1777; August 22, 1777.

DESERTED from the *Lewis* galley, *Samuel Wharton,* about 20 years old, has sandy coloured hair, and had on and took with him common sailors clothes. Also *Henry Overstreet,* about 25 years old, and is very talkative. Whoever secures the said deserters, so that I get them again, shall have 20 dollars reward for each.

    CELEY SAUNDERS. capt.

 The Virginia Gazette, Purdie, August 15, 1777; August 22, 1777.

DESERTED from the *Safeguard* galley, *William Farrell* about 5 feet 8 inches high, has an impediment in his speech, sore eyes, and is red headed; had on when he went away an old shirt, and woolen trousers. Also *Charles Elder,* a *Scotchman,* which may easily be discovered from his dialect, about 5 feet 8 inches high, and wears his own hair; had on a blue jacket, and black breeches. Whoever secures the said deserters, so that I get them again, shall have 10 dollars reward for each. GEO: ELLIOTT, captain.

The Virginia Gazette, Purdie, August 15, 1777; August 22, 1777.

DESERTED from capt. *John Lewis's,* company of colonial troops the following soldiers, who were enlisted in *Bedford. Henry Fear,* about 40 years old, 5 feet 6 or 7 inches high, a tailor by trade, *Philip Atkins,* 5 feet 9 or 10 inches high, about 30 years old, and of a dark complexion. *James Boyd,* about 25 years old, 5 feet 6 or 7 inches high. *James Jordan* (alias *William Johnston*) about 20 years old, 5 feet 3 or 4 inches high. Whoever secures the above deserters, so as they join their company, or delivers them at capt. *Lewis's* warm springs, *Augusta* county, shall have 20 dollars reward for each, and reasonable charges. J. MUCKLEHENNY, lieut.

The Virginia Gazette, Purdie, August 15, 1777; August 22, 1777.

LEFT in possession of Samuel Young, by a Man that calls his Name Joseph Plaster, a black MARE, about five Years old, naturally inclines to pace, is middling well built, and has the letter P artificially and curiously mark'd on the left shoulder; who said he belonged to Old York, and deserted from the Raleigh; he was taken up by the Committee of Lyme, and afterwards made his escape, he is about 25 Years of Age, five Feet, four Inches high, short black Hair, and had on snuff coloured Cloaths; any Person proving their Property to said Mare & paying costs may have her by applying at Gunthwait in Cohos.

The Freeman's Journal, Or New-Hampshire Gazette, August 16, 1777; August 23, 1777.

DESERTED from Capt. Fry's Company, in Col. Cilly's regiment, Andrew McDaniel, about five feet six inches high, 25 years of age, an old Country-man, something pock marked, dark complexion.— Whoever will take up said Deserter, and send him to his regiment, shall have five Dollars reward, and necessary charges pay'd by me, Joshua Thomson, Ensign,

The Freeman's Journal, Or New-Hampshire Gazette, August 16, 1777; August 23, 1777.

YESTERDAY afternoon left their several places of residence in this town, where they were out (upon their own earnest request at labour) for their own benefit, two prisoners, viz, Robert Johnson Collins, a serj. in a company in Gen. Delancey's brigade, taken by Col. Meigs at Long-Island, appears like a civil honest man, was of a pretty fair skin

and countenance, had short brown hair, about 5 feet high, about 24 years of age, wore a short blue coat, white shirt, and check'd trowsers, by trade a weaver; also one Joshua St[arr], a tory prisoner, belongs to Stanford, in this State, about 22 or 23 years of age, above middling for bigness and stature, had short brown hair, grey eyes, near sighted, and wore when he went away a lightish brown coat, check'd or white shirt, and check'd tow long-trowsers, a down guilty look, odd cast with his eyes. As Collins appeared greatly desired to get back again to his friends at Long-Island, it is most probable that he will attempt that way, it is hoped every friend to his country will use his best endeavours to stop and return them; and whoever shall receive one or both, shall have a reasonable reward and all necessary charges paid,
      by EZEKIEL WILLIAMS, Commis. Prisoners. Hartford, Aug. 13, 1777.
The Connecticut Courant, And Hartford Weekly Intelligencer, August 18, 1777; August 25, 1777.

LAST sabbath night escaped from Charles Granger, of Suffield in the state of Connecticut, one Stephen Pangman, a prisoner of war taken at Long-Island in May last; he lately belonged to Stamford, and went from there to Long-Island, about six months ago, is about twenty one years old, short of stature, dark hair, his right hand contracted and finger crooked by a burn he received when a child; had on a dark brown coat with white buttons, white woolen vest and breeches, and thread stockings, he stole from said Granger and carried away with him a gun and bayonet, a pair of with stockings, and twenty four shillings in bills, it is apprehended that he is gone towards New-York, and that he intends to pass for one of our militia on the road. Whoever will take him up and secure him in any goal in this state, and give notice the the subscriber, shall have five Dollars Reward and necessary charges paid,
      By   EZEKIEL WILLIAMS, Commis. Prisoners.
      Hartford, Aug, 11, 1777.
The Connecticut Courant, And Hartford Weekly Intelligencer, August 18, 1777; August 25, 1777; September 1, 1777; September 8, 1777.

      TEN DOLLARS Reward.
      June 10th, 1777.
DEserted from my company in Col. Chandler's regiment, an inlisted soldier, named Chapman Judson, born in Woodbury, about 27 years of age, about 5 feet 9 inches high, dark complexion, blue eyes, and black hair, and a scar on one of his cheeks. Whoever will take up said

deserter, and return him to me, or to any other officers in the regiment, shall receive the above reward, and all necessary charges
        paid by   *Nath. Stoddard*, Capt.
The Connecticut Journal, August 20, 1777; September 2, 1777.

DESERTED from Capt. Thomas Arnold's Company, on his March from Coventry to Peck's-Kill, one Moses Smith, seventeen Years old, 5 Feet 11 inches high, blue Eyes, brown Hair, light Complexion, a Tanner by Trade, born in Scituate, in the State of Rhode Island. Whoever takes up said Deserter and conveys him to Col. Christopher Green's Regiment in Coventry, in the State of Rhode Island, or to Pecks Kill, shall have ten Dollars Reward, and all necessary Charges
        paid by   Thomas Arnold Capt.
The Connecticut Gazette; And the Universal Intelligencer, August 22, 1777; August 29, 1777; September 5, 1777.

DESERTED some time past from Capt. Abijah Savage's company, Col. Henry Sherburne's regiment, one Samuel Mozner, a Soldier 22 years old, 5 feet 10 inches high, well made, light complection, light coloured hair and eyes, said Mozner formerly lived in Frederickburgh, in the State of New-York. A reward of ten Dollars is offered to any person, who shall secure said deserter in any goal, or return him to Peek's-Kill, and all necessary charges paid by
        ABIJAH SAVAGE, Capt.
                                      AUGUST 1, 1777.
The Connecticut Gazette; And the Universal Intelligencer, August 22, 1777; August 29, 1777; September 5, 1777.

                                  New London, Aug. 5, 1777.
DESERTED from Capt. James Smith's company in Col. Ely's regiment, Isaac Fanes, belonging to Voluntown, a pretty well set fellow, about 23 years old, dark complection, dark grey eyes, black hair; had on a dark brown coat:—Whoever will take up said Deserter and return him to his regiment in New London, or secure him in any goal in this State, so that he may be had, shall receive Five Dollars reward and all necessary charges,
        paid by   Joshua Bottum, Lieut,
The Connecticut Gazette; And The Universal Intelligencer, August 22, 1777.

DESERTED the 27th of June from Capt. John Ellis's Company, Col. Sherburne's Regiment, now stationed at Fort Montgomery, the following soldiers, viz. Joseph Culver, Sergeant, 22 Years of Age, 5

Feet 7 Inches high, round Face, dark short Hair, black Eyes, a sprightly active Man; Nathan Stoddard, Corporal, 23 Years of Age, 5 Feet 8 Inches high, well Built, square Face, dark Complexion, black Eyes, dark short Hair; Elisha Fanning, Corporal, 21 Years of Age, 5 Feet 7 Inches high, slim Built, light Complexion, short light Hair, each belonging to Groton, in the State of Connecticut. A Reward of 5 Dollars and Charges paid is offered for each of the above Soldiers, except Culver, for whom a Reward of 15 Dollars is offered, as he has been guilty of the vilest Ingratitude to his Officers, exclusive of Desertion. Whoever will take up said Deserters and return them to the Regiment, or confine them in any Goal in the United States, shall receive the above Reward.
    Per JOHN ELLIS, Capt.
The Connecticut Gazette; And The Universal Intelligencer, August 22, 1777; August 29, 1777.

COMMITTED to *Spotsylvania* jail, on the 9th of this instant (*August*) as a deserter, *John Malady* (or *Malony)* who says he was enlisted by lieut. *Catlett.*
The Virginia Gazette, Purdie, August 22, 1777; September 12, 1777.

DESERTED from the *French* Company in *Williamsburg,* ANDREW DANIEL, about 20 Years old, 5 Feet 2 Inches high, short reddish Hair, speaks a little broken *English,* went off without Regimentals, had a long smooth Vissage. Whoever apprehends said Deserter shall have TEN DOLLARS Reward, paid by the commanding Officer, of said Company at *Williamsburg.*
    LAGIRORUETE.
The Virginia Gazette, Dixon and Hunter, August 22, 1777; August 29, 1777.

EDWARD VALENTINE, serjeant in capt. *Pierce's* company of artillery, is hereby ordered to repair to his company at *Portsmouth* immediately.
  By order of col. *Harrison,*
    CHRISTIAN HOLMER, major in the said battalion.
The Virginia Gazette, Purdie, August 22, 1777.

THE following Persons belonging to Capt. Amasa Soper's Company, in Col. Marshal's Regiment, viz. Andrew Garret, of Sandwich; Fortune Cunkery, of Eastown, a Negro man; are hereby ordered to

join Capt. Marshall, of said Regiment, at Boston, by the 15th. of September, in order to join their own Company, otherwise they will be deemed Deserters.
            AMASA SOPER. Capt.
The Boston-Gazette, and Country Journal, August 25, 1777; September 1, 1777; September 15, 1777.

DEserted from my Company in Colonel Henry Jackson's Regiment, a Frenchman by the Name of Simon Duzier. He is 5 feet 8 inches high, brown complexion, black Eyes, and dark Hair, is pitted with the Small-Pox, and wears a blue Coat, with red Facings. Any Person that will bring him to our Rendezvous, at Mr. Loring's, in King-Street, shall receive TWENTY DOLLAS Reward.
            N. JARVIS, Captain.
The Boston-Gazette, and Country Journal, August 25, 1777; September 1, 1777; September 15, 1777.

Freehold, Monmouth County,
New-Jersey, Aug. 21.
            TEN DOLLARS REWARD.
DESERTED from Capt. John Burrowes's company, in Col. David Forman's regiment of Continental troops, on the 6th of July last, a certain GEORGE SHADE, about twenty-four years of age, five feet eight inches high; has light coloured hair and blue eyes, one of his legs thicker than the other occasioned by its being broke: It is supposed he is on board one of the vessels of war on Delaware river. Whoever will apprehend the said deserter and secure him, so that he may be had again, shall receive the above Reward and all reasonable charges.
            JOHN BURROWES, Captain.
Dunlap's Pennsylvania Packet or, the General Advertiser, August 26th, 1777.

SARATOGA, June 19, 1777.
ARTIFICERS deserted on the retreat from Ticonderoga, under the command of Col. JEDUTHAN BALDWIN, Esq: Chief Engineer of the Northern Department, in the service of the United States of America; the following persons, viz.

Capt. *Thayer's* Company Of Carpenters.	Places of Abode.
William Walker,	Boston, Massachusetts.
Benjamin Ingersoll,	do. do.
William Blaney,	Roxbury, Massachusetts.
Mathew Co[c]ks,	Cambridge do.

David Turner,	Scituate,	do.
Benjamin Vassel,	do.	do.
Elisha Holbrook,	Weymouth,	do.
Athanasias Lewis,	Hingham,	do.
Ebenezer Lewis,	do.	do.
Joshua Dunbar,	do.	do.
John Fowles, jun.	Woburn,	do.
John Fowles,	do.	do.
John Muchmore,	Sawko,	do.
William Fellows,	do.	do.
Edward Wheelar,	Jericho,	do.
Solomon Wright,	Williamstown,	do.
Stoddard Cady,	Brimfield,	do.
Moses Little,	Hampstead, N. Hampshire.	
Levi Webster,	do.	do.
Joseph Dowe,	do.	do.
John Keyes,	Wilton,	do.
Ezra Johnson,	do.	do.
Daniel Willson, carried away a public hand-saw,	Keen,	do.
Abel Brown,	Hollis,	do.
Eleazer Fisher, carried away a public hand-saw,	Woodstock, Connecticut.	
Jarvis Sammis,	Long-Island, New York.	
John Arnold, deserted before the retreat.	Boston, Massachusetts.	

JEDEDIAH THAYER, Captain.

Capt. *Baton's* Company, of Blacksmiths.	Places of Abode.
Moses Kinniston,	Amsbury, Massachuettts,
Solomon Lowel,	R[ ]w[ ]y do.

EZRA EATON, Captain.

It is requested that the committees and selectmen, would take up the above named persons, and send them to their duty in the Northern Army, in which service they were inlisted, and passed muster, to serve until the first day of January next, 1778.

The Continental Journal, And Weekly Advertiser, August 28, 1777.

THIRTY DOLLARS REWARD.

DESERTED from lieut. Samuel M'Pherson, on his way to camp, on the 23d day of August, a certain THOMAS LONG, belonging to col. John H. Stone's regiment of foot: The said Long is about twenty-two

years of age, about six feet one or two inches high, of a swarthy complexion, long black hair; had on, when he went away, a country cotton coat, white jacket, country cotton breeches, thread stockings, and country made shoes. Whoever will apprehend the said Long, and deliver him to Mr. James Fernandes, in Charles county, shall receive the above reward, and reasonable charges.
The Maryland Gazette, August 28, 1777.

DESERTED the 16th instant (*August*) from my quota of state troops, *Francis Depak,* a *Frenchman,* 5 feet 3 or 4 inches high, who had on a blue lapelled coat with a silver shoulder knot, a check shirt, and *Russia* drill breeches. It is probable he may be gone towards *Petersburg,* as he came from that place. Whoever delivers the said deserter to the commanding officer in *Williamsburg* shall have ten dollars reward.
     EDWARD DIGGES, lieut.
The Virginia Gazette, Purdie, August 29, 1777; September 5, 1777.

     Vanshaick's Island, August 25, 1777.
DEserted the service of the United States, from the regiment commanded by Col. Thomas Marshall, and Capt. Josiah Smith's company, two inlisted soldiers, who have each lately served as serjeant-majors, viz. *Abiel Brintnall,* born in Marshfield, in the county of Bristol, and State of Massachusetts, 23 years old, 5 feet 9 inches high, ruddy complexion, dark hair, grey eyes; said Brintnall has formerly been detected in counterfeiting Massachusetts bills, and is very handy with his pen. *Seth Stebbins,* born in Wilbraham, 22 years old, 5 feet 8 inches high, has lately had the small-pox, and is much marked. Any person who is friend enough to his country, and honest enough to detect and secure such robbers of the public, so that they may be returned to their regiment, shall receive *Five Dollars* Reward, and all necessary charges
   paid by JOSIAH SMITH, Capt.
The Boston-Gazette, and Country Journal, September 1, 1777; September 8, 1777; September 15, 1777.

STOLEN on Saturday the 9th instant, out of the house of the subscriber in Reading, one pale blue worsted coat and vest, with pale blue worsted lining in the fore parts, the backs lined with striped flannel, with horn buttons on the coat, painted blue, the vest had mohair buttons on it, one pair mixt blue and white homespun breeches, with yellow flour'd buttons on them, one raizor, one hone,

and one pair cissors. One James Hamilton, a soldier who deserted the night before the things were stolen, from Danbury, is suspected to have stolen the above things. Said Hamilton is about 5 feet high, about 34 years old, grey headed. Whoever takes up said thief, with the stolen goods, shall receive two dollars reward, and all reasonable charges
from   ISAAC HAMBLETON.

Reading, August 10 1777.
The Connecticut Journal, September 2, 1777; September 9, 1777.

TWENTY DOLLARS REWARD.

D*ESERTED from the Brigantine* Resistance, Samuel Chew, *Commander,* Samuel Culver. *He is a lusty well set, of a down, or Indianish look, by Trade a Mason, and is supposed to be lurking about Groton. Whoever will take up the said Deserter, and send him on Board the above named Brig, or secure him in Goal, that I may have him again, or send him on Board any of the United States Ships, so that he may serve the Time he Inlisted for, shall be intitled to the above Reward, and all necessary Charges*
paid by   SAMUEL CHEW.

Brig Resistance, New-London, *August* 24, 1777.
The Connecticut Gazette; And The Universal Intelligencer, September 5, 1777; September 12, 1777.

Twenty DOLLARS Reward

FOR apprehending of *Richard Bishop,* a deserter from my quota of state troops; he is about 5 feet 9 inches high, rather slim, has dark hair, and had on a blue coat turned up with red. He is now lurking about in *Charles City* county, where he has a family, and at one *Perkins Thomson*'s. I will give the above reward if the said deserter is delivered to the commanding officer in *Williamsburg.*
JOHN DUDLEY, lieutenant.

The Virginia Gazette, Purdie, September 5, 1777; September 12, 1777; September 19, 1777.

Twenty dollars reward.

I SOME time ago enlisted *Pater Pritchett* into the 14th regiment who has since secreted himself, and will not join my company; he is about 24 years of age, 5 feet 9 or 10 inches high, very well made, has dark hair, and is supposed to be lurking about the upper end of *Dinwiddie* county. Whoever will apprehend him, and secure him so that he is made to join the regiment, shall be entitled to the above reward.
PETER JONES.

155

The Virginia Gazette, Purdie, September 5, 1777; September 12, 1777.

DESERTED from the 2d *Virginia* Regiment in *New Jersey,* the following Soldiers, *viz. Francis Dryskil,* an *Irishman* 35 Years of age, 5 Feet 10 Inches high, short light Hair, well made, chews Tobacco, and very fond of Liquor; took off with him his regimental blue Coat, with white Binding.— *Strawther,* 5 Feet 7 1/2 Inches high, red Hair, and much freckled; he lived some where about *Williamsburg,* served in Capt. *Nicholas'*s Company the Campaign at *Norfolk,* was discharged in *August* 1776, and enlisted into the same Company again. *Benjamin Jones,* 5 Feet 10 Inches high, dark Complexion, well set, black Beard, and short Hair; it is imagined; that he is lurking about *Baltimore,* as his Parents live nigh that Town. *Joseph Bryant,* 5 Feet 9 Inches high, fond of Liquor, and has a remarkable Scar on one of his Lips; he was enlisted in *King George* County, *Virginia,* and it is imagined he may be taken there, as his Presents live in the said County. *William Denny,* an *Irishman,* about 30 Years of Age, 5 Feet 7 Inches high, round shouldered, light Hair, much pitted with the Smallpox, and fond of Liquor, *John Saunders,* an *Irishman,* about 18 Years of Age, 5 Feet 6 Inches high, short light Hair, and smooth faced. *John Stokes,* a *Virginian,* about 30 Years of Age, short dark Hair, round Face, and fond of Liquor. *Thomas Conneran,* an *Irishman,* 20 Years of Age, 5 Feet 5 Inches high, short black Hair. *Richard Lewis,* an *Englishman,* 35 Years of Age, 5 Feet 6 Inches high, short dark Hair, much marked with the Smallpox; he formerly lived in *Loudoun* County, *Virginia, Thomas Trap,* Serjeant, 30 Years of Age, 6 Feet high, dark Hair slim made, pitted with the Smallpox, talks in a whining Manner; his Wife, who was heavy with Child, went off with him, *Philip Ragan,* Corporal, 22 Years of Age, 5 Feet 7 Inches high, brown Hair, speaks fierce, of a dark Complexion. *Brice Ragan,* a Private, Brother to *Philip,* near his Size, 20 Years of Age, fair Complexion, of an agreeable Look. *Henry Mace,* a Private, 5 Feet 8 Inches high, well set, fair faced, had a blue hunting Shirt when he went off; the Serjeant, Corporal, and *Philip Ragan,* carried of their Regimentals of Blue with white Worsted Binding; they, with *Mace,* were enlisted into Captain *Alexander* 's Company, and may be taken in *Frederick* County, *Virginia.* EIGHT DOLLARS Reward for each Man, to be paid by
ALEXANDER SPOTSWOOD. Col. 2d *Virg.* Reg.

The Virginia Gazette, Dixon and Hunter, September 5, 1777; September 12, 1777; October 10, 1777.

DESERTED from the *Hero* galley, some time in *August,* William Miller, a *Scotchman,* formerly belonging to capt. *Stevenson*'s company of the 8th regiment, enlisted at *Fort Pitt.* He is about 5 feet 9 inches high, has a very innocent look, and had on when he deserted a *Scotch* bonnet. Whoever delivers him to me shall have 20 dollars reward.
      PHILIP CHAMBERLAIN, capt.
The Virginia Gazette, Purdie, September 5, 1777; September 19, 1777; September 26, 1777.

STOLEN on Saturday 9th instant, out of the house of the subscriber in Reading, one pale blue worsted coat and vest, with pale blue worsted lining in the fore parts, the backs lined with striped flannel, with horn buttons on the coat, painted blue, the vest had mohair buttons on it, one pair mixt blue and white homespun breeches, with yellow flour'd buttons on them, one raizor, one hone, and one pair cissors. One James Hamlinton, a soldier who deserted the night before the things were stolen, from Danbury, is suspected to have stolen the above things. Said Hamlinton is about 5 feet high, about 34 years old, grey headed. Whoever takes up said thief, with the stolen goods, shall receive two dollars reward, and all reasonable charges
    from ISAAC HAMBLETON.
            Reading, August 10, 1777.
The Connecticut Journal, September 10, 1777; September 17, 1777.

DESERTED from my company in the 2d *Virginia* regiment, *James Brown,* about 22 years old, of a fair complexion, and about 5 feet 10 inches high. I expect he is in *North Carolina.* Whoever delivers the said deserter to a continental officer shall have 20 dollars reward.
      FRANCIS TAYLOR, capt.
The Virginia Gazette, Purdie, September 12, 1777; September 19, 1777.

        ESSEX County, *August* 6, 1777.
THIS is to inform Capt. *Samuel Hawes,* of the 2d *Virginia* Regiment, that some Time in *September* last I was indulged with a Furlough from Brigadier General *Lewis,* for the Recovery of my Health, and have ever since been afflicted with a tedious Spell of Sickness, which has taken away the Use of my Limbs, so that I have never been able to

join my Company. And whereas I understand that some treacherous Persons have been very busy in advising Capt. *Hawes* to advertise me as a Deserter, which I hope will not be the Case, as he known me to be true and faithful Soldier, and was always ready and willing to serve my Country at all Times. During my Sickness I suffered greatly for the Want of Money to subsist on; and, being so circumstanced, I made several Applications to my Officers for Money to support me in my Sickness, but never was supplied with any.
     REUBEN GIBSON.
The Virginia Gazette, Dixon and Hunter, September 12, 1777; September 19, 1777.

DESERTED from the state troops at *Portsmouth, Thomas Short,* who is a native of *Virginia,* and has a family in *Chesterfield* county, where he is supposed to be lurking. The said *Short* is about 5 feet 8 or 9 inches high, well made, dark complexion and dark hair, is fond of drink, and very talkative when intoxicated. I will give ten dollars reward on his being delivered to the commanding officer at *Portsmouth* or *Williamsburg.*
     FRANCIS SMITH, capt.
The Virginia Gazette, Purdie, September 12, 1777; September 19, 1777; September 26, 1777.

     140 *DOLLARS Reward,.*
DESERTED from col. *William Grayson*'s regiment, the following soldiers, *viz. John Russell,* 21 years of age, 5 feet 6 inches high, light hair, hazel eyes, thin visage, and fair complexion. *George Russell,* 19 years of age, 5 feet 8 or 9 inches high, sandy hair, blue eyes, fair complexion, and slow of speech. *William Harness,* 20 years of age, 5 feet 10 inches high, light hair, blue eyes, and very fond of drink. Upon his enlistment, he obtained a furlough for 20 days; having failed to meet agreeable thereto, I am informed he has made for some of the northern states. *Joseph Younger,* about 24 years of age, 5 feet 9 inches high, yellow curled hair, gray eyes, and thin visage. *Abraham Childress,* 30 years of age, 6 feet high, short black hair, gray eyes, and fair complexion. *James Kyle,* 21 years of age, 5 feet 8 inches high, black curled hair, remarkable large nose, swarthy complexion, and by trade a hatter. The four first mentioned enlisted with me in *Pittsylvania* county, the next two in *Halifax,* and the last in *Charlotte.* I will give the above reward for the whole, or 20 dollars for each, on their being delivered to any continental officer on their march to head quarters, or to myself at *Peytonsburgh* in *Pittsylvania* county.

RO. RAKESTRAW, 1st lieut.

N. B. The three first mentioned have since enlisted with capt. *John Dooly,* and are gone with him to *Georgia,.*

The Virginia Gazette, Purdie, September 12, 1777. See *The Virginia Gazette,* Purdie, October 10, 1777.

DESERTED from on board the brig *Northampton,* at *Frazer's* Ferry, on *Mattapony,* the 4th instant, *John Anthoney,* a stout well made fellow, *Portuguese* born, and as dark as a mulatto; he is rather knock-kneel, and had on a *London* brown coat faced with red. Also *Osmond Sandal, Englishman,* very much pock marked, a stout well made fellow with short light hair; also *Thomas Brown,* an *Englishman,* very round shouldered with a large *Roman* nose, and very gray eyes. Also *Thomas Jeffery,* a lad of about 19, thin visage, a smooth face, and short light hair. *Thomas Brown* has a smooth face and short black hair. Whoever will apprehend the said deserters, and deliver them to me on board the said brig, shall receive ten pounds reward for each of them.
FRANCIS BRIGHT

The Virginia Gazette, Purdie, September 12, 1777.

PETER MAY, the 3d, being drafted by the commissioned officers of the militia in Stoneham, and warned to march under Capt. Abraham Foster, of Reading, in Col. Ballard's regiment, but has deserted. Said Peter is about 5 feet 6 inches high, something dark complexioned, with black curled hair. Any person that will bring him to Capt. Foster, in the northern army, or to the subscriber in Stoneham, shall receive Six Dollars, and all necessary charges,
paid by me, ABRAHAM GOULD, Captain.

The Boston-Gazette, and Country Journal, September 15, 1777; September 22, 1777; September 29, 1777.

DESERTED from the ship Union, and said to be about Santee, a French carpenter, named Jean Rotier, about 5 feet 7 inches high, very brown complexion, long roman nose, and wears his hair, which is brown. Whoever apprehends and delivers him on board the said ship, or gives such information that he may be taken, shall a reward of Fifty Pounds currency, from   E. ROCHE.

The Gazette Of The State Of South-Carolina, September 15, 1777; September 30, 1777.

STOL'N from the subscriber's waggon, on the road leading from Charlestown westward, near sergeant Campbell's place, about the 1st of March last. A sorrel roan HORSE, 8 years old near 14 hands and an

half high, a blaze in his face, branded BE in one on the near shoulder and buttock, and 75 on the off buttock and shoulder, hath remarkable large quarters, round body, trots heavy, and carries low: supposed to be taken by one Sarhuel More, a deserter from Col. Thomson's regiment, and carried towards Georgia. Whoever contrives the said horse to his owner, on the head of Pacolet river, near the North Carolina line, shall have Fifty Pounds currency reward, or Twenty-Five Pounds if delivered to Capt. John Bowie at Fort Charlotte.
   BAYLIS EARLE.
The Gazette Of The State Of South-Carolina, September 15, 1777;

DESERTED the Service of the United States of America from Col. James Wesson's Regiment, WILLIAM BATMAN, an old Countryman, 5 Feet 4 Inches high, dark Hair. Any Person who will take up said Deserter, so that he may be returned to his Regiment, shall have TWENTY DOLLARS Reward. and necessary Charges,
   paid By SAM. CARR, Capt.
The Independent Chronicle and the Universal Advertiser, September 18, 1777; September 25, 1777.

DEserted from Capt. Keys's company, Col. John Ely's regiment, one Aholiab Branch, who lately lived in Killingly, in the State of Connecticut; is about 21 years old, 5 feet 7 inches high. Whoever will take up said Branch, and return him to the subscriber, or confine him in any goal in the United States, so that he may be brought to Justice, shall have eight Dollars reward, and necessary charges,
   paid by ASA LYON, Lieut.
 N. B. Said Branch received half his bounty and has never joined the regiment, and is supposed to have inlisted at Providence, under
   Lieut. Zadock Williams.
         N. London, Sept 16, 1777.
The Connecticut Gazette; And The Universal Intelligencer, September 19, 1777; October 3, 1777.

   FAIRFAX *country*, Virginia, *Aug*. 27, 1777.
DESERTED from capt. *Thomas Weft's* company of the 10th *Virginia* regiment, commanded by col. *Edward Stevens,* the following deserters, *viz. Jeremiah Brown,* of *Fairfax* country, aged 28 years, 5 feet 11 inches high, slender made, dark complexion and eyes, by trade a carpenter. *Hezekiah Matteny,* aged 22 years, 5 feet 10 inches high, slender made, light hair, a shoemaker by trade. *James Maddox,* aged 27 years, 5 feet 8 inches high, light complexion, close made, a planter. *Henry Jones,* aged 17 years, 5 feet 5 inches high, slender

made, light complexion, a planter. *Charles Potter,* aged 18 years, 5feet 4 inches high, light complexion, close made, a planter. *Davis Ratcliff,* aged 20 years. 5 feet 7 inches high, close made dark complexion, a planter. *Edward Meeks,* aged 30 years, 5 feet 6 inches high, close made, light complexion, a planter. *John Hayly,* aged 23 years, 5 feet 8 inches high, close made, dark complexion, a tailor *John Smith,* an *Englishman,* aged 30 years, 5 feet 6 inches high, close made, dark complexion, a wheel-wright. *John Williamson,* aged 19 years, 5 feet 9 inches high, close made, dark complexion, a planter. *William Roberts,* an *Irishman,* aged 30 years, 5 feet 7 inches high, light complexion, a planter. *William Anderson,* an *Englishman,* aged 28 years, 5 feet 6 inches high, close made, dark complexion, a planter. *George Johnson,* an *Englishman,* aged 25 years, 5 feet 5 inches high, slender made, dark complexion, a blacksmith. *Joseph Stouton,* of *Loudoun* county, aged 28 years, 5 feet 10 inches high, slender made, dark complexion, a planter. *James Rush,* aged 21 years, 5 feet 6 inches high, slender made, light complexion, a planter. *Richard Crop,* of *Prince William* county, aged 18 years, 5 feet 7 inches high, close made, dark complexion. One hundred and sixty dollars reward will be given for the above deserters, or ten dollars for each, if delivered to the commanding officer of the regiment, or to me in *Fairfax* county.

    CHARLES LEWIS BROADWATER, lieut.
 The Virginia Gazette, Purdie, September 19, 1777; September 26, 1777; October 3, 1777; October 10, 1777.

   MATTHEW JACKSON, absenting himself from the second division of *Mecklenburg* militia, I do hereby offer a reward of ten dollars to any person who may deliver the said *Jackson* to the commanding officer at *Portsmouth* before my division be released from the service.
    JOHN BURTON.
 The Virginia Gazette, Purdie, September 19, 1777.

JOHN LUCAS, *William Askins,* and *Richard Brinn,* of *Westmoreland,* and *Smith Stevens* of *Northumberland,* draughts for the fifteenth *Virginia* regiment, having failed to attend, or submit themselves (being previously summoned) are hereby advertised as deserters, and a reward of SIX POUNDS will be paid for each, on their being delivered to me, or to any other continental officer.
    GEORGE LEE TURBERVILLE, Capt.
    fifteenth Virginia battalion.

The Virginia Gazette, Purdie, September 19, 1777; September 26, 1777; October, 10, 1777.

TWENTY DOLLARS REWARD

FOR apprehending *Edward Sage* and *John Freeland,* two Deserters from my Company, in Colonel *Harrison's* Regiment of Artillery. *Sage* is a likely will made Man, about 5 Feet 10 Inches high, has lost one of his under Eyelids, and has a Scar on the same Side of his Nose. *Freeland,* a likely Man, near the same Size as *Sage,* much marked with the Smallpox. They have both been bred to the Sea. I will give the above Reward to any Person that will deliver them at *York* or *Portsmouth,* or secure them in any Gaol in this State.
WILLIAM MURRAY, Captain.
The Virginia Gazette, September 19, 1777; September 26, 1777.

DESERTED *from Col.* Henry Jackson's *Regiment the following soldiers—John Warren, 40 years old, light complexion, grey eyes, dark hair, 5 feet 4 and 1-2 inches high, by trade a shoemaker, born in Bristol, old England.*

John Smith, 27 years old, light complexion, grey eyes, dark short hair, 5 feet 9 inches high, born in old England, brought up to the sea.

John Goodale, 21 years old, light complexion, grey eyes, dark short hair, pitted with the small pox, 5 feet 8 & 1-2 inches high, born in old England.

James Hisket, 29 years old, light complexion, grey eyes, dark hair, 5 feet 7 & 1-2 inches high, born in old England, has lived 3 years in Smithfield.

Daniel Spinney, 20 years old, 5 feet 7 inches high, dark complexion, grey eyes, brown hair, born in Portsmouth, New-England, trade a brick- maker.

James Bridges, 25 years old, 5 feet 8 inches high, light complexion, deep grey eyes, brown hair, born in Ireland, by trade a woolcomber.

William Russel, 28 years old, 5 feet 9 inches high, light complexion, blue eyes, dark hair, well made, born in Londonderry, in the State of New-Hampshire.

John Wilson, 27 years old, 5 feet 8 inches high, dark complexion, grey eyes, short light hair, well made, born in Scotland, a Seaman.

Alexander Smart, about 22 years old, 5 feet 7 inches high, light complexion, blue eyes, light short hair, well made, pockt mark'd, born in Scotland.

John Pettye, 18 *years old*, 6 *feet high, light complexion, blue eyes, brown hair, belongs to Dartmouth, in this State, by trade a shoemaker.*

John Smith, 20 *years old*, 5 *feet* 2 & 1-2 *inches high, grey eyes, light colour'd hair, pitted with the small-pox, has a projection under the shoulders, born in Sheepscut, Massachusetts Bay, labourer.*

John Crane, 46 *years* & 5 *months old*, 5 *feet* 5 *inches high, fresh complexion, dark eyes, black hair, has a scar on his forehead, pitted with the small pox, born in Philadelphia.*

George White, 28 *years old*, 5 *feet* 7 & 3-4 *inches high, light complexion, dark blue eyes, short dark hair, scar over both eyes, born in Glocester, Old England, Seaman.*

Alexander Collier, 29 *years old*, 5 *feet* 6 *inches high, dark complexion, blue eyes, dark short hair, by trade a cabinet maker.*

The friends to the public are strenuously urged to use their influence to apprehend and send said Deserters to the regiment on Dorchester *heights, and are offered a reward of* TWENTY DOLLARS *each, for so signal a service to the public.* JAMES CAREW, *Adjutant.*

N. B. Captains of Privateers and Merchantmen are charged at their peril not to conceal or carry off any of the above Deserters.

The Boston-Gazette, And Country Journal, September 22, 1777; September 29, 1777; October 6, 1777.

DESERTED from Col. Wylly's regiment, stationed at this post, on the 2d instant, William Matthews, a soldier, 27 years old, 5 feet 11 inches high, light eyes, dark hair and complexion; wore away a light brown uniform coat, lappel'd with dark red, a white hat, with other clothing mostly old.

Whoever will apprehend said soldier and return him to the regiment shall have eight dollars reward and all charges.

HENRY CHAMPION, Capt.

Camp at Peeks-Kill, Sept 4, 1777.

The Connecticut Courant, and Hartford Weekly Intelligencer, September 22, 1777; September 29, 1777.

DESERTED from Col. John Durkee's Regiment, one JOHN WHEATON, a transient Person, aged 36 Years, dark Complexion, dark blue Eyes, dark brown Hair, 5 Feet 9 Inches high—Whoever will take up said Deserter, and return him to his Regiment, or secure him in any Goal, so that he may be brought to Justice, shall have Five Dollars Reward, paid by me

EBEN. LESTER, Ensign.

Norwich, Sept. 22, 1777.

The Norwich Packet and the Connecticut, Massachusetts, New-Hampshire, and Rhode-Island Weekly Advertiser, From September 15, to September 22, 1777; From September 22, to September 29, 1777; From October 13, to October 20, 1777.

WHEREAS Mr. Lee Peck was advertised by me as deserting the company under my command, on the 24th of April last, which company was then stationed at Fort Trumbull, in New-London.—These may certify that said advertisement was occasioned by wrong information, and that his outstaying the time of his permit, was through unavoidable necessity, occasioned by sickness. Wherefore his character ought to be exculpated from any ill impressions they may be made in the minds of any one from the said advertisement. JABEZ BEEBE, Captain.

New-London, September 19, 1777.

The Connecticut Gazette; And The Universal Intelligencer, September 26, 1777; October 3, 1777.

SHOULD George Batson *(a soldier who enlisted in capt.* Massie's *company of regulars in the sixth* Virginia *regiment) fail to join the continental troops in* Williamsburg *on* Monday *next, he may depend on being treated as a* deserter; *and I here offer a reward of TEN DOLLARS to any person who will deliver him to the commanding officer in* Williamsburg.

By order of capt. Massie.

JAMES TAYLOR, *serjeant in*

capt. Massie's *company sixth* Virg. *reg.*

The Virginia Gazette, Purdie, September 26, 1777. See *The Virginia Gazette*, Purdie, November 21, 1777.

WILLIAMSBURG, College Camp, *Sept.* 18, 1777.
REUBEN REASON, deserter from my company of state troops, about five feet six inches high, of a ruddy complexion, with short black hair, fluent of speech, and remarkably fond of his horsemanship and dress, quitted this camp about a fortnight ago, and is supposed to have enlisted into a light horse company of this state. Whoever delivers him to the commanding officer here shall be rewarded agreeable to law.

JOHN POPE, Captain.

☞ All those of the quotas of Captain *Pope,* Lieutenants *Fields, Minor,* and *Clayton,* who have received furloughs, are hereby ordered to repair, by the expiration of them, to this place.

JOHN POPE. Captain.
The Virginia Gazette, Purdie, September 26, 1777; October 10, 1777; October 17, 1777.

DESERTED from Capt. Walcott's Company, in Col. Marshall's Regiment, James Lewis, 5 Feet 8 Inches high, 25 years old, short black Hair, light Complexion, blue Eyes, pitted with the Small-Pox, had on a blue Coat with red Facings, white Waistcoat and Breeches, and black Stockings. Whoever will take up said Deserter, and commit him in any Goal, or return him to his said Regiment, shall have Eight Dollars Reward, paid by
J. SAVAGE, Lieut.
The Boston-Gazette, and Country Journal, September 29, 1777; October 6, 1777; October 13, 1777.

DESERTED from my Company in Col. Wyllys's regiment, lying near head-quarters at Peeks-Kill, one James Jeffers, is about five feet and nine inches high, 28 years old, dark complexion, grey eyes and dark short hair, a native of Ireland, had on or carried with him a light brown regimental coat much soiled, waistcoat of ditto, brown linnen breeches. Whoever will take up and confines said deserter, or returns him to the regiment shall have five dollars reward and necessary charges paid, by
JOHN BERNARD, Capt.
N. B. He has formerly been known and passed by the name of James Smith.

Peeks-Kill, August 27, 1777.
The Connecticut Courant, and Hartford Weekly Intelligencer, September 29, 1777; October 7, 1777.

DESERTED from Peeks Kill the 4th of September from Capt. John Bernard's company Col. Wyllys's regiment, one John Ledgard, a French neutral, but talks good English, a thick set fellow, dark Hair, light complexion, 32 years of age, 5 feet 9 inches high: he wore away a dark brown coat. Whoever will return said deserter to the regiment, or confine him in any of the continental goals, shall have eight dollars reward and all necessary charges
paid by, AARON BUTLER Ens.
The Connecticut Courant, and Hartford Weekly Intelligencer, September 29, 1777; October 7, 1777; October 21, 1777.

DESERTED from Capt. Stoddard's company, Col. Vose's regiment, one Amos Cock, 28 years of age, five feet seven inches high, of a dark

complexion, very much pitted with the small pox, talks very quick, very red eyes, occasioned by hard drinking. Also, John Roberts, 5 feet 10 inches high, 30 years of age, red complexion, long hair with a large hair mole on his left cheek, an Irishman, talks very thick. Also, David Jones, this country born, 5 feet 6 inches high, of a light complexion, a lean slim fellow, about 19 years of age. Whoever will take said Deserters and send them to their regiment in the northern army above Albany, or confine them in any goals in the States and give information do that they may be had, shall have six dollars reward for each, and all necessary charges paid,
    by ABIATHAR ROBINSON. Lieut.
The Connecticut Courant, and Hartford Weekly Intelligencer, September 29, 1777; October 7, 1777.

WHEREAS Ebenezer Williams, about 24 years of age, about 5 feet 7 inches high, who said he belonged to Lynn, wore cloth colour'd cloaths, red hair pitted with the small-pox, has a remarkable mark which covered the left side of his face, and very much disfigur'd him, belonging to Col. James Wesson's regiment, Capt. Blanch[er]'s company, some time since obtained a furlow from Lieut. Abner Graves, and the period of his joining his corps long since has expired. This is to notify said Williams, that unless he immediately joins his company he will be deemed and treated as a deserter. Also deserted from Petersham, one John Casey, an old countryman, belonging to said company, supposed to be 34 years of age, about 5 feet 4 inches high, had black hair, wore snuff coloured cloths. Whoever will take up said deserter and return him to his regiment shall have three dollars reward, and all necessary charges
    paid, by ABNER GRAVES, Lieut.
                Athel, August 4, 1777.
The Connecticut Courant, and Hartford Weekly Intelligencer, September 29, 1777; October 7, 1777; October 21, 1777.

ON the night after the 15th of September, made his escape from Mr. Abijah Roe's of Simsbury, one Robert Mallen, a prisoner of war, a Highlander of the 71st regiment; had on when he went away a short regimental coat and vest, long tow cloth trowsers, and the Scotch bonnet; is about 19 years old, grey eyes, short well set, short curl'd sandy hair, something freckled, rather slow of speech, and of few words. And on the 21st of September made his escape over the pickets at Hartford goal, one Alexander Adams, a Highlander of the 71st regiment; is a short lad, red hair, had of a brown coat with red cuffs, Scotch bonnet, light gray eyes. Also escaped from Hezekiah Ketchum,

the 26th of September, one John Blake, a prisoner of war, taken at Long-Island; about 26 years old, about 5 feet high, dark complexion, black hair; had on a brown coat, a red jacket, white trowsers, and felt hat. Whoever will take up and secure either of the above runaways in any goal in this or neighbouring states, and inform the subscriber, shall have five dollars reward for each, from
    Ez'l WILLIAMS, Commissary of Prisoners.
        Hartford, September 19, 1777.
The Connecticut Courant, and Hartford Weekly Intelligencer, September 29, 1777; October 7, 1777. See *The Connecticut Courant, And Weekly Intelligencer*, August 11, 1777, for Adams.

DESERTED from East Hartford, one Thomas Welch, about 26 years of age, 5 feet 7 inches high, short black hair, a thick stocky fellow, he had on red soldiers cloaths or nankeen, or rifle frock.—Whoever will take up said deserter and return him to Hartford, or secure him where he may be found, shall have five dollars reward and necessary charges
    paid by SAMUEL WADSWORTH.
The Connecticut Courant, and Hartford Weekly Intelligencer, September 29; 1777; October 7, 1777.

DEserted from Capt. Elisha Lee's Company, in Col. Durkee's Regiment, a transient Person who calls himself David Wilson, a thick set Fellow, about 5 Feet 6 Inches high, light Hair and light Eyes, crooked Nose, a rough looking Fellow and much given to Drink, is a Scotch-man, and of the Appearance of a Sailor, by Trade a Nailor. Whoever will apprehend and secure him ton any Goal, so that he may be had, shall receive five Dollars Reward, and all necessary Charges
    paid by DANIEL WAIT. Lieut.
The Connecticut Gazette; And The Universal Intelligencer, October 3, 1777; October 17, 1777.

DESERTED last *February,* from Captain *Nat. Burwell*'s company of artillery, STEPHEN KELSEY, about five feet eight or ten inches high, of a swarthy complexion, has light hair, a down look when spoke to, an impediment in his speech, and is supposed to be gone to *N. Carolina.* Whoever delivers him to the commanding officer in *Williamsburg* shall have TWENTY DOLLARS reward.
    WILLIAM MEREDITH, Capt. Lieut.
The Virginia Gazette, Purdie, October 3, 1777; October 10, 1777; October 17, 1777.

DESERTED from my company of continental artillery, JOHN NUTTLE, five feet five or six inches high, twenty one or twenty two years of age, has light hair, was bred to the sea, and is supposed to be gone to *Philadelphia.* Whoever delivers him to the commanding officer of the continental troops at *York* or *Portsmouth* shall have TWENTY DOLLARS reward.
      N. BURWELL, captain of artillery.
 The Virginia Gazette, Purdie, October 3, 1777; October 10, 1777; October 17, 1777.

DESERTED from my Quota of State Troops at *Williamsburg,* THOMAS GRUME, who is a Native of *Virginia,* and has a Family in *Orange* County, though I believe he is lurking about *Gloucester,* as chief of his Relations live there, and I understand he went that Way when he went off. The said *Grume* is about 5 Feet 10 or 11 Inches high, well made, of a dark Complexion, and short brown Hair. I will give 20 Dollars Reward on his being delivered to the commanding Officer at *Williamsburg.*
      NATHANIEL WELCH, Lieut.
 The Virginia Gazette, Dixon and Hunter, October 3, 1777.

      WILLIAMSBURG, *Sept.* 18, 1777.
DESERTED from the *Mecklenburg* company of regulars belonging to this state the following soldiers, viz. *James Hudson, Thomas Sutton, Garner Green, Richard Melton, Nehemiah Matthews, Nathan Russel, and Page Pucket,* natives of said county. If they will return in a month from this date, and deliver themselves to the commanding officer in this city, they shall receive their bounty money, and be excused; but should they continue out after that time, a reward of TEN DOLLARS will be given for each of them.—Deserted likewise, *John Thomas,* a blacksmith, who lately worked in *Amelia* county; *William Harris,* who said he came from *Culpeper*; *John Harris,* and *William Harris*; two brothers from *Carolina.* TWENTY DOLLARS will be given for each of them, and it is hoped that all wellwishers to the *American* cause will be active in taking them, as they are vile offenders. *Thomas* has enlisted with two or three officers, and the other three have received very considerable sums of money to take other mens places.
      ISAAC HOLMES, Ensign.
 The Virginia Gazette, Purdie, October 3, 1777; October 24, 1777.

DESERTED from the State Troops at *Williamsburg,* RANDOLPH WAKER, who is Native of *Virginia,* and it is supposed he will go to *Buckingham* County to his Father; he is about 5 Feet 4 Inches high, and light coloured Hair. I will give 10 Dollars Reward on his being delivered to the commanding Officer at *Williamsburg.*
     DAVID BALLEW, Lieut.
 The Virginia Gazette, Dixon and Hunter, October 3, 1777.

ONE hundred and thirty DOLLARS reward for apprehending ESDALE COMES, JOHN LUNSFORD, JAMES LEE, EVAN OWENS, PETER EADES, JAMES MARDERS, CHARLES REEVES, JOHN CHILCOTT, BURDITT MILLS, SIMON PERRY, MICHAEL WELSH, EVAN PAYNE (a mulatto) EPHRAIM OWENS, and JOHN CASH. The said *Cash* removed, some time after the draught, into *Loudon* county, near the *Marsh* there; and it is requested of all officers, civil and military, to make diligent search after him. As the above men were draughted, I cannot give any particular description of their size, dress, or features. They failed meeting after proper notice was given, and therefore I will give the above reward, or TEN DOLLARS for each, if delivered to me at *King George* courthouse.
     JOHN TANKERSLEY, Lieut.

 ☞ WILLIAM CAMPBELL, an *Irishman,* a shoemaker by trade, about 35 years old, 5 feet 7 inches high, of a fair complexion, dark hair, and much pitted with the smallpox, who enlisted last *December* into the regular service, and took the bounty money, I will give TWENTY DOLLARS reward for, if delivered to me, or any continental officer.
 The Virginia Gazette, Purdie, October 3, 1777.

DESERTED from the *Manly* galley, two men, *viz.* JOHN HARFORD, a sailor, who is about thirty years old, five feet eight or nine inches high, has short black hair, a very dark skin, is much addicted to liquor, and very talkative when so; had on when he went away a pair of canvas trousers, and old jacket, and a check shirt. WILLIAM WILKINS, a serjeant of marines, and formerly enlisted by captain *John C. Cocke*; he is about twenty five years old, five feet seven or eight inches high, and had on when he went away an old pair of white *Virginia* cloth breeches and cotton shirt. Whoever delivers the said men on board, or secures them so that I get them, shall have TWENTY DOLLARS reward.
     WILLIAM SAUNDERS, Captain.

The Virginia Gazette, Purdie, October 3, 1777; October 24, 1777.

TEN DOLLARS Reward.

DESERTED from Capt. *John Winslow's* Company of the Artillery, commanded by Maj. *Ebenezer Stevens, James Morrisson,* alias *Donnel Mc Laine,* supposed to be a Highlander last year; about 5 feet 9 inches high, light curl'd hair, stupes a little, and is very slow in speech, is 21 years of age; had on when he went away, a blue coat faced with white, a red waistcoat, a pair leather breeches and white stockings. Any person apprehending said deserter and forwarding him to camp, shall receive Ten Dollars reward, and all necessary charges paid by me,   *John Winslow,* Capt. of Artillery.

Camp near Still-Water, Sept. 22, 1777.

N. B. The above fellow deserted the night before last.

The Boston-Gazette, and Country Journal, October 6, 1777.

ON Saturday last came to the house of Zachariah Mather of Torringford, one Roswel B[l]a[re], said he belonged to Lebanon, but was afterwards found to be a deserter from the Continental army, and was taken into custody in order to be returned to the regiment, but has since made his escape; he is about 5 feet 10 inches high, red hair, had on a waistcoat made of a blanket, and striped woolen vest, one pair of leather breeches, and butternut colour'd stockings, white shirt. He also stole a butternut colour'd great-coat, with some white mixt with it, an outside waistcoat, with pewter buttons, a pair of worsted seam'd stockings, and a pen knife and ink stand. Whoever will take up said villain and secure him so that he may be brought to justice shall have all necessary charges paid, by

ZACHARIAH MATHER.

Torringford, Oct. 6. 1777.

The Connecticut Courant, and Hartford Weekly Intelligencer, October 7, 1777; October 21, 1777; November 11, 1777.

DESERTED from Wethersfield, John Watson, who on the 19th of September inlisted himself a soldier in Col. Samuel B. Webb's regiment, and had a furlough go to Paq[uak]nock in Windsor, and was to return the 22d to Wethersfield; he was about 20 years old, 5 feet 7 inches high, brown hair, bluish eyes, fair complexion, a small powder mark over his left eye, and a little pitted with the small pox. He took away with him a bay trotting mare, her hind feet white, a star in her forehead, and a small slip on her nose. Whoever will take up said deserter and thief and secure him in any of the continental goals, or

return him to me the subscriber in Wethersfield, shall have ten dollars reward and necessary charges paid,
> EDWARD BULKLEY, Capt.
>
> September 25, 1777.
The Connecticut Courant, and Hartford Weekly Intelligencer, October 7, 1777; October 21, 1777; November 11, 1777.

WHEREAS a certain *John Wells* enlisted with me the twenty second of *September,* and has since secreted himself, and has not appeared at the place of rendezvous, I therefore offer a reward of TWENTY DOLLARS to any person that will deliver the said *Wells* to me in *Willliamsburg,* or any continental officer.
> ROBERT THOMPSON, ensign
> in the fourth *Virg.* reg.

The Virginia Gazette, Purdie, October 10, 1777.

> 140 DOLLARS Reward.

DESERTED from Col. *William Grayson's* regiment, the following soldiers, viz. *John Russell,* 21 years of age, 5 feet 6 inches high, light hair, hazel eyes, thin visage, and fair complexion. *George Russell,* 19 years of age, 5 feet 8 or 9 inches high, sandy hair, blue eyes, fair complexion, and slow of speech. *William Harness,* 20 years of age, 5 feet 8 inches high, dark hair, and fair complexion. *Reuben Farrington,* 20 years of age, 5 feet 10 inches high, light hair, blue eyes, and very fond of drink. Upon his enlistment, he obtained a furlough for 20 days; but having failed to meet agreeable thereto, I am informed he has made for some of the northern states. *Joseph Younger,* about 24 years of age, 5 feet 9 inches high, yellow curled hair, gray eyes, and thin visage. *Abraham Childress,* 30 years of age, 6 feet high, short black hair, gray eyes, and a fair complexion. *James Kyle,* 21 years of age, 5 feet 8 inches high, black curled hair, remarkable large nose, swarthy complexion, and by trade a hatter. The four first mentioned enlisted with me in *Pittsylvania* county, the next two in *Halifax,* and the last in *Charlotte.* I will give the above reward for the whole, or 20 dollars for each, on their being delivered to any continental officer on their march to head quarters, or to myself in *Peytonsburg,* in *Pittsylvania* county.
> RO. RAKESTRAW, 1st Lieut.

N.B. The three first mentioned have since enlisted with Capt. *John Dooley,* and are gone with him to *Georgia.*

The Virginia Gazette, Purdie, October 10, 1777; October 24, 1777. See *The Virginia Gazette,* Purdie, September 12, 1777.

ONE HUNDRED DOLLARS REWARD.

DESERTED from the 5th *Virginia* regiment, the following soldiers, *viz.* JESSE MEEKS, thick and well made, and 5 feet 8 or 9 inches high, WILLIAM ARCHER, about the same height, with red hair, and much freckled. Whoever delivers the said deserters to the commanding officer at *Williamsburg* shall have to dollars for each.

RICHARD C. ANDERSON

The Virginia Gazette, Purdie, October 10, 1777; October 17, 1777; November 14, 1777.

This Forenoon, (previous to Col. Henry Jackson's Regiment marching to the Southward) Thomas Lake was hung at the Bottom of the Common for Desertion.

The Freeman's Journal, Or New-Hampshire Gazette, October 11, 1777.

TWENTY DOLLARS REWARD.

DESERTED from the ship *Tarter,* lying at *Fraser's* ferry, *Mattapony* river, THOMAS POWELL, about 5 feet 3 inches high, about 25 years old, has a dark complexion nose a remarkable large upper fore tooth, and was seen in *King George* county, where he enlisted with Lieut. *John Tankersley,* by the name of *Thomas Newton.* I expect he will go to George town in *Maryland,* as that was his place of residence. Whoever delivers the said deserter on board the ship *Tarter,* or to the jailer of *Fredericksburg,* shall have the above reward, and necessary charges, paid by

RICHARD TAYLOR, Capt.

The Virginia Gazette, Purdie, October 17, 1777.

DESERTED from my company in the second *N. Carolina* continental battalion, JOHN RIGS, about five feet six inches high, has a thin visage, black hair, and a down look. He afterwards enlisted with Capt. *Thomas Bracey* in the colonial service, at *Portsmouth* and when I applied for him to Capt. *Thomas Bracey,* producing the said *King's* receipt for the bounty, and a certificate for his having been legally sworn before a justice, he refused to deliver him up till he had a trial, and before that came on he made his escape from the guard at *Portsmouth.* Whoever secures the said deserter, so that I get him again, shall have TWELVE DOLLARS reward.

MANLOVE TARRANT Capt.

The Virginia Gazette, Purdie, October 17, 1777; October 24, 1777.

As it is not improbable I may be advertised as a deserter, I have thought proper, in my own Justification, should that be the case, to advertise the lieutenant's receipt for the man I had hired to take my place, which man has been since refused by Capt. *Harris. Baxter Folkes.* Received of *Baxter Folkes* a certain *Lewis Laren,* as a soldier in the continental army, for the term of three years, or during the war, in order to exempt the said *Baxter Folkes* from the service of a soldier in the continental army, agreeable to an act of Assembly for the more speedily completing the quota of troops for the commonwealth of *Virginia,* and other purposes.

HEROD GIBBS, 2d lieut. 15th *Virg.* reg.—

Sept. 15, 1777.

The within named *Baxter Folkes* was one of the soldiers fixed upon by the commissioners of the county of *Chesterfield,* on *Friday* the 5th of *September* 1777, as a soldier to complete the company to be raised in the said county.

HEROD GIBBS, 2d Lieut. 15th *Virg. reg.*

Sept. 15, 1777.

The Virginia Gazette, Purdie, October 17, 1777.

ON *Saturday* night last, the 4th instant (*October*) broke jail at at *Dumfries,* a certain SAMUEL THOMAS, whom I enlisted in *August* as a soldier in the service of the United States of *America,* where he was committed for having unlawfully taken or stolen, from *Alex: Doyle,* merchant, a sum of money, which was discovered upon him, and restored to the proprietor. I will give TWENTY DOLLARS reward to any person who will deliver him to Col. *David Mason* at head quarters in *Williamsburg* to the commanding officer at *Alexandria.* He is about 5 feet 7 inches high, 22 or 23 years old, well featured, wears his hair, and says he was born in *Augusta,* of *Irish* extraction, to which country he may probably repair.

JOHN CRITTENDEN, 15th *Virg. reg.*

The Virginia Gazette, Purdie, October 17, 1777.

EDWARD CLARKE, and Stephen Hudson, *who absented themselves without leave, are hereby ordered to repair to their company immediately, otherwise they will deemed* deserters, *and treated as such.* ISAAC HOLMES, ensign.

The Virginia Gazette, Purdie, October 17, 1777.

DESCRIPTION of three men deserted from his Majesty's ship Centurion, Capt. Richard Brathwaite, Commander, WILLIAM LEADBERRY, born at St. Margets, Kent, 22 years of age, 5 feet 6 inches high, wore his own black hair, fresh complexion, had on a pea jacket, and cock'd hat, no trowsers on, slim built.

BENJAMIN BEAMES, born at Albany, in America, 21 years of age, 5 feet 5 inches high, brown hair, fair complexion, had on a brown jacket, and trowsers; snub nose.

JOHN CRAIG, born at North Shields, 20 years of age, about 5 feet 2 inches high, black hair, ruddy complexion, stout built, pitted with the small pox, had on a blue jacket, and trowsers.

N. B. There shall be paid the sum of FORTY SHILLINGS sterling, to the person or persons who shall apprehend each of the above people, or or producing a certificate of their being confined on board any of his Majesty's ship at New-York.

October 17, 1777.

Rivington's New-York Loyal Gazette, October 18, 1777; October 25, 1777.

RUN-away from Head Quarters, about the 5th instant, with the following valuable articles, the infamous, loquacious SAMUEL ELY, of Somers, formerly an itinerant preacher, and auctioneer of the gospel. This inhuman, plundering villain may be distinguished by his being constantly cloathed with a face of brass, and armed with a lying tongue in his own vindication and defence, when most guilty.

ARTICLES.

A number of silk and worsted hose, one British officers coat, one gold diamond ring, one pair of shoes, a number of holland shirts, several pair of breeches, (one of which he sold to the prisoners for solid coin) one gold eppalet, one lawn apron, a considerable quantity of linnen, some engineers instruments, a pock book, and many other articles too numerous to mention; all of which he knew to be in direct opposition to general orders.

It is earnestly requested of all committees of safety and others of authority in the neighbouring towns, to apprehend the said Ely and convey him to this place, or confine him so that he may be brought to justice, for which they shall receive ten dollars reward and have all necessary charges allowed them.

By order of the Court of Enquiry,
WILLIAM WILLIAMS, President.

The Connecticut Courant, and Hartford Weekly Intelligencer, October 21, 1777.

DESERTED from me the subscriber one James Brown, an Irishman, by trade a weaver, a soldier in the continental army, belonging to Capt. Stephen B[   ]'s company, Col. Charles Webb's regiment, about 24 years of age, 5 feet 9 inches high, lightish complexion, dark short curl'd hair; had when he went away a light colour'd fustian coat, and a silk waistcoat almost worn out, a dark brown pair of breeches, flopt hat, all except one side, a pair of square shoe buckles, wash'd with silver. Whoever will take up said Brown and return him to me, shall have ten dollars reward, and all necessary charges
          paid, by   ENOCH MERRIMAN, Serjeant.
The Connecticut Courant, and Hartford Weekly Intelligencer, October 21, 1777; November 11, 1777.

DESERTED out of my Company in Major Elijah Hyde's Regiment of light Horse from the State of Connecticut, now in the Continental Army in the northern Department, one Benjamin Gary, belonging to Lebanon in said State, is a well built Fellow, about 5 Feet 10 Inches high, dark Complexion, brown Hair, about 30 Years of Age, had on a light brown Coat, with Buff Facings, trimmed with white Vellum, a yellow lincey Lace round the Crown of his Hat, wears a Pair of Gaters or half Boots; it is said he has sold his Horse, Saddle and Bridle, and carried off his Saddle Baggs on his Back with a Pair of Pistols in them. Whoever will return said Deserter to the Subscriber at Head-Quarters shall have one Dollar Reward paid by me,
          JAMES GREEN, Capt.
                        Stillwater, October 8, 1777.
The Connecticut Gazette; And The Universal Intelligencer, October 24, 1777; October 31, 1777.

DESERTED from the *Page* galley, a certain CORNELIUS THOMPSON, by trade a blacksmith, 5 feet 4 or 5 inches high, pretty thick made, has a dark complexion, and dark hair, which curls I have reason to believe he is lurking about the lower end of *Fauquier* county, near my house, as his family lives there, Whoever secures the said deserter, and delivers him to *Eleazer Callender* Esq; commander of the *Dragon* at *Fredericksburg,* or on board any of the state vessels, shall have twenty dollars reward.
          JAMES MARKHAM, Capt.
The Virginia Gazette, Purdie, October 24, 1777; October 31, 1777.

DESERTED from my quota of the state artillery, JOHN DESHONCLE, a *Frenchman,* who speaks bad *English,* and is about 5 feet 2 or 3 inches high; had on when he deserted a long snuff coloured coat, with an old hat and trousers, I imagine he may be gone to *South Quay,* in order to go out of the state with one of his countrymen, as I enlisted him at *Portsmouth* from a *French* vessel there. Whoever delivers him to Col. *Muter,* or to the subscriber at *Hampton,* shall have twenty dollars reward.
      JAMES W. BRADLEY, Lieut.
 The Virginia Gazette, Purdie, October 24, 1777; October 31, 1777; November 14, 1777.

         YORK, *October* 16, 1777.
DESERTED on *Thursday* the 9th of this Instant, JAMES KING, 5 Feet 10 Inches high, black Hair, blue Eyes, had on a blue Coat, white Waistcoat and Breeches, and white Hat. He purchased from *John Gibbs* a black Stud Horse about 13 ½ Hands high. I will give TWENTY DOLLARS to any Person that will deliver him to any continental officer.
     FRANCIS MENNIS, Lieut. 1st *Virg.* Regt.
 The Virginia Gazette, Dixon and Hunter, October 24, 1777; October 31, 1777.

   Mecklenburgh County, Virginia, Sept. 17, 1777.
ON Thursday the 2d of this instant September, about three hours before day, were taken out of my pasture on Roanoke River,
   Two very valuable Chariot Horses,
both good bays, one rather brighter than the other, 5 or 6 years old, near or about 4 feet 10 Inches high, the brighter bay has one or more white feet, a large or streak in his face, hanging mane on the near side, a switch not docked, pretty much wind galled for a young horse, and as he has been much worked lately in a chariot is chased in several places with the harness, and is tolerably square built. The dark bay is also rubbed with harness is rather thin made, has a long blaze or streak in his face, bench kneed, and is a little eat-hamm'd.—The above horses are supposed to be stolen by one Drury Thomson, a deserter from Charlotte County, in this State, who is thought to be endeavoring to pass to the New- purchase, in the State of Georgia, where I am told his father John Farley Thomson lives. The said Drury Thomson is better than 6 feet high, remarkably strong and active, has black hair and eyes and was dressed when he went off in white Virginia cloth, but has with him a blue coat. I will give Five pounds

for each of my horses, delivered at my house, and Ten pounds for conviction of the thief.
                    PEYTON SKIPWITH.
    N. B. The bright bay was not branded, the dark bay is supposed to be branded on the near shoulder with T.E. encircled by a scroll in the shape of a heart.
    The Gazette Of The State Of South Carolina, October 28, 1777; November 4, 1777; November 11, 1777.

WHEREAS I understand that Capt. *Isaac Hicks's* Lieutenant has informed Col. *David Walker* that I belong to the *Georgia* service, and, Capt. *Hicks* being now in that state, his report may gain credit, I do hereby forewarn any officers to interrupt me till the Captain's return, as I have not a farthing of the county's money, and will then make appear that I am not a deserter.
                    HENRY DANIEL.
    The Virginia Gazette, Purdie, October 31, 1777; November 7, 1777.

                One hundred and fifty DOLLARS *Reward.*
FOR apprehending the under mentioned deserters, *viz. William Davis, John Amos, Elias M'Grooder,* and *Jesse Lowe,* of *Powhatan,* and *Richard Dean, Jesse Bradley, Allegana M'Guire, John Rowland, Martin Blake, George Bandy, Moses Robertson,* and *Anderson, M'Guire,* of *Cumberland,* draughts for the tenth *Virginia* regiment, who having failed to attend, or submit themselves (being previously summoned) are hereby advertised as deserters, and the above reward will be given for apprehending them, or twenty dollars for each, on their being delivered to me, or any other continental officer. *Josiah Clarke,* and *James Dorum,* natives of *Buckingham,* who enlisted themselves with me, I will give twenty dollars reward for apprehending either of them.
                  SAMUEL BASKERVILLE, Lieut.
              10th *Virginia* battalion.
    The Virginia Gazette, Purdie, October 31, 1777; November 7, 1777; November 14, 1777.

MITCHELL COLLINS and JOHN SWEPSTON, late inhabitants of *King & Queen,* and now soldiers in Col. *Grayson's* regiment, are ordered to repair to *Dumfries* immediately, to join their corps, or they will be deemed deserters, and treated accordingly.
                  R. BUTLER.
    The Virginia Gazette, Purdie, October 31, 1777.

DESERTED from my Company of State Troops in the 2d Regiment, the 1st of this Instant *(November)* a certain *Jesse Critmore,* a Draught from *Norfolk* County, who had been exchanged by Col. *Mason* for another Man in my Company some few days before to go to the Northward. Whoever takes up said Deserter, and delivers him to me, or commits him to the public Gaol shall receive the usual Bounty of 20 Dollars Reward.
      JOHN LEWIS, Captain.

☞All those enlisted in my Company, who have not joined it, or who are out on Furlough, are desired to attend at the Barracks, near *Williamsburg,* without loss of Time, otherwise they may expect to be deemed Deserters, and advertised as such.
 The Virginia Gazette, Dixon and Hunter, November 7, 1777; November 21, 1777.

      Thirty DOLLARS Reward.
FOR apprehending and delivering to some continental officer, or securing in any jail in this state, *Anthony Rain, Ren Dejarnett,* and *Bury Lewis,* three deserters from my quota of the *Prince Edward* draughts, or ten dollars for other of them.
    HEZEKIAH MORTON, Lieut. 12th *Virg.* reg.
 The Virginia Gazette, Purdie, November 7, 1777

DEserted from Capt. Lieut. John Lambert's Company, in the Continental Service, Henry White, a Dutchman, about 5 feet 8 inches high, sandy Hair, red Complexion, much Pock broken. Had on a blue Coat, trim'd with red, and a white Woolen Waistcoat and Trowsers. Whoever will take up and return said Deserter to the Subscriber in Boston, shall have TWENTY DOLLARS Reward paid by me JOHN LAMBERT. Capt. Lieut.
N. B. He has taken two Bounties.
 The Boston-Gazette, and Country Journal, November 10, 1777; November 17, 1777; November 24, 1777.

        Springfield, Nov, 7, 1777.
WHEREAS Colonel SKEEN is well known to be a notorious Enemy to our Country's Liberties, and has broke his Faith of Capitulation, and gone directly contract to General GATES's positive Orders to him in particular, when attempting to go to Albany against Orders—when General Gates took from him his Sword, and ordered him to go directly to Boston with the English Troops, which was to go by the shortest Rout—He has stroled away thro' the Country to Hartford, where he said he was taking his own Way to Boston, but is mistrusted

to be going to Long or Rhode Island.—Therefore it is recommended and desired that every Friend to the Country will apprehend said Offender, wherever he may be found, and closely confine him in some State Goal till General Gates's farther Pleasure & Orders may be known about him.
     EBENEZER LEARNED, B. G.
 The Boston-Gazette, And Country Journal, November 10, 1777; *The Connecticut; And the Universal Intelligencer,* November 14, 1777.

DESERTED from Canaan, on the 25th day of September instant, a soldier inlisted in my company, in Col. Chandler's regiment, named John Watson, about 5 feet 6 inches high, grey eyes, brown hair, well set, slim built, about 25 years of age; had on when he went away a blue sailor's jacket, red and white under jacket, white tow cloth over-halls. Whoever shall take said deserter and return him to his regiment, or secure him and send word so that me may be returned to his duty, shall have five dollars reward and all reasonable charges
    paid, by JESSE KIMBALL, Capt.
            Cannan, September 27, 1777.
 The Connecticut Courant, and Hartford Weekly Intelligencer, November 11, 1777; November 18, 1777; December 2, 1777.

WHEREAS, about two months ago, I left *Patrick Welch,* seaman, sick in the hospital at *Portsmouth,* since which I am informed he has recovered his health, and is walking about the said town, careless of duty, I do hereby order him to repair on board the *Henry* immediately, now on her station in *Mobjack* bay, otherwise he will be deemed a deserter.   ROBERT TOMPKINS, Captain.
 The Virginia Gazette, Purdie, November 14, 1777; November 28, 1777; December 5, 1777.

DESERTED from Capt. *Peter Jones's* company of regulars, raised in *Dinwiddie* county, the following soldiers, *viz. Elleck Wills, John Randol, John Bishop, James Burchet, Samuel Browder, Frederick Browder, Jacob Bott, Joel Johnson Stow, William Williamson, John Graves Thrift, John Cawdle* and *John Sangster.* Whoever delivers the said deserters to me in *Dinwiddie,* or to the commanding officer in *Williamsburg,* by the 25th of this instant (*November*) shall have ten dollars reward for each, and all reasonable expenses paid.
     DAVID WALKER, Lieut.

The Virginia Gazette, Purdie, November 14, 1777; November 21, 1777.

DESERTED from the *Manly* galley, two negro men, the property of Mr. *Willis Cowper* of *Suffolk,* one named PASS, the other CAMBRIDGE. *Pass* is about four feet eight inches high, of a very yellow complexion, shout and well made, and has a remarkable scar near one of his knees, occasioned by the cut of a glass bottle. *Cambridge* is about four feet seven inches high, of a black complexion, and has a very pleasing countenance. Whoever secures the said negroes, so that I get them again, shall have twenty dollars reward for each.　　WILLIAM SAUNDERS.
The Virginia Gazette, Purdie, November 14, 1777.

DESERTED from Col. *Gibson's* regiment of state troops, JOHN HIX, a soldier who enlisted with me in *Cumberland* county. Whoever delivers him to the commanding officer in *Williamsburg,* or to me in *Powhatan* county, shall have ten dollars reward.
　　ROBERT H. SAUNDERS, Lieut.
The Virginia Gazette, Purdie, November 14, 1777.

DESERTED from *Gosport,* DANIEL MURPHY, a soldier in Col. *Harrison's* regiment or artillery. He is an Irishman, five feet five or six inches high, well made, of a ruddy complexion has a down look, and dark hair; had on when he went away a blue coat turned up with red, white jacket and breeches. Twenty dollars will be given to any person who delivers him to the commanding officer at *Portsmouth.*
　　THOMAS DIX, Lieut Artillery.
The Virginia Gazette, Purdie, November 14, 1777; November 21, 1777; November 28, 1777.

DESERTED from Capt. *Samuel Scott's* company in the *Georgia* service, the following soldiers, *viz. William Warren, John Pounds, Benjamin Turner, Philemon Crain, William Butler, William Fulcher, Elisha Gipson, William Bartlett, Thomas Gimbe, William Fidler, James Hunt, John Scates, William Watkins, John Draper, Joshua Butler, Thomas Butler* and *Timothy Warren,* from *Halifax* county *David Haley, Solomon Porter, William Lake, John Christie, William Stewart, Benjamin Lawless, George Brock, Archibald Silvey, Benjamin Tilleson, William Robinson, Henry Vinceson, George Ballard, John Brock, Daniel Bence, Thomas Jones,* and *Thomas Crawley,* of *Pittsylvania; Samuel Beasley, Moses Wade,* and *William Correll,* from *Prince Edward.* From Capt. *Hunter* 's company, in the said service, *Edward Ferguson, Isham Dikes, Obadiah Ferguson, Ambrose Lucas, John Johnson, William Bartley, John McClay, William Woodkough, Alexander Barclay, David Womock, William Johens, William Zackley, Daniel Tulley, Moses Battally, James Randal, Francis Gaines, Francis Hopkins, William Prince,* and *John Wales.* Any of the above deserters who come to *Prince Edward* courthouse, and deliver themselves to an officer there that will be appointed to receive them, shall be kindly received, and meet with a free pardon.

The Virginia Gazette, Purdie, November 14, 1777; November 21, 1777.

WILLIAMSBURG, *Nov* 1, 1777.
LEWIS SEALE *Culpeper,* and *Reuben Jones* of *Fauquier,* whose furloughs have expired some time, are ordered to repair to head quarters immediately, or send certificates of their inability to do, so, otherwise they will be deemed deserters, and treated accordingly.— The representatives of *George Dorton* and *John Dalton,* deceased, late soldiers in my company, are desired to apply to me for what wages, are due to them.
     BENJ. POLLARD, Capt.
The Virginia Gazette, Purdue, November 14, 1777; November 21, 1777.

YORK town, *Nov.* 3, 1777.
JAMES WESTON, of *Brunswick* county, who obtained furlough till the first of *October,* but failing to return, is hereby advertised as a deserter, and a reward of twenty dollars will be given for delivering him to any continental officer. He is about six feet high, has light hair and eyes, and served in the campaign at *Norfolk* in Capt. *Meade*'s company of the second *Virginia* regiment.
    FRANCIS MENNIS, Lieut. first *Virg.* reg.
The Virginia Gazette, Purdie, November 14, 1777; November 28, 1777; December 5, 1777.

THE Hon. Board of War having directed me to order all the troops in this quarter, who are to join the grand army, immediately to proceed to the Northward, I hereby give notice to the officers that they are to march their several quotas to the town of *Lancaster* in *Pennsylvania,* there to remain till fitted for the field.—I take this opportunity again to address myself to the several County Lieutenants and other militia officers of this state, and earnestly request them to exert their utmost endeavours in apprehending and forwarding to this station, or to the general rendezvous, all draughts or deserters from their respective counties, there being a large proportion of those men not yet collected; not it is practicable for the continental officers within this state to perform such signal service to their country, unless assisted effectually by the officers of the militia.—And whereas, inconsequence of instructions from his Excellency General *Washington,* I lately promised a free pardon to all deserters who would return to their duty in a limited time (many of whom availed themselves of the generous offer) but there are still some so daring and obstinate as to remain out, and risk every thing rather than an honourable return to their duty, I hereby offer a reward of THIRTY DOLLARS for apprehending either of the following soldiers, *viz. Samuel Sammons, Isham Underhill,* and *Gideon Mason,* of *Sussex* county, the two former in Capt. *Edmunds*'s company, the latter in Capt. *Manson*'s fo the XVth regiment; and the same reward for *Lewis Charles,* jun. of *Brunswick,* and *Levin Phillips* of *Nansemond,* the former a soldier in the XVth, the other in the IVth *Virginia* regiment. And for all deserters brought to head quarters in this city, or delivered to some proper continental officer, the takes up may depend upon receiving a generous reward, besides what the law allows. —

Given at head quarters, *Williamsburg, Nov.* 12, 1777.

DAVID MASON. Col. XVth *Virg.* reg.

The Virginia Gazette, Purdie, November 21, 1777; November 28, 1777; December 5, 1777.

Forty DOLLARS *Reward.*

DESERTED from Capt. *Thomas Massie's* new recruits for the sixth *Virginia* regiment, the following soldiers, viz. *George Batson,* an *Englishman,* much pitted with the smallpox, five feet eight or nine inches high, was enlisted in *Williamsburg,* but have been informed he ran away from his master in *North Carolina. William Harris,* a mulatto fellow, about five feet eleven inches high, the veins in his legs being much broke, appear in knots, he was enlisted in the lower end of *New Kent,* but expect he is lurking about *Charles City.* Whoever delivers the said soldiers to the commanding officer in *Williamsburg* shall receive the above reward, or twenty dollars for either. By order of Capt. *Massie.*

JAMES TAYLOR, serjeant.

The Virginia Gazette, Purdie, November 21, 1777; November 28, 1777. See *The Virginia Gazette,* Purdie, September 26, 1777, for Batson.

DESERTED from the *Norfolk Revenge* gallery, a negro man named HARRY, about twenty eight years of age, well set, and very likely. Capt. *Calvert* bought the said negro from Mr. *Southall* in *Williamsburg.* Whoever takes him up, and delivers him to me at *Hampton,* shall receive eight dollars.
                      WRIGHT WESTCOTT.
The Virginia Gazette, Purdie, November 21, 1777; November 28, 1777.

DESERTED from my quota of state troops, PRESLEY GARNER, about sixteen years old, five feet two inches high, has dark hair, and stoops in his shoulders. I have since informed that he enlisted with Lieut. *Thomas Pollard,* on board of Capt. *Calvert* 's galley. Whoever delivers the said deserter to the commanding officer in *Williamsburg* shall have ten dollars reward.
                      WILLIAM LAWSON, Lieut.
The Virginia Gazette, Purdie, November 21, 1777; November 28, 1777.

WHEREAS a number of German prisoners have been receiv'd into families in this and the neighbouring towns, by their own desire, and after having been cloathed have deserted.—'Tis therefore desired that is any of them are found lurking about town or country, they may be taken up and sent to me, in order to be put on board the prison-ship for their ingratitude; and all reasonable charges shall be paid.
    Also, three prisoners have made their escape from the hospital, viz.— *Thomas Silk*, alias, *Old Ginger*, a seaman who had on a blue coat, is 5 feet 6 inches high, about 40 years of age, a deceitful villain, often shewing his private parts to deceive people, and telling how he was abused, which is very black, and it was done by his own hand to get to the hospital, for to make his escape.— *Thomas Dix*, a British soldier, 5 feet 9 inches high, about 35 years old, had on a Continental coat, which he took and left his at the hospital.—*John Cunningham*, a British soldier, 5 feet 10 inches high, about 28 years of age, wore away a cloth coloured sailor jacket.
    The above are great villains, and it is desired that all friends to their country will exert themselves to find them, that they may be taken up and brought to my office, and receive their punishments; and they shall be well rewarded for their trouble, by
                    ROB. PIERPONT, Commissary of Prisoners.
                                 Boston, November 28, 1777.

The Connecticut Gazette; And The Universal Intelligencer, November 27, 1777; December 4, 1777; December 11, 1777; *The Boston-Gazette, And Country Journal*, December 1, 1777; December 8, 1777.

Sixty DOLLARS *Reward.*
DESERTED from the *Mecklenburg* company of state troops, *Edward Clark, Stephen Houston,* and *Edward Clark.* [sic] Whoever delivers the said deserters to the commanding officer at *Williamsburg* shall receive the above reward, or twenty dollars for either of them. It is hoped that all wellwishers to themselves and their country will be active in apprehending the above deserters, and also those of the same company who were advertised in former paper by Ensign *Holmes.* The soldiers belonging to the same company, who were indulged with furloughs, are earnestly requested to repair to this place immediately, or they will be considered as deserters, and treated as such, except those who have furloughs for a longer time than they have been absent, or are rendered unable by a low state of health.
WILLIAM BASKERVILLE, Lieut.
The Virginia Gazette, Purdie, November 28, 1777; December 12, 1777; December 19, 1777.

DESERTED from the IVth *Georgia* battalion, the following soldiers, *viz. James M'Cormick* about five feet four inches high, about twenty seven years old, of a fair complexion, has dark coloured hair, gray eyes, by trade a shoemaker, and Born in *Ireland. James M'Farland,* a *Scotchman,* twenty three years old, five feet five inches high, has blue eyes, fair hair and complexion, and a tailor by trade. *John Mitchell,* five feet five inches high, twenty one years old, fair complexion, brown hair, gray eyes, a shoemaker, and born in *Ireland, John Hodges,* a *Scotchman,* thirty years old. Five feet nine inches high, brown hair, blue eyes, dark complexion, and is a sailor. *Conor Sullivan,* serjeant, an *Irishman,* twenty five years old, five feet six inches. high, brown hair, black eyes, dark complexion, a weaver by trade. Twenty dollars reward for each.
BERNARD PATY, Lieut. IVth *Georgia* battalion.
The Virginia Gazette, Purdie, November 28, 1777; December 19, 1777.

One Hundred and Twenty DOLLARS Reward.
FOR apprehending the following deserters, from *Charles City* county, *viz. Perkins Thomson,* jun, who is twenty five years of age, of a yellow complexion, a shoemaker by trade, and is lurking about a place

called *Fountain's* creek, in *Brunswick* country. *James Miles, William Miles, William Bond, John Arthur* (alias Smith) and *Benjamin Brown* are now lurking about in *Charles City.* We will give the above reward if the said deserters are delivered to the commanding officer in *Williamsburg,* or twenty collars for each. Also to inform *John Major,* jun., and *Edward Brown,* who are draughts from the *aforesaid* country, that unless they come in to their duty by the tenth of *December,* they will be advertised as deserters, and treated as such.
      JOHN DUDLEY, Lieut.
      BENJ. EDMONDSON, *Ensign.*
WHEREAS *Samuel Black,* of *Henry* country enlisted himself as a soldier some time last *July* with Ensign *Thomas Bush,* and has failed to join his company, according to orders, I hereby offer a reward of twenty dollars to any person that will bring him to head quarters in *Williamsburg,* or deliver him to any state officer.
      AMEROE DUDLEY, Capt.
  The Virginia Gazette, Purdie, November 28, 1777.

      Sixty DOLLARS *Reward.*
DESERTED from Captain *John Lewis*'s company of state troops in the Second State regiment, the following soldiers, *viz. Philip Atkins,* about five feet nine or ten inches high, who I have heard is gone towards *Carolina. James Jurden,* (alias *William Jonesten*) a tailor by trade, about five feet three or four inches high. They were all enlisted in *Bedford* county. Whoever secures the said deserters, so as they may join their company, or sends them to the commanding officer at *Williamsburg,* shall have the above reward, or twenty dollars for each. JOHN M‘ELHENY, Lieut,
  The Virginia Gazette, Purdie, November 28, 1777; December 19, 1777.

SEVENTY dollars reward for the following soldiers, *viz. Randol Luvsey, Heartwell Harrison, Jesse Williams, Samuel Brasington, Joe Butler,* mulatto, *Jack Stuart,* do. *Phil. E[van]s,* do. who were draughted out of *Prince George* county. For each of the above men I will give ten dollars, and pay and expences if delivered to the commanding officer in *Williamsburg,* or to the subscriber in *Prince George* county.
     BENJAMIN GREEN, Ensign XIV *Virg.* reg.
  The Virginia Gazette, Purdie, November 28, 1777.

FLUVANNA county, *October* 22, 1777.
WHEREAS I enlisted with *George Thomson,* then of *Albemarle* county, Lieutenant in Capt. *Brown*'s company for the colonial service, upon the express condition, that if I was ever ordered out of the state of *Virginia* I should then be immediately discharged by the said *Thompson* from any further service; and whereas, some time in the month of June last, there were orders for the first regiment of the state troops, to which I belonged, to join General *Washington*, upon which I applied to Mr. *Thompson* for a discharge, agreeable to the terms of enlistment, who refused to give one, aledging it was out of his power, but at the same time acknowledged my right to such a discharge, I therefore publish this advertisement to inform the Governour and Council, or any other power that may have a right to determine the matter, that I shall be ready to attend any place for that purpose, though I should acknowledge it a great indulgence to have it determined in *Fluvanna* county, where the evidences are, as it would save trouble and expense.
ADAM COUSINS.
The Virginia Gazette, Purdie, November 28, 1777; December 5, 1777.

SNOW Creek, *Henry country, October* 27, 1777
DESERTED from *Fort Salter's,* in the *New Purchase* of the state of Georgia, the following soldiers, *viz. Benjamin Meggerson,* serjeant, from *Buckingham.* John *Webster* and *David Jennings,* corporals, from *Prince Edward. Joel Holland* from *Cumberland. John Ramay, Thomas Church,* and *Jesse Mills,* from *Amherst. Joseph Lawrence,* and *Ambrose Hutcheson,* from *Henry. James Navarre,* from *Halifax. Andrew Clark,* from *Loudoun.* Likewise James Smith, and *Wallace Dunston,* mulattoes, from *Halifax.* The above soldiers being chiefly enlisted by Capt. *John Baird* of the state of Georgia. it is not in my power at present to give a description of them, but expect they have mostly returned to their respective counties. I have in orders from Col. *Elbert,* of the 2d *Georgia* battalion of continental troops, to offer a free pardon to all deserters that voluntarily give themselves up to me and return to their duty; and I do farther offer a reward of twenty dollars for each of the above mentioned soldiers to be delivered to me, or any other continental officers of the state of *Georgia.*
SHEM COOK, Capt. 2d *Georgia* battalion
The Virginia Gazette, Purdie, November 28, 1777; December 19, 1777.

WHEREAS *James Skelton of Charlotte,* who enlisted with *William Dickson,* an officer in the continental service, upon condition that he himself continued the service, but as he threw up his commission, the said *Skelton* paid back the bounty money, and gives this publick notice that he is clear of the said *Dickson.*
The Virginia Gazette, Purdie, November 28; December 12, 1777.

RICHARD USREY, *Gideon Hogg (alias Boar) Julius Layne, William Melion, Overton Baker, Nathan Talley, son of Micajah, Heneley Grubbs, John Clopton, William Goodman, John Mallery, Claiborne Good, Francis Tyler, Benjamin Sanders, John Frazer, Nathaniel Harris, Hezekiah Ford, James Howard, Thomas Stanley, jun. Elijah Alvis, Thomas Stanley, son of John, draughts from the Hanover militia,* for the XIVth regiment, falling to appear at the appointed me, are hereby advertised as deserters, and a reward of twenty dollars will be given for each man, on their delivery to the commanding officer at *Williamsburg.* JOHN B. JOHNSON, Lieut.
The Virginia Gazette, Purdie, November 28, 1777; December 19, 1777.

JOHN STILL, of the County of *Gloucester,* and ISAAC OLDHAM, of the *Isle* of *Wight,* are ordered to repair to Head Quarters immediately, or they will be deemed Deserters, and treated as such.
FRANCIS MENNIS, Lieut. 1st *Virg.* Regt.
The Virginia Gazette, December 5, 1777; December 12, 1777.

DETECT PUBLIC ROBBERS!
TEN DOLLARS REWARD for each.
DESERTED the service of the United States, from Colonel DAVID HENLEY'S regiment, and Lemuel Tresscott's company, from Litchfield, in Connecticut, one JOSEPH BUTLER, of Concord; 19 years of age, 5 feet 8 inches high, dark hair, brown complexion, and grey eyes. He is supposed to be at Concord, at this time; as his father dwells there. Also, WILLIAM STRAW, 21 years of age, 5 feet 3 inches high, born in Sandown, in this State, brown hair, fair complexion, and grey eyes. The two last, deserted at Morristown, New-Jersey, and are gone, it is supposed, to Sanford, at the entrance of Casco-Bay.

All Persons, who have the good of their country at heart, are hereby called upon to use their utmost endeavours, in detecting the above named villains, and to secure them in some goal of the United States, or send them to their regiment at Boston.

Any person or persons, who shall receive the above traitors, so that they may be brought to justice, shall receive the above reward, and all necessary charges,
    paid by me, W. CURTIS, Major.
                Boston, Dec. 11, 1777.
The Independent Chronicle and the Universal Advertiser, December 11, 1777; December 19, 1777.

DESERTED from the second *Georgia* battalion of continental troops, *James Harrifield,* about thirty five years of age, from *Prince Edward* county. *Hawkins Briant,* about twenty one years of age, from *Bedford* county. *Thomas Moore.* about twenty five years of age, from *Brunswick* county, *Charles Breeks,* about nineteen years of age, from *Loudoun* county. *John Cock,* about twenty five years of age, from *Halifax* county, but understand he is gone to an uncle's of his on *Meherrin* river. *Joseph Ingram* a *Scotchman,* from *Lunenburg* county. *Edward James,* about twenty years of age, who I understand is at one of his sister's in *James City* county, near *Cartwright*'s ordinary. I will give one hundred and forty dollars reward for the whole of them, or twenty dollars for each, if delivered to me in *Prince Edward* county, near the courthouse.
      JESSE H. WALTON, Capt.
 ☞ Any of the deserters who will return to their duty in fifteen days will have a free pardon.
 The Virginia Gazette, Purdie, December 12, 1777.

DESERTED from Capt. *John Winston's* company of the XIVth regiment, *William Gunter,* five feet six or seven inches high, thick and well made. and about forty years of age. A reward of twenty dollars will be given on his delivery to the commanding officer at *Williamsburg.*   JOHN B. JOHNSON, Lieut.
 The Virginia Gazette, Purdie, December 12, 1777; December 19, 1777.

DESERTED from the subscriber at Hartford, one Bartholomew Davis, late of Windsor, belonging to the continental army, about 5 feet 6 inches high, grey eyes, about 30 years of age, had on a pale blue coat, small round hat, brown breeches, went off on a small sorrel horse. Whoever will apprehend said deserter and secure him, so that he may be bro't to his corps in Col. Chandler's regiment shall have ten dollars reward and all necessary charges
    paid, by SAMUEL MATTOCKS, Capt. .
                 Dec. 14, 1777.

The Connecticut Courant, and Hartford Weekly Intelligencer, December 16, 1777; December 30, 1777.

Annapolis, December 16, 1777.
BROKE gaol on the night of 13th day of this instant, December, the following persons, viz,

HUGH DEAN, a Scotchman, committed on suspicion of being a tory, about twenty-five years of age, five feet six inches high, of a brown complexion, dark brown hair, dark eyes, and his nose turns up a little; had on when he made his escape, an old brown coat and waistcoat, buckskin breeches half worn, castor hat, and country made shoes, several shirts, and sundry pairs of stockings, and is supposed to have had several half joes and other gold about him.

HENRY HUGHES, committed on suspicion of felony; he is a solder in the train of artillery, an Englishman, about forty years of age, about five feet four or five inches high, of a sallow complexion, brown hair, stoops a little in his walk, battle ham'd, and chews tobacco; he had on a light coloured coat and waistcoat, old leather breeches, old hat, and half worn long quartered shoes.

Whoever takes up and secures the above prisoners, so that they may be had again, shall receive the sum of twenty pounds currency, or ten pounds like money for either of them, paid by

THOMAS DEALE, sheriff of Anne-Arundel county.
The Maryland Gazette, December 18, 1777; December 25, 1777.

WILLIAMSBURG, *December* 18, 1777.
JOHN JONES, of *Henrico* County, aged about 20 Years, 5 Feet 9 or 10 Inches high, with light coloured Hair, having failed to join my Company, I do hereby offer a Reward of 10 Dollars to any Person who will deliver him to the commanding Officer at this Place.— *William Richardson,* and *Stephen Bailey,* are ordered to join their company immediately (sickness excepted, in which Case they are to get the same certified by a Magistrate) otherwise they will be deemed Deserters, and treated accordingly.

B. C. SPILLER, Capt. State Troops.
The Virginia Gazette, Dixon and Hunter, December 19, 1777.

WILLIAM ELAM, *of* Amelia *County,* David Johnson, *and* Solomon Jones *of* Brunswick *County, who enlisted under me in the State Artillery, are hereby ordered immediately to repair to* Hampton *Garrison, or they will be deemed* Deserters, *and treated as such.*

WILLIAM JENNINGS, *Lieut. Artillery.*

The Virginia Gazette, Dixon and Hunter, December 19, 1777.

DESERTED *from the* Manly *Galley two Marines, viz.* James Hodges *about* 30 *Years of Age,* 5 *Feet* 8 *or* 9 *inches high, has short brown Hair, very dark Skin, and talks soft; had on when he went off, an old* Virginia *Cloth Coat and Breeches, and an Osnabrug Shirt;—the other* Isaac Carlton *about* 20 *Years of Age,* 5 *Feet* 7 *or* 8 *Inches high, has short black Hair, and dark Skin, has an Impediment in his Speech when he talks fast, had on when he went off, a* Virginia *Cloth Jacket, a Cotton Shirt, and long Trousers; they both carried off with them a good many Clothes, unknown to the Officers on Board. These Men were formerly enlisted in the Service by Capt.* John C. Cocke, *and put on Board the* Manly *by Order of the Commodore. Whoever takes the said Men up, and delivers them on Board, or secures them so that I may them, shall receive* 20 *Dollars Reward for each.*
   WILLIAM SAUNDERS, Captain.
The Virginia Gazette, Dixon and Hunter, December 19, 1777; December 26, 1777.

AS Capt. *Ancram* has left a list of his Men recruited for this State with me, therefore desire every Man who enlisted under him to repair immediately to *Hampton* Garrison, or they will be deemed Deserters, and will be treated as such. The Names of the Men are as follow; *John Harvey, William Davids, Matthew Harvey, James Cradock, Peter Green Raines, Christopher M'Gehee, John Chapman, Henry Ledger, Stripling Lester, Ed. Peters, Robert Peters, James Tucker, Joseph M'Micken, Thomas Mitchell, John Mitchell, Matthew Roberts.* and *John Taylor.*
   JOHN MAZARET, Capt. Artil.
The Virginia Gazette, Dixon and Hunter, December 19, 1777.

DESERTED from the 3d *Georgia* Battalion of Continental troops *Caleb Hunter,* from *Amelia* County, about 23 Years of Age, 5 Feet 9 Inches high, well made, and of a dark Complexion.—*Obediah Ferguson,* appears to be about 17 Years of Age, 5 Feet 4 Inches high.— *Isham Dyke,* about 18 Years of Age, 5 Feet 8 Inches high, thin Visage, and of a dark Complexion.—*John Johnson,* about 25 Years of Age, 5 Feet 5 Inches high, very dark Complexion, much addicted to Liquor, and then talkative.— *Ambrose Luthas,* about 21 Years of Age, 5 Feet 10 Inches high, of a dark Complexion, sloops in his Shoulders, and slender made; the above were all in Soldiers Dress.— *David Womath,* about 16 Years of Age, 5 Feet 9 Inches high.— *William*

Bartlett, about 24 Years of Age, very bald.— *John Moore Clay,* about 20 Years of Age.— *William Woodruff,* about 40 Years of Age.— *Alexadder Bortlett,* [sic] about 18 Years of Age.— *William Jones,* about 25 Years of Age.— *Andrew King,* about 26 Years of Age, I expect said *King* is on *Clinch* River, and as I know him to be a great Villain, will give 40 Dollars for him, and 20 Dollars for each of the others, if delivered to me in *Prince Edward* County, or any Officer belonging to the Regiment. If any of the above Soldiers will come and deliver themselves up to any of the Officers belonging to the State, they shall have a free Pardon.
          THOMAS SCOTT, Capt.
The Virginia Gazette, Dixon and Hunter, December 19, 1777.

DEserted from Capt. James Bancroft's Company, in Col. Michael Jackson's Regiment, Thomas Fitch, a Native of this Town, aged 30 Years, about 5 Feet 10 Inches high, of a sandy Complexion, and a little Pock mark'd: Had on when he absconded, a pale blue Regimental Coat, faced with Red, and a Gold Appalet on his Right Shoulder. Whoever apprehends and confines him in any of the Continental Goals, or give Information to me at the Widow Fadro's Tavern, shall be entitled to Ten Dollars Reward.
          Wm. STORY, Lieut.
                                        Boston, Dec. 20.
The Boston Gazette, And The Country Journal, December 22, 1777.

DESERTED from my Quota of State Troops, JAMES BARKER of *Buckingham,* he appears to be upwards of 40 Years old, 5 Feet 7 or 8 inches high, well set, short black Hair, one of his Knees larger than the other, by trade a Shoemaker. Whoever delivers the said *Barker* to me or any State Officer, shall have a Reward of 10 Dollars, and all reasonable Charges paid.
          RICHARD CRUMP, Lieut, Art.
The Virginia Gazette, December 26, 1777.

                    TWENTY DOLLARS REWARD.
DESERTED from the 9th *Virginia* Regiment, a certain SAMUEL DAY, enlisted in *Powhatan* County, but says he was born in *Albemarle,* and has lived in *Georgia,* or *Carolina* for some Time, he is about 30 Years old, 5 Feet 7 or 8 Inches high, of a dark Complexion and well made. I will give the above Reward to any Person who will deliver him to the Commanding Officer in *Williamsburg,* or to any Officer going to the Grand Army with Troops.

NATH: G. MORRIS, Capt. 9th *Virg* Regt.
The Virginia Gazette, Dixon and Hunter, December 26, 1777.

DESERTED from Capt. *Bressie's* company of State troops, serjeant *Joshua Campbell, Edmund Love, Charles Smith,* and *William Gregory,* who was enlisted from *North Carolina* State.— *Campbell* is 5 Feet 8 Inches high, about 22 years of age, with light hair.— *Love* is about 5 Feet 4 or 5 inches high, yellow hair, and of a dark complexion.— *Smith* has very dark hair and complexion, about the same height of *Love.*—*Gregory* is 5 Feet 10 inches high, about 27 years of age, light hair and complexion.— *James Johnston,* 35 years of age, 5 feet 8 inches high, light hair and complexion, stoops in his walk, and he formerly kept a school.— *John Wayles,* who was enlisted in *Princess Anne* county, 5 feet 9 or 10 inches high, about 30 years of age, light hair and complexion. I will give a reward of 30 dollars for serjeant *Campbell* and *William Gregory,* and 20 dollars for each or the others, delivered at *Portsmouth.*
JOHN HUDSON, Lieut.
The Virginia Gazette, December 26, 1777.

1778

Rye, December 13, 1777.
DESERTED from Capt. Abijah Savage's company, Col. Henry Sherburne's regiment, Jonathan Clark, light hair and eyes, about 5 feet 8 inches high, belongs to Hartford, Five Miles, in Connecticut. Whoever will take up said deserter and bring him to his regiment, or confine him in Hartford goals and give notice thereof, shall have five dollars reward and all necessary charges paid,
by ABIJAH SAVAGE, Capt.
The Connecticut Courant, and Hartford Weekly Intelligencer, January 6, 1778.

MADE their escape from Leesburg, Virginia, the following people, viz. ISAAC JOHNSTON, about twenty years of age, about 5 feet ten inches high, smooth face, and dark hair. BENJAMIN KING, a well made man, about five feet eight inches high, pitted with the small-pox, and appeared to be a middle-aged man. JOHN PORTER, a stout fellow, near six feet high, and about twenty two years of age. All the above mentioned prisoners were born in the neighbourhood of Shrewsbury in the Jerseys, and were taken by General Sullivan on Staten-Island: each had on a green coat, a white waistcoat and breeches. Whoever brings them to me in Leesburg, or confines then in any gaol, shall receive what the law allows.

     S. THOMSON MASON,
      Commissary of Prisoners for Loudoun County.
The Pennsylvania Packet or the General Advertiser, January 14, 1778.

DESERTED the 14th inst. from his Majesty's Brigantine Dunmore, Lieut. John Wright, commander, Patrick Campbell, an able seaman, born in Glasgow, about 25 years of age, sandy hair, fresh complexion, slightly pitted with the small pox, and freckled; has a down look, and speaks broad Scotch, had on when he went away, a blue upper and under jacket, white shirt, long trowsers, and a round hat, with narrow gold binding. Whoever secures the above deserter in the Provost of this city, or gives such information as they he can be secured, shall receive Five Guineas reward, by applying to Mr. Gilchrist at No. 1015 in Water-street, near the bottom of Dover-street. All masters of vessels, and others, are hereby warned not to ship, or harbour the said Campbell, as in so doing they will incur the severest penalties.
 The Royal Gazette, January 17, 1778.

     TWENTY DOLLARS Reward.
            Jan. 12, 1778.
DESERTED, from a recruiting party of the Fourth Maryland regiment, now in Baltimore-Town, a certain NATHAN HALE, about 5 feet 9 inches high, thin and meagre, looks very sickly, and says he deserted from the British New Levies. Had on their uniform, a long green coat, lined with white flannel, with white buttons, and old leather breeches; he has a small wound on one of his shins, which he says he received at Brandywine. He had with him a pass from Gen. Woodford, giving him liberty to go to any of the States. It is suspected he is gone to Virginia, as he belonged to a Virginia regiment, before he was taken by the enemy.—Whoever takes up said deserter and delivers him to me in Baltimore, shall have the above reward, and reasonable charges.
    SAM. SMITH, Lieut. Col. 4th Maryland Reg.
 The Maryland Journal, and the Baltimore Advertiser, January 20, 1778.

RAN away on the 6th Inst. from, the BRITANIA, a Victualler, two Apprentices, one named NATHANIEL BOLTON, the other THOMAS YOURS.[*sic*]—Whoever shall apprehend both or either of then shall receive FIVE DOLLARS Reward from
    RALPH YOUNG, Master.

Newport, January 8, 1778,
All Masters of Vessels and others, hereby cautioned against harbouring or concealing said Boys.
The Newport Gazette, January 22, 1778.

DESERTED from *Leesburg* the first of last *October, Hugh M'Comick,* a continental soldier belonging to the 16th regiment of guards commanded by Col. *William Grayson,* the said soldier had a wife in *Buckingham* county. Whoever delivers the above deserter to the commanding officer at *Williamsburg* shall receive a reward of 30 dollars.   THOMAS H. DREW, Lieut.
The Virginia Gazette, Dixon and Hunter, January 23, 1778.

GEORGE ELLIOT, *Robert Gilles, William Lyons, William Francis,* jun. draughts for *York* County, failing to appear at the time appointed, I hereby offer a reward of twenty dollars for each of them, being delivered up to the commanding officer in *Williamsburg,*
AUGUSTINE TABB, Lieut. State Regt.
The Virginia Gazette, Dixon and Hunter, January 23, 1778.

DESERTED from the Adventure Victualler, JOHN MASON, Master, JOHN WILDE and PHILIP DOWYER, the former 5 Feet 10 Inches high, well set, and wears his own Hair—had on when he went away two waistcoats, one Red the other Brown, and Pair pf long Dufil Trowsers—the other, a thick short Man, swarthy complexion, wore a blue jacket, Dutch Cap, long Trowsers, and short Hair.—TEN DOLLARS will be given for apprehending the above Persons, so that they may be conveyed on Board the Adventure or to the Provost.
JOHN MASON.
Newport, January 21st, 1778
The Newport Gazette, January 29, 1778.

DEserted from my company, in Col. Johnson's regiment, belonging to the state of Connecticut, John Tew, 23 years of age, a transient person, 5 feet 9 inches high, of a light complexion, has brown hair, grey eyes, and a long nose; had on a brown great coat, a buff cap, leather breeches, and overalls.

David Eanos, a transient person, 5 feet 6 inches high, of a light complexion, has grey eyes; had on a ragged great coat, and leather breeches.

Also Ichabod Randall, 16 years of age, 5 feet 3 inches high, of a ruddy complexion, and has light eyes; had on a blue great coat, a close bodied coat faced with red, and leather breeches; he belongs to Voluntown, in Connecticut.

Whoever takes up said deserters, and returns them to said regiment in Providence, shall have Three Dollars reward for each, and necessary charges, paid by

MOSES BRANCH, Capt.

January 29, 1778.

The Providence Gazette; And Country Journal, January 31, 1778; February 7, 1778; February 14, 1778. See *The Connecticut Gazette; And The Universal Intelligencer*, February 20, 1778, for Eanos/Enos.

DESERTED from Capt. Joshua Truffin's Company, in Col. Henry Sherburne's Regiment, NATHAN MARTIN, about 40 Years of Age, 5 Feet 9 Inches high, dark Complexion. Whoever will take up said Deserter, and return him to his Regiment at Fish-Kill, or secure him in any Goal in the United States, shall have FIVE DOLLARS Reward, and all necessary Charges paid,

EPHRAIM CARY, Ensign.

December [3]0, 1777.

The Connecticut Gazette; And The Universal Intelligencer, February 13, 1778.

STOP THIEVES!

CAME to the house of the subscriber, on the 25th of January 1778, one JAMES HAMILTON, about 5 feet and an half high, well sett, black short curled hair, black eye brows, light blue eyes, can read and write well; had on when he went away, a white out-side jacket, with one button on each sleeve, at the wrist, a pair white breeches, much wore, a pair blue and white stockings, his left thumb (upper joint) put out, so that he can slip it in or out Likewise, one PATRICK BRIAN, about 6 feet high, a sprightly well limbed man, short strait brown hair, light blue eyes, speaks broad: had on when he went away, a green coat faced with red, and yellow buttons, a white coarse linen shirt, a pair white cloth breeches, almost new, a pair blue and white clouded stockings, a good felt hat, with a metal button thereon: Both these fellows were Irishmen, said to desert from the 22d regiment of Rhode-Island the 6th day of September last, and had passes from Governor Cook at Providence, to go into the country to get work; they tarried with me till Friday the 30th ult. (after dinner) then went off without paying for their board, and carried off one white Holland shirt and sundry other things, to the value of 22 or 23 dollars.—Whoever will take up said villains, and bring them to Norwich or New-London jail, so that justice may be done them, shall have SIX DOLLARS reward, and all necessary charges paid by me

    EBENEZER GROVER.

Norwich, February 2, 1778.
The Norwich Packet and the Connecticut, Massachusetts, New-Hampshire, and Rhode-Island Weekly Advertiser, February 16, 1778.

    Goshen (in Litchfield County) Jan. 31. 1778.

RANAWAY from said Goshen on the night after the 25th of January instant, two persons, both Irishman, one named *Peter Golden*, about 23 years old, light complexion, about 5 feet 8 inches high, short hair; had on and carried with him an old felt hat, grey coat, vest, and breeches, pair of grey woolen stockings, pair of white ditto, pair of white thread ditto, striped Holland shirt, black velvet stock, square copper shoe buckles. The other *John May*, he belonged to the 40th regiment is about 28 years old, and carried with him a felt hat, light brown surtout bound with white, grey coat lined with brown tammy, black home made vest & breeches, pair of black woolen stockings, two pair of blue and white ditto, on pair white thread ditto, two pair of shoes, pewter shoe buckles, silver knee buckles, striped Holland shirt, two white linnen shirts. It is supposed the said prisoners are endeavoring to escape to the enemy, as they had parted with most if not all their regimentals before they went off. Whoever will secure said prisoners and send them to Hartford to the care of Ezekiel Williams, Esq; commissary of prisoners, or to the subscriber at said Goshen, shall be well rewarded.

    EBEN'R MORTON.

The Connecticut Journal, February 18, 1778.

DESERTED from Capt. Sharaway's company, Col. Prentice's regiment, one William Hall, a soldier 5 feet 8 inches high, well set, long black hair and black eyes, had on a small round hat, an old short blue coat, leather breeches, & white shirt, he is an indian born but is scarce to be known from a white man. Whoever will take up said deserter and return him to his regiment or confine him & give due notice, so that he may be had, shall receive ten Dollars reward, with necessary charges

    paid by me Darius Peck, Ensign.

The Connecticut Gazette; And The Universal Intelligencer, February 20, 1778.

DESERTED on the 23d inst. David Enos, a transient person, 5 feet 6 inches high, light complexion, grey eyes, had on when he deserted, a ragged great coat, leather breeches, very ragged. Whoever takes up said deserted, and returns him to Col. Johnson's regiment, in Providence shall have three Dollars reward & all necessary charges paid by Moses Branch, Capt.
Providence, Jan. 19th 1778.
The Connecticut Gazette; And The Universal Intelligencer, February 20, 1778. March 6, 1778. See *The Providence Gazette; And Country Journal*, January 31, 1778, for Eanos/Enos.

DESERTED *from my company, in Col. Thomas Craft's regiment of artillery, in the service of the State of Massachusetts-Bay, James Grace, a native of Georgetown, in the County of York, 5 feet 8 inches high, 22 years of age, dark complexion, short dark hair, dark eyes, & carried with him when he went away, a regimental blue coat faced with red, blue waistcoat and breeches. Any person that will apprehend said deserter shall have* 20 *dollars reward, and all necessary charges paid by* JONATHAN EDES, *Capt. Artill'y.*
The Boston-Gazette, And Country Journal, March 2, 1778; March 9, 1778; March 16, 1778.

DESERTED from the second state regiment, the following soldiers, viz. *Benjamin Jacobs, George Brushwood, Thomas Moore, Christopher Carlton, William Allen, Arthur Watts, Robert Singleton, John Mash*, jun. *Robert Moore, George Moore, William Atkins, David Farinholtz, John Wheatly,* jun., *John Batts, Henry Wilmore, Albian Gordian, William Rainey, Benjamin Philips, James Mitchell, Majo O'Dear,* and *Thomas Bohannan.* For the first mentioned nineteen deserters twenty dollars will be given for each, and forty dollars each for the two last mentioned.
H. DUDLEY, Captain.
The Virginia Gazette, Purdie, March 6, 1778.

Forty DOLLARS Reward.
DESERTED from Col. *Harrison's* battalion of continental artillery, two soldiers, *viz. Peter Layland,* about thirty years old, five feet nine or ten inches high, has a down lock, and stoops much in the shoulders, with red brown hair; he obtained a furlough of Col. *Harrison,* last *July,* to go to *Northumberland* county for twenty days. *John Fisher,* about twenty four years of age, five feet seven or eight inches high, has light brown hair, and is of a fresh complexion; he obtained a furlough of Col. *Carrington* last *October,* for twenty five days, to go

to *Westmoreland* county. Both the above deserters carried away regimental clothes, blue coat faced with red, and white waistcoat and breeches. Whoever delivers the above deserters to the commanding officer in *York* or at *Williamsburg* shall have the above reward, or twenty dollars for each.
      JOHN DANDRIDGE, Capt. of artillery.
  The Virginia Gazette, Purdie, March 6, 1778.

                 Feb. 17, 1778.
      TEN DOLLARS REWARD.
TAKEN out of the house of the subscriber at the New-Mills near Mountholly, the 13th inst. at night, a SILVER WATCH, with a silver face, maker's name C. Rigdel, London. As a certain John Kelly, alias John Wheeler, who said he was a light horseman and had lately deserted from the British army, lodged at the subscriber's house that night, he is *suspected* of the theft: He is about five feet eight or nine inches high, and had on a blue great coat, light coloured ditto under it, green jacket, and linen trowsers. Whoever takes up the *real* thief so that he may be brought to justice, and secures the Watch for the owner, shall have for the Watch only SIX DOLLARS, and for the thief FOUR DOLLARS, with reasonable charges,
    paid by THOMAS PLATT.
  The New-Jersey Gazette, March 11, 1778.

Deserted from FORT TRUMBULL, in New-London, the 10th Instant, one JOHN DEXTER, a Soldier about 5 Feet 8 Inches high, thick built, light complexion, walks lame, wore a light colour'd Surtout, and a white Hat; he says he belongs to East Greenwich, in the State of Rhode-Island. Whoever will take up said Deserter and return him to me at said Fort shall have TEN DOLLARS Reward, and all necessary Charges
    paid by ADAM SNAPLEY, Capt.
               NEW-LONDON, March 11, 1778.
  The Connecticut Gazette; And The Universal Intelligencer, March 13, 1778; March 20, 1778; April 3, 1778.

      RUN from the NELLY
Victualler, ANDREW STALKER, Master, EDWARD CARPENTER, 5 Feet 5 Inches high, thin Visage, and marked with the Small Pox: Had on a blue Jacket and old Surtout Coat, flop'd Hat and short Hair.— JOHN VIAT, a Boy about 16 Years old, had on a blue Jacket, Dutch Cap, and short Hair.—A Reward of THREE DOLLARS will be given for discovering them, so as said Master may get them again.—All Masters of Ships are forbid harboring them as there will be strict search made them.
  The Newport Gazette, March 19, 1778.

Fish Kill, Feb. 5, 1778.
DEserted, on their March from Farmington to this Place, from my Detachment of Artillery, belonging to Col. John Crane's Battalion, as follows, viz. Serj. Thomas Rouse, of Capt. Perkin's Company, 26 Years of Age, 5 Feet 7 Inches high, long brown Hair, blue Eyes, dark Complexion, a double upper Lip, belonging to Long-Island, a Cordwainer by Trade, had on when he went away, a light green short outside Jacket, white Flannel under Jacket, a Pair of homespun light colour'd Breeches, a round Hatt, and a Pair of white Yarn Stockings. Corporal Benjamin Leach, of the same Company, 23 Years of Age, 5 Feet 10 Inches high, curl'd black Hair, blue Eyes, a Carpenter by Trade, belonging to New-England, had on when he went away, a white Surtout, short dark outside Jacket, white Flannel under Jacket, a Pair of white swanskin Overhauls, and a round Hatt.—Also, Jacob Evens, a Matross in Capt. Sargent's Company, 23 Years of Age, 5 Feet 10 Inches high, short black Hair, dark Eyes, dark Complexion, belonging to Swansey, in New-England, had on when he went away, a black regimental Coat, red under Jacket, dark woollen Overhauls, and a regimental Hatt. Whoever shall take up said Deserters and confine them in any Goal, or deliver them to any Officer of the Artillery in Boston, or Camp at Head Quarters, shall receive TWENTY DOLLARS Reward for each, by me
    JAMES HALL, Lieut. of Artillery,
The Connecticut Gazette; And The Universal Intelligencer, March 20, 1778; April 10, 1778.

RAN away last Tuesday morning, from the subscriber living in Front-street, between Arch and Race streets, an apprentice boy named JOSEPH CHASE; he is about fourteen years of age, stout made, and has the New England dialect, being born at Boston. He had on when he ran away, a blue coat and jacket, coarse short, and pepper and salt coloured beeches. He is a deserter from Washington's army, about which he is very fond of talking. Whoever brings him to his master, shall have SIXPENCE reward, and the sweepings of the shop board.
    HUGH M'CONNAL.   March
The Pennsylvania Evening Post, March 23, 1778.

    TWENTY DOLLARS REWARD,
FOR delivering to the commanding officer in *Williamsburg, James Wilson,* who having failed to joined the regiment agreeable to orders, is considered as a deserter. He is about 23 years old, 5 feet 8 inches high, has short black hair, and is remarkable for having lost the first joint of the little finger on the left hand.

GRANVILLE SMITH.
The Virginia Gazette, Purdie, March 27, 1778.

DESERTED from my company of state artillery, the following soldiers, *viz*. *Thomas Moody,* about twenty one years of age, of a brown complexion, and is from *Lunenburg*; had on when he went away a blue coat turned up with yellow, blue waistcoat, and brown cloth breeches. *Richard Asuleck,* about sixteen years of age, five feet six inches high, and is from *Halifax* ; had on when he went away a large blue coat, and brown waistcoat. Whoever apprehends the said deserters, and delivers them to the commanding officer at *Williamsburg,* or in *York,* where they deserted from, shall receive twenty dollars for each.
HENRY QUARLES, Capt. S. Artil.
The Virginia Gazette, Purdie, March 27, 1778.

DESERTED from Saratoga, the 4th of November 1777, from Capt. Abner Seeley's company, in Colonel Seth Warner's regiment; Experance Trescott, belonging to the Town of Hanover in the state of New-Hampshire, about 5 feet high, about 20 years of age light complexion, short hair, something slim: Whoever will take up said deserter, and convey him to the regiment, shall have six dollars reward, and reasonable charges paid by me.
JONATHAN PAYNE, Lieut.
The Connecticut Courant, and Hartford Weekly Intelligencer, April 7, 1778.

DEserted from the Continental service, in Col. Lee's regiment, Charles Wheaton, 5 feet 6 inches high, he is about 21 years of age, slim built, or a light complexion, has dark eyes, and long dark hair: Had on when he went away a blue coat, light coloured waistcoat and overalls, and a small round hat. Whoever will take up said deserter, and return him to the subscriber, or secure him in any gaol in the United States, shall receive Six Dollars reward, and all necessary charges, paid by JESSE SANDERS, Lieut.
Swansey, April 7, 1778.
The Providence Gazette; And Country Journal, April 11, 1778; April 18, 1778; April 25, 1778.

MADE his escape from Windsor, one Stuart Mason a British prisoner, he is about 23 years of age small of Stature, fair complexion, a large scar under his chin.—Whoever will bring said fellow to the Goal in Hartford shall have a handsome reward and necessary charges paid by

EZEK. WILLIAMS Com. Prisoners.

N. B. As sundry other of the prisoners particularly two of the Stages, taken last year on Long Island have also ran away; it is hoped that all friends of their country will keep a good look out for all such fellows travelling without a pass.

The Connecticut Courant, And The Weekly Intelligencer, April 14, 1778.

DESERTED, two Indians named James Yocake and Samuel Wampey, they inlisted with and deserted from a serjeant of Col. Charles Webb's regiment when on their march to join said regiment in Pennsylvania. Said Yocake is about 6 feet 2 inches high long favored bushy head of hair. Wampey is 5 feet 7 or 8 inches high well set, fair complexion, hd on an old blue coat, his under dress unknown. Said Yocake had on a dark brown coat and a lightish vest; they have been seen in some part of Granville since they deserted, and it is expected they will soon steer for Rhode-Island or Stockbridge and from there to the Northward. Whoever will take up said deserters and deliver them to the subscriber at Simsbury send them secured to the regiment or secure them in any Continental goal, shall receive 25 dollars reward for each, and charges paid, by JAMES ANDREWS, Lieut.

N. B. It is to be feared they have done some mischief they have the serjeants clothing with them.

The Connecticut Courant, and Hartford Weekly Intelligencer, April 21, 1778.

DESERTED from my Custody, on the 16th Day of April instant, one Samuel Taber, jun. a detached Soldier for the Continental Service, belonging to the Militia Company under my Command. Said Taber is of a middling Size, light Complexion, wears his own light brown Hair. Whoever will take up said Deserter and deliver him to Col. John Durkee in Norwich, or to any other Continental Officer who has Orders to take such detached Soldiers into the Service, shall be well rewarded, and all necessary Charges paid by JONATHAN CALKINGS, Capt.

New-London, April 21, 1778.

The Connecticut Gazette; And The Universal Intelligencer, April 24, 1778; May 1, 1778.

ONE HUNDRED DOLLARS, AND ALL REASONABLE EXPENCES PAID,

FOR apprehending and delivering at this garrison JOHN BATES, a soldier of the 6th *Virginia* continental regiment, who is under sentence

of a general court martial to be shot for desertion, and inducing others of his fellow soldiers to the like villainous practice. He made his escape on *Tuesday* night last from the public jail with fetters on his legs. The said *Bates* is about 25 years age, a likely fellow, rather call. He is well known to the southward for his many base practices, and will probably attempt to reach *Georgia,* where he has lived for several years. He has given a list of a number of horses and other articles he has, with his confederates, stolen, and of the persons from whom taken, and in what manner disposed of. Any Gentleman who have reason to suppose they have suffered by him, or his accomplices, may perhaps be informed, by applying to the subscriber, of his circumstances as may enable them to regain their property. And it is hoped, that as said *Bates* has been a notorious villain, the greatest exertions will be made for apprehending and securing of him, that justice may be done the public.
          DAVID MASON, Col. 15th regt.
          HEAD QUARTERS, *Williamsburg, April* 19, 1778.
The Virginia Gazette, Dixon and Hunter, April 24, 1778

THE subscriber informs the public, that his son, Benjamin Commins, a minor, is non compos mentis, and incapable of acting for himself; all recruiting officers are therefore notified not to inlist him, as he will not answer for the service in any respect. Said Benjamin has been already inlisted oftener than once, and have trifled away the bounty, the officer or the public has lost it, as he would not pass muster.
          JOSEPH COMMINS.   Coventry, April 21, 1777.
The Providence Gazette; And Country Journal, April 25, 1778; May 2, 1778.

RAN-AWAY from the subscriber, on Sunday the 26th inst. the following persons, viz.. .GEORGE SNYDER, a German, who was taken prisoner; he is about six feet high, and had on a red coat faced with blue. Whoever secures said persons, shall have Ten Dollars   for each. JOHN BARNEY, junr.
          Norwich, April 27, 1778.
The Norwich Packet, April 27, 1778. See *The Norwich Packet,* May 4, 1778.

INLISTED into Capt. Abel Holden's Company, Col. Nixon's Regiment, sometime about the third of March last, one Edward Adams about Thirty Years of age about five feet eight inches high light Complexion, sandy hair, a fine voice, something of a thin spair man, and is an old countryman, has made his home chiefly at Spencer, same

year he took a large hire for a man of said town, and after being paid, he set out for Sudbury or Watertown, and to return in a few days but has not yet joined his Company. Whoever will take up said Adams and return him to his company or confine him in any goal, and send word to his company, shall have Thirty Dollars, reward, and all reasonable charges
    paid by JOEL OREEN, Lieut.
              April 7th 1778.
The Massachusetts Spy: Or, American Oracle of Liberty, April 30, 1778; May 7, 1778. See *The Massachusetts Spy: Or, American Oracle of Liberty*, May 21, 1778.

SIXTY DOLLARS REWARD.

DESERTED from Capt. *De Laporte,* DeLaporte, Capt. the following soldiers, *viz. Patrick Cary,* an *Irishman,* about 5 feet high, has chestnut coloured hair, round face, blue eyes, flat nose, small mouth, has the mark of a sore upon his leg, and is about 25 years old; had on when he went away a brown coat and breeches, and dark jacket. *Henry Ingot,* surnamed *La Fuillade,* a *Frenchman* about 5 feet 3 inches high well made has dark hair, gray eyes, hawked nose, about 27 years old, and was lately enlisted at *Edenton. Prittraud,* surnamed *Coeur de Roy,* a *Frenchman,* about 4 feet 10 inches high, round face, chestnut coloured hair, gray eyes, and flat nose. Whoever delivers the said soldiers to the commanding officer in *Williamsburg,* or to the said Capt. *De Laporte,* shall receive the above reward, or twenty dollars for each.
    The Virginia Gazette, Purdie, May 1, 1778.

FORTY DOLLARS REWARD.

RAN-AWAY from Norwich Goal, on Sunday the 26th inst. the following persons, viz....GEORGE SNYDER, a German, who was taken prisoner, at the northward last year by Gen. Arnold's army, and has been on parole in this town for some months past; he is full six feet high, well set, about twenty-five years of age, light complexion, light coloured hair, talks bad English, and is pitted with the small-pox: Had on a red regimental coat faced with blue, the buttons on the same marked 2[ ], a brown jacket, leather breeches, and an old felt hat.—Went off at the same time, PATRICK KELLY....Whoever will take up any of the above persons, and return them to the subscriber, or confine them in any goal in this State, shall have FOUR POUNDS reward for each.
JOHN BARNEY, junr. Gaoler. Norwich, April 27, 1778.

The Norwich Packet, May 4, 1778. See *The Norwich Packet*, April 27, 1778.

STOLEN out of the stable of Philemon Sanford of Goshen, in Litchfield County, the night after the 20th of April instant, a MARE, 13 hands and a half high, ten years old, of a bay colour, large black mane, lying the right side, with a black tail, good carriage, a good pace and trot, shoe before toe cork'd, a white spot under the saddle; she has a remarkable bunch of a considerable bigness on the inside of each hind foot near the huff.—Also at the same time stolen from Jonathan Wadhams of said Goshen, a good hunting saddle, with a cloth housen of a lightish colour, green fringe. The thief is supposed to be a transient fellow who came to Goshen about six months age, calling his name David Foreman, about 21 years old, well set, pretty fleshy, rather taller than middling, short straight light brown hair, has of late usually worn white jacket and breeches, a blue coat faced with white in the regimental mode, he being a soldier that lately received 100 l. for inlisting into the Continental army, as also white blanket surtout.—Whoever will secure and return said Mare shall have Five Dollars Reward, and Two Dollars for said Saddle, with all necessary charges, and also Ten Dollars Reward with necessary charges for securing said Thief, in any of the public goals, so that he may be brought to justice, paid by
   JONATHAN WADHAM, PHILEMON SANFORD.
          Goshen, April 21, 1778.
WHEREAS the above named David Foreman is retained to me as an inlisted soldier in the Continental army, and hath neglected to obey my orders for marching to join said army—I apprehend him to have deserted said service. Whoever therefore will apprehend said Deserter, and return him to me in Litchfield in Connecticut, or secure him in any Continental goal, and notify me, shall have Ten Dollars Reward, and reasonable charges paid by,
   BAZELEL BEEBE, Recruiting officer of the
   6th brigade of the Continental Military.
         Litchfield, April 21, 1778.
The Connecticut Journal, May 6, 1778; May 13, 1778; *The Connecticut Courant, And The Weekly Intelligencer*, May 26, 1778. Minor differences between the papers. The *Courant* spells the deserters last name as Furnam in one place, and Farnam in another, and Beebe's first name appears as Bezaleel in the *Courant*.

DESERTED from my quota of *Virginia* artillery, *James Brown,* an *Irishman,* about five feet ten inches high, twenty three years of age, a little marked with the smallpox, and I understand has been seen at *Newbern* in *N. Carolina.* I will give fifty [dollars to the person] who will deliver him to me at Fort Ste[phen   ] officer.
[   ]ley, Capt. *Virg.* Art.
The Virginia Gazette, Purdie, May 8, 1778.

MATTHEW LIGHTFOOT ANDERSON, *Thomas Bowler, George Hiatt,* and *Thomas Grunsell,* belonging to the *Virginia* artillery, stationed at Fort *Stephen,* whose furloughs are expired, are desired to join their company immediately, or they will be deemed deserters, and treated accordingly.
NIC. GEO: MOEBALLE, Capt. *Virg.* Art.
The Virginia Gazette, Purdie, May 8, 1778.

FIFTEEN DOLLARS REWARD.
DESERTED [   ] ship *Tarter, Thomas Shore,* a [   ] twenty years of age, about five feet ten [   ] *Richmond* county, but probably is lurking [   ] in *Lancaster.* Whoever will deliver him on [   ] shall have the above reward.
RICHARD TAYLOR, Capt.
The Virginia Gazette, Purdie, May 8, 1778.

APRIL 22, 1778.
THE following soldiers, belonging to Col. *Charles Harrison's* regiment of artillery, are ordered immediately to *York* garrison, to join with the party from *Celey's,* in order to march for the grand camp. I shall certainly march by the 14th instant; and if they should not get to *York* by that time, they must repair immediately to *Fredericksburg,* or If I should be gone from thence, proceed on till they join me. *Thomas Kemp* of *Gloucester, Thomas Hulm, William Brown, William Haynes, Richard Sherwood, George Wilson, John Brown,* of *Dinwiddie,* and all others who have not joined the regiment, those who fail meeting at the appointed place, without shewing me just cause for so doing, may expect to be treated as deserters.
By order of the Colonel.
WHITEHEAD COLEMAN, Capt. Lieut. Art.
The Virginia Gazette, Purdie, May 8, 1778.

At a General Court Martial held in this Town, last Friday, Thomas Harrison, of Col. Tupper's Regiment, being convicted of Desertion, was sentenced to be shot on the 21st Instant. The above

Harrison is the notorious Villain well known in this State, by the Names of Williams, Johnson, Steel, &c. &c.

The Independent Chronicle and the Universal Advertiser, May 14, 1778. See *The Continental Journal, And Weekly Advertiser*, May 21, 1778, and *The Connecticut Gazette; And The Universal Intelligencer*, July 17, 1778.

HEAD QUARTERS Boston, May 20, 1778.

ESCAPED last night from the Main-Guard, THOMAS HARRISON, alias STEEL, alias WILLIAMS, alias many other names, under sentence of death—He is a man of midling stature; had both his ears crop't, black hair, which hangs pin'd over them, and turns back on his forehead, on which is a scar where he was formerly branded, black eyes, light complexion, something pock-broken, and about thirty years of age. It is supposed that he is secreted somewhere in town.

Whoever will apprehend said HARRISON, &c. and return him to the Main-Guard, shall have the thanks of the General, and ONE HUNDRED DOLLARS Reward.

By order of Major General Heath,
DANIEL LYMAN, A. D. C.

☞ *The several Printers of the Public Papers are desired to Insert the above.*

The Continental Journal, And Weekly Advertiser, May 21, 1778; *The Independent Chronicle and the Universal Advertiser*, May 21, 1778. See *The Independent Chronicle and the Universal Advertiser*, May 14, 1778, and *The Connecticut Gazette; And The Universal Intelligencer*, July 17, 1778.

INLISTED into Capt. Abel Holden's Company, Col. Nixon's Regiment, some time about the third of March last, one Edward Adams about Thirty years of Age about five feet eight inches high light Complexion, sandy hair, a fine voice, something of a thin specimen, and is an old countryman, has made his home chiefly at Spencer, same year he took a large hire for a man for said town, and after being paid, he set out for Sudbury or Watertown, and to return in a few days but has not yet joined his Company. Whoever will take up said Adams and return him to his company or confine him in any goal and send word to his Company, shall have Thirty Dollars reward, and all reasonable charges

paid by   ABEL HOLDEN, Capt.

The Massachusetts Spy: Or, American Oracle of Liberty, May 21, 1778. See *The Massachusetts Spy: Or, American Oracle of Liberty*, April 30, 1778.

PROVIDENCE, May 8th, 1778.
LAST Night made his Escape from the Provost Guard, in Town, MICHAEL MANLEY, a Deserter from Col. Alden's Regiment of the Massachusetts-State, he lately belonged to Gen. Burgoyne's Army, had on when he made his Escape, a light colour'd Grey Coat, very ragged, is about 5 Feet 10 Inches high, has short black curl'd Hair, light Complexion, black Eyes, and is mark'd with the Small-Pox: 'Tis supposed he'll attempt to join the Enemy on some Part of the Continent. Any Person that will return said Deserter to Providence, shall have THIRTY DOLLARS Reward, and all necessary Charges paid, by applying to Col. PECK, Adjutant-General of the Army in the State of Rhode-Island.

The Connecticut Gazette; And The Universal Intelligencer, May 22, 1778; May 29, 1778; *The Providence Gazette; And Country Journal*, May 23, 1778; *The Connecticut Courant, and the Weekly Intelligencer*, May 26, 1778. Minor differences between the papers.

RUN away from Simsbury on the 6th instant, a British soldier, named John Bates, belonging to the 24th regiment, about 5 feet 6 inches high, thick-set well-shaped, had a large scar on his left cheek, wore and took with him a felt hat, brown coat red waistcoat with regimental Buttons, leather breeches, white stockings, two checkt linnen shirts. Whoever will secure said run away in any prison and give information or bring him to Hartford, shall have 5 dollars reward and all necessary charges paid, by   Ez'l. Williams, Dep. Com. Pris.

May 15, 1778.

The Connecticut Courant, And The Weekly Intelligencer, May 26, 1778.

DESERTED from Capt. Judd's company, Col. Wylly's regiment, one DANIEL CAHER or CASOR, born in Glasgow in the Kingdom of Scotland, 5 feet 6 inches high 39 years of age, black curl'd hair, had on a brownish long skirted coat, he says he has lived some years in Glasgow in the state of the Massachusetts Bay, and some time in the state of New Hampshire; said CAHER is very soft and easy in his conversation and inclines to loquaciousness. Any person that will take up said fellow and secure him in any goal or send him to his regiment at West or North-River, shall receive 10 dollars reward and all necessary charges paid by

Wm. JUDD, Capt.   April 30.

The Connecticut Courant, And The Weekly Intelligencer, May 26, 1778.

RUN away from the *Diligence* galley, *Richard Tolley,* a *Scotchman,* about five feet high, much pock marked, and has very light hair. Had on when he went away a white cloth jacket, and a white fulled cap. He pretends to be a seaman, and is very talkative. Whoever apprehends the said *deserter,* and secures him so that he may be again taken into the naval service of this state, shall have ten dollars reward.
          JOHANNES WATSON.
The Virginia Gazette, Purdie, May 29, 1778; June 12, 1778.

DESERTED from my Company, in Col. Crary's Regiment, in the Service of the State of Rhode-Island, John Rynes, born in Ireland, about 5 Feet 11 Inches and an Half high, has light Eyes, sandy Hair, somewhat freckled, and pitted with the Small-Pox, drinks freely, and is very saucy when disguised with Liquor. Whoever will take up said Deserter, and return him to his Regiment, or commit him to any Gaol in the United States, shall have Fifteen Dollars Reward, and all reasonable Charges, paid by me,
       ABRAHAM TOURTELOT, Capt.
                                      Gloucester, April 23, 1778.
The Providence Gazette; And Country Journal, May 30, 1778; June 6, 1778.

               DESERTED from my company,
in Col. Stearns's regiment of guards, a soldier named John Holbrook, about twenty years of age, of a dark complexion, whoever will take said Holbrook, and return him to my company, shall be handsomely rewarded for their trouble,
          by THOMAS WHIPPLE, *Capt.*
                                             Rutland, May 27.
The Massachusetts Spy: Or, American Oracle of Liberty, June 4, 1778.

RUN away the 26th of May, inst. one John Tom an Irishman belonging to the 21st British regiment, taken at the Northward in September last by trade a Blacksmith, had on when he went away a short blanket coat, striped vest, tow cloth trowsers, about 5 feet 6 inches high, light complexion, 21 years of age fore teeth rotten. Whoever will take up said runaway, and secure him in any goal or return him to the subscriber, shall have 5 dollars reward and all

necessary charges paid,
> by Ez'l WILLIAMS Dep. Commiss. Prisoners.
> Hartford, June 2, 1778.

The Connecticut Courant, and the Weekly Intelligencer, June 9, 1778.

WILLIAM ROTHAM, Mathew Griffen, Edward Thomson jun. Reuben Phelps, Ephras Saunders, Joshua Holcom jun. Silas Phelps, Ichabod Strickland, Abner Griffen, Jonathan Adams jun. Jesse Negus, David Phelps and Joshua [   ]in, of the Town of Simsbury. Samuel Way, and Elihu Barber of Harwinton. Merrit Blakely and Nathan Gillet, of Salisbury. Jeremiah House, Lemuel Deming, and Abraham Baley of Canaan. Tho's Wilcox Richard Bristal Aaron Baldwin, and Abraham Hand of Cornwall. Dudley Roberts, Jabez Whitmore, Preserved Marshall, Joel [ ]arks, Amos Hinman, Timothy Lee and James Lowree of Farmington, have been returned to me legally detached for the Continental army, until the [ ]t day of January next, and have been properly warned to join the army, and have refused to obey said warning and have absented. Therefore any person who will take up and deliver any of the above persons to me at Litchfield, shall be intitled to 5 dollars reward, for each, and necessary charges paid,
> by me BEZALEEL BEEBE.
> Recruiting Officer for the 6th brigade
> Litchfield, May 28, 1778.

The Connecticut Courant, and the Weekly Intelligencer, June 9, 1778. See *The Connecticut Courant, and Hartford Weekly Intelligencer*, June 30, 1778, for Adams.

> NINETY-FIVE DOLLARS Reward.

JUST come to hand, a large assortment of draughted mens names, to fight their friends, the ministerial army, which will in a few days be exposed to the public at the printing office; among others the following are a sample, viz. John Hunt, jun. Matthew Royce, Jonathan Blackley, David Blackley, Robert Hurtbut, Gideon Hurlbut, jun. and John Whited Gold, all of Woodbury, and belonging to Capt. Adam Hurlbut's company.— Noah Starkey & Samuel Still, draughted men from Col. Worthington's regiment, Say-Brook, had a furlough for four days to visit their families, and since have forgot to return: As the above mentioned men have eloped, any person who will bring them back to their duty, that they may receive present pay and provision, shall be intitled to Ten Dollars reward for each, and all necessary charges.—Also Stephen Scribner, who was draughted from Capt. Lockwood's company, Norwalk, and since inlisted has unadvisedly gone off with himself, Five Dollars reward for him, and necessary charges. ELI LEAVENWORTH, Capt.

New-Haven, June 8, 1778.

The Connecticut Journal, June 10, 1778, July 1, 1778.

DESERTED from my command in Col. Peabody's Regt. from New-Hampshire to Rhode-Island, one Jotham Sayer of Hawke in the State of New-Hampshire, who left the main guard at Providence on the night of the 17th of this instant, said deserter to about 5 feet, 9 inches high, slim bodied, with large legs and thighs, wears his own hair, which is light coloured, had on a light coloured coat, with red faceings, and is of a light complexion. Whoever shall take up said deserter, & convey him to me the subscriber at Providence, or confine him in any goal so that he may be returned, shall have 20 Dollars reward, and all necessary charges paid

by me, EZEKIEL GILE, Capt.

Providence, May 20th, 1778

The New-Hampshire Gazette, Or, State Journal, and General Advertiser, June 16, 1778. See *The Norwich Packet and the Connecticut, Massachusetts, New-Hampshire, and Rhode Island Weekly Advertiser*, June 22, 1778, for Sayer/Sawyer.

DESERTED,

FROM the Jenny transport, John Ready, a Frenchman, he is about 21 years of age, 5 feet 4 ½ inches high, dark complexion, and black hair, which he wore tied in a blue and white handkerchief, had on when he went away, a black coarse hat, a white coloured coat bound; also taffeta at the pockets, a white waistcoat on which is several spots of tar, a pair of old long trowsers, much wider than commonly wore, and a pair of new pumps, with a pair of buckles not fellows. Whoever will secure the said deserter, and give notice to William Hamilton, on board, laying near Bedlow's Island, shall receive eight dollars reward.

The Royal Gazette, June 17, 1778; June 20, 1778.

PROVIDENCE, MAY 30.

On Thursday last John Fretter, for inlisting three several times into the service of the United States, taking as many bounties, and finally attempting to desert to the enemy, while under sentence to be punished, was executed here, pursuant to the judgment of a Court-Martial. Jotham Sawyer, a centinel, who had the charge of said Fretter when he deserted, and went off with him, was whipped one hundred lashes.

The Norwich Packet, June 22, 1778; *The Providence Gazette; and Country Journal,* May 30, 1778. See *The New-Hampshire Gazette,* June 16, 1778, for Sayer/Sawyer.

OLIVER BARNS of Litchfield and Azariah Bradley of Winchester have been returned to me as legally detached for the Continental army, and after proper warning have refused to join said army. Therefore, any one who will take up said persons and deliver them to me at Litchfield shall be entitled to a reward of five dollars each, and necessary charges paid,
     by BEZALEEL BEEBE, Recruiting Officer
      for the 6th Brigade.
The Connecticut Courant, and Hartford Weekly Intelligencer, June 23, 1778; June 30, 1778.

THIS may notify whom it may concern that Jonathan Addams jun. who was advertised in the Connecticut Courant, as being returned to Major Bebee recruiting officer for the 6th brigade, as one that was legally detached for the continental army, until the first of January next, and properly warned, and had refused to march, and absented himself: he the said Addams never was legally detached for said service, nor properly warned for long before, and at the time of detaching for said service, the said Addams was removed from this state to the State of Vermont, and hath never returned since, therefore it would be injurious to treat him as one that was detached. Certified by us.
    JONATHAN ADDAMS, EZEKIEL ROBARTS
    THOMAS ADAMS Jun. JOSIAH CASE the second
            Simsbury, June 23, 1778.
The Connecticut Courant, and Hartford Weekly Intelligencer, June 30, 1778; July 7, 1778. See *The Connecticut Courant, and the Weekly Intelligencer,* June 9, 1778.

JOHN SWANEY, of Lyme, having entered for a Cruise in the Ship Warren, and has neglected to repair on Board. Whoever will take up the said Swaney, and deliver him on Board the said Ship in Boston Harbour, shall have TWENTY DOLLARS Reward,
    paid by JOSHUA HEMPSTED, jun.
            Boston, July 1, 1778.
The Connecticut Gazette; And The Universal Intelligencer, July 10, 1778.

DESERTED from the *Safeguard* galley, *Dominick Vential,* a native of *Minorca,* talks *English* pretty well, and is about five feet one or two inches high. It is supposed he is gone to *Smith Quay,* therefore all masters of vessels are forewarned from carrying him away, or employing him. Whoever secures him, so that I get him again, shall have thirty dollars reward.
    GEORGE ELLIOTT, Captain.
The Virginia Gazette, Purdie, July 10, 1778.

DESERTED from the schooner *Sally,* now lying at *Burwell* 's ferry, ISRAEL AUSTIN, a sailor, about 5 feet 10 inches high, with a thin visage, much freckled, and has red hair. I have reason to believe he has made towards *Richmond,* where, I am told, he intends to be married. I will give fifty dollars reward to any person that will deliver the said deserter to Capt. on board the said schooner, or to the subscriber at *Suffolk,* who intends to sail in the aforesaid schooner.
    G. ANDERSON.
The Virginia Gazette, Dixon and Hunter, July 10, 1778.

THOMAS TAYLOR, *Thomas Harvey, William Davis, Matthew Harvey, James Cradock, Peter Green Raines, Stripling Lester, James Tucker,* and *John Mitchell,* enlisted by Capt. *Ancram* for the state artillery, and by orders from the Governor were turned over to my company, are ordered to join immediately in *York* garrison, otherwise they will be deemed deserters, and treated accordingly.
    CHARLES de KLAUMAN, Capt. S. Artillery.
The Virginia Gazette, Dixon and Hunter, July 10, 1778.

WHereas Charles Woodruff, of Litchfield, Brewen Baldwin of Goshen, Nathaniel Canfield, Reuben Hicok, Joseph Martin, Ebenezer Green, Timothy Goodrich, of Woodbury. Eseck Allen, Fithan Case, Daniel Wilcox, Roswel Skinner, of Simsbury, Uriah Seymour, Seth Steal, [sic] John Spencer, New Hartford, Thomas Jones, of Berkhemsted, Samuel Clark, of Canaan. Levi Hart, James Root, Thompson, of Farmington, being legally detach'd and properly ordered to join my Company in the Army under General GATES, and refused to join: Whoever shall take all or either of the above named Persons, and bring them to me at the White Plains, or secure them in any public Goal, and certify me, shall receive Twenty Dollars for each, and all necessary Charges
    paid by *James Judson,* Lieut. in
    Maj. Skinner's Reg. Militia L. H.

The Connecticut Journal, July 15, 1778; July 22, 1778; July 29, 1778. See *The Connecticut Courant, and Hartford Weekly Intelligencer*, July 21, 1778. See *The Connecticut Journal*, July 29, 1778, for Levi Hart.

WHEREAS Phero Towley, Nathan Phelps, Clark Baldwin, of Newtown, and Augustus Pulling, John Sherwood, of Ridgefield, and Nehemiah Banks, William Buckley, Amos Sherwood, of Fairfield, Joseph Smith, of Norwalk, and Bowers How, of Middlesex, and William Stone of Reading, has been lawfully detached, and have neglected their Duty in joining their Company, and marching according to orders: any Person that will take up the before mentioned Persons, and bring them to their Company or Regiment, or confine them in any Goal, and give Notice to the Commanding Officer of the Company now at White-Plains, shall receive Twenty Dollars Reward an all necessary Charges by me Capt.
Ezekiel Hull, of Maj. Skinner's Regiment.
The Connecticut Journal, July 15, 1778; July 22, 1778; July 29, 1778.

THIRTY DOLLARS REWARD.
DESERTED from Capt. Whitney's company, in Col. M'Clellan's regiment, three soldiers, by the names of AARON FISH, JOHN NORMAN, and ABNER GREER: said Fish belong'd to Groton, 21 years of age, something small, well built, light complexion, light hair and blue eyes, is a taylor by trade, and is something crippled in his hands by a burn: said Norman and Geer belong'd to Preston, Norman is about 17 years of age, small of stature, dark complexion, and black eyes; Geer is about 16 years of age, small of stature, light complexion, light hair and light eyes. Whoever will take up said deserters and return them back to their company at New-London, shall be intituled to the above reward, or ten Dollars for each, and all reasonable charges paid: WILLIAM WHITNEY, Capt.
New-London, July 9, 1778.
The Connecticut Gazette and the Universal Intelligencer, July 17, 1778; July 24, 1778.

BOSTON, July 9.
As the Public are desirous of knowing whether *Steel*, alias *Williams*, alias *Harrison*, &c. &c. who was Shot for Desertion on the Common on Tuesday last, made any Discoveries relative to his Life, or Family, from which he descended, we have procured the following Circumstances from a Gentleman who attended him to the Place of

Execution, viz.—That he appeared more anxious about his future State, as he walked from the Prison to the Common, then he had done at any Time before—often crying out "Lord Jesus have Mercy on me." And lamented that he was born to "follow his Coffin to his Grave," He denied repeatedly that he had ever been guilty of Murder; but confessed that his Life had been notoriously wicked. The Particulars of which he chose not to mention, because he did not think that such Relation would be any real benefit to the World. At the same Time he voluntarily confessed, that he had been guilty of Crimes for which he deserted to die. When asked, whether he was will to tell what his *real* Name was, he answered, That he wished that his Friends might never know the shocking End to which he came; and therefore chose to secret his Name, in Order to prevent that distress which they would feel upon being informed that he died a shameful Death. This Answer had much Weight in it, the Request was not repeated, But the Prisoner declared, that R. I. were the initial Letters of his real Name: Which two Letters were put upon his Coffin at his desire. He said, that he had but little Fear on his Mind about Death; but that he was shocked at the Prospect before him "I am going, said he, either to eternal Happiness, or to eternal Misery." His last Words were, "Lord Jesus have Mercy on me."

The Connecticut Gazette; And The Universal Intelligencer, July 17, 1778. See *The Independent Chronicle and the Universal Advertiser*, May 14, 1778, and *The Continental Journal, And Weekly Advertiser*, May 21, 1778.

WHereas Charles Woodruff, of Litchfield, B[re]wen Baldwin of Goshen, Nathaniel Canfield, Reuben Hicock, Joseph Martin, Ebenezer Green, Timothy Goodrich, of Woodbury, Eseck Allen, Fithan Case, Daniel Wilcox, Roswel Skinner of Simsbury, Uriah Seymour, Seth Steel, John Spencer, of New Hartford, Thomas Jones, of Farmington, being legally detached and properly ordered to join my Company in the Army under General GATES and refused to join: Whoever shall take all or either of the above named Persons, and bring them to me at the White Plains, or secure them in any public Goal, and certify me shall receive Twenty Dollars Reward for each, and all necessary Charges paid by JAMES JUDSON,
Lieut. in Major Skinner's Regt. Militia L. H.

The Connecticut Courant, and Hartford Weekly Intelligencer, July 21, 1778; July 28, 1778. See *The Connecticut Journal*, July 15, 1778.

DESERTED from the Ship WARREN at Boston, ELNATHAN MASON, belongs either to Stonington or Groton. Whoever will return him to the said Ship, or on Board any Continental Vessel, shall have TWENTY DOLLARS Reward, and necessary Charges paid.
JOSHUA HEMPSTED, JUN.
Boston, July 1, 1778.
The Connecticut Gazette; And The Universal Intelligencer, July 24, 1778; July 31, 1778.

TWENTY GUINEAS Reward.
WHEREAS WILLIAM WILLMAN, has absconded from this city, on account of defrauding some Merchants, by a forged indorsation of bills: Whoever will apprehend the said William Willman, so as he may be brought to justice, shall receive the above reward, by applying to Messrs. Samuel and Levy, No. 356, Hanover-Square, or at Mr. George Graham's, No. 209, Queen-Street. Said Willman has passed for a considerable time as a cornet of the 17th light dragoons, about five feet five or six inches high, stout made, and dark complexion. He had with him when he went away, and wears frequently a green coat, the uniform of the above regiment; at other times, a scarlet coat of the same uniform, nankeen jacket and trowsers, and slouch'd hat, with a black feather.—He left this city on Saturday the 18th instant, and is reported to have left Red-Hook, on Long-Island, the Monday following. He is supposed to pass at present under the name of Lieut. Greaves.

☞It is expected he will attempt to make his escape to the rebels, from the East end of Long-Island, or other convenient place there.
The Royal Gazette, July 25, 1778; July 29, 1778; August 1, 1778; August 5, 1778; August 8, 1778; August 12, 1778; August 15, 1778; *The New-York Gazette; and the Weekly Mercury*, July 27, 1778. Minor differences between the papers.

WHEREAS I stand advertised in the Connecticut Journal of New-Haven, July 15th, by James Judson, Lieut. in Major Skinner's regiment of militia L. H. for refusing to join said company in the army under General Gates.

I take this method to inform the public, that the above scandalous aspersion is without foundation, for I here publicly declare, that I never did directly or indirectly refuse joining the above company, nor did I ever think I had a right to join them; as by a Resolve of Congress, any two persons providing an able bodied man, for the Continental army, during the war, were excused from the present duty of that company; that Resolve being complied with by Simeon Smith

and myself, as appears by the annex'd certificate, I think myself highly injured, and particularly so, as I am a true friend to liberty, and my country, and have always been ready and willing to turn out in defence of them, with my fellow countrymen, according to the laws of the United States. As I am a young man who values my character more than life, hope the public will judge the matter impartially.
Farmington, the 6th of March, 1778.
SAMUEL Hotchkiss, of Farmington, in the county of Hartford, this day inlisted himself in the army of the United States of American, to serve during the present war in my company, Col. Wyllys's regiment; and that Simeon Smith and Levi Hart, both of said Farmington, hired and procured the said Hotchkiss to inlist as aforesaid.
Certified per Wm. JUDD, Capt.
The Connecticut Journal, July 29, 1778. See *The Connecticut Journal*, July 15, 1778.

DESERTERS.

DESERTED from his Majesty's ship LIZARD,
 ISAAC COOPER, 5 feet 7 inches high, of a brown complection short dark brown hair.
 PHILIP BECKETT, 5 feet 8 inches high, of a fair complection, much freckled, short black hair.
 SAMUEL SMITH, 5 feet 6 inches high, of a dark complection, strait black hair.
 The above Deserters it is imagined are lurking about New-York.
 A reward of FORTY SHILLINGS STERLING, will be given to any person apprehending and securing any one of the before-mentioned deserters, by applying to Mr. RIVINGTON, who is directed to pay ONE GUINEA for each, brought to his house, besides the above allotted sum of Forty Shillings for apprehending Deserters.
 The Royal Gazette, August 8, 1778; August 12, 1778; August 15, 1778.

STOLEN,

The property of an officer of the 4th regiment,
A complete new Uniform, with silver engraved buttons, silver epaulets, three paid silver shoe-buckels, a plain gilt doulde rased watch, a great quanitity of shirts and wearing apparel, the shirts marked F. D. by a Frenchman native of Bayonne, six feet high, pale complexion, very thin sickly face, light hair, about thirty years of age, had on a scarlet jacket, round hat, trowsers and half boots, called himself LE JEUNESSE, but his real name is Barnard du Verdier, is

supposed to be hid in town. He was seen lately enquiring for a boat to carry him to Jersey.

Whoever can give intelligence so as the offender may be brought to justice shall receive five guineas reward, by applying to the paymaster of the 4th regiment; or where any of the above articles may have been sold, shall be rewarded in proportion.

N. B. He came from Philadelphia with the army, and says his master is dead.

The Royal Gazette, August 8, 1778.

SIXTY DOLLARS Reward.

DESERTED July 31st, 1778, from Capt. James Duncan's company, Colonel Moses Hazen's Regiment, the following persons, viz. *John Fitzgerald*, an Irishman, about five Feet five Inches high, fair Complexion, grey Eyes, short brown Hair, about 21 Years of Age; he is supposed to be near Danbury, Connecticut.—Also *Jesse Lewis*, born in Rhode-Island, about five Feet six Inches high, dark Complexion, short black Hair, black Eyes, about 28 Years of Age, a well set likely fellow; it is thought he has made for New Lebanon where his parents are supposed to live. Whoever apprehends said deserters and brings them to their Regiment, shall have the above Reward, or thirty dollars for either of them, and reasonable Charges paid,

by me,   PALMER CADY, Lieut.

White Plains, August 5th, 1778.

The Connecticut Journal, August 12, 1778; August 29, 1778, *The Connecticut Courant, And The Weekly Intelligencer*, August 25, 1778; September 1, 1778.

Five Dollars REWARD.
DESERTED

FROM the William transport, George Stupart, Master, a boy between thirteen and fourteen years of age, named ISAAC TAPPAN; had on when he went away, a red flannel jacket spotted black, canvas trowsers and a Dutch cap. Short hair and a good deal marked with the small pox. All masters of vessels are particularly requested not to ship said boy, he being an apprentice: Any person who will take up said boy and deliver him to Captain John M'Lean, of the Lord Howe, privateer, shall receive the above reward.

The Royal Gazette, August 12, 1778.

DESERTED,
From his Majesty's Ship GALATEA,

LOUIS PINARD, five feet seven inches high, stout made, black hair, sallow complexion, and has a cast in one of his eyes. He commonly wears a red and white striped linen jacket and trowsers, and a narrow gold laced hat. Whoever apprehends the said Deserter, and secures him so that he may returned to his Ship, shall receive the reward offered by act of parliament.
The Royal Gazette, August 12, 1778; August 15, 1778.

CHARLES-TOWN.

Eloped from me in the night of the 11th of April last, my wife Angelica Elizabeth Baour, with one Peter Bourdajau, of Hillsborough township, a deserter from the service of this state; they took with them a horse and other effects (my property) to the value of 7 or 800 pounds. This is to forwarn all persons from trusting my said wife or any other person in my name, as I shall pay no debt contracted without my written order. I offer two hundred pounds reward so any person who will secure the said Bourdajau in any goal, so that he may be brought to justice, exclusive of the public reward for apprehending deserters. He is about 5 feet 5 or 6 inches high, thin faced, has a long nose, black curled hair, brown complexion, is slim made, and speaks both French and English; my wife is a short thick made woman, brown complexion, red faced, marked with the small-pox, and has black hair she speaks good English, and a great deal of French when she pleases, and is very bold.
JOHN EYMERIE.

Hillsborough Township, July 5.
The Gazette of the State of South-Carolina, August 12, 1778.

WHEREAS *Abraham Bulkley*, a soldier in my company of militia, being legally detached, & properly ordered, to join a company under the command of Captain Eliphalet Thorp, in Colonel Mosely's regiment militia at White Plains, in the army under General Gates; and said Bulkley having absconded, and neglected to join the aforesaid company and regiment: Notice is hereby given, that whoever will take said deserter, and carry him to his company now at Horse-Neck, or secure him in any public goal, and notify me shall receive Twenty Dollars, & other necessary charges from me,
STEPHEN WAKEMAN,

Fairfield, August 5, 1778.
The Connecticut Journal, August 19, 1778; August 26, 1778.

THIRTY DOLLARS REWARD.
THE house of the subscriber, living in Amwell township Hunterdon county, was robbed on the night of the 15th instant, (August) of a silver watch, with a China face, number 421, maker's name forgot, and number 44 on the outside case; pale blue broadcloth coat, lapell'd jacket and breeches; a shirt and pair of blue woollen stockings, with white tops. The above things were stolen by an Irishman named John Ramson, (a soldier who was left sick after the army cross'd the Delaware) about 5 feet 9 or 10 inches high, very much hump back'd and appeared to be about 25 years of age.—The above reward will be given to any person that secures the thief and the articles, and reasonable charges, by
     CASPER BEAR, near Ringo's tavern.
                August 17, 1778.
 The New Jersey Gazette, August 19, 1778.

DESERTED from the continental service, Nathan Duning of Reding, about 5 feet 9 inches high, light complexion, light eyes, light long hair, had on a red coat, silver knee and shoe buckles; he [lef]t to join his regiment at West Point last May, but supposed to steer for Susquehannah. Whoever will take up said fellow and return him to Col. Samuel Webb's regiment, or confine him in any goal, and give information to me, shall have ten dollars reward and necessary charges paid, by JOSEPH GILBERT, Serjt.
                Aug. 15, 1778.
 The Connecticut Courant, and Hartford Weekly Intelligencer, August 25, 1778.

           Hebron, August 15, 1778.
THESE may certify that Ebenezer Haughton, jun. who hath been detached and returned to me the subscriber to serve in the Continental army, hath produced a certificate signed by Samuel Wadsworth, a recruiting officer in Col. Samuel B. Webb's regiment, dated the 23d day of May, that he the said Haughton had hired an able bodied man to serve in his stead until the first day of January next.
     SAMUEL GILBERT, Capt.
 The Connecticut Courant, And The Weekly Intelligencer, August 25, 1778.

DESERTED from my company, Col. Warner's regiment, on the 15th of January 1778, one Christopher Chestor, (a serjeant) well set, about 22 years old, 5 feet 8 inches high, long brown hair, grey eyes, one of his upper fore teeth missing and small soft beard, long favoured

belonging to New-London; rather bashful and slow of speech. Whoever will take up said deserter and return to his regt. [or] the state of Vermont, shall have ten dollars reward, and all reasonable charges
paid, by me SIMEON SMITH, Capt.
Bennington, May 4, 1778.
The Connecticut Courant, and Hartford Weekly Intelligencer, August 25, 1778.

DESERTED from my company, in Col. Warner's regiment on the 26th of January 1778, one Aanias Pottage, an Indian fellow well built 5 feet 10 inches high, talks good English, about 33 years old, his upper fore teeth missing, belonged to [Can]aan, in Connecticut, hath since his desertion inlisted into a company of militia some time last May [for] 8 months, and gone to Fish Kill. Whoever [will] take up said Pottage and return him to his regiment in the State of Vermont shall have ten dollars reward and all necessary charges,
paid by   SIMEON SMITH, Capt.
Bennington, June 20, 1778.
The Connecticut Courant, and Hartford Weekly Intelligencer, August 25, 1778.

Newtown, State of Pennsylvania, Aug. 22, 1778.
WAS some time past, and now in gaol at this place, the following persons, viz. John Ross, says he belongs to the 10th Virginia regiment, in Capt. Stevens' company: Abraham Lawell, says he belongs to Colonel Baylor's regiment of light dragoons, in the service of this State; and John Walter, who says he belongs to Colonel Dayton's regiment, in the service of the State of New-Jersey. The officers concerned are desired to send for them and pay charges.
THOMAS HUSTON, Gaoler.
The New-Jersey Gazette, August 26, 1778.

DESERTED.
From the First New-Jersey Regiment.
A Certain Theophilus Cummins, about 21 years of age, five feet six inches high, supposed to be near New-Germantown,—Also a certain William Erwin, about 17 years of age, and about the same height as Cummins, of said regiment. Whoever secures either of the above, and delivers them to any continental officer, or confines them in any gaol and gives notice thereof, shall receive Twenty Dollars for each, and One Shilling per mile to Camp, paid by me
JOHN V. ANGLIN, Capt.   Aug. 28.

The New Jersey Gazette, September 2, 1778; September 16, 1778.

Philadelphia, September 3.
Yesterday ----- McMullen, a soldier, was executed in this city for desertion.
The Pennsylvania Gazette, September 5, 1778.

DEserted *from the Regiment formerly Commanded by Col. William R. Lee, Company now Commanded by Lieut. Samuel Cogswell, Steward Black, about 6 Feet High, dark Complexion. Joseph Black, about 5 Feet 9 Inches high, dark Complexion, both from Oakham in this State. Joseph Henry, 6 Feet high, light Complexion, Murraysfield. James Hunt, 5 Feet 10 Inches high, light Complexion, a Hatter by trade, from Lexington. Thomas Sawtill from New Brantree, about 5 Feet 3 Inches high, Light Complexion, Whoever will Apprehend the above Deserters or any of them, and bring them to Boston, or confine them in any Goal, so that they may be returned to the Service of their Country; shall receive a handsome Reward, and all necessary Charges paid.* DANIEL LYMAN, *A. D. C.*
The Boston-Gazette, And Country Journal, September 7, 1778.

One Hundred Dollars Reward.
STOLEN from the subscriber, living in Suffield, about eighty or ninety pounds Continental bills. The thief calls his name James Briges, but will likely change it, says he deserted out of Boston just before it was shut up, and has since been in the American army: Had on when he went away, a gray colour'd Coat, Buckskin Breeches check shirt, blue Stockings, felt hat, is about 5 feet 10 inches high, much pock broken, something stocky speaks broad, walks grand, is an Irishman, and understands combing wool. Whoever will take up said thief and money, so at the owner may have the money and secure the thief in any of the goals, or bring him to Suffield in Connecticut, in Hartford county shall receive the above reward or for the thief only shall receive 60 dollars, and all necessary charges paid by me,
AARON HALLADAY.
The Connecticut Courant, and Hartford Weekly Intelligencer, September 8, 1778.

DESERTED from my Company, in Col. *Thomas Crafts's* Regiment of Artillery, one Thomas Smith, a Native of George-Town, a well set Man, 5 Feet 8 Inches high, 26 Years of Age, dark Complexion, dark

Hair, dark Eyes, had on a blue Coat faced with red, blue Waistcoat and Breeches. Whoever will apprehend said Deserter and return him to his Regiment, shall have Twenty Dollars Reward,
   paid by me JONATHAN W. EDES, Captain.
The Independent Chronicle and the Universal Advertiser, September 10, 1778; September 17, 1778.

DESERTED from my Company in Col. Meigs's Regiment, *Isaiah Blakslee* and *Jesse Tharp*, some Time in July last, Blakslee is about 28 Years of Age, about 5 Feet 9 or 10 Inches high, of a dark Complexion, with black Hair and grey Eyes, is rather slim built, and carries his head a little forward; had on when he went away, a brown Jacket, a check'd linen Shirt and Trowsers. Tharp is about 26 or 27 Years of Age, about 5 Feet 6 or 7 Inches high, of a light Complexion, has light brown Hair and grey Eyes, a wide Mouth and broad fore Teeth, some of which stand out rather farther than the Rest, one of his Ankles is larger than the other, and his Foot turns a little inwards, occasioned by a Cut he received in his Ankle in his Youth; he had on when he went away a butternut colour'd Jacket, white linen Shirt and Trowsers. Whoever shall take up said Deserters, and secure them in any of the Goals in these States, or bring them to me, shall have Twenty Dollars Reward, and all necessary Charges paid, and for either of them Ten Dollars,
   by me JOSEPH MANSFIELD, Capt.
           White Plains, August 16, 1778.
The Connecticut Journal, September 23, 1778; September 30, 1778.

This day Patrick MacMullen was executed upon the Commons in this city. He was a deserter from the British, and had deserted from several Continental regiments. He was so hardened and insensible of his unhappy situation, that when the executioner put the rope around his neck, he smiled, and said it was strong enough to hang any man, and behaved with like unaccountable indifference to the last moment.
Thomas's Massachusetts Spy Or, American Oracle of Liberty, September 24, 1778; *The Boston-Gazette, And Country Journal*, September 28, 1778. The *Gazette* spells the man's name as M'Mullen.

Forty Shillings Reward.
DESERTED from his Majesty's Ship the Brune, James Syze, a Portugueze, by birth, speaks broken English, of a black swarthy complexion, black eyes, and Raven black long hair, about thirty years

of age, five feet ten inches high, an active stout made man to appearance.

The Royal Gazette, September 26, 1778.

DESERTED from town, county, *John Gri[ffiths,]* thirty years old, five feet eight inches high, who says he lived in *Lancaster c*ounty, and is of no [troop]. He has a thin visage, is addicted to drink, and when drunk very talkative. Whoever delivers the said deserter to me at *Petersburg,* or to any officer in the first regiment of light dragoons, shall have twenty dollars reward.
     JOHN WHITE, Cornet.
  The Virginia Gazette, Purdie, October 16, 1778

DESERTED from Capt. Goodwin, on their March from Boston to New-London, the following Persons, viz.

Thomas Gray,	*John Blamer,*	*Joseph Rustin,*
William McKever,	*James Louther,*	*James Johnse,*
Henry Thomas,	*James Downey,*	*William Ward,*
Samuel Killey,	*William Taylor,*	*Michael Knox,*
John Allensby,	*Griffeth Roberts,*	*Thomas Fortune,*
James Roseberry,	*Samuel Other[lt]brow,*	*Alexander Hellon,*
James Tier,	*John Smith,*	*William Noble,*
Thomas Parker,	*William Prian,*	*Seal Chandler,*
John Moss,	*Robert Moss,*	*James Camby,*
John Cillet,	*William Grant,*	*James Sandler,*
Alexander McCloud,	*Dominick Harbenson,*	*William Eton,*
Markalm Walcom,	*Anthony Roose,*	*Edward Christin*

All Prisoners of War to his Excellency Count De Estaing, and being ordered to New-London for an Exchange to be made for French Prisoners, made their Escape, and prevents the Count De Estaing having the Benefit of such an Exchange: I therefore require all Officers, civil and military, to exert themselves to apprehend all or as many of the above (being British sailors) as is in their Power, and confine then in any Goals or Guard-ships, acquainting Mr. THOMAS SHAW, Deputy Commissary for Navy Prisoners at New-London, or the Subscriber at Rutland.
    JOSHUA MERSERAU, D. C. G. of Prisoners, (and
     Commissary for the Count De Estaing.
        NEW-LONDON, *October* 24, 1778.
 The Connecticut Gazette; And The Universal Intelligencer, October 30, 1778; November 6, 1778; November 20, 1778.

BROKE Goal, and made his Escape, in the Town, on Tuesday, the 20th instant, one *Thomas Moore*, a Sailor, about 28 Years of Age, born in England, about 5 Feet 6 Inches high, had on a red out-side Jacket, and striped Trowsers. He was committed to Goal for Debt, and for deserting from the Continental Ship Alliance. Whoever will return him to the Subscriber, shall have 20 DOLLARS Reward.
    JOSEPH OTIS, Deputy-Goal-Keeper.
                Boston, October 28, 1778.
The Independent Chronicle and the Universal Advertiser, November 5, 1778.

DEserted from my Company, one William Money, a Negro, belonging to the Town of Walpole, and hired for said Town for the Term of eight Months. He is about 24 Years of Age, and about 5 Feet 6 Inches high.—Also one Joseph Hunt, some Time in August, on his Way from Dorchester to Peeks-Kill; he is about 20 to 25 Years of Age, and about 5 Feet 10 Inches high, a stout well-built Fellow; he is supposed to have returned back to Dorchester again. Whoever will take up said Deserters, and bring them to Camp, at West-Point, shall receive TEN DOLLARS Reward for each.
    JOHN ELLIS, Capt.
               West-Point, October 20, 1778.
The Boston-Gazette, And Country Journal, November 9, 1778; November 16, 1778; November 23, 1778.

DESERTED, from the second *Georgia* regiment of continental troops, THOMAS MARTIN, about 22 years of age, 5 feet 9 or 10 inches high, a resident of *Chesterfield* county. Also THOMAS OWEN, near Col. *Cole's*, in *Albemarle,* about 27 years of age, well made, about 5 feet 7 inches high, very subject to drink, and when drunk quarrelsome. They are both natives of *Virginia.* A reward of FORTY DOLLARS will be given for each of the said deserters if conveyed to *Chesterfield* courthouse, and all reasonable expences paid, by
    GEORGE HANCOCK, Capt. 2d battalion.
The Virginia Gazette, Dixon and Hunter, November 13, 1778.

WILLIAM CALWILL, a British Prisoner, hired of me the Subscriber, on Saturday the 13th of November, one Horse and one Mare; the Horse was about 5 & ¼ hands high, and of a red colour, with a yellow mane and a short square tail, *also* a white spot in his forehead, trots and canters well; the Mare was of a black colour, and about 14 hands high; the Mare was for his servant to ride on, the Horse and Mare had on each a good saddle & bridle, the smallest and neatest saddle was on

the Horse. Said Caldwill is a likely genteel fellow, had on when he went away, a light colour'd coat and a pair of royal ribb'd breeches, he wore a cockade in his hat, and a hanger by his side: he was taken in a sloop of war by a privateer out of Marblehead; said Calwill is a headstrong fellow, and very generous in company. Whoever will take up and secure said Calwill, the Horse, Bridle and Saddle, so that I the Subscriber shall have them all again, shall have One Hundred & Fifty Dollars Reward, or Fifty Dollars only, for the Horse.
    Paid by me DAVID PARKER.
The Boston-Gazette, And Country Journal, November 30, 1778; December 7, 1778; December 14, 1778.

      PROVIDENCE, November 28.
 Monday last John Bushby; a soldier of Col. Vose's regiment, was shot here for desertion. He had been three several times under sentence of death for the like crime, and was twice pardoned.
 The Independent Chronicle and the Universal Advertiser, December 3, 1778.

           Philadelphia, December 3.
The Supreme Executive Council have issued their pardon to Joseph Wilson and John Lawrence, who were sentenced to be shot for desertion.
 The Pennsylvania Gazette, December 3, 1778.

DESERTED from the company under my command in Col. McClellan's Regiment of Connecticut State Troops, a Soldier named PHILIP MINARD, about 17 Years old, 5 Feet 8 inches high, dark complexion, dark short Hair, dark Eyes. Whoever will take up said Deserter and return him to his regiment of company, at New-London, shall have TEN DOLLARS Reward, and all necessary charges
    paid by me LEE LAY, Capt.
         NEW-LONDON, 2d Dec. 1778.
 The Connecticut Gazette; And The Universal Intelligencer, December 4, 1778; December 11, 1778.

     Deserted from Captain WILLIAM
Scott's Company, in Colonel DAVID HENLEY's Regiment, *John Vauner*, aged 20 Years, 5 Feet 8 Inches, fair Complexion, curled short light Hair, belonging to Londonderry in New Hampshire: *John Mitchell*, aged 20 Years, 5 Feet 8 Inches, dark Complexion, short dark brown curled Hair, belonging to said Derry, with a little Impediment in his Speech; and *John Wilson*, late of Burgoyne's Army

aged 26 Years, 5 Feet 11 Inches, fair Complexion, short red curled Hair. Whoever apprehends said Deserters, or either of them, and secures them in any of the Goals on the Continent, or return them to the Regiment at Providence, shall receive SIXTEEN DOLLARS for each of them, and all necessary Charges paid by me
JOHN NEWSMITH, Lieutenant in
Colonel DAVID HENLEY's Regiment.
The Independent Chronicle and the Universal Advertiser, December 10, 1777; December 17, 1777.

DESERTED some Time in November last, from the 4th Continental Regiment, commanded by Col. JOHN DURKEE, Esq; one Isaac Basset, of Canterbury, 22 Years old, a stout well built Fellow, of about 5 Feet 8 Inches high, light Complection, and short brown hair. Also one Comfort Chappel, belonging to New-London, a well built Fellow, of midling Stature, dark Complection, with short dark Hair, about 20 Years old. Also one John Miller, of Lyme, about 19 years old, small of Stature, light Complection, short brown Hair, and is a very sprightly active Soldier. Also the well known Allen Pratt, from Middletown, lately an Apprentice at Lebanon, a small dirty Soldier, about 18 Years old, yet has the Countenance of near 30, of a dark smutty insignificant Countenance, noted for being lousy, and having an unsoldierlike Appearance, yet to the first Appearance is possessed of much good Nature, and has distinguished himself in the Duty of a Soldier. Also Ely Wigger, of Stonington, a stout well built Fellow, of midling Stature, dark Complexion, and short dark Hair.

N. B. All the above mentioned Soldiers carried with them a Suit of Regimental Cloaths, the Coat dark brown with red Facings, light brown Vest and Breeches, trim'd with Continental Buttons marked U S A. It is supposed they are lurking about in some Part of the State with an Intent to go a privateering, consequently all Masters of Vessels are hereby cautioned against harbouring concealing or carrying off said Soldiers. Whoever will apprehend said Deserters, and commit them to Goal, or convey them to the Regiment, shall have FIFTY DOLLARS Reward, or TEN DOLLARS for each of them,
paid by PHINEHAS BECKWITH,
Serjeant of (the 4th Continental Battalion,
by Order of Col. Durkee.
The Connecticut Gazette; And The Universal Intelligencer, December 11, 1778; December 18, 1778.

1779

DESERTED from his Most
Christian Majesty's Hospital, on Roxbury-Neck, one STEPHEN VERDIER, aged 2[3] Years, 5 Feet 3 Inches, brownish complexion, short cut chesnut Hair, having a blue Jacket, with two Blankets which he has stolen; he [   ], is said, to Salem in Company with two other Frenchmen. Whoever apprehends said Deserter, or either of the two other Frenchmen, and secures him or them in the Goals on the Continent, or returns said Deserter to the French Hospital, shall receive TWENTY DOLLARS reward, and all necessary Charges.
By order of the H[   ] VALNAIS esq;
Vice Agent of the Royal Navy, and Vice Consul of France.
NEBON, Secretary, Mrs. BROWN's, Water-Street.
Boston, October 18, 1779.
The Independent Chronicle and the Universal Advertiser, January 14, 1779.

DESERTED from Capt. Paine Converse's Company, in Col. M'Clellan's Regiment, JACOB WHITE,
a tall Fellow, about 18 Years old, light Complexion. Whoever will take up said Deserter and cause him the join the Regiment now at New-London, shall have a Reward of Ten Dollars, paid by me,
PAINE CONVERSE, Capt.
New-London, January 6, 1779.
The Connecticut Gazette; And The Universal Intelligencer, January 15, 1779.

DESERTED
FROM the Horse Department belonging to the Royal Artillery, RICHARD SHEY, about 5 feet 8 inches high, brown complexion, brown hair, stout made, about 46 years of age, had on when he went away a brown short coat.
JAMES M'MUNNIGAN, about 5 feet 5 inches high, black complexion, black short hair, marked with the small pox, aged about 25 years, had on a short brown jacket with collar and cuffs, and a blanket coat.
HUGH DAVIES, about 5 feet 7 inches high, well made, of a dark complexion, had on a blue great coat, with a red collars. And

JAMES JUKE, about 5 feet 8 inches high, fair hair'd and fair complexion, about 20 years of age, had on a claret coloured coat and waistcoat.

A Reward of TWO GUINEAS is hereby offered to any person who will bring any of the said deserters to the Office of Ordnance opposite St. Paul's church. It is imagined they have been enticed to go on board some privateer, or other vessel. This public notice is given to all owners and masters of privateers and other vessels, that they may depend on the most severe and rigourous treatment upon conviction, that the law will admit.

The Royal Gazette, January 19, 1779.

DESERTED from Capt. Elijah Blakman's company, Col. Henry Sherburne's regiment, Nathaniel Montgomery, sergeant, aged 22 years, 5 feet 10 inches high, has black hair and eyes, of a dark complexion; had on, when he went away, a dark brown coat, faced with yellow, a green vest, and brown overalls. Also John Payne, a soldier in the same company, aged 20 years, has light coloured hair, is of a fair complexion, 5 feet 8 inches high; has a like uniform with the other.—Whoever will take up said deserters, and return them to the regiment, or secure them in any gaol, and give information, shall have Forty Dollars reward, or for either of them Twenty Dollars, and necessary charges,

    paid by JOHN SMITH, Lieut.

Bristol, Feb. 2, 1779.

The Providence Gazette; And Country Journal, February 6, 1779.

STOLEN out of the house of WILLIAM DIBLEY, inn-keeper in Chesnut-street, this morning, (February 15) the following articles, viz. A silver watch, the outside case marked with a cypher W D, has a steel chain, a Cornelian seal set in gold, the top part mounted with silver, another seal with W D engraved thereon, a hunting key. One pair silver shoe buckles, open work'd, on an oval kind, worn nearly smooth: one pair plain silver knee ditto. Two table-cloths marked W D. Supposed to be taken by a certain Daniel White, a soldier belonging to Capt. Scott's company in Gen. Putnam's corps: He is a thick chunky fellow, about five feet five inches high, dark bushy hair, wears a blue regimental coat faced with red, and buttons marked U S, a white flannel jacket and drawers, coarse white linen stockings, and shoes almost new. Whoever takes up and secures said thief, with the things above mentioned, shall receive Forty Dollars reward, or in

proportion for any part thereof. It is requested, should they be offered for sale, that they and the person who offers them may be stopped.
WILLIAM DIBLEY.
The Pennsylvania Packet or the General Advertiser, February 16, 1779; February 20, 1779; February 25, 1779.

DESERTED from the 8th Connecticut Battalion, about the 1st of January last, TOM GAGE, a Negro Fellow, about 21 Years old, slim built, much pitted on the Nose with the Small-Pox, speaks broken English, had on a red regimental Coat.—Whoever will bring said Tom to the Regiment in General Parson's Brigade, or confine him and send me Word, will serve the Public, and be intitled to Eight Dollars Reward, and necessary Charges,
paid by   DANIEL BARNS, Capt. Lieut.
Reading, February 3, 1779.
The Connecticut Journal, February 17, 1779; February 24, 1779; March 3, 1779.

PROVIDENCE, *February* 19 1779.
ESCAPED from the main guard in this town, about nine o'clock in the evening of the 18th instant, a certain WILLIAM CROSSING, who says he is a Captain in Whitman's corps of tory refugees; and JOSEPH CASWELL, of said Crossing's company, who were captured at Seconnet. CROSSING is about 40 years old, 5 feet 9 inches high, has a light complexion, light blue eyes, short hair, is marked with the small-pox, and is a man of great activity; was dressed in a brown velvet coat, red waistcoat and breeches, and a furr cap. CASWEL, is about 40 years old, 5 feet 7 or 8 inches high, full fac'd, well set, very dark complexion'd, has a remarkable black bushy beard, wears his hair short, and was clothed with a blue coat and waistcoat, and dark brown breeches.—Whoever will apprehend and secure the abovementioned villains, shall receive Two Hundred Dollars Reward or One Hundred Dollars for either of them.
Published by order the honorable Major Gen. Sullivan.
WILLIAM PECK, Adj. Gen. I. R. I.
The Norwich Packet, February 22, 1779; March 1, 1779; March 8, 1779; *The Connecticut Gazette; And The Universal Advertiser*, March 5, 1779.

DESERTED from Capt. Reuben Slayton's Company, Colonel William Shepards Regiment, at Providence, the 27th of February, JOHN CLARK, an Irishman, has dark coloured Hair, large blue Eyes, a malicious Look, and is something pitted with the Small-pox; had on a

blue Coat with white Facing, white Jacket and brown Over-alls, and cock'd Hat bound with white, and carried with him his Arms and Accoutrements. Whoever will take up said Deserter, and send him to the Regiment above mentioned, or give Notice to any of Col. Shepard's Officers shall have Thirty Dollars Reward, and all necessary Charges
     paid by SAMUEL DANFORTH, Lieut.
The Connecticut Gazette; And The Universal Intelligencer, March 5, 1779; March 12, 1779; March 18, 1779.

        Camp, near Reading, March 4 1779.
DEserted from Capt. T. Munson's Company, 8th Connecticut Battalion, *James Willcocks*, Corporal, about 5 Feet 10 Inches high, well set, makes a soldier-like Appearance, light brown Hair, blue Eyes, supposed to be at Farmington; the Authority (of which Place) are requested to secure him, or should any other, they may expect 15
    Dollars, per me, A. BENJAMIN, Lieut.
The Connecticut Journal, March 10, 1779; March 17, 1779; March 31, 1779.

WHEREAS the following soldiers have deserted from the third continental regiment, stationed in the state of *Georgia,* and now lurking in this state, to the great prejudice of the common good of *America* ; this is therefore to acquaint them, that if they will voluntarily join their regiment by the first of *May* next, that they shall be pardoned, and receive their pay and clothing that may be due them, otherwise if they fail to accept of this indulgence, I will give forty dollars reward for each deserter which shall be secured in any of the jails of this commonwealth after the above date. All soldiers who are on furlough in this state or otherwise, are ordered to repair to *Purysburg, South Carolina,* immediately.
   Given under my hand
    this 21*st day of* February, 1779.
      RAWLEIGH DOWNMAN, 3d continental regt.
Return of the deserters names, deserted from the 3d continental regiments, since its arrival in the state of *Georgia.*
FIRST COMPANY.
Calep Hunter, Corporal, *Isham Dychs, Obediah Ferguson, William Bartley, Philemon Burks, John M'Clay, William Wooderosse, Ambrose Lucas, Roger Tandy, John Johnson, Alexander Bartley, David Womack, and William Jones.*

THIRD COMPANY.
Charles Jones, James Randolph, Moses Batley, Francis Gams, Francis Hopkins, John Wills, James Berry, Patrick Cochran, James Page, and John Johnston Florry.
FOURTH COMPANY.
Anthony Williams, Thomas Jones, John Canterbury, Jun., *John Thomas, James Smith, John Thompson, John Hailey, James Cunningham, William Price,* and *William Musteen.*
FIFTH COMPANY.
Henry Donnel, Omes Walker, Benjamin Steward, Thomas Williams, Alexander Rise, William Hepper, James Cook, James Brakeen, Benjamin Edmundson, and *James Butler.*
SIXTH COMPANY.
David Johnson, Munford Wilson, Joseph Burnet, Joseph Stacy, William Atkins, Seward Price, Joseph Smith, William Smith, Henry Lee, John Bates, and *Guthridge Garland.*
SEVENTH COMPANY.
John Vaughan, Daniel Murray, John Sadler, Daniel Toley, Samuel Crawford, William Zidlidge, John Wells, John Carney, and *John Culember.*
EIGHTH COMPANY.
John Philip, Richard Brown, John Nash, Champness Tearry, Joseph Clark, John Soleham, John Oldham, John Bowens, Richard Brim, James Brunsfield, John Hewett, William Eastes, Richard Shores, James Burns, William Dearin, John Turley, John Bentley, Jesse Bradley, Peter Jones, Godfrey Burnet, and *Benjamin Edmonson.*

The Virginia Gazette, Dixon and Nicolson, March 12, 1779.

DESERTED,
From His Majesty's Ship ARDENT.

THOMAS PRATT, a Seaman, 5 feet 10 inches high, well made, wears his own dark hair, has a cut in his left cheek, had on when he left the Barge a blue jacket, white shirt, and round hat.

WILLIAM WATSON, a Seaman, 5 feet 6 inches high, well set, wears his own brown hair pretty long, tied behind, pitted with the small pox, and had on when he left the Barge a brown jacket, stripped cotton shirt, and round hat.

Whoever secures the said Deserters do that they may be brought to justice, shall receive TEN GUINEAS for either, about the bounty of Forty Shillings Ster. allowed for apprehending deserters.

S. W. CLAYTON.

The Royal Gazette, March 17, 1779; March 20, 1779; March 24, 1779.

EIGHTY DOLLARS REWARD

FOR apprehending the following deserters belonging to the *Virginia* state garrison regiment of infantry now stationed near *Williamsburg, Thomas Tisdale*, a *Virginian*, born in *Hanover* county, about 23 years old, 5 feet 8 inches high, brown complexion, brown hair, black eyes, had on when he went away a blue regimental coat turned up with red, a red jacket and breeches. *Charles Valentine*, a mulatto, born in *Surry* county, *Virginia*, 28 years old, 5 feet 9 inches high, well made, had on the same uniform as above. *James Collier*, a *Virginian*, born in *King & Queen* county, 16 years of age, 5 feet 2 1/2 inches high, fair complexion, light hair, blue eyes, and well made, had on same uniform as above. *John Bunns*, a *Virginian*, born in *King & Queen* county, 16 years old, 5 feet 2 inches high, light eyes and brown hair, with the same uniform as above. Whoever apprehends the said deserters, and conveys them to the commanding officer at *Williamsburg, York, Hampton,* or *Portsmouth*, shall have the above reward, or 20 dollars for either of them.

Given under my hand at head quarters
Williamsburg, *March* 13, 1779.
EDWARD WALLER, Capt. Com. S. G. R.

The Virginia Gazette, Dixon and Nicolson, March 19, 1779; April 2, 1779; April 16, 1779. See *The Virginia Gazette*, Dixon and Nicolson, May 1, 1779, for Tisdale and Valentine. The May 1 ad refers to Valentine as a "free negro".

DESERTED *from the State Regiment of Artillery, lately commanded by Thomas Crafts, Esq; the following non-commissioned officers and matrosses, viz.*

BOMBADIERS.

James Grace, Georgetown, *William Crawford,* Eastward, *Jeduthen Wyman,* Lancaster, *Alexander Willson,* Worcester, *Levi Stutson and George Tate,* Boston, *John Norcutt,* Middleboro', *Simeon Hale,* Scituate, *and Jacob Porter,* Weymouth, *and Thomas Achison.*

GUNNERS.

Ebenezer Hollis, Weymouth, *Nehemiah Thomas,* Marshfield, *and Spencer Vose,* Milton, *and — Haley.*

DRUMMERS.

Abiel Abbot, Andover, *and Doctor Edwards, Foreigner*

MATROSSES.

William Wood, Virginia, *Prince Norton*, Marthas Vineyard, *John Vaughan*, Dorchester, *James Dunton*, Weymouth, *John Tuckerman*, Boston, *Peleg Hearsy*, Leicester, *Solomon Burges*, Harvard, — *Seger*, Leicester, *Thomas Giles*, Boston, *John Weld*, & *Benjamin Weld*, Roxbury, *Jacob Smith*, Worcester, *David Thompson*, Newbury, *Bennet Hodgekins*, Virginia, *John Adams*, Marblehead, *Ebenezer White*, Middleboro', *Ebenezer Chamberlain*, Charlton, *Bela Gardner* & *Jacob Gardner*, Abington, — *Howard*, Braintree, — *Knowlton*, Middleboro', *James Cushing*, Pembroke, — *Weld*, Dorchester, *Thomas Nicholls*, Boston, *John Fuller*, Lancaster, *Benjamin Warner*, *and Elijah Priest*, Harvard, *John Butler*, Concord, *James Newhall*, Lynn, *Ephraim Norcutt*, & *Zenas Norcutt*, Middleboro', — *Blanchard*, America, *Francis Peabody*, Middleton; *also the following Foreigners, George Fie*, — *Sanders*, — *Jacobs*, — *John McConnell*, *Francis Wiggon, William Griffith, Arthur Thomas, Conrad Kramer, Wm. Reinwald, Nath. Witechurch*, — *Lawson*, —*Walker*, — *Adams*, — *Johnson*, — *Jones, William Witman, Peter Lagirt, John Franks, Edward Lawson, John Blake, Henry Sherder, John Hardwick, Powell Buckard, John Barker, Thomas Greenway, Hugh Hayes, and John Huet; and John Clark of* Mendon.

If they will return to their duty by the last day of March instant, they shall be received and pardoned; otherwise they may depend on being treated as the military law directs. They were dressed in a blue uniform Coat, turned up with red, white waistcoat & breeches; many of them carried off their Arms, which is the property of this State. The Selectmen and Committees of the several towns in this State, are desired to secure said Deserters, and send them to Head Quarters, at Boston.

PAUL REVERE, Lt. Col. Artillery.

Castle-Island, March 6, 1779.

The Commission Officers [sic] of said Regiment who have had leave to resign, are desired to leave their inlisting papers with the Secretary of Council, as their pay-rolls cannot be passed upon until this is done, and to leave the arms belonging to the State, now under their care, with Col. Burbeck, at the Laboratory, who will give them a receipt for the same.

PAUL REVERE, L. C. A.

BOSTON, *March* 8, 1776. [*sic*]

The Boston Gazette, And Country Journal, March 22, 1779.

STOL'N from the subscriber's wagon, on the road leading from Charlestown westward, near sergeant Campbell's place, about the 1st of March last. A HORSE, 8 years old, near 14 hands and half high, a

blaze in his face, branded BE in on the near shoulder and buttock, and 75 on the off buttock and shoulder, hath remarkable large quarters, round body, trots heavy, and carries low: supposed to be taken by one Samuel More, a deserter from Col. Thomson's regiment, and carried towards Georgia. Whoever contrives the said horse to his owner, on the head of Pacolet river, near the North Carolina line, shall have FIFTY POUNDS currency reward, or TWENTY FIVE POUNDS if delivered to Capt. John Bowie at Fort Charlotte.
    BAYLIS EARLE.
The Gazette Of The State Of South-Carolina, March 24, 1779

             Newport, March 17. 1779.
      DESERTED
  From this TOWN, a few DAYS ago,
JOHN KERBER, the Gunsmith of Major General de HUYN's Regiment, about 36 Years of Age, of a middling Size, and very pale Complexion. He left his Charge as a Rogue, taking with him several Tools belonging to the Regiment, and other Things, viz. Two Silver Watches, which he stole from his Friends, Silver Handled Swords, Buckles, &c. which he had to mend.—Therefore, every Person is warned against this false, perjured, and thievish Fellow.—Any Person that will give any certain Intelligence to the Regiment of the aforesaid Tools or other stolen Things (which are supposed not yet carried off from this Island) shall be well rewarded, and his or her Name kept secret.
    The Newport Gazette, March 25, 1779.

STOLEN from the subscriber, on the 26th instant, by a deserter from the British army, A blue GREAT-COAT, with a white velvet cap, and two pair silver SHOE-BUCKELS: He's a lusty fellow, about 26 years old, with a grey dull eye; he wore a red coat, white jacket and breeches, the buttons on his coat had the number of his regiment.—Whoever will secure said thief and articles, shall have Ten Dollars reward, and necessary charges,
    paid by J. DOUGLAS. *Plainfield, March* 29, 1779.
  The Norwich Packet and the Connecticut, Massachusetts, New-Hampshire, and Rhode-Island Weekly Advertiser, March 29, 1779; April 13, 1779.

    TWO HUNDRED DOLLARS Reward.
STOLEN from the subscriber, living in Somerset County, State of New-Jersey, about the 21st of February last, by a certain Henry Rush, the following articles.—

A woman's gold watch and key, the watch has a gold face, chased case, representing Pompey's head shewn to Caesar, maker's name supposed to be Wilsman, London; on the key is represented a hautboy. fiddle, flute, trumpet, &c. lying across each other; also a blue regimental coat, turned up with red, silver epaulet, (made out of knee garters) the coat is lined throughout with white durant, except the skirts which turn up, and about four inches the fore part, which is red shalloon; the buttons are white-flowered, (two or three lost) hooks and eyes, in the fore part, are some of black wire, twisted, some single white wire; also a white twilled vest and breeches, the vest lined with white fustian, the breeches not lined, buttons white flowered; all which clothes he went off in;—likewise a full welted hunting saddle, not half worn, the tree has been broke, and is mended by a piece of iron clinched on the inside; the saddle cloth, blue long ells, with a stripe of white cloth, three quarters of an inch wide, sewed round near the edge, and lined with tow linen; a bridle, the reins tied to the bit.— The said fellow was born in Philadelphia, has straight hair, a scar on one side of his face, is very talkative, and speaks both the English and German very well; it is expected he will endeavour to pass for an officer, as he has procured himself a sword, and an old commission. He is now deserted from Capt. Heer's troop of light horse, and it is supposed he is gone to Goshen, in the State of New-York, as he has said his mother lived there, or to Albany, where he is well acquainted.—Whoever will secure the said thief in any of the State's gaols, shall receive one hundred dollars reward, and all reasonable charges, and for the watch, one hundred dollars more, paid by
          JOHN J. SCHENK.
          Somerset County, State of New-Jersey,
                                      March 1, 1779.
   The Royal Gazette, April 3, 1779.

DESERTED from my company of state artillery, THOMAS ROBERTSON, an *Englishman* a short well made man, with a bald head, and some of his teeth out before, carried away with him, a blanket and suit of regimentals. Whoever delivers the said deserter to the commanding officer at *Williamsburg,* or *York,* shall receive 20 dollars reward.— *Richard Armstrong* is ordered to join his company immediately, or he will be considered and treated as a deserter.
HENRY QUARLES, Capt. Lieut.
   The Virginia Gazette, Dixon and Nicolson, April 9, 1779, May 1, 1779.

ONE HUNDRED DOLLARS REWARD.

DESERTED from *York* garrison, THOMAS ORTON, about 30 years of age, near 6 feet high, slender made, pitted with the smallpox, speaks thick, and a little through his nose, has a down look; had on when he went away, a blue coat turned up with red, and red waistcoat and breeches. Whoever takes up the said deserter, and delivers him to the commanding officer at *Williamsburg, York, Hampton,* or *Portsmouth,* shall have the above reward.

     GIDEON JOHNSTON, Lieut.

The Virginia Gazette, Dixon and Nicolson, April 9, 1779; May 1, 1779.

ONE HUNDRED DOLLARS REWARD.

DESERTED from *Williamsburg, Stephen Hawk* and *William Thompson,* both *Englishmen*; they were enlisted on the new establishment to serve in the continental army 18 months, in the room of draughts for the said city. HAWK is very stout, five feet five inches high, has dark brown hair, round shoulders, a down look, and pitted with the smallpox, he pretends to be a sailor, and said he was on board the *Randolph* frigate when she was lost. THOMPSON is five feet seven inches high, has dark brown hair, a pale thin face pitted with the smallpox, and several red spots about his mouth and nose, he is a nailor by trade and commonly wears a leather apron, very talkative when in liquor, and is well known in *Suffolk* and *Portsmouth.* Any person who will apprehend the said deserters and deliver them to the commanding officer of the militia of this city, shall have the above reward, or fifty dollars for each.

The Virginia Gazette, Dixon and Nicolson, April 9, 1779, April 16, 1777; May 1, 1779. April 16 ad ends with:

☞ *John Mitchell, James Waters, William Stone,* and *Jean Lozerat,* are hereby ordered to return to the commanding officer of this place immediately, otherwise they will be deemed deserters and treated accordingly. See *The Virginia Gazette*, Dixon and Nicolson, May 22, 1779.

ONE HUNDRED DOLLARS REWARD.

ABSCONDED from his master, a few nights ago, a Hessian deserter, named CHARLES ———, (his sirname not recollected) a handsome young fellow, about twenty-one or twenty-two years of age, five feet six or seven inches high, fair complexion, and dark brown hair: He took with him a light blue short coat, a jean coatee lined with Persian, six or seven ruffled shirts, the same number of stocks, four pairs of

silk stockings almost new, a few pairs of thread stockings, a white casimer waistcoat, a pair of Russia sheeting trowsers, four pocket handkerchiefs, and a pair of boots. The shirts, stocks and stockings are marked D. L. Whoever will secure the said servant in any gaol on the Continent, shall receive the above reward from the Printer.
    The Pennsylvania Packet or the General Advertiser, April 27, 1779; May 4, 1779; May 8, 1779.

    FOUR HUNDRED AND FIFTY DOLLARS REWARD.
THIRTY dollars for each of the following deserters will be paid to any person, who apprehends and brings any of them to Williamsburg *garrison.* James Egmon *from* York *county, 19 years of age, 5 feet 6 inches high, of a dark complexion, brown hair and dark eyes, he is supposed be enlisted in the light horse, and stationed at* Winchester. Charles Valentine, *a free negro from* Surry, *of a long stature, talks very smooth and is very merry when a little in liquor, it is thought he is with his wife in said county.* Philip Miller, *a* German, *about* 20 *years old, of a fair complexion, light hair, gray eyes, and a middle stature, a cooper by trade and is supposed to work at* Alexandria. John O'Deer, *from* King & Queen, *about* 16 *years old, fair complexion, black eyes, and a pleasant countenance, short stature, a cooper by trade, he is supposed to be at his home.* Thomas Johnson, *an* Irishman, *of a fair complexion, thin visage, middle stature, a sailmaker by trade, is very apt to get drunk and is very talkative, he commonly wore a long blue surtout coat above his regimentals.* Andrew Wilson, *a* Scotchman, *28 years old, of a fair complexion, long stature, brown hair, gray eyes, he was acquitted last fall in the general court, deserted with new regimentals on.* Marshal Delasie, *a fifer, born in* France, *21 years old, fair complexion, well made, spoke broken* English, *deserted in his uniform.* Wilson Jackson, *from* Nova Scotia, *33 years old, is gray bearded, long stature, looked very pale and speaks low, is apt to get in liquor.* William Thompson, *an* Englishman, *45 years old, of middle stature, pale complexion, brown hair, is very apt to get drunk.* Thomas James, *a* Portuguese, *29 years old, short stature, a tailor by trade.* Samuel Hamond, *25 years old. 5 feet 7 inches high, fair complexion, well made, talks low, was enlisted at* Hampton *by Ensign* Millbank, *and deserted from there.* Harwell Randolph, *from* Prince George, *30 years old, of a dark complexion, black hair middle stature, and talks rather filly.* Thomas Tisdale, *from* Hanover *county, 23 years old, brown complexion, brown hair, black eyes, middle stature, used to drive a wagon for this garrison; he is supposed to be with his wife in said county.* John Armstrong, *from* Maryland, *29 years old, of a*

swarthy complexion, long stature, black hair and black eyes, has been a long time with the Indians, *is very apt to get drunk, deserted in a hunting shirt.* John Lawrence, *from* Richmond, 21 *years old,* fair complexion, black hair, very pleasant countenance well made, is rather dull of hearing, wears his uniform.

If the above mentioned deserters will deliver themselves up and return to their duty in this garrison by the 20*th of* May, *a free pardon shall be granted to them; but if they are apprehended, they shall be punished as* deserters *by the rigour of the martial law.*
    Given under my hand this 22d day April, 1779.
              EDWARD WALLER, Major. S. G. R.
    The Virginia Gazette, Dixon and Nicolson, May 1, 1779; May 8, 1779. See *The Virginia Gazette,* Dixon and Nicolson, March 19, 1779, for Tisdale and Valentine. The March 19 ad refers to Valentine as a mulatto.

AS *William Deane* a soldier belonging to the state garrison regiment, got leave of absence the 23d of *January* for six days, and has never returned yet, I have great reason to think he never intends to return. I will therefore give 20 dollars reward to any person that will bring the said *Deane* to the commanding officer at *Williamsburg.*—
∴ Likewise all soldiers belonging to the state garrison regiment whose furloughs are out, and has not returned, must return to the garrison immediately or they will be deemed as deserters.
              E. DIGGES, Capt. S.G.R.
    The Virginia Gazette, Dixon and Nicolson, May 1, 1779.

              TWENTY DOLLARS REWARD.
DESERTED May 10, 1779, from Annapolis, a certain JOHN BOWER, a new recruit for the first Maryland regiment; he is about twenty years of age, five feet five or six inches high, was born in England, but has been from there about eight years: he had on, when he went away, a blue plush coat, red waistcoat, blue breeches, felt hat, and a pair of osnabrig trousers. Whoever takes up the said deserter, and delivers him to any officer of the Maryland line, or to me at Annapolis, shall receive the above reward from
              JOSHUA LAMB, R. S.
    The Maryland Gazette, May 14, 1779; May 21, 1779.

            THREE HUNDRED DOLLARS REWARD
DESERTED from *Williamsburg,* six recruits, who were enlisted on the new establishment to serve in the continental army 18 months, in the room of draughts for the said city, *viz. Stephen Hawk,* 5 feet 5

inches high, very stout, has dark brown hair, round shoulders, a down look, and pitted with the smallpox, he pretends to be a sailor, and said he was on board the *Randolph* frigate when she was lost. *William Thompson,* 5 feet 7 inches high, has a pale thin face pock pitted, and has several red spots about his mouth and nose, he is a nailor by trade and commonly wears a leather apron, very talkative when in liquor, and is well known in *Suffolk* and *Portsmouth. John Mitchell,* about 6 feet high, pock pitted, ruddy complexion and has short dark brown hair, he commonly wears a round hat bound with gold lace, but as he had a variety of clothes it is impossible to discribe his dress, he said he came from *Baltimore,* and had served three years in the Continental army as a serjeant in one of the *Maryland* battalions. *William Stone,* about 5 feet, 7 or 8 inches high, large eyes dark hair, by trade a blacksmith very talkative when in liquor, had on when he went away, an old light coloured cloth coat, blue jacket and leather breeches, he is well known in *James City* and *Dinwiddie* counties. *James Waters,* about 5 feet, 7 or 8 inches high, pock pitted, short dark brown hair, stout and well made, by trade a plaisterer, commonly wears a light coloured newmarket coat, white flannel jacket, leather breeches, and a round hat. *Jean Lazerat* a *Frenchman* about 5 feet 8 or 9 inches high, slim made, dark complexion, black hair commonly cued, he speaks broken *English,* had on when he went off, a dark brown jacket, white linen waistcoat and breeches, a cocked hat, and new shoes and stockings. Any person who will apprehend the said deserters and deliver them to the commanding officer of the militia of this city, shall have the above reward, or fifty dollars for each.

The Virginia Gazette, Dixon and Nicolson, May 22, 1779; May 29, 1779; June 5, 1779. See *The Virginia Gazette,* Dixon and Nicolson, April 9, 1779.

POUGHKEEPSIE, May 17.

On Saturday the 8th instant, was executed at Albany, pursuant to his sentence, *William Hooghteling,* for sundry robberies whereof he was convicted. This unhappy youth began his evil practices by desertion, from one of the continental regiments raised under the directed of this state, to which he declared he was induced by his-step father, and others of the family; this induced him to the necessity of skulking and secreting himself until he was induced to join a banditti of robbers.—Let his fate be a warning to others, not to persuade those who have plighted their faith for the defence of their country, to violate their solemn engagements, lest their latter end should be like his.

The Connecticut Courant, And the Weekly Intelligencer, May 25, 1779; *The Connecticut Journal*, May 26, 1779; *Thomas's Massachusetts Spy Or, American Oracle of Liberty*, May 27, 1779.

THREE HUNDRED DOLLARS REWARD.

Port-Tobacco, May 10, 1779.

Stolen, out of the Subscriber's Plantation, on the 25th of April last, a light bay HORSE, about 14 hands and a half high, with a mealy nose, one hind foot white, a star in his forehead, nicked in the tail, trots and gallops, and if branded, unknown. There is great reason to believe a certain John Chapman (a deserter from one of the Virginia regiments) stole him. The said Chapman is about 5 feet 6 or 8 inches high, thin visage, light short hair, curled in his neck, and had with him a claret-coloured coat, turned up or edged with red, one pair of black breeches, edged with ditto, one pair of jean ditto, one pair of brown ditto, two pair of thread and one pair of yarn stockings, three white shirts, a new fan-tail hat, and a large iron stock-buckle. He was seen with the Horse, at Queen-Anne, on the 26th of April, offering him for sale. One hundred Dollars will be given for bringing home the Horse, with reasonable charges; and the above reward, upon conviction of the

Thief, by WALTER PYE.

The Maryland Journal, and Baltimore Advertiser, May 25, 1779.

Forty Dollars Reward.

Deserted last night from the Artillery Park at Pluckemin, JOHN FLAGLEY, a Matross belonging to Capt. Bauman's Company, in Col. LAMB's Battalion of Artillery, born in Ireland, twenty-sox years of age, five feet eight inches high, brown hair, blue eyes, pretty fat, very talkative and exceeding good natured when in liquor; had on when he deserted, a brown jacket (having left his uniform coat) white woolen undercloaths, a regimental hat, by occupation a farmer, and is supposed to be gone either to the Nine Partners in New-York State, or Philadelphia.

Also DESERTED at the same time, and supposed to be went with FLAGLEY, WILLIAM ROBINSON, born in Pennsylvania, a Matross, belonging to Capt. Lee's Company, in said Battalion, twenty two years of age, about five feet eight or nine inches high, light eyes, short brown hair, slim built and thin visaged. Whoever secures the said Deserters, so as they may be brought to justice, shall receive the above reward, or TWENTY DOLLARS for each, from the

subscribers, SAMUEL DOTY, Lieut. Artillery, or
JAMES LEE, Capt. Artillery.

The Pennsylvania Journal, and Weekly Advertiser, May 26, 1779; June 30, 1779.

TWENTY DOLLARS REWARD.

STOLEN from the subscriber, in Roxborough township, Philadelphia county, an indented boy named RUDOLPH CREASEL, son of Andrew Creasel, paper-maker, a deserter from the Continental army, residing at or near Paul Traiger's, paper-maker, about three miles from Reading in Berks county. He was taken away by his mother, is about thirteen years of age, and had on when taken away, a tow shirt and trowsers, old brown jacket, and an old hat without the brim. Whoever will discover who conceals or harbours said boy, so that they may legally be brought to justice, shall have the above reward: Also FIFTEEN PENCE for said boy, if brought home to his master.

HUGH CRAWFORD.   *May* 26.

The Pennsylvania Packet or the General Advertiser, June 1, 1779; June 5, 1779; June 15, 1779.

DESERTED from on Board the Ship Oliver Cromwell, the following Persons, viz *Jedidiah Norton, of Middletown; Samuel Thrasher,* of *Ditto; Joseph Carter,* of *Plainfield; Anthony Francis, a* Portugese, swarthy Complexion, his Hair tied behind; *Peleg Sanford,* of *Rhode-Island*; *James Richards,* a Native of *Boston*, taken on Board the *Sheriah* Privateer, out of New-York, and voluntarily entered on Board, light complexion, sandy bushy Hair, about 5 Feet 8 Inches high, 24 or 25 Years old, stocky well built, had on when he went away a blue out side Jacket, white flannel lining, round felt Hat, and long Ticklinburg Trowsers. Trowsers. Whoever will take up the above Persons, or any of them, and deliver them to the Commanding Office at New-London, shall receive Fifty Dollars Reward, and all necessary Charges

paid by   NATH'l SHAW, Agent for the State.

The Connecticut Gazette; And The Universal Intelligencer, June 3, 1779; June 10, 1779.

DESERTED from the Continental Service, the following Soldiers, viz—*James Parker,* about 36 Years of Age, about 5 Feet 10 Inches high, light Complexion, dark straight Hair; had on when he went away, a blue Coat and light-colour'd Waistcoat.— *James Smith,* about 28 Years of Age, about 5 Feet 7 Inches high, something slim, dark Complexion, dark straight Hair, something pitted with the Small-Pox; a Leather Breeches Maker.— *Baptist Knight,* about 25 Years of Age, 5 Feet 10 inches high, well built, light Complexion, light Hair; had on when he went away light colour'd Cloaths; Sadler by Trade.—*William*

Rogers, about 30 Years of Age, 5 Feet 5 Inches high, has dark straight Hair, very much pitted with the Small-Pox; had on when he went away, brown Cloaths.— *Edward Kelly*, about 6 Feet high, has had the Small-pox, about 30 Years old, something round shoulder'd, dark Complexion, *Thomas Spendergreess*, about 25 Years, old light Complection, often the worse for Drink.

Whoever will take up said Deserters and secure them in any of the Goals on the Continent, and will send Notice thereof to Col. *John Webster*, Muster-Master in Cheshire, in the State of New-Hampshire, shall receive *Fifty Dollars* for each, and all necessary Charges
           paid by said   Col. *John Webster*.

N. B. As large Bounties were paid them, it is hoped all Persons will exert themselves to secure said Villains.

The Boston Gazette, And Country Journal, June 7, 1779; June 14, 1779; June 21, 1779.

DESERTED from Col. SHEPARD'S regiment, General GLOVER's Brigade, stationed here at Providence— *Nathan Gilmore*, a private 25 years of age, 5 feet 10 inches high, light hair, light complexion, blue and white uniform, a Foreigner; *Daniel Hurley*, a private, 25 years of age, 5 feet 10 inches high, darkish red hair, light complexion, blue and white uniform, a Foreigner; *Daniel Taylor*, a drummer, 19 years of age, 5 feet 8 inches high, light hair, ruddy complexion, white and blue uniform, belongs to Worthington, exceeding well cloathed; *Thomas Allen*, a private, 21 years of age, 5 feet 6 inches high, light hair, light complexion, blue and white uniform, belongs to New-London; *William Cowen*, a corporal, 22 years of age, 5 feet 10 inches high, sandy hair, light complexion, blue and white uniform, belongs to Rochester, carried with him a brown coat, faced with blue, green breeches, and brown overalls; *Prince Bacon*, a private, 20 years of age, 5 feet 10 inches high, dark hair, dark complexion, blue and white uniform, belongs to Sandwich, goes a little stooping; *Alexander Johnson*, a corporal, 23 years of age, 5 feet 10 inches high, dark hair, dark complexion, blue and white uniform, belongs to Nantucket; *Abner Howes*, a corporal, 26 years of age, 5 feet 10 inches high, dark hair, dark complexion, blue and white uniform, belongs to Wellfleet, goes a little stooping; *James Masterman*, a private, 30 years of age, 5 feet 9 inches high, dark brown hair, florid complexion, belongs to Barnstable; *Francis Luce*, a private, 20 years of age, 5 feet 9 inches high, light hair, light complexion, cloth coloured and blue uniform, belongs to Rochester; *Robert Steele*, drum-major, 22 years of age, 5 feet 9 inches high, light hair, light complexion, blue and white uniform, belongs to Boston, carried with him a fringed linnen coat, white breeches, several ruffled shirts, and white stockings; *John Robinson*, fife-major, 20 years of age, 5 feet 9 inches high, dark hair, darkish complexion, white and blue uniform, belongs to Kingston; considerably pitted with the small-pox, carried with him a fringed linnen coat, several ruffled shirts; *Samuel Eggleston*, a private, 27 years of age, 5 feet 10 inches high, black hair, darkish complexion, belongs to Murrayfield. Whoever will apprehend and secure all or either of the above deserters, and return them to their regiment in Providence, shall receive the reward, allowed by Congress for apprehending deserters, and all necessary charges paid, by   WILLIAM SHEPARD, Col.

Providence, May 26, 1779.

N. B. All officers, civil and military, are requested to be aiding and assisting in taking said deserters. All masters of vessels, either in public or private service, are desired not to take any of the above-mentioned deserters into employ; if any are already employed, they are requested to give information of, and immediately return them.

The Independent Chronicle and the Universal Advertiser, June 10, 1779.

DESERTED from the second Connecticut Regiment, Gen. Huntington's Brigade, LEVI CHOSTER, a well built handsome fellow, five feet ten inches high, black eyes and hair, belongs to East Windsor. LEVI LEE, of the same Regiment 6 feet 10 inches [*sic*] high, light hair, eyes and complexion. And WM. LANE, of said Regiment, thick set well built fellow, 5 feet 9 inches high, light hair and complexion. Lee and Lane, belong to New London. Whoever shall take up said deserters, and secure them, so that they may be brought to their duty, shall receive Fifty Dollars Reward, for either of the above deserters, and all necessary charges, paid by
ICHABOD HINCKLEY, Capt.

N. B. Said Lee is an old offender, as this is the third time he has deserted since he belonged to this Regiment.

The Connecticut Courant, And The Weekly Intelligencer, June 15, 1779; June 22, 1779. June 22 ad shows Lee as 5 feet 10 inches.

DEserted from Capt. Gid. Westcott's company, Col. Elliott's regiment of artillery, JOHN ARMOND, a Frenchman, about 30 years of age, 5 feet 3 inches high, of a dark complexion, has dark hair, and blue eyes: Had on when he went away, a blue regimental coat, faced with red, green waistcoat and breeches: He is a slim fellow and talks broken. Whoever will take up said deserter and return him to his company, or confine him in any gaol of the United States, shall have One Hundred Dollars reward and reasonable charges,

    paid by ISAAC PITMAN, Capt. Lt. Artillery.

Providence, June 16.

The American Journal And General Advertiser, June 17, 1779; June 24, 1779; July 1, 1779.

To the PUBLIC.

EVERY defrauder of the public must be looked upon as a capital offender, and it is the duty of every member of society to assist in detecting and punishing such offenders. Every soldier in the army may be considered as your servant, who, if he deserts your service, ought to be reduced to obedience. For, this reason your particular attention is desired to the following advertisements.

Deserted from my battalion in the service of the United States of America, now stationed at North-Kingstown, the following persons, viz. Robert Knowlton, of Dartmouth, 5 feet 9 inches high, light complexioned, has blue eyes, sandy short hair, 35 years of age. John Simmons, of Boston, fifer, dark complexioned, has blue eyes, short dark hair, much pitted with the small-pox, 4 feet high, 11 years of age. John Wyer, of Merrimack, 5 feet 7 inches high, dark complexioned, has short black hair, 20 years of age. William Lewis, of Beverly, fifer, 5 feet 5 inches high, brown complexioned, has short black hair, thick set, 16 years of age. Richard Dresser, of Scarborough, 5 feet 9 inches high, has dark hair, and is dark complexioned. William Mooney, of Boston, 5 feet 10 inches high, fair complexioned, has red hair, 20 years of age. Peter Cummings, of Andover, 5 feet 9 inches high, dark complexioned, has brown hair, 39 years of age. Patrick Catherwood, of Boston, 5 feet 8 inches high, dark complexioned, has black hair, 23 years of age. Joseph Habb, of Peterborough, 5 feet 4 inches high, dark complexioned, has black hair, 23 years of age. William Burke, of Stamford, 5 feet 9 inches high, dark complexioned, has brown hair, 32 years of age. Richard Tinsley, drummer, from Marblehead, 4 feet 10 inches high, dark complexioned, has brown hair, 15 years of age. Enoch Bailey, serjeant, from Newbury, 5 feet 9 inches high, light complexioned, has light hair, sandy hair, 24 years of age. Benjamin Witt, serjeant, from Worcester, dark complexioned, has dark eyes, dark hair, 5 feet 10 inches high, 26 years of age, John Beard, of Providence, serjeant, 5 feet 10 inches high, dark complexioned, has light eyes, dark hair, 32 years of age. Thomas Wadden, of Marblehead, drummer, 5 feet 5 inches high, light complexioned, has dark eyes, dark hair, 20 years of age. John Fullerton, of Pomfret, 5 feet 6 inches high, light complexioned, has light eyes and sandy hair, 36 years of age. John Matthews, of Scarborough, 5 feet 6 inches high, light complexioned, has light eyes, and sandy hair, 24 years of age. Ezra Whitcom, of Lancaster, 5 feet 9 inches high, light complexioned, has light eyes, sandy-hair, 24 years of age. Lemuel Tucker, corporal, from Falmouth, 5 feet 9 inches high, dark complexioned, has black eyes, black hair, 29 years of age. William Stapler, of Sudbury, 5 feet 7 inches high, light complexioned, has blue eyes, sandy hair, pock-marked, 23 years of age. Nicholas Brune, a Frenchman, 5 feet 4 inches high, dark complexioned, has black eyes, black hair, 23 years of age. Peter Jew, a Frenchman, 5 feet 4 inches, dark complexioned, has grey eyes, dark hair, 21 years of age. Alexis Bear, a Frenchman, 5 feet 4 inches high, light complexioned, has blue eyes, light hair, pock-marked, 17 years of age. Emon Gennet, a Frenchman, 5 feet 4 inches high, dark complexioned, has black eyes, black hair, 20 years of age. John Barns, an Englishman, 5 feet 10 inches high, light complexioned, has blue eyes, light hair, pock-marked, 33 years of age. Edward Redford, an Englishman, 5 feet 6 inches high, dark complexioned, has blue eyes, black hair, pock-marked, 25 years of age. Yone Le Turk, a Frenchman, 5 feet 2 inches high, dark complexioned, has black eyes, black hair, his right arm shorter than the left. John Coate, a Frenchman, 5 feet 4 inches high, dark complexioned, has grey eyes, black hair, pock-marked, his eyes bloodshot, 22 years of age. Samuel Pomroy, of Black-Point, 5 feet 4 inches high, dark complexioned, has black hair, 18 years of age. James Kearnes, an Englishman, about 5 feet 9 inches high, pock-marked, has grey eyes, short sandy hair. Caleb Howard, of Warwick, 5 feet 7 inches high, has light hair, light complexioned, thin favoured, 20 years of age. Jacob Bullock, of Rehoboth, 5 feet 8 inches high, has dark hair, dark complexioned, hasel eyes, his head standing forward, his fore teeth gone, 21 years of age. Abraham Shippey, of Smithfield, 5 feet 9 inches high, has light hair, light complexioned, blue eyes, round shouldered, 20 years of age. James Briggs, of Durham, 5 feet 9 inches high, swarthy complexioned, dark hair, hasel eyes, 25 years of age. Peleg Loring, of Raynham, 5 feet 7 inches, light complexioned, has blue eyes, brown hair, 27 years of age. William Roper, an Englishman, 5 feet 6 inches high, well made, swarthy complexioned, has long chestnut coloured hair. Edward Hunt, of Boston, 6 feet high, light complexioned, has light hair, blue eyes, 35 years of age. John Grey, of Connecticut, 5 feet 9 inches high, freckled, has sandy hair, 28 years of age. Samuel Cashell, an Englishman, 5 feet high, swarthy complexioned, has dark short hair, 25 years of age. Joseph Wilkinson, an Irishman, 6 feet high, pock-marked, has short dark hair, 35 years of age. Jotham Libby, of Scarborough, formerly a serjeant, 5 feet 9 inches high, light complexioned, has light hair, 50 years of age. William Bolton, of Becket, 5 feet 9 inches high, has dark hair, dark eyes, and of a dark complexion, freckled, 30 years of age. John Rittor, of Lunenburg, 5 feet 7 inches high, dark complexioned, has dark hair and eyes, 20 years of age. Benjamin Alds, of Merrimack, 5 feet 9 inches high, dark complexioned, has dark hair, blue eyes, 19 years of age. Daniel Balcom of Attleborough, 5 feet 7 inches high, ruddy faced, has dark hair, blue eyes, 35 years of age. Joshua Austin, of Dartmouth, 5 feet 8 inches high, dark complexioned, has black hair and eyes, 33 years of age, John Noonon, of Boston, 5 feet 7 inches high, freckled, has red hair, light eyes, 30 years of age. John Eclitee, a Frenchman, 5 feet 7 inches high, dark complexioned, has dark hair and eyes, 25 years of age. William Stewart, of Merrimack, 5 feet 9 inches high, swarthy complexioned, has dark hair and eyes, 22 years of age. Oliver McLane, of Dedham, 6 feet high, light complexioned, has light hair, 25 years of age. James Cuff, an Englishman, 6 feet high, strait bodied, pock-marked, with a blemish in one eye, 24 years of age. John Bryant, an Irishman, 5 feet 11 inches high, stout bodied, light complexioned, has light hair, pock-marked, 25 years of age. Thomas Bushel, an Irishman, 6 feet high, strait bodied, swarthy complexioned, has dark hair, bow-legged, 30 years of age. Philip Targee, of Swansey, 6 feet high, swarthy complexioned, has dark hair, grey eyes, 30 years of age. David Enos, of North-Kingstown, 5 feet 7 inches high, dark complexioned, has brown hair, 25 years of age. Josiah Hunt, of Scarborough, 5 feet 5 inches, light complexioned, has light hair, blue eyes, goes with his head forward, 19 years of age, Emanuel Lawrel, a Frenchman, 5 feet 7 inches high, dark complexioned, has dark hair and eyes, 35 years of age. George Patch, of Newbury, 5 feet 6 inches high, has light hair, light complexioned, 21 years of age.

It is hoped that no person will harbour or conceal any of the above named deserters, but that every friend to the army, and in the interest of the United States, will use their utmost endeavours to apprehend and bring them to justice.

Any person who shall take up and secure any of the said deserters, so that they may be returned to their regiment, shall receive a reward of twenty dollars for each, and all necessary charges,
    paid by me, HENRY JACKSON, Colonel.
    Barber's Heights (North-Kingston) June 15, 1779.

N. B. Many of the above deserters are gone off with a design to enter on board privateers. It is therefore desired, that all persons residing in sea-ports will assist (as far as in their power) in detecting and apprehending them.

The Providence Gazette; And Country Journal, June 19, 1779; July 26, 1779; July 3, 1779.

DESERTED from the Ship WARREN the Night of the 22d, THOMAS DOUGLASS, 26 Years of Age, 5 Feet 6 Inches high, short dark brown Hair, ruddy Complection, stout and well made, carried away with him a crimson Silk Waist-Coat, a short whitish Coat, a black Silk Handkerchief, a Pair of blue Breeches, a Pair of grey ribb'd Stockings, a Pair of turn'd Pumps, Silver Buckles, and a Pinchbeck Watch, all which he stole from Alexander Hamilton, belonging to said Ship. Whoever will secure the above Deserter and Thief and return him to said Ship, or secure him in any Goal, shall receive TWO HUNDRED DOLLARS Reward, and all necessary Charges
         paid by   JOSHUA HEMPSTED, jun.
New-London, June 23, 1779.
The Connecticut Gazette; And The Universal Intelligencer, June 24, 1779. See *The Connecticut Gazette; And The Universal Intelligencer*, July 8, 1779, for Douglass.

DESERTED from the ship *Dragon* the following men, *viz. William Angel; Joseph Angel, Thomas Manes, James Jenings, Edny Coats, Thomas Coats, William Edwards, Thomas Pope, John Walker,* all of *Lancaster* and *Northumberland* county, *Edward Swan* from *Maryland, Thomas Wood* and *Able Springs,* mulattoes. I will give 60 dollars for each to any person that will secure them in any jail, or deliver them on board of any vessel belonging to the navy in this state, and all reasonable expences allowed.
         JAMES MARKHAM.
☞ All those that have been indulged with furloughs are requested to return to their duty immediately, or they will deemed as deserters and treated as such; and all those deserters that will return to their duty by the 20th of *July,* will be received without any punishment.
The Virginia Gazette, Dixon and Nicolson, July 3, 1779; July 10, 1779.

Hartford, June 19, 1779.
ESCAPED from the goal last Tuesday afternoon; 3 prisoners of war, viz. Joseph Bradly, a tall lusty man, perhaps near 40 years old, was a serjeant of grenadiers, very poorly cloathed, his outside covering was a very poor almost worn out blue great coat. Another named Thomas Slate, a sailor, also a tall lusty man, about the same age. The other is a Thomas Ward, who was taken up at Waterbury and returned. It is

hoped they may be taken up and returned, and when I am informed of it necessary charges shall be paid,

        by   E. WILLIAMS, Dep. Com. Pris.

The Connecticut Courant, And The Weekly Intelligencer, July 6, 1779.

        ONE HUNDRED DOLLARS REWARD,

Whereas *John Wight* of *Dedham,* in the county of *Suffolk,* and State of *Massachusetts Bay,* being one of the militia for said state, was to serve nine months from the time of his joining the army, which was on the 7th day of July, 1778; and he being put in the company under my command, in Col. Putnam's regiment, on the 29th day of the same month, deserted from said company and regiment, and carried away with him one of the Continental guns, &c. and has been absent from his duty ever since; and he being lately advertised for said crimes by the said Col. Putnam, was taken into custody by me, to be convey'd to the army, to carry back said gun, &c. and to serve his term; but being encouraged and assisted by some persons known to me, the said John on the 29th instant broke away from me, and is supposed to be concealed by the same persons, in said Dedham:—Therefore, all militia officers, committees of correspondence, and committees for raising soldiers, and all others, are desired to assist in securing the said John Wight, so as he may be return'd to his duty, as they would avoid the encouragement of such abominable practices in future; and one hundred dollars shall be paid to any person that shall apprehend the said John Wight, and bring him to me, or commit him to any goal in this state, that he may be conveyed to the army to serve the remainder of his term, and return the arms he brought away, or be otherwise proceeded with agreeable to rule and order.

        JOSEPH MORSE, Capt. in Con'l army.

        Natick, June 30.

The Continental Journal, And Weekly Advertiser, July 8, 1779; July 15, 1779; July 22, 1779.

BROKE out of the County Goal in New-London, the Night after the 5th Inst. one THOMAS DOUGLASS, 25 Years old, 5 Feet 6 inches high, has short brown Hair, ruddy Complexion; strait and well made; had on a brown Holland Coattee and linen Breeches; committed for Theft and Desertion from the ship WARREN. Whoever will return him to the Subscriber, shall have TEN DOLLARS Reward.

        NATHAN BALEY, ju. *Goaler.*

        NEW-LONDON, JULY 6, 1779.

The Connecticut Gazette; And The Universal Intelligencer, July 8, 1779; July 14, 1779; July 28, 1779. See *The Connecticut Gazette; And The Universal Intelligencer*, June 24, 1779.

Philadelphia, July 9.
THE following articles are supposed to be stolen by a certain JOHN Kline, a deserter belonging to the tenth Pennsylvania regiment, viz. A mare and saddle, the mare branded on the left side **O**. two cheeses, fatts and all; a pair of boots, two pots with butter, a green silk jacket, a great-coat, an old quilted white petticoat, and a quantity of needles. Whoever has lost the said articles, by proving their property and paying the charges may have them again,
by applying to WILLIAM RADIGER, Constable.
The Pennsylvania Packet or the General Advertiser, July 10, 1779; July 15, 1779; July 20, 1779.

DESERTED FROM Lieut. Col. Stacy's Company, in the 6th Massachusetts Regiment; Samuel Wheeler, Corporal, 24 Years of Age, about 5 Feet 5 Inches high, light Brown Hair, light Complexion, an Inhabitant of Boston, and a Baker by Trade. Whoever will take up said Deserter, and send him forward to his Regiment, shall have Thirty Dollars Reward, and all necessary Charges paid by the Subscriber.
WILLIAM CURTIS, Lieut.
Fort Alden, 14th June, 1779.
The Boston Gazette, and Country Journal, July 12, 1779; July 19, 1779.

SIXTY DOLLARS Reward.
RUN away from the subscriber, living in Eastown, Northampton county, on Sunday the 4th inst. an apprentice LAD, named CONRAD COOK, by trade a blacksmith, a Hessian, about 19 years of age, about 5 feet 10 inches high, slim made, pock-marked, brown long hair: He took with him when he went away, a blue broad-cloath coat, a blue jacket, leather breeches, linen overalls, a pair of white breeches, blue stockings, white cotton stockings, a pair of pumps, and carved yellow metal buckles, has a stock, white, handkerchief and a wool hat. Whoever apprehends said runaway and delivers him to the subscriber, shall receive the above reward.
GEORGE ERUFRIDT.
N. B. He has a pass as a deserter from the British army.
The Pennsylvania Journal, and Weekly Advertiser, July 14, 1779.

DESERTED from the *Prince* of *Wales American Regt.* on the 8th inst. JOHN DERUCE, native of Block-Island, a thick well set Man, with a ruddy complexion; and robbed his Captain of 170 DOLLARS.—He is about 24 years of age, 5 Feet 4 Inches high; and was a Deserter from Col. Jackson's Regt. in the Rebel Service.—Whoever apprehends the said Deserter and will deliver him to the Regiment, shall Receive 40 DOLLARS REWARD, besides his MAJESTY'S allowance for apprehending Deserter.

Newport, July 22d. 1779.

The Newport Gazette, July 22, 1779; July 29, 1779; August 12, 1779.

Hillsborough, July 18, 1779.

BROKE out of Somerset county gaol last night, James Erwine, about 40 years old, sandy hair, a very down look, pale face and ugly visage, a native of Ireland, about 5 feet 9 inches high, he was confined on suspicion of committing murder. Also Henry Caster, a likely young man, about 21 years old, said he had served his time to a Doctor in Philadelphia, about 5 feet 6 inches high, brown curled hair; was taken up near Bonem-town, on his way to the enemy. Also Henry Winn, a young man, well built, of a light complexion, about 5 feet 9 inches high, belonging to Gen. Maxwell's brigade; was taken up for desertion. Any person apprehending the said runaways, and returns them to said gaol, shall have Thirty Dollars for each, and all reasonable charges, paid by me

PETER DUMONT, Sheriff.

The New Jersey Gazette, July 28, 1779; August 4, 1779.

Broke out of the Goal at Salem, on the Night of the 25th Instant, the noted *Isaac Taft,* in the Continental Service, who has been convicted three Times for hireing Men into said Service, and has receive his Punishment the last at Salem, and has the Marks of Part of his Punishment streak'd on his Back: He is a thick well made Fellow, light Complection, and short light Hair, 26 Years of Age, 5 Feet 10 Inches high—Also *George Stacnon,* a soldier Col. Jackson's Regiment, dark Complection, black Hair, about 5 Feet 10 Inches high; and two Negro Fellows, Prisoners of War, taken by the Ship Hunter.—Whoever shall take up any, or all of the above named Prisoners, and confine them in any Goal within the United States of America, shall receive ONE HUNDRED DOLLARS Reward for each of them,

by me, MICHAEL FARLEY, Sheriff.

Ipswich, July 26, 1779.

The Independent Chronicle and the Universal Advertiser, July 29, 1779, August 5, 1779; September 2, 1779. See *The Boston Gazette, And The Country Journal*, November 8, 1779, for Taft.

DESERTED three of the recruits from *York* county, to wit. *Brian Bickerton* an *Englishman,* pitted with the smallpox, about 5 feet 6 inches high. *Anthony Murvey* a *Frenchman,* very likely, 5 feet 7 or 8 inches high. *Francis Basnitt* an *Englishman,* very much pitted with the smallpox, is 5 feet 6 inches high. Whoever will deliver the above deserters to the county Lieutenant of *York,* shall receive a reward of THREE HUNDRED DOLLARS, or ONE HUNDRED DOLLARS for each.
    The Virginia Gazette, Dixon and Nicolson, August 7, 1779; August 14, 1779; August 21, 1779.

MADE his escape from a guard at Maidenhead, in New-Jersey, on their way to Head-quarters, a certain JOHN CLINE, about 5 feet 7 or 8 inches high, a very dark complexion, and squints; he had on a lapelled jacket of brown cloth, without sleeves, a check shirt, black stocking breeches, has one pair of white woollen stockings, and no shoes. Whoever secures the above-mentioned Cline, and lodges him in any gaol, or delivers him to any guard of continental troops on their way to Head-quarters, shall receive the thanks of their country, and a proper compensation.
    N. WHITE, Lieut. 10th Penn. Regt.
N. B. Said Cline was graced with handcuffs when he made his escape.
                                                                     Aug. 15.
    The New Jersey Gazette, August 18, 1779.

                ONE HUNDRED DOLLARS REWARD
FOR each of the following deserters from the snip TARTAR, *viz. Matthew Nightengale, John Taylor, Ellis Edwards, Motto Pickerin, Patrick Hopkins, Thomas Mains, George Day,* and *Augustine Boyd,* all of *Wicomic* parish, *Northumberland* county; *Richard Timberlake* and *William Darby* of *Lancaster* county; *John Bass* of *Middlesex; John Marshall, Daniel Grant,* and *Dennis Obrian,* there is reason to believe are gon\e to *North Carolina.* The above reward will be given for each of the above deserters, on their being delivered on board any armed vessel belonging to this state.
                THOMAS GRANT.
        CHICKAHOMANY SHIP-YARD, *September* 10, 1779.
    The Virginia Gazette, Dixon and Nicolson, September 11, 1779; September 18, 1779; September 25, 1779.

AUGUST 29, 1779.

DESERTED, three of the recruits from *Prince William* county, to wit: ANDREW MURPHEY, an *Irishman,* 5 feet 7 or 8 inches high, well made, black hair, a large black beard, had on a round hat, brown cloth sailors jacket, check shirt, and a pair of osnabrug trowsers. JAMES MILLER, an *Englishman,* 5 feet 8 inches high, of a swarthy complexion, short brown hair, curls before, well made, had on a white coarse cloth jacket, cotton shirt, and osnabrug trowsers. ROBERT WOODERFIELD, an *Englishman,* 5 feet 11 inches high, fair complexion, short light hair, well made, much given to liquor, lost his foreteeth, had on an old white shirt slit on the shoulders, a pair of bed ticking trowsers, and a pair of old shoes. Any person apprehending the above deserters, shall receive 150 dollars, or 50 dollars for each upon
    delivery to WILLIAM LINTON.
The Virginia Gazette, Dixon and Nicolson, September 11, 1779; September 25, 1779; October 2, 1779.

DESERTED about 12 o'clock last night from Col. Angel's regiment of Continental troops, one COVEL LARKENS, belonging to Hopkinton, State of Rhode-Island, 22 years old, 5 feet 2 inches high, dark complexion, black hair, has a scar on his right jaw; had on when he went away, a felt hat, rifle frock and overhauls. Also THOMAS SARLS, belonging to Stonington, State of Connecticut, 18 years old, 5 feet 5 inches high, fresh complexion, dark brown hair, has a mole upon his left breast, well built; had on when he went away, a white coat, jacket and overhauls. Also JOSEPH CONGDON, belonging to Hopkinton, State of Rhode-Island, 17 years old, 5 feet 8 inches high, dark brown hair, light complexion; had on when he went away a small felt hat, rifle frock and overhauls. Whoever will take up said deserters and return them to their regiment, or secure them in any goal of the United States, and send word to the Colonel of said regiment, so that they may be had by their officers, shall receive a reward of TWO HUNDRED DOLLARS for each soldier, and all necessary
    charges paid. JERE. OLNEY, Lt. Col. Commandant.
      North-Kingston, (Rhode-Island) Sept. 16. 1779.
N. B. Said deserters will it is supposed endeavour to get on board some armed vessel. All masters of vessels are forbid transporting said deserters from the continent, on penalty of suffering the consequence.
    NATHAN WHITTELSEY,
      Quarter-Master to said Regiment.

The Connecticut Gazette; And The Universal Intelligencer, September 22, 1779; September 29, 1779; October 6, 1779; October 13, 1779.

DESERTED from Capt. Cone's Company, Col. Jonathan Wells' Regiment, a Soldier who called his Name *James Ailes*, of a dark Complexion, short black Hair, has an Impediment in his Speech, wore away a dark coloured Surtout and a red Waistcoat. Any Person that will take up said Deserter, and bring him to said Regiment, or secure him so that he may be returned to Camp before the 10th of October, shall receive FORTY DOLLARS Reward, and all necessary Charges, paid by SIMEON DRAKE, Lieutenant.

New-London, September 11, 1779.

The Connecticut Gazette; And The Universal Intelligencer, September 22, 1779; September 28, 1777; October 13, 1779.

DESERTED.

FROM the *Prince of Wales's American* Regiment, THOMAS FOSTER, by trade a Shoemaker, born in Dorchester, near Boston, he is about 5 Feet 11 Inches high, 35 years of age, black Eyes, dark complexion, and dark Hair, has followed his occupation in Newport, for some years, and left behind him a Wife and four Children.—Whoever apprehends him so as that he may be brought to the Regiment will RECEIVE TEN DOLLARS, from the Commanding Officer, over and above the King's Bounty.

The Newport Gazette, September 23, 1779.

THIRTY DOLLARS Reward.

DESERTED on Monday the 20th Day of *Sept.* Instant, from my Company in Col. *Jonathan Welles's* Detachment of Militia, stationed at New-London, one *ELISHA ALLEN*, of Hartford West-Division, (as he said), about 24 Years old, is well built, 5 Feet 10 Inches high, light Hair and light Complexion, something mark'd with the small pox, he was inlisted for two Months. Whoever will take up said Deserter and convey him to me at New-London, or secure him in any of the state Goals, so that he may be have, shall have the above Reward, and all necessary Charges

paid by   JOHN WOOD, Capt.

New-London, Sept. 27, 1779.

The Connecticut Gazette; And The Universal Intelligencer, September 29, 1779; October 13, 1779; October 20, 1779.

TWENTY DOLLARS REWARD.

BROKE out of this gaol a certain Edward Morfit, who was put in for deserting from his party of British prisoners who were going to New-York to be exchanged. Whoever takes up said Morfit, and secures him, so that he may be exchanged, shall be entitled to the above reward. JOHN JAMES.
Keeper of Trenton gaol.   Sept. 24.
The New Jersey Gazette, October 13, 1779.

Deserted from the Ship Ranger,

RIchard Lee, a Marine on Board the said Ship Ranger, 20 Years of Age, 5 Feet 7 Inches, brown Complexion, born in Ireland, Resident in Portsmouth.

John O'Brian, ordinary Seaman, 24 Years of Age, 5 Feet 6 Inches, brown Complexion, born in Ireland, Resident in Portsmouth.

Whoever will take up said Deserters, and secure them, so that they may be put on Board said Ship, shall receive 200 Dollars Reward, or 100 for either of them.

THOMAS SIMPSON. Portsmouth, October 26. 1776.
The New-Hampshire Gazette; Or, State Journal, and General Advertiser, October 26, 1779; November 2, 1779.

TWO HUNDRED DOLLARS Reward.

DESERTED, Newburgh, October 29th, 1779, from Capt. Robert Walker's Company, Second Battalion Artillery, *John Peet*, a Corporal, about 25 Years of age, 5 feet 7½ Inches high, dark Complection, black Hair, and grey Eyes, round shouldered, and stoops in his Walk, by Trade a Joiner, born in America.—*John Wells*, a Corporal, 30 Years of Age, 5 Feet 8 Inches high, dark Complexion, dark Hair & grey Eyes, a little pitted with the Small-Pox, by Trade a Blacksmith, born in America.— *Joseph Eldridge*, 28 Years of Age, 6 Feet high, fair Complexion, brown Hair & grey Eyes, has an Impediment in his Speech which may be discovered by conversing with him, bred to the farming Business, born in America.— *Thomas Davenport*, about 27 Years of Age, 5 Feet 11 Inches high, dark Complexion, short black curl'd Hair, dark Eyes, addicted to Liquor, bred to the Seas.—They wore away black Coats faced with red, but 'tis very probable they may change their Dress. Whoever takes up and secures the above Deserters so that they may be had again, shall receive the above Reward, or Fifty Dollars for either of them, and all necessary Charges paid by
ROBERT WALKER. Capt. 2d Bat. Artillery.

The Connecticut Journal, November 3, 1779; November 10, 1779; November 17, 1779; November 24, 1779; December 1, 1779.

I Ebenezer Pelton, jun. of Groton, a Continental Soldier in Col. Starr's Company and Regiment, Gen. Huntington's Brigade, did by the Instigation of the Devil, on the 22d Inst. steal a large from Mare, from Dr. Peter Hays, of Danbury, for which Sin I beg the forgiveness of God and the Public. I desire this may be published in the New-London Papers, as the Public may be informed of my Villainy.
          EBENEZER PELTON, 2d.
                                  Groton, October 26, 1777.
In Presence of John Morgan, Benjamin Hicks, Mary Fanning.
    The Connecticut Gazette; And The Universal Intelligencer, November 10, 1779; November 17, 1779.8

DESERTED from my company in the Hessian Regiment of Losberg, in the night of the 7th instant, a Soldier named JOHN ANSELL, a native Frenchman, 24 years old, five feet one inch high, marked with the small-pox, when he went off he wore his regimentals, a blue coat faced with orange. It is likely the above deserter may be concealed either in this city or Long-Island, whoever should discover him in desired to give notice to the regiment of Losberg.
          de ALTENBOCKUM, Captain.
                              Camp near New-York, Oct. 10, 1779.
    The Royal Gazette, November 10, 1779.

DESERTED the 16th inst. from Capt. Adam Shapley's company of artillery, at Fort Trumbull, one THOMAS BUCK, about 17 years of age, 5 feet 4 or 5 inches high; had on when he went off, a brown jacket, white flannel overhauls, and check shirt. Whoever will take up said deserter and return him to his company at Fort Trumbull, shall have Sixty Dollars, and all necessary charges.
    Also deserted from his post at Black-hall, one Sergeant William Winslow, a talkative person, of a sandy complexion. Whoever will take up said Winslow, and secures him in any gaol in this State, and give notice thereof, shall have Five Dollars reward.
          RICHARD CHAPMAN, Lieut. Art.
              Fort Trumbull, (New-London) November 17, 1779.
    The Connecticut Gazette; And The Universal Intelligencer, November 17, 1779; December 8, 1779.

255

ONE HUNDRED DOLLARS REWARD,
DESERTED from this city, SAMUEL CHESTER, an *Irishman*, about 5 feet 7 or 8 inches high, dark hair and eyebrows, hazle eyes, his hair tied behind, down look, of a brown complexion, a weaver by trade, and said he came from *York*; his dress, a short brown coat, white waistcoat and breeches, blue stockings, and a round hat I will give the above reward to any person who delivers the said deserter to me in *Williamsburg,* or secures him in any jail so that get him again.
EDWARD D[IGGES] [   ]R.
The Virginia Gazette, Dixon and Nicolson, November 20, 1779

WILLIAMSBURG, NOVEMBER 20.
On Saturday last, Andrew Wilson, alias John Williams, alias John Gordon (who enlisted three different times, and deserted as often) was shot at the barracks, near this city, agreeable to his sentence.
The Virginia Gazette, Dixon and Nicolson, November 20, 1779.

November 22, 1779.
DESERTED from *Richmond* the 15th of *October* last, two recruits who enlisted in the continental army for eighteen months, under the act of Assembly passed the last winter. *Robert Tate,* a *Virginian,* who enlisted as substitute for a division in *Henrico* ; he is about 27 years of age, 5 feet 8 inches high, fair complexion and by trade a blacksmith. *John Wash,* who enlisted as substitute for a division in *Louisa* ; he is about 25 years\ of age, 5 feet 11 inches high. I will give a reward of one hundred dollars for the above deserters, or fifty for either of them. THOMAS WILLIAMSON.
The Virginia Gazette, Purdie, November 27, 1779; December 18, 1779; December 25, 1779.

DESERTED from Fort Griswold, one THOMAS CARRAL, a soldier in the artillery company, he is about 5 feet 11 inches high, a thick stout built fellow, with sandy hair and light eyes, said he belonged to Dudley, in Massachusetts State. Also one NATHAN AUSTIN, of Preston, a small slender fellow, speaks quick. Whoever will take up said deserters and return them to the Fort, shall have One Hundred Dollars for Carral, and all necessary charges paid, and One Dollar for Austin, by   WILLIAM LATHAM, Capt. Artillery.
Groton, 26th November, 1779.
The Connecticut Gazette and the Universal Intelligencer, December 1, 1779; December 8, 1779.

DESERTED from on board his Majesty's ship Robuste, JAMES RUTHERFORD, aged about 21 years, 5 feet 3 inches high, brown complexion, light brown hair, brown jacket; place of abode, Newcastle. Left the ship's long-boat November 21.

 WILLIAM WALLER, aged about 21 years, 5 feet 4 inches high, brown complexion, a mole under his left cheek, dark brown hair, blue jacket; place of abode, Whitby. Left the long-boat November 21.

 JOHN RIDLEY, aged about 23 years, 5 feet 7 inches high, brown complexion, pitted with the small-pox, flaxen hair, tied; place of abode Newcastle.

 ALEXANDER COWANS, aged about 20 years, 5 feet 2 inches high, fair complexion, white coloured hair; place of abode Newcastle.

 ☞The two last left the ship about a month ago.

 If any of the above men will deliver themselves up to any of his Majesty's ships, within four days of the date hereof, they shall be pardoned;—otherwise, any person who apprehends them, shall receive FORTY SHILLINGS Sterling for each man.

The Royal Gazette, December 1, 1779.

DESERTED from the Horse Department of the Royal Artillery, on command at Staten-Island, MICHAEL FUTCHER, five feet eleven inches high, fair complexion, fair hair, slight made, by trade a Blacksmith; had on when he went away, a short red jacket, round hat and feather in it. Whoever apprehends said deserted, by giving information at the Officer of Ordnance opposite St. Paul's Church, Broad Way, will be handsomely rewarded for their trouble. It is expected he is on board some privateer. Whoever harbours or conceals him will be prosecuted to the utmost rigour of the law.

 Likewise THOMAS KEMPTON, about 45 years of age, 5 feet 4 inches high, yellowish cast, sandy hair, had on when he went away a red coat.

The Royal Gazette, December 22, 1779; January 1, 1780; January 5, 1780. Kempton is not listed in the first ad.

1780

400 Dollars Reward.

DESERTED from the French King's Frigate Negress, lying in the Harbour of New-London, on the 9th Instant, a Frenchman named —— Charleonnier, about 45 Years old, 5 Feet 4 or 5 inches high, slim built, dark Complexion, black short Hair and black Beard, had on a gold Wire in his left Ear; had on a round Hat, a sailor's Jacket of brown Cloth, white Vest, blue coarse cloth Breeches, supposed to have carried with him a pair of large sailor's Boots. Whoever will take up and return said Deserter to Capt. Landolphe, in New-London, shall have the above Reward, and all necessary Charges paid.

New-London, Jan 11, 1780.
The Connecticut Gazette; And The Universal Intelligencer, January 12, 1780.

ON the night after the 9th instant, Litchfield county goal was broke and the following prisoners made their escape, viz. Thomas Knap, confined for treason, of a middling size short black curled hair, black eyes, quick spoken, a fellow of great address. Also, William Thompson, confined for theft, lately belonged to Col. Sheldon's regiment of Light Dragoons, a small likely looking fellow, about 22 years of age. Also, William Simmons, confined for treason, a young fellow about 22 years of age, thick set, appears to be and ignorant worthless fellow. Also, Eno. Blakesley, confined for desertion for the continental army. The Cloaths of the above cannot be described, as they have lately made some exchanges. Whoever will apprehend and return the above prisoners to said goal again shall have for Knap 50 dollars, and for Thompson and Simmons 20 dollars each as a reward; and for Blakesley the thanks of the public's humble servant,

LYNDE LORD Sheriff.   Litchfield, Feb. 10, 1780.
The Connecticut Courant, And The Weekly Intelligencer, February 15, 1780; February 22, 1780.

Extract of a Letter from Litchfield, Feb. 10.
"*You have doubtless heard that the house of Caleb Mallery of Washington was consumed by fire last Thursday night, and five persons, viz. Mr. Mallery, his wife, and three children all burnt in it, which was the whole of the family that was at home that night: and this day one Barnet Davenport, (who was a hired man to said Mallery at the time) was committed to our goal, and confesses he knocked Mr. Mallery and his wife on the head, robbed the house, and then set it on fire, and when said Davenport was taken up was cloathed in Mr. Mallery's cloaths.*"

The Connecticut Courant, And The Weekly Intelligencer, February 15, 1780. See *The Connecticut Gazette, And The Universal Intelligencer*, February 16, 1780, and *The Connecticut Journal*, February 16, 1780.

Stop a Murderer.
ON the night after the 3d last, was destroyed by Fire, the Dwelling House of Caleb Mallery, of this Town, Caleb Mallery, his Wife, and

three small Children were consumed with the House, (the whole Family except one Davenport.) It is supposed that one *Nicholas Davenport*, as he called himself, his true Name is *Barnard Davenport*, a Deserter from the American Army, a stout well built Fellow, about five Feet ten Inches high, light Complexion, hard favoured, light Eyes, about Twenty Years of Age, a Native of New-Milford, plundered the House, murdered the Persons, set Fire to the House, and then run-away by the Light of it. Every Friend to Justice, the Ties of Society, and the Laws of God and Man, is earnestly requested to use every Method and Means to apprehend the aforesaid [Villai]n—Whoever shall apprehend the Perpetrator of this horrid Villainy, will be generously rewarded, and all necessary Charges paid, and receive the Thanks of every Friend of Mankind in General.

Washington, Litchfield County,
State of Connecticut, Feb. 8, 1780.

The Connecticut Gazette, And The Universal Intelligencer, February 16, 1780. See *The Connecticut Courant, And The Weekly Intelligencer*, February 15, 1780, and *The Connecticut Journal*, February 16, 1780.

NEW-HAVEN, February 16.

The following are all the particulars we have been able to collect of a most barbarous murder, committed at Washington, in this State. On the night of the third inst. the dwelling house of Mr. Caleb Mallery, a wealthy farmer, of that town, was observed to be on fire, but standing remote from neighbours, it was not discovered until the house was nearly destroyed; and as none of the family were to be found, it was concluded at first, that they had all perished in bed, while asleep; it consisted of Mr. Mallery, his wife, and three grandchildren, and one Barnard Davenport, a youth of about 20, a native of New Milford, who had for some time been in the employ of Mr. Mallery. On searching the rubbish, after the fire was out, the bones of Mr. Mallery, his wife, and the children, were found near the apartment where they lodged, but as the bones of Davenport, who lodged in another part, could not be found, and several other circumstances made it strongly suspected that he had murthered the family, robbed the house, and then set it on fire, to hide his villainy. We hear he has been taken up, and committed to Litchfield gaol, and owns he is guilty of the black crimes of having first inhumanly murthered Mr. Mallery, then Mrs. Mallery, and two of the children, while in bed, and after plundering the house, set it on fire, and that he heard the child, whom he had spared for a more painful death, calling for help, from the flames. The mother of the children being from home, escaped the unhappy fate of the rest of the family.

The Connecticut Journal, February 16, 1780. See *The Connecticut Courant, And The Weekly Intelligencer*, February 15, 1780, and *The Connecticut Gazette, And The Universal Intelligencer*, February 16, 1780.

THREE HUNDRED AND FIFTY DOLLARS
REWARD.

BROKE out of the county goal in Boston, on the night of the 23d instant, the following prisoners, viz. George Harris, aged 23, about 5 feet 5 inches high, dark complexion, black hair, wore a light coloured waistcoat, blanket trowsers.— John Downs, aged 30, about 5 feet 6 inches high, reddish complexion, round face, black short hair, had on a blue short jacket, dirty leather breeches.—James Bardine, aged about 30, near 6 feet high, much pitted with the small pox, black hair tyed behind, wore a blue jacket, long trowsers.— John Brine, aged about 25, near 5 feet 8 inches high, light complexion, brownish hair tyed behind, of a thin make, wore red short coat, jacket and breeches the same.— Michael Raylay, (alias Fahay) aged 28, about 5 feet 7 inches high, light complexion, brownish hair, short full faced, wore a red coat, waistcoat and breeches. All the above are Irishmen.

John Wyman (born in Woburn, in this State) aged about 26 years, 5 feet 8 inches high, light complexion, wore brown long clothes. Thomas Gleason (born in this State) aged 26 years, about 5 feet 7 inches high, light complexion, short hair, wore long brown clothes. The above men are deserters from the Continental army.

Fifty Dollars reward will be paid to any person who shall apprehend either of the above men, and secure them in any goal within this State, upon notice being given to
JOSEPH OTIS, Jun. Dep. Goaler.
The Boston Gazette, and Country Journal, February 28, 1780.

DESERTED from the Continental Frigate Trumbull, lying in this Harbour, one JOHN BURTIS, about 5 Feet 10 Inches high, about 21 Years old, swarthy Complexion, black long Hair and black Eyes, the Eyelid of this right Eye hangs a little lower than the other, slim Built, has a Scar on one of his Cheeks; stole and carried with him, a pale blue Coat and Jacket with white Edging, a Pair of white Corderoy and blue Velvet Breeches, large round Beaver Hat, bound with Velvet Binding, clouded worsted Stockings, and a Quantity of other Cloathing; & about eight Pounds in hard Money. Whoever will apprehend said Fellow with the Cloathing shall have FIVE

HUNDRED DOLLARS Reward, or TWO HUNDRED and FIFTY for either of them, and all necessary Charges
           paid by BENJAMIN HAYDEN.
                               New-London, March 7th, 1780.
The Connecticut Gazette; And The Universal Intelligencer, March 12, 1780; March 29, 1780.

BROKE GOAL, on Saturday night, the 26th of February, a certain JAMES M'FARLAND, about five feet eight inches high, dark complexion; had on when he went off, a brown regiment coat, faced with red, and buckskin breeches. Also GEORGE TAYLOR, about six feet high, fair complexion. And RICHARD MATTHEWS, about five feet ten inches high, of a dark complexion: Both dressed in light coloured cloth coats, and white cloth waistcoats: They are deserters from Burgoyne's troops, and were taken up making their way to New-York. A reward of FIFTY DOLLARS, and all reasonable charges, is hereby offered to any person who will secure the abovementioned James McFarland: He was committed for receiving stolen goods.
           JAMES GREGG, Goaler.
                                          March 22, 1780.
The Pennsylvania Gazette, and Weekly Advertiser, March 22, 1780; March 29, 1780; April 5, 1780; April 12, 1780.

One Thousand Dollars reward, or One Hundred and Fifty for each.
DESERTED from my company of state artillery, stationed in *York* garrison, the following soldiers, *viz: John Johnson,* an *Irishman,* about 5 feet 8 or 9 inches high, well made, black eyes, blue coat faced with red, brown waistcoat and breeches, loves to drink, and at that time will boast of his manhood. *John Lewis,* an *Englishman,* about 5 feet 6 or 7 inches high, fair complexion, short brown hair, pitted with the smallpox, had on the above uniform. *William Black,* an *Irishman,* about 5 feet 7 or 8 inches high, has a particular cast in his eyes, short brown hair, had on the above uniform with a pair of sailors trousers. *Peter Luthie,* a *Frenchman,* speaks broken *English,* 5 feet 4 or 5 inches high, short brown hair, has a surly look, had on the above uniform. *Christopher Magee,* an *Englishman* about 5 feet 7 or 8 inches high, loves liquor, and at that time will be apt to rangle, short brown hair, pitted with the smallpox, had on the above uniform. *George Fitzpatrick,* an *Irishman* about 5 feet 4 or 5 inches high, much pitted with the smallpox, slender made, short brown hair, and on the above uniform. *Thomas Newton,* an *Irishman,* about 5 feet 10 or 12 inches

high, full faced, very lusty made, short hair, and had on the above uniform. I will pay the above reward if delivered to the commanding officer at *Williamsburg, York, Hampton,* or *Portsmouth.*
                GIDEON JOHNSTON, Capt. St. Art.
The Virginia Gazette, Dixon and Nicolson, March 25, 1780; April 1, 1780; April 8, 1780.

DESERTED from my company of state artillery in *March* last, *John Rodmore,* an *Englishman,* about 5 feet 8 inches high, short brown hair, stoops a little in shoulders, has a down look, had on a blue coat faced with red, and brown waistcoat and breeches. He stole a blanket, sheet, and pair of red sagothy breeches. Also *William* [   ] a *Dutchman,* about 5 feet 6 or 7 inches high, [   ] made, has a lively countenance, and formerly lived in *Orange* county. He had furlough which has expired, and unless he joins his regiment within 15 days after the date hereof, will be treated as a *deserter*; and One Hundred Dollars given for him, as well as *Rodmore,* on being delivered to any officer in the regiment to which they belong.
                SAM. BLACKWELL, Capt. S. A.
The Virginia Gazette, Dixon and Nicolson, April 8, 1780.

                              Reading, April 17, 1780.
                  Five Hundred Dollars Reward.
BROKE goal last night, a certain PETER PHILIPS, who was committed for passing counterfeit continental currency; had on a sky-blue lincey coat, lincey jacket, and an old hat; he is of a black complexion, and has a bad countenance. Also JOHN WOLFKILL, who was committed for deserting from the army; he belongs to the third Virginia regiment. Whoever apprehends the said villains, so that they may be had again, shall be entitled to the above reward,
            paid by   HENRY HAFFA, Sheriff.
The Pennsylvania Gazette, and Weekly Advertiser, May 3, 1780; May 10, 1780; May 17, 1780; May 24, 1780.

Extract of a letter from West Point, dated April 23.
    In this day's orders, the sentence of death is published against William Burtis, son to the late landlord Burtis, of White-Plains. He is a youth of genteel appearance, good address, and sprightly turn, of a rich and reputable family: he is about 29 years of age, has a mother and sister living near White-Plains: his crime is being a second time detected as a spy. Likewise, one Lakeman, who deserted from Danbury, 1778, and was recruiting as a Lieutenant in the British service. They are to be executed next Wednesday.

The Connecticut Courant, and Hartford Weekly Intelligencer, May 5, 1780.

One Hundred Dollars Reward.
THE house of the subscriber, living in Griggs-Town, Somerset county, was robbed last night by a soldier who calls himself William Leary, of the following articles; a brown broadcloth coat; a white cloth vest, with gold lace on the edges; an old fashioned snuff coloured broadcloth jacket; yellow plush breeches; buckskin ditto; a half worn narrow rimmed beaver hat; silk cap; two striped linsey petticoats; a black silk bonnet; a check apron; a pair of women's linen stockings; a pair of men's woollen stockings; two stocks and a steel stock-buckle; a linen shirt, and six linen caps. Said Leary is about five feet some inches high, has lightish hair, pale blue eyes; had on a blue regimental coat with red facings, white jacket and striped overalls. Whoever takes up the above thief, and secures the goods so that the owner gets them again, and the thief be convicted, shall have the above reward and all reasonable charges.
PETER WYCKOFF.

May 5, 1780.

The New Jersey Gazette, May 10, 1780.

ONE HUNDRED DOLLARS REWARD.
LAST night escaped from the subscribers with whom they were permitted to work in Hartford, MICHAEL MURREY and JOHN SCOVEL both prisoners of war. Said Murry is a short thick set fellow, about 5 feet 6 inches high, dark complexion, small eyes, short curl'd black hair; had on a dark brown out side jacket, short under vest and overhalls of the same kind, an old bever hat, small brim'd, old check shirt much town, is about 20 years of age, a native of Ireland. Scovel is a short thick set fellow, about 5 feet 6 inches high, light complexion, large white eyes, short strait brown hair; had on an old outside vest much torn, short under vest both lightish brown, a pair of corduroy breeches, old shoes, a pair of mixt blue and white cotton stockings, an old coarse white shirt, small round hat, was born near Horseneck. Whoever will take up and confine said prisoners or send them to the goal in Hartford, shall have 50 dollars for each.
ELIAKIM FISH. STEPHEN AUSTIN.

Hartford, May 15, 1780.
The Connecticut Courant, And Hartford Weekly Intelligencer, May 16, 1780; May 30, 1780.

THREE HUNDRED DOLLARS REWARD.
DESERTED, from the upper Cross-Roads, Harford county, Maryland, a certain HENRY REDING, an Irishman, talks Irish, and speaks country-like, belonging to the 4th Maryland Regiment, about 5 feet 4 inches high, of a brown complexion, has dark brown hair, and has lost one of his fore teeth: had on and took with him, a blue regimental coat with white lining, edged with yellow, plain metal buttons, a green handle [ ]eau, silver-mounted, a black leather belt, with brass buckle, the end tipped with brass, a piece of fine Irish linen containing 25 yards, the property of the subscriber; he is suspected to be gone back to Redstone or Kentuck. Whoever secures said deserted, shall be entitled to the above reward.
   EDWARD OLDHAM, Captain.   May 8, 1780.
The Maryland Journal, and Baltimore Advertiser, May 16, 1780.

THREE HUNDRED DOLLARS REWARD.
DESERTED from a detachment of Col. Benjamin Flower's regiment of artillery and artificers, under the command of Major Joseph Eayres, at Springfield, in Massachusetts State, Louis Lafever, of French extraction, speaks broken English, 23 years of age, dark complexion, 5 feet 8 inches high, a thick built fellow, it is supposed he is gone to Boston.—Also, Thomas Cox, Joseph Baker, Adam Brindle, Robert Long, James Keltey and John Henrey, all of the said company. Said Thomas Cox, 22 years of age, 5 feet 8 inches high, by trade a carpenter, black hair, very much pitted with the small pox; Joseph Baker, 25 years of age, 5 feet 8 inches high, fair complexion, a genteel built fellow; Adam Brindle, 27 years of age, fair complexion, a stout built likely fellow; Robert Long, 22 years of age, 5 feet 8 inches high, a stout built fellow; James Keltey, 26 years of age, 5 feet 9 inches & half high, a Blacksmith by trade, dark complection; John Henry, 29 years of age, by trade a Carpenter, 5 feet 4 inches high, fair complexion, born in Shutesbury, Bay State.

Whoever will take up the said Deserters, and secure them in any goal, or send them to their respective company, now in Springfield, shall receive the above reward, or FIFTY DOLLARS for each, and all reasonable charges paid, by me,
   NATHANIEL CHAPMAN, Captain of A. & A.
The Boston Gazette, and Country Journal, May 22, 1780; May 29, 1780.

CHATHAM, May 17.
We are informed, that at Newtown, Sussex county, on the 16th inst. John M'Coy, and Robert Maxwell, deserters from the convention

troops, were convicted of bulgary, [*sic*] committed in Greenheage; that the Friday ensuing M'Coy was executed, and the other respited till the 9th of June next. We are told they appeared extremely penitent, expressed confident hopes of salvation, and, at the place of execution, made the most solemn protestations of their innocence of the accusation for which they were to suffer. The unhappy man died in charity, he said, with all men, and hoped that after his death, the world might have due testimony of his integrity.—
The New-York Gazette; and the Weekly Mercury, May 29, 1780.

Springfield, June 3 1780.
Broke Goal, one Edward John, about 45 Years of Age, 5 Feet 8 inches high, dark Complexion, short built, by Trade a Blacksmith, an Old Countryman. He belonged to the Regiment of Artillery and Artificers, in Capt. Richard Faxon's Company, and was committed for Desertion. Whoever will secure said John in any Goal on the Continent, shall have *One Hundred Dollars* Reward, and all necessary Charges
      paid by   RICHARD FAXON.
The Boston Gazette, and Country Journal, June 12, 1780; June 19, 1780; June 26, 1780.

550 *Continental Dollars Reward.*
ON the evening after the 30th of May instant, Litchfield County Gaol was broke open, and the following prisoners made their escape, viz. JOHN WELCH, a deserter from the British, an Irishman; confined for murder, thick set, about 21 years old....Whoever will apprehend and return the above prisoners, to said goal again, shall have as a reward for Welch... 100 dollars,
      paid by   LYNDE LORD, Sheriff.
      Litchfield, May 31, 1780.
N. B. The Cloathing of the above fellows cannot be described.
The Connecticut Courant, And The Weekly Intelligencer, June 13, 1780; June 20, 1780.

On Friday last was executed at camp, near the grand parade, James Coleman of the 11th Pennsylvania regiment for repeated desertion and forgery. Ten more of different regiments were under similar sentence, but for many important reasons were by the commander in chief fully pardoned.
The Connecticut Gazette; And The Universal Intelligencer, June 16, 1780.

WHEREAS Daniel Yeomans, a Deserter from the Continental Army, on being discovered and about to be taken, made his escape, left in the road a small bay Mare, Saddle and Bridle, supposed to be unjustly taken from some person. The owner may have them by proving his property and applying to the subscriber.
                    ABNER WAY.
                                      Wallingford, May 12, 1780.
The Connecticut Courant, And The Weekly Intelligencer, June 20, 1780.

                    CHATHAM, June 21.
  On Saturday last was executed for desertion at camp, a soldier belonging to the Jersey brigade; and on Monday three spies shared the same fate.
The New-Jersey Gazette, June 28, 1780.

                      DESERTED.
FROM the 64th Regimental Store at Coenties Market; RICHARD HUTCHINSON, private Soldier in the 64th regiment, born in Ireland, about 5 feet 7 inches high, short curly hair, much freckled in the face; had on when he went off, a crimson coloured jacket, a pair of new duck trowsers, (was lately on board the General Pattison privateer.)— Whoever will give information of the said Hutchinson, to Serjeant M'Donald at the said store, so that he may be apprehended, shall receive five Guineas Reward. All Masters of ships are hereby warned not to harbour the above-mentioned Hutchinson, at their peril.
                M. WOOD, Ensign, 64th Regt.
The Royal Gazette, July 5, 1780.

                State of New-Hampshire, Strafford.
RAN-AWAY, on Monday July 9th, from the town of Lee, TWO IRISHMAN, who had inlisted in the Continental service, viz. James Sullivan, about 45 years of age, with black hair, blue coat with a red plush cap, light coloured knit breeches—and William McKilsener, about 35 years of age, had on a brown coloured homespun coat and jacket, light coured [*sic*] hair and bald head: Whoever will apprehend said persons, or inform where they may be found and brought to justice, shall have all necessary charges paid, and a handsome reward, by applying to Zaccheus Clough, or the Selectmen of said town.
                    Lee, July 17, 1780.
The New-Hampshire Gazette; Or, State Journal, And General Advertiser, July 22, 1780; July 29, 1780; August 5, 1780.

DESERTED from Col. Levi Wells's Regiment, Capt. Lay's Company of State Troops, one FRANCIS JANNES, an inlisted Soldier, the Town he belongs to is not known; he is about 5 Feet 8 Inches high, light Complection, a little freckled. Whoever will take up said Soldier, and return him to his Regiment, or confine him in any Gaol, shall have Five Hundred Dollars Reward, and all necessary Charges
    paid by me, JOSHUA RAYMOND, Lieut.
              Greenwich July 17, 1780.
The Connecticut Journal, July 27, 1780; August 3, 1780.

RUNAWAY NEGROES!

ON the 26 Inst. two Negroes were taken up in the Sound near the West End of Fisher's-Island in a Canoe, and supposed to have absconded from their Master or Masters, and intending for Long-Island; one of then says his Name is Prince, and the other Gillam. Prince is about 45 Years old, large and well set, had on a grey Jacket, Towcloth Shirt and white Hat; says he belongs to John Williams, Esq. of Stonington. Gillam is 19 Years old, small and very black and likely; had on a blue Camblet Coat and brown Cloth Overalls, says he came from Swansey; but it's said was lately inlisted in the Continental Army; they are both committed to Goal. The Owner may have them, paying Charges, by applying to
    JAMES HOLT, in New-London.
The Connecticut Gazette; And The Universal Intelligencer, July 28, 1780.

Four HUNDRED DOLLARS Reward.

DESERTED on Sunday last (the 30th July) from New-London, an enlisted Soldier in the three Months Service, a Native of Ireland, named JAMES CASE, Case, James but some Times calls himself M'KINSEY, he is a short thick set Fellow, between 40 and 50 Years of Age, is very talkative, wears a large brim'd lopt Hat, striped Shirt and Trowsers, without Shoes, was seen on his way to Rhode Island. Whoever will take up and return said Deserter to New-London Fort or to Captain Ely's Company in Colonel Wells's Regiment, shall have the above Reward and all necessary Charges
    paid by DAVID HILLHOUSE, Ensign.
            New-London, August 1st. 1780.
The Connecticut Gazette; And The Universal Intelligencer, August 4, 1780; August 18, 1780.

STEPHEN MINER, Junr. of the 1st Company in the fifth Regiment of Militia, of the State of Connecticut, being reasonably and duly

detached agreeable to Orders, and directed to march and join the Continental Army, hath deserted or concealed himself to avoid his Duty, he is a well proportioned Youth, of a good Countenance, about 18 Years Old, and about 5 Feet 5 Inches high, his Eyes of a lightish Colour. Whoever will secure said Deserter in any public Goal, and give notice thereof, or forward him to the commanding Officer of said Company, in Windham, that he may be forwarded to do his Duty, shall receive a reasonable Reward and necessary Expences
        paid by   NEHEMIAH TINKER, Capt.
July 30, 1780.
The Connecticut Gazette; And The Universal Intelligencer, August 4, 1780; August 18, 1780.

        Broke out of Goal last Thursday
Morning, James Ryder Mowet, about 5 feet 9 inches high, had on a short green coat, trimmed with narrow gold lace, striped trowsers, light complexion.— David Mowet, about 5 feet 6 inches high, had a brown coat, round hat, very red face.— Samuel Chapman, had a green short coat, trimmed with narrow gold lace, a fur cap, wore boots, short curl'd hair, about 5 feet 10 inches high, very full fac'd, prisoners of war....Whoever will take up any of the above persons and secure them, so that they may be brought to justice, shall have Five Hundred Dollars reward for each, by
        JOSEPH OTIS, Dept. Goaler.
Boston, Aug. 5, 1780.
The Boston-Gazette, And The Country Journal, August 7, 1780; August 14, 1780; *The Independent Chronicle and the Universal Advertiser*, August 10, 1780; August 17; August 24, 1780. Minor differences between the papers.

        TRENTON, JULY 26.
    On the night of the 14th inst. Serjeant Bainbridge, of the New Levies deserted from Staten Island, and brought off Captain Steward's wife, two privates, six horses, and a considerable sum of hard money.
The Connecticut Courant, And The Weekly Intelligencer, August 8, 1780.

DESERTED the evening after the 6th instant, from the guard stationed at Litchfield, under my command, a soldier belonging to Col. Durkee's regiment of the Connecticut Line, Moses Gates, by name, about 22 years of age, about five feet 7 inches high, dark complexion, short dark hair, for some time past resided at New Hartford; had on when he went away, a white frock, streaked linen shirt, dark brown

cloth breeches, white woollen stockings, wore a felt hat cockt up, and took with him a small pack. Whoever will take up said deserter, and return him to the subscriber at Litchfield, shall have ten shillings State's money reward, and all necessary charges
paid by me   EZRA SMITH, Lieut.

Litchfield, August 7, 1780.

The Connecticut Journal, August 10, 1780; August 17, 1780; August 24, 1780.

1000 DOLLARS REWARD.

Deserted, one *John Dayen,* who was inlisted for the town of Roxbury, to serve six months in the Continental army; said Dayen is about five feet seven inches high, of a brown complexion, aged 22 yers, formerly belonged to Charlestown. Whoever will apprehend said deserter, and secure him in any goal, or deliver him to Capt. LEM. MAY, shall have the above reward, and all necessary charges paid.

Roxbury, July 19.

The Independent Chronicle and the Universal Advertiser, August 10, 1780.

DESERTED from Capt. Bell's Company, Col. Beebe's Regiment, William Shippen, lately resident in Salisbury: 5 feet 7 inches high, thick set, lightish brown hair, judged to be about 22 years of age; supposed to be gone into the State of Vermont. Also, one William Winslove, lately resident of Woodbury, about 5 feet 10 inches high; tho't to be about 25 years of age. Whoever will take up either or both of said deserters, and secure them so that they may be had, shall have Twenty Shillings reward for each, and forty shillings each, if they will deliver them at the regiment, and all reasonable charges paid.
JESSE BELL, Capt.

Horse-Neck, July 28, 1780.

The Connecticut Courant, And The Weekly Intelligencer, August 22, 1780; August 29, 1780.

EPAPHRODITUS LOVLAND and DANIEL EMMONS, of the sixth Company of Militia, in the 12th Regiment of the State of Connecticut, being reasonably and duly detached agreeable to Orders, and directed to march and join the continental Army, have both deserted or concealed themselves to avoid their duty. The said Lovland is about five feet nine inches high, light Complexion and eyes, about 23 Years of Age. Said Emmons, is a short thick set Man, about five feet high, light Complexion and Eyes. Whoever will secure said Deserters in any public Goal and give notice thereof or forward them to the Subscriber,

shall receive a reasonable Reward and all necessary Charges
        paid by CHARLES MILLER, Capt.
                              Colchester, Aug. 9, 1780.
The Connecticut Gazette; And The Universal Intelligencer, August 25, 1780; September 8, 1780; September 15, 1780.

RUN-AWAY from the Subscriber, a certain THOMAS KELVIN, Prisoner of War to the United States: had on when he went away, a Tow Cloth Coat, Vest and Breeches, a brass Button to his Hat: about five Feet six Inches High, dark curl'd Hair. Whoever will up and return said Prisoner to EZEKIEL WILLIAMS, Esq. Commissary of Prisoners, shall have all reasonable Charges
        paid, by Wm. JEPSON.
                              Hartford, August 26, 1780.
The Connecticut Courant, And The Weekly Intelligencer, August 29, 1780; September 5, 1780.

SIXTY DOLLARS REWARD, to any person that will take and bring to me, or secure in Litchfield goal Jonas Leach of Torrington, who was detached to serve in the Connecticut Line in the Continental Army until the last of December next, and all necessary charges paid,
        by   ELIJAH GAYLORD, Capt.
                                      August 18, 1780.
The Connecticut Courant, And The Weekly Intelligencer, August 29, 1780.

                              New-London, 29 Aug. 1780.
DEserted this Day from Fort Trumbull, one Robert Brown; he is part white and part Indian, about 5 feet 8 or 9 inches high, had on when he went away a white tow shirt, short under jacket the fore part brown and back part red, a dark brown coat, knit breeches, and a round hat, one of his legs has been broke, and two of his fore teeth are out; he is very talkative. Whoever will take up said deserter and return him to Fort Trumbull, shall have Three Hundred Dollars reward, and necessary charges, paid by me,
        ADAM SHAPLEY, Capt.
The Connecticut Gazette; And The Universal Intelligencer, September 1, 1780; September 8, 1780; September 15, 1780; September 22, 1780.

DESERTED the 19th of July, from my company of militia, in Branford, in Col. Russell's regiment, in Connecticut, one David Frisbie, a soldier drafted for six months, for the Continental army; he

is a stout thick set man, about forty years of age, lightish colour'd hair, a cooper by trade. Whoever will take up said deserter, and return him to me, the subscriber, shall have three hundred dollars reward, and all necessary charges
                  paid by me BENJAMIN BALDWIN, Capt.
                                  Branford, September 4, 1780.
The Connecticut Journal, September 7, 1780; September 14, 1780.

                  Broke out of the Goal in this Town, on the Night of the 3d Instant, the following British Officers, Prisoners of War, viz.—Capt. *Thomas Sandford*, Lieut. *Hugh Davis*, and Lieut. *John Miller*. Said *Sandford* had on a Red Coat, trimmed with Silver, and nankeen Waistcoat and Overalls, about 5 Feet 9 Inches high, brown Hair; *Davis* and *Miller* had on short green Coats trimmed with narrow Gold Lance, and Nankeen Waistcoat and Overalls, about 5 Feet 9 Inches high, brown Hair.—Whoever will apprehend any of the above Persons, and secure them so that they may be brought to Justice, shall have 400 Dollars reward for each,
                  By   EPHRAIM JONES, Dep. Goaler.
                                    Concord, September 4, 1780.
The Continental Journal And Weekly Advertiser, September 7, 1780; September 14, 1780; *The Independent Chronicle and the Universal Advertiser*, September 7, 1780; September 14, 1780; September 21, 1780. See *The Connecticut Journal*, September 14, 1780, and *Thomas's Massachusetts Spy Or, American Oracle of Liberty*, September 14, 1780.

JOEL PRATT, of the 8th company in the 7th regiment of militia of this State, having been reasonably and duly detached agreeable to orders, & directed to march to join the Continental army, hath deserted or concealed himself to avoid his duty. Said Pratt is about 18 or 19 years of age, light complexion, light hair and light eyes, slim & small of a likely look. Whoever will secure said deserter in any public goal and give notice thereof or forward him to the commanding officer of said company in Say-Brook, that he may be forwarded to his duty, shall receive Forty Shillings lawful money, and necessary charges
                  paid by   DAN PLATTS, Capt.
The Connecticut Gazette; And The Universal Intelligencer, September 8, 1780; September 15, 1780.

Tuesday last James Duncan, a Soldier belonging to Col. Greene's Regiment, was shot at Rhode-Island for Desertion.
The Providence Gazette; And Country Journal, September 23, 1780.

South Kingstown, Sept. 18, 1780.
I This day having returned to me, by the Committee of this town, Samuel Taylor and Judith [*sic*] Cartwright, jun. as persons detached by said Committee for filling up the Continental battalions of this State, they having notice of the same, and not appearing or procuring a substitute. According to an act of this State, I promise a reward of Three Hundred Pounds for each, to any person or persons who will apprehend the abovesaid persons, and deliver them to Colonel Greene's regiment.
THO. POTTER, jun. Lieut. Col. Com.
The American Journal And General Advertiser, October 21, 1780; October 28, 1780; *The Providence Gazette; And Country Journal*, October 25, 1780; November 1, 1780.

JOHAN MICHAEL TILOKE, who deserted from the Hessian Yagers, may hear of his Wife by inquiring at Edes's Printing Office, in State-Street, Boston—She requests the Printers in the other States to insert the above.
The Boston-Gazette, And The Country Journal, October 30, 1780.

New-London, December 5, 1780.
DESERTED from Fort Trumbull, the 27th of November last, one THOMAS GREEN, a transient person, says he deserted from the British fleet in Gardner's Bay about the middle of September last, is about 21 years of age, of a middling stature, light complexion, has been wounded in one of his legs by a musket ball, has a double row of teeth, and is a native of Great-Britain; stole and carried away with him a grey coloured great-coat, a dark brown straight bodied coat with white lining, an under jacket and a pair of overhauls of a buff colour, three check'd flannel shirts, and three pair stockings. Whoever will take up said deserter and return him to Fort Trumbull, shall have Three Hundred Dollars reward, and necessary charges,
paid by ADAM SHAPLEY, Capt.
The Connecticut Gazette; And The Universal Intelligencer, December 12, 1780; December 26, 1780; January 2, 1781.

DANIEL JACKSON, a soldier in Baylor's light dragoons, requested a few moments before his death, that this method should be taken to inform his wife, who lives near Springfield in New-Jersey, that he was executed the first of May last, at George-Town in South-Carolina, for desertion.
     J. STITH, Captain Baylor's dragoons.
The New Jersey Gazette, December 13, 1780.

          Hartford, December 18, 1780.
LAST night the county goal was broke open, and the following prisoners made their escape, viz. ENOCH JOHNSON, JAMES WILSON, FRANCIS NOBLE, and DANIEL FAIRCHILD, Traitors. DARLING SEALECK, NATHAN SEALECK, HEREKIAH SCRIBNER, ARCHIBALD HIGENS, Prisoners of War. Whoever will take up said prisoners, and secure them, so that the subscriber can get them into his custody again, have HANDSOME REWARD and reasonable charges.
     WILLIAM BARNARD, Goaler.
The Connecticut Courant, And The Weekly Intelligencer, December 26, 1780.

    Two Thousand Dollars Reward.
      RAN AWAY,
 On Sunday last, from the subscriber, in Mendham
     township, Morris county,
A NEGRO MAN named JOE, about 30 years of age, five feet eight inches high, one leg a little shorter than the other, part of one of his great toes cut off, lost some of his foreteeth, and his back is much scarified and in lump by whipping.—Also a handsome NEGRO WENCH, 18 years of age, with her Child about six week old, which from some of its clothes being found, she is supposed to have killed. The Negroes went off with one *Slight*, a soldier belonging to the 2d Pennsylvania regiment, and they stole, and took with them, a variety of clothes, and two horses, the one a bay, four years old, the other a grey, seven years old, and have switch tails. The soldier stole a written discharge, in the name of William Nelson, whom he will probably personate. Whoever takes up the said Negroes and horses, so that the owner may get them again, shall have the above reward, or Twelve Hundred dollars for the Negroes only, and Eight Hundred for the horses, or in proportion for any or either of them, and reasonable
   charges, paid by   EBENEZER BLACKLY, jun.
               Dec. 22, 1780.
   The New-Jersey Gazette, December 27, 1780.

Three Hundred Dollars Reward.
DESERTED from Capt. Mead's company the 12th instant, Benjamin Bonnel, John Burnett, and John Yherts, belonging to the 1st Jersey regiment. Any person that will apprehend and secure the above deserters, shall be entitled to the above reward.
    G. MEAD, Capt.   December 19, 1780.
The New-Jersey Journal, December 27, 1780.

1781

DESERTED from my Company, in Col. John Mead's Regiment, about the 9th of January instant: JOHN LOMISS and JOHN MIRAMBL[R]. Lomiss is a short thick set fellow, about 30 years of age, a blemish on his left eye, belongs to Hartford West Division. Mirambl[r] is an Irishman, about 28 years of age, something pock broken; belongs to Roxbury in Woodbury. Whoever will take up said deserters, or either of them, and return them to their regiment, at Greenwich, shall receive Forty Shillings, State Currency,
    and all necessary charges
      by ISAAC POMEROY, Capt.
          Greenwich, January 13, 1781.
The Connecticut Courant, And Weekly Intelligencer, January 23, 1781; February 13, 1781.

DESERTED the 1st last from New London one John Robinson, enlisted by the 25th class of Stonington, s a soldier for the continental army, he is 4 feet 5 inches high, [*sic*] red hair, grey eyes, one of them is cross'd, 22 years old, very much pitted with the small pox; it is supposed he is gone to Rhode Island to enlist a second time. Whoever will take up said deserter and secure him in any gaol, or deliver him to said class, shall have One Hundred Dollars reward, and all necessary
    charges paid by
      —— Williams, Esq; head of said class.
          New-London, February 25, 1781.
The Connecticut Gazette; And The Universal Intelligencer, March 2, 1781; March 9, 1781; March 16, 1781.

    Eight Dollars Reward.
DESERTED from the subscriber's Independence Company, JAMES HARDY, 5 feet 5 inches high, from Ireland, 25 years of age, of a dark complexion, can speak several languages, says he is a peruke maker, and it is supposed will change his name: He had on his regimentals when he left the company. Whoever apprehends the said deserter, and

confines him in the main-guard of this city, or brings him to my quarters at the sign of the ship, in the Bowery, shall receive the above reward.

All masters of privateers are desired not to harbour him at their peril.   ANDREW FORSHNER.

March 10, 1781.

The Royal Gazette, March 14, 1781.

DESERTED from Gloucester, an Indian Man, named ROBERT WIRE, who inlisted in the Continental Army for three Years, to serve for the State of Rhode Island.—He is a short, thick Fellow, about 27 Years of Age; had on when he deserted an old brown Coat, a Flannel flower'd Jacket, Red Baize or Shag Overalls, white Yarn Stockings, new Shoes with Straps, but Strings tyed in them. Whoever will take up said Deserter and commit him to Providence Goal, in said State. shall receive Thirty Silver Dollars reward and all necessary Charges paid by me,   ASA KIMBALL, Major

Providence, March 13, 1781.

The Boston Gazette, And The Country Journal, March 19, 1781; April 2, 1781.

The following is an Extract of his Excellency General Washington's Orders of the 17*th Instant.*

ALEXANDER McDOWALL, late Lieutenant and Adjutant of Colonel Welles's Regiment of the State Troops of Connecticut, having been, by a General Court-Martial of the Line, held at Hartford the 7th Day of March, 1781, whereof Colonel Heman Swift was President, found guilty of *Desertion to the Enemy*, and by the said Court Martial sentenced to suffer Death for the same, agreeable to the 6th Section of the first Article of War; which Sentence is ordered to be put in execution of Wednesday the 21st instant, at Hartford, between the Hours of Ten in the Forenoon and Three in the Afternoon of the same Day.

The Connecticut Courant, And The Weekly Intelligencer, March 20, 1781; *The Norwich Packet and the Weekly Advertiser The Boston Gazette, And The Country Journal*, March 26, 1781. See *The Connecticut Courant, And The Weekly Intelligencer*, March 27, 1781.

One Thousand Dollars Reward.

BROKE out of Burlington gaol, on the night of the 6th inst. the following persons, JOHN WORKMAN, (advertised in the

Pennsylvania papers for breaking out of Easton gaol) about five feet nine or ten inches high, dark complexion, pitted with the small pox, about thirty-four years of age. JOHN KETCHUM, five feet eleven inches high, stoops when he walks, a deserter from the 6th Pennsylvania regiment. THOMAS M'CALVEY and JOHN HANLY, formerly belonging to the Pennsylvania line. Whoever secures the said John Workman in any gaol, shall have FIVE HUNDRED and FIFTY DOLLARS, and ONE HUNDRED and FIFTY for each of the other three, with all reasonable charges,
    paid by me RALPH PRICE, Gaoler.

March 7, 1781.

The New Jersey Gazette, March 21, 1781.

HARTFORD, March 27.

Last Wednesday Alexander McDowall, late Lieutenant and Adjutant in Colonel Wells's regiment, was executed in this town, pursuant to his sentence, for Desertion to the Enemy.

The Connecticut Courant, And The Weekly Intelligencer, March 27, 1781; *The Connecticut Journal*, March 29, 1781; *The Norwich Packet and the Weekly Advertiser*, March 29, 1781. See *The Connecticut Courant, And The Weekly Intelligencer*, March 20, 1781.

      James Neil, of the corps of
Artillery, deserted the 10th inst.—He was a native of Great Britain, 5 feet 10 inches in height, well form'd, ruddy complexion, and short brown hair.—In addition to the premium (by the honourable Congress) for apprehending deserters, ONE GUINEA will
    be given by W. SARGENT, Capt. 3d Bat. Art.

The Independent Chronicle and the Universal Advertiser, March 29, 1781.

DESERTED *between Leicester and Springfield, JOHN-WILLIAM JOHNSON, a soldier engaged for three years in the Continental army, for the town of Western, in the county of Worcester, called himself a Dutchman, aged 25 years, five feet five inches high, dark complexion, called himself a farmer. Whoever will take up said deserter, and confine him and give information to the subscriber, shall be paid all necessary charges, and a handsome reward, according to a resolve of the General Court.*

    SETH WASHBURN, Superintendant for the
    (county of Worcester.

Leicester, March 26, 1781.

The Massachusetts Spy: Or, American Oracle of Liberty, March 29, 1781; April 5, 1781; April 19, 1781.

DESERTED the 5th last from Woodstock, one John Senior, a negro or mulatto, enlisted by the 25th class of Woodstock as a solder for the Continental army, he is about 5 feet 4 inches high, darkish curled hair, something thick built, a little round shouldered, and 18 years old. Whoever will take up said deserter and secure him in any public goal, or deliver him to said class, shall have Three Dollars reward in silver, and all necessary charges paid,
                by   HENRY CHILD, head of said class.
                                        Woodstock, March 9, 1781.
The Connecticut Gazette; And The Universal Intelligencer, March 30, 1781; April 13, 1781.

RUN AWAY a few days ago from the regiment of Brunswick Dragoons, at Flat-Land, on Long Island, a Black named Prince Dermen, Drummer in said regiment, about five feet ten inches high, stout built, had on a suit of light blue cloaths quite new. Whoever will secure him so that he may be brought back, or delivered over to any non-commissioned officer of the said regiment, shall receive a proper reward for so doing; and every one is forbid concealing him at their peril.
    The Royal Gazette, April 18, 1781; April 28, 1781.

                        SPRINGFIELD, *April* 15, 1781.
            DESERTED from the Barracks at
Springfield, JOHN STILL, an Irishman 33 years old, 5 feet, 8 inches high, red hair, light complexion, and little freckled, apt to get drunk, badly cloathed, hired by Great-Barrington.—PETER EVANS, 16 years old, 5 feet, one inch high, light complexion, hired by West-Springfield.—SETH BROWN, 20 years old, 5 feet 9 inches high, dark complexion, 1 squint eye, hired by Melford, in the County of Worcester. All the good people throughout this Commonwealth, are desired to exert themselves to detect and secure the above-mentioned Deserters, as they wish to prevent the infamous and abominable practice of Desertion, and thus render an essential service to their
            Country.   WILLIAM SHEPARD, Col.
    ☞The several Printers in this Commonwealth, are desired to Publish the above in their Papers.
    The Boston Gazette, And The Country Journal, April 30, 1781.

RETURN OF DESERTERS FROM FOURTH PENN'A, COMMANDED BY WILLIAM BUTLER, CARLISLE, JUNE 6, 1781.

Closs, John, sergeant; age thirty; bricklayer; Ireland; sprained.
Carcass, Conrad, age forty-nine; shoemaker; Pennsylvania; German descent.
Carney, John, age twenty; tobacconist; Ireland.
Conway, James, age twenty-nine; Ireland.
Cashedy, William, age twenty-two; Ireland; pox marked.
Daily, John, age thirty; tailor ; Ireland; Lancaster.
Hendry, John, age twenty-five; Ireland.
Hunt, Thomas, age twenty-seven; shoemaker; ruptured.
Leed, Jacob, age twenty-five; Pennsylvania; Lancaster.
McCann, William, age thirty; tailor; Ireland; squints and addicted to strong drink.
McLau, David, age thirty; Ireland; addicted to strong drink.
Malcolm, Charles, age twenty-two; Ireland.
Martin, Patrick, age thirty-one; tailor; Dublin, Ireland; addicted to strong drink.
Marshall, William, shoemaker; Ireland.
O'Narra, Francis, Ireland; very much of a blackguard.
Pew, Eli, shoemaker; Pennsylvania.
Shoemaker, John, tailor; Pennsylvania; Easton; German.
Smith, John, age twenty-nine; shoemaker; England.
Smith, Peter, age thirty; Ireland; pitted with smallpox.
Spinkhouse, Anthony, age twenty-eight, tailor; Spain; has a great turn for dealing.
Travis, Andrew, age twenty-five; Dublin; formerly of Second Penn'a .
Tronzo, Jacob, age forty; Germany.
Walker, Samuel, age sixteen; drummer; of Lancaster, Pennsylvania.
Wilkinson, Christopher, age twenty- five; England.

John B. Linn and Wm. H. Egle, eds. *Pennsylvania Archives* 2nd. Ser., vol. 10, (Harrisburg: Clarence M. Busch, 1896), 536-537.

DESERTED,

A few days ago, from the Lieutenant of Caecil county, MICHAEL BARKER, born in Ireland, five feet nine inches high, twenty-eight years of age, fair complexion, light brown hair, the letters M. B. marked on the outside of his left hand, much addicted to drink, and when drunk very abusive: he wore a new castor hat, old black broad cloth coat, linen waistcoat, white corduroy breeches and thread stockings. 'Tis likely his wife may travel with him, she is a short young woman, and red hair. Whoever takes up and delivers the said deserter to the subscriber, or to Col. Henry Hollingsworth, at the Head of Elk, shall receive a reward of SIXTEEN MARYLAND STATE DOLLARS.

JOHN D. THOMPSON, Lieut. Caecil county.

May 28, 1781.

The Pennsylvania Journal; and the Weekly Advertiser, June 20, 1781; June 27, 1781.

DESERTED from the Third Connecticut Regiment, commanded by Samuel B. Webb, Esq; PRINTICE STORES; aged 23 years, 5 feet 10 inches high, well set, dark brown hair, light eyes, light complexion, pited with the small-pox, born in Wethersfield, in Connecticut. Any person that will apprehend said Stores, and return him to the regiment, or safely lodge him in any gaol in these States, shall receive ONE GUINEA REWARD.

E. HOPKINS, Capt. in 3d. Regt.

Hutts, Connecticut Camp, High-Lands, June 17, 1781.

It is probable that Stores may produce a discharge from the three years service, but he has been legally tried, and found to have inlisted during the war. E. H.

The Connecticut Courant, And Weekly Intelligencer, July 3, 1781; July 10, 1781.

STOLEN from the subscriber, the night after the 25th of June last, a light brown STONE HORSE, nine or ten years old, about 14 hands high, trots and canters, lame in his fore feet, newly shod before; supposed to be taken by one JOHN SELAH, a Continental soldier, about five feet four inches high, dark complexion, twenty-four years old. Whoever will take up said horse and thief, and deliver them to the subscriber, shall have FIVE DOLLARS, hard money, reward, and all necessary charges paid, or Three Dollars or either the horse or thief.

OLIVER BELDING,

Lenox, July 2, 1781.

The Connecticut Courant, And Weekly Intelligencer, July 10, 1781; July 17, 1781; July 31, 1781.

DESERTED from Coventry, one NATHAN CLAP, an Indian Fellow, about 5 feet 7 or 8 inches high, hath lately taken up preaching, said Clap inlisted into the Continental army, as a recruit for the town aforesaid—Whoever shall take up said deserter, and give information to the subscriber, shall have ten dollars reward and all necessary charges paid, by   THOMAS BROWN.

Coventry, August 28, 1781.

The Connecticut Courant, And Weekly Intelligencer, September 4, 1781; September 11, 1781.

THE solder, Conrad Riel of the Hessian regiment Prince Charles, Major General de Gosen's company, was missed in the evening of the 8th of this month, and it is supposed that he conceals himself in this city; it is therefore desired that in case he is found out, to deliver him to Serjeant Reis, of the said regiment, in Queen-Street, No. 191, opposite Mr. Hegeman's, and their favour will be thankfully acknowledged.
The Royal Gazette, September 12, 1781.

DESERTED from Norwich, the 15th instant, one EZRA HOLBROOK, who inlisted in the room of one Isaac Tracy, from Capt. Waterman's Company, and Col. Rogers's Regiment.—Whoever shall take up said Deserter, and delver him to the subscriber, or to the commanding officer at Fort-Griswold, shall have three Dollars Reward, and all necessary charges paid by
    ELISHA LEFFINGWELL, Ensign.
      Fort Griswold, in Groton, Sept. 20, 1781.
The Connecticut Gazette; And The Universal Intelligencer, September 21, 1781; September 28, 1781; October 5, 1781.

DESERTED from my company, in Col. Bailey's regiment, now doing duty at Newport, the following persons, viz. THOMAS EVERTON, who came from the town of Gloucester, had on, when he went away, a red coat, white waistcoat, black breeches, about thirty years of age.—PETER CRANDALL, belonging to Exeter, a stout built fellow, with rather a down look, about thirty-six years of age.—AMOS BENNET, who came from the town of Exeter, a stout well made fellow, very much pitted with the small-pox, strait hair, supposed to be about thirty six years of age, said fellow carried off a number of cartridges with him. Whoever will apprehend all or either of said deserters, and secure them or him in any of the gaols of the United States, or return either of them to me, at Newport, shall receive FIVE SILVER DOLLARS reward for each, and all necessary charges paid.
    J. S. TAYLOR, Lieut.
          Newport, Sept. 28, 1781.
The Newport Mercury, September 29, 1781; October 6, 1781.

September 19, 1781.
MADE their escape, from Montgomery County gaol, last night, the following prisoners, viz. SAMUEL CAYE, about 65 years of age, 5 feet 4 inches high, and has a down look. Had on, a country linen coat, blue and white striped linen jacket, good shoes, an old hat, has but one tooth in his head, was whipt last court, and shows the marks. Also, JOHN CARLTON, a deserter from the army, talks much on the Irish dialect, about the same height of Caye. Had on an old coat, and ragged trousers.—Whoever secures the said prisoners, in any gaol, shall receive a Reward of Five Pounds, specie; and if delivered to the subscriber, reasonable charges, or in proportion for either,
SAMUEL NICHOLS,
Sheriff of Montgomery County.
The Maryland Journal; and Baltimore Advertiser, October 2, 1781; October 9, 1781; October 16, 1781.

DESERTED from the six month's draught, in Sharon, one JOHN BARSLEY, jun. about 21 years old, 6 feet high, slim built, black hair and eyes. Whoever will take up said deserter, and return him to the subscriber, shall receive One Hundred Dollars reward, and all reasonable charges.   ADONIJAH GRISWOLD, Capt.
Sharon, September 11, 1780.
The Connecticut Courant And The Weekly Intelligencer, October 3, 1780; October 10, 1780.

At the supreme judicial court, held at Barrington, in the county of Berkshire, on the first Tuesday of October instant, one James Hewit was indicted for damning the Congress, and uttering insolent and threatning expressions against the inhabitants of these states; upon his being brought to the bar he informed the court that he had been an officer in the British army, and had deserted after the surrender at Saratoga: The court was further informed that he had married a wife of considerable property in that county. The Sheriff was ordered to secure him in Irons, and to transmit him to the order of the Governor, to be dealt with as a prisoner of war. This order was very agreable to the auditory, who behaved in court with a peculiar decency.
The Massachusetts Spy: Or, American Oracle of Liberty, October 11, 1781.

BROKE away from his guard, MICHAEL JERISON, a prisoner belonging to the Armoury Company, in the Continental service; commanded by Captain WILLIAM BARTON, at Springfield. He is an Irishman, about 40 years of age, five feet eight inches high, short dark brown curled hair; formerly worked with Col. Pomroy of North-Hampton, at the armoury business, but lately from Colchester, in Connecticut.—Whoever pprehends [*sic*] said deserter, and delivers him to the subscriber in Springfield, or confines him in goal, and notify the subscriber, so that he may be dealth with according to the regulations of the army, shall receive TWO HUNDRED DOLLARS reward and all necessary charges

   paid by me WILLIAM BARTON, Capt. Armoury.

Springfield, October 3, 1780.

The Connecticut Courant, And The Weekly Intelligencer, October 17, 1780; October 24, 1781.

Camp, Peek's-Kill, Nov. 4, 1781.
DESERTED from Lieut. Col. Commandant Webb's regiment of levies, from Suffolk and Middlesex counties, Lieut. Nathaniel Loring of Holliston, & took with him a soldier by the name of Nathan Wood, of the same town.—Also deserted from on command at Fish-Kill, the following soldiers, viz. David Bailey, George Am[s], and Peter Haynes, of Malden, Stephen Colburn of Medford, and John Doty of Braintree, the 27th ult. And this day deserted, William Foster, Samuel Foster, and Jesse Nicolls of Reading; Jesse Hopkins and Samuel Eames of Wilmington; Josiah Stearns, of Billerica; Nathaniel Harwood of Chelmsford; Samuel Tidd, Benjamin Lock, William Russell, Jacob Richardson, and Pomp Baldwin of Woburn; likewise Stephen Easton of Ashford.—It is earnestly desired that the commanding officers of the respective regiments of militia, to which they belong, will do their duty: And that the respective towns would make them return their bounty, as most of them had not been in camp for more than one month.

The Boston Gazette, and Country Journal, November 19, 1781;
The Independent Chronicle and the Universal Advertiser,
November 22, 1781. Minor differences between the papers.

STOLEN from the subscriber in the night of the 13th inst. by a British deserter, who calls his name Henry Brown, about 5 feet 7 or 8 inches high, says he was born in Germany, but speaks good English, had on a pale blue short jacket, light coloured cloth breeches, white woolen stockings, checked woolen shirt, and stole from the subscriber, a red duffil great coat, a light coloured surtout, a pair of green plush breeches, a holland shirt, two pair of worsted stockings of a greyish colour, a pair of channel pumps, a pair of boots, a pair of silver buckles, a napkin marked E. I. and a considerable sum in hard cash, and sundry articles too tedious to mention. Whoever takes up said

thief shall be handsomely rewarded and charges
paid by me JONATHAN HEBARD, of Windham.
Danbury, November 13th, 1781.
The Connecticut Courant, and Weekly Intelligencer, November 20, 1781; November 27, 1781.

DESERTED about the 10th of September last, from the Matross Company under my Command, one JOHN SHIPMAN, of Saybrook, about 19 Years of Age, of a light Complexion, about 5 Feet 5 inches high. Also ROBERT BROWN, of East-Haddam, a Molatto Fellow, about six or seven and twenty Years of Age, has lost some of his fore Teeth, is about 5 Feet 8 Inches high, has been hurt in one of his Legs by a Horse. Whoever will take up said Shipman and Brown, and return them to Fort Trumbull, shall have THREE DOLLARS Reward for each, and all necessary Charges
paid by me,   ADAM SHAPLEY, Capt.
New-London, November 27, 1781.
N. B. Notice is hereby given to the non-commissioned Officers and Soldiers that belong to the above Company, to immediately join it without the least Delay, by Order of Col. M'Clellan.
The Connecticut Gazette; And The Universal Intelligencer, December 7, 1781.

DESERTED from a boat belonging to his Majesty's ship Otter, the 8th instant, lying at the market wharf, CHARLES KERR, the coxswain of the boat, aged 18 or 19, about 5 feet 4 or 5 inches high, slender made, and marked with the small pox; had on when he went away, a new blue cloth jacket with white buttons. Whoever will apprehend him, and carry him on board his Majesty's ship Sandwich, at Gadsden's wharf, shall receive *Three Guineas*, over and about what his Majesty allows for apprehending deserters. It is supposed he has been enticed away by some recruiting part, or master of a ship, any master of a vessel or others, who shall be found having inticed him away, or concealed him, shall be punished as the law directs.
JOHN CRANSTOUN.
Otter, Five Fathom Hole, December 10, 1781.
The Royal South-Carolina Gazette, From December 12, to December 15, 1781.

1782

CHATHAM, December 26.
Last Sunday night....a party of volunteer militia, under the command of Capt. Jeroldman, came down by the way of Hackinsack

to Bergen, where they made prisoners of Captains Harding and M'Michael. The latter deserted from our army in 1780, and was taken out of a flag last spring, and confined in irons in Morristown gaol; but, through a stratagem of his wife, made his escape.

The Providence Gazette; And Country Journal, January 12, 1782.

COMMONWEALTH OF MASSACHUSETTS,
BY HIS EXCELLENCY
JOHN HANCOCK, Esquire,
Governor of the Commonwealth of Massachusetts.

WHEREAS it hath been represented to me by the Sieur De LE TOMBE Consul General of France, That the following Sailors and Mariners have deserted from his Most Christian Majesty's ship the Cibelle, viz. Charles Savale, Louis le Marquis, Pierre Gerbaux, Pierre Tillet, Jean Bapteste Vilgouain, Jean Tousraiut Aubert, Antoine-Thomas Sire, Nicholas Pierre Piquet, Jean Paris, Jerome Lahouw, Pierre Baudet, Salvat Casuave, & Jacques Rostin, and requesting that effectual measures may be taken to detect them and prevent any future desertions. Any whereas, duty as well as interest, call loudly upon the inhabitants of this State to afford every assistance requisite for apprehending the deserters aforesaid.

I have therefore by and with the advice of the Council, thought fit and proper to issue this Proclamation, requiring all officers, civil and military, and others in the government whom it may concern, to do their utmost for apprehending and securing the deserters aforesaid, as well as all others who have heretofore or may hereafter desert from any ships or vessels belonging to his most Christian Majesty. And all commanders of armed ship and other vessels, are hereby cautioned against shipping or conveying away on board their ships or vessels, any deserter or deserters are aforesaid; and all persons whatsoever are cautioned against harbouring to concealing any deserters, as they would avoid the penalty of the law for so doing.

GIVEN at Boston, the 12th day of January, in the year of our Lord 1782, and in the sixth year of the Independence of the United States of America.

JOHN HANCOCK.

By His Excellency's command, JOHN AVERY, Secretary.

The Boston Evening Post, January 19, 1782; *The Independent Ledger, and American Advertiser*, January 21, 1782.

DESERTED,
FROM the *William* Navy Victualler, *Thomas Randall*, Master, on the 24th instant, JOHN ROBINSON, an apprentice, a stout lad, born in Scotland, has a large scar on his right temple in the form of a horse-shoe, pitted with the small pox, dark hair; had on when he went away a blue upper and white under waistcoat and a Dutch cap. Whoever will apprehend and carry him on board said ship, lying near the men of war below White-Point, shall receive one GUINEA reward.
    THOMAS RANDALL.   *January 26th,* 1782.
The Royal South-Carolina Gazette, January 23, to January 26, 1782; January 26, to January 30, 1782.

    Newtown, Bucks county, February 3, 1782.
BROKE GOAL on the night of the 1st instant, the two following persons: ASSHA PARENT, a county born, convicted of horse stealing, and committed for treason, about 23 years of age, 5 feet 10 inches high, slender made, dark brown hair, thin visage; had on a small round beaver hat half worn, a yellowish coloured worsted coat, a light coloured broadcloth waistcoat, blue woolen trowsers, and a pair of good shoes.
  WILLIAM HARRIS, Harris, William who says he is a British deserter, born in Scotland, about 21 years of age, 5 feet 6 or 7 inches high, brown hair turned up before, had a light infantry cap with white hair in the comb, an old short regimental coat faced with blue, a blue short waistcoat, a pair of dirty buckskin breeches, old blue stockings and half worn shoes with brass buckles.
  Whoever apprehends the above described Prisoners, and brings them to the Goal of the county, or secures them in any Goal, shall receive EIGHT DOLLARS for each,
    paid by me, JAMES GREGG, Goaler.
The Pennsylvania Packet or the General Advertiser, February 9, 1782.

    Richmond, January 26.
  Yesterday were executed here, pursuant to their sentence, James Robinson, for burglary, and John Chapman, alias Timberlake, for horse stealing. Reuben Griffin, a deserter, under sentence of death for horse stealing, was pardoned, and was ordered to join his regiment.
The Pennsylvania Journal, and the Weekly Advertiser, February 16, 1782.

DESERTED from the Devonshire, *Samuel Tetherly* Master, Two Sailors, one named *Rees Hopkin,* wearing his own hair, five feet six

inches high, the fore-finger of his right hand frost-bitten; the other named *James Patterson*, a Dutchman, about five feet three inches high. Whoever will secure said persons, so that they may be had again, shall receive TWO GUINEAS reward for each. Apply to the Printers.
The Royal South-Carolina Gazette, From March 13, to March 16, 1782.

BOSTON, March 15, 1782.
THIRTY DOLLARS Reward.
FOR apprehending and securing a certain *George Brown*, aged 23 years, 5 feet 7 inches high, light complexion, blue eyes and brown hair, laborer, inlisted for the town of Woburn for the term of three years—and deserted from this Rendezvous in October last.
The above reward and reasonable charges will be paid by
T. ROBINSON, Ensign 1st Regt.
Assistant to Major PETTENGILE.
The Boston Gazette, And the Country Journal, March 18, 1782; April 1, 1782; April 8, 1782.

RUN AWAY on the evening of the 15th instant, my hired man JOHN ROWLAND LENOX, who before this lived with me some time as my hostler, served me faithful and well untill this time, is a good looking fellow, about five feet ten inches high, talks broad and open English, stammers a little, dark coloured hair, his foretop carelessly turned back, handsomely pitted with the small pox, fair complexion, about 25 years of age, is a deserter from the British army; well cloathed, in white plain home made cloth waistcoat, vest and over alls; stole a likely black Horse, fourteen hands and an half high, white star in his forehead, marked with a Dutch brand TB, about twelve years old, has lost one eye, marked on his hoof if not worn out by Webb. He stole the following things besides said horse, viz. One exceeding genteel pair of plated jointed Stirrup Irons, one pair plated spurs, one genteel plated curb bridle, two pair steel common stirrups, half a dozen fine razors, some of them in a shagreen pock-book, with scissors, &c. two watch coats, one a light brown lined with green baize, the other a new dark brown Bath-Coating, a number of stockings, silk and linen handkerchiefs, five linen shirts, and a number of other articles of wearing apparel, most of them marked with the initials of some of my family's name's. Whoever will take up the said thief, and secure him, shall have eight Dollars reward, and eight Dollars for the things, and all necessary charges paid, by their humble servant,
JOSEPH WEBB.   Wethersfield, April 16, 1782.

The Connecticut Courant, and The Universal Weekly Intelligencer, April 19, 1782; April 30, 1782. See *The Connecticut Gazette; And The Universal Advertiser*, April 19, 1782.

RUN away on the evening of the 15th instant, my hired man JOHN ROWLAND LENOX, who before this lived with me some time, a good looking fellow, of about 32 years of age, talks broad and open, dark coloured hair, his foretop turned back, handsomely pitted with the small-pox, fair complexion, about 5 feet 11 inches high, dressed in white plain cloth, home made, white overhalls; stole dark brown great coat, a number of stockings, a number of pocket handkerchiefs, some linen shirts, a genteel pair of plated swiveled stirrups irons, a plated bridle bit, a genteel pair of plated spurs; also a number of raisors in a black leather case like a pocket-book, and a number of other articles;—also a black horse, with one eye. Said horse is 14 ½ hands high, about 12 years old, a good trotter. The fellow also stole and carried off a gun; by which it is supposed he will turn up said horse and endeavour to pass with a gun and knapsack as a soldier; he is a deserter from the British army, and likely gone towards Rope-ferry. Whoever will secure the thief and things, shall be handsomely rewarded by their humble servant,
    JOSEPH WEBB. Wethersfield, April 16, 1782.
The Connecticut Gazette; And The Universal Advertiser, April 19, 1782. See *The Connecticut Courant, and The Universal Weekly Intelligencer*, April 19, 1782.

WHEREAS on Friday last, one William Lameson, aged 28 Years, 5 Feet 7 Inches high, light Complexion, grey Eyes, and brown Hair, Labourer, enlisted for the Term of three Years for the Town of Salem, having on Callico Clothes, hired of the Subscriber a Horse and Chaise to go the Watertown, but has not yet returned—The Horse was or a Sorrel Colour with a white Face, Trots and Paces; the Chaise painted Yellow, with a white Lining. Whoever will bring the Man, Horse and Chaise to the Subscriber, shall have TWENTY DOLLARS Reward, or the Horse and Chaise only Ten Dollars, and all reasonable Charges
    paid. JOHN NEWELL. Boston, May 20, 1782.
The Boston Gazette, and Country Journal, May 20, 1782.

DESERTED.
From the French frigate Sybille, in Chesapeake bay.

PETER MARIE, about thirty years old, very near five feet high, nimble and stout made, pitted with the small-pox, brown hair, speaks English tolerably, and was clad all in brown when he went off.

JOHN CHA, about twenty-five years old, remarkably well shaped, fresh complexion, a hooked nose, and speaks good English; had on when he went off, a fine blue cloth jacket with blue buttons, lapells and cuffs of blue camblet. This man, as well as Peter Marie, had just been released from prison at New-York.

FRANCIS RIGAUDEN, five feet nine inches high, with light brown hair, and some scars on his face.

Whoever secures the above-mentioned deserters, shall receive a reward of THREE FRENCH GUINEAS for either of them, from the Adjutant-General of the French Army.

The Virginia Gazette, or, The Weekly Advertiser, May 25, 1782.

DESERTED from this post on Wednesday night last, three Recruits for the Continental Army, viz. Jacob Beyer, 22 years old, five feet nine inches high, blue eyes, red hair, light complexion. Peter Boice, 20 years old, five feet eleven inches high, black eyes, dark hair and complexion. Peter Stephens, 22 years old, five feet seven inches high, blue eyes, dark hair, dark complexion. Also, four Recruits on Thursday night last, one day's march from this post on their road to camp, viz. John Dewsey, 21 years old, five feet five inches high, black eyes, black hair, dark complexion, and John Francis Fournier, 26 years old, 5 feet five inches high, blue eyes, black hair, light complexion; both Frenchmen, well dressed, speak bad English. David Huff, 23 years old, five feet six inches and a half high, grey eyes, black hair, light complexion, and Moses Parker, 23 years old, five feet nine inches high blue eyes brown hair, light complexion. Whoever detects said deserters, or either of them, shall be entitled to the reward of the State for that purpose, viz. TWENTY DOLLARS

each, and expences paid.

SETH BANISTER, Capt. 4th Mass. Regt. M. M.

Springfield, June 4, 1782.

The Massachusetts Or The Springfield and Northampton Weekly Advertiser, June 4, 1782; June 11, 1782; June 18, 1782.

DESERTED, Caesar Augustus, black driver to the horse department of the Royal Artillery, about five feet high, very much bandy-leg'd; had on when he went away, a regimental blue coat with a red collar, red waistcoat, linen trowsers and round hat. Whoever apprehends the said deserter, shall receive one Guinea reward, by applying to the office of the horse department, No. 16, Nassau Street. It is suspected

that he is gone to Bergen Point, or on board some of the vessels in the harbour. Whoever harbours or conceals the said deserter, shall be prosecuted as the law directs.
The Royal Gazette, June 15, 1782.

Extract of a letter from Albany, June 6.
This day one Canfield will be Executed at Saratoga, according to the sentence of a General Court Martial. Said Canfield in a native of Northampton, in the Commonwealth of Massachusetts, deserted from the first New-Hampshire regiment and joined the most infamous Major Rogers's Rangers, came with a party to No. 4, to take some intelligent person, and was fortunately taken, with four others. He seems to be a hardened wretch and insensible of his unhappy state.
The Connecticut Journal, June 20, 1782.

DESERTED from this post on the 24th ult. WILLIAM SHIELDS, a solder enlisted for three year's service in the Continental Army, thirty-three years old; five feet nine inches high, grey eyes, black hair, light complexion; had a printed discharge from the Pennsylvania line signed by General Wayne, and it is probable will inlist again. Whoever will take up and secure said deserter shall be entitled to the reward of the State viz. Twenty Dollars and expences paid.
SETH BANISTER, 4th M. R. M. M.
Springfield, June 29, 1782.
The Massachusetts Gazette Or The Springfield and Northampton Weekly Advertiser, July 2, 1782; July 9, 1782; July 16, 1782.

To the PUBLIC.
WE the subscriber having by evil counsel undertaken a wicked scheme, and in its tendency ruinous to the cause of America, as well as our own characters; impressed with a deep sense of the wickedness of our purposes, and hoping that a humble confession will in some degree atone therefor, do in this public manner declare, that we were persuaded by one FOSTWICK, of Bolton, in the county of Worcester, to list for three years service in the continental army by fictitious names, and did give false accounts of ourselves with design to deceive the continental muster-masters, and were to share the promised bounty of 60 l. each with FOSTWICK, then assume our real names, and return to our respective homes to enjoy the fruits of our wickedness; but, by the scrutinous examination at mustering we were detected in our designs, have most sincerely repented of them, and hoping the candid world (in consideration of our future good behaviour) will throw the veil of charity over the folly of unguarded youth, do humbly

ask the pardon of the public, the muster master and all good men for our intended imposition. We also have willingly and cheerfully paid twenty dollars each as smart money to be appropriated to public use in advertising deserters, detecting deceivers, &c. at the discretion of the Muster-Masters.

Witness our hands,
GERSHOM BROWN, jun. ELIAS SWAN.

Springfield, June 27 1782.

N. B. The above-mentioned villain, FOSTWICK, after seducing Brown and Swan, to join in his nefarious schemes, on the detection of the villainy, took the first opportunity to make his escape, leaving the others in the trouble he himself created, and clandestinely conveyed a hat belonging to Swan and a pair of silver shoe buckles the property of Swan.

It is hoped every friend to justice will use his endeavors to bring to condign punishment so attrocious an offender.

The Massachusetts Gazette Or The Springfield and Northampton Weekly Advertiser, July 2, 1782; July 9, 1782; *The Boston Gazette, And The Country Journal,* July 22, 1782. The *Boston Gazette adds:*

The above Fostwick, *was in this town last week, and very narrowly escaped being apprehended. People are cautioned to be on their guard, lest they should be taken by him.* Boston, July 22.

DESERTED on the road from this post to camp, two recruits, viz. SOLOMON DECKAR, 19 years of age, 5 feet 6 and a half inches high, grey eyes, obrown [sic] hair, light complexion, had on a red coat, and is a lad of great assurance, says he formerly belonged to Poughkeepsie. WILLIAM GRANT, 19 years old, 5 feet 5 inches high light blue eyes, light hair and complexion. They stole Sergeant King's knapsack, who commanded the party, with all his baggage, in which was a consolidated State Note the Property of Mr. JAMES COLBY.

Whoever will detect the villains will do a great service to the cause; prevent their further imposing on the good people; and be entitled to the reward of the Commonwealth of Massachusetts for that purpose.

SETH BANISTER, Capt. 4th Mas. Reg't, M. M.

Springfield, July 13, 1782.

The Massachusetts Or The Springfield and Northampton Weekly Advertiser, July 16, 1782.

WHEREAS *ROBERT FELTON* and *RICHARD BURK,* soldiers having inlisted and mustered for the town of Middleton, having on the

15th ult. obtained my liberty to be absent from this rendezvous eleven days, on a certain Capt. MOSES STONE, being bound for their appearance, at the expiration of the above limited term: And as said soldiers do not yet appear, this is to request Capt. STONE to deliver said soldiers to me, at my quarters in Worcester immediately, to prevent further trouble.

E. THORP, Capt. 7th M. R. M. M.

Worcester, July 16, 1782.

The Massachusetts Spy: Or, American Oracle of Liberty, July 18, 1782; July 25, 1782; August 1, 1782.

DESERTED from this post on the 16th instant, a recruit for the Continental Army. Called himself THOMAS TOUPER, twenty years old, five feet two inches and a half high, dark eyes, black hair, dark complexion. He was brought to this post by one RAWSON, for the town of Montague. It is natural to suppose the cheat to the public was previously concerted, as said TOUPER did not remain in town three hours and RAWSON left him. He was much scrupled at mustering, by RAWSON affirmed that he was himself, and this his hire was mostly left in the hands of his class. This is therefore to request them, if friends to their country, to exert themselves with said hire to detect the deserter, or put a better man in his room.

SETH BANISTER, Capt. 4th Mas. Reg't, M. M.

Springfield, July 23, 1782.

The Massachusetts Or The Springfield and Northampton Weekly Advertiser, July 23, 1782; August 6, 1782.

CHATHAM, July 17.

Last Friday one Cooke, a soldier in the second regiment, was hung at camp for the reiterated crimes of desertion and theft.

The Massachusetts Spy: Or, American Oracle of Liberty, August 1, 1782.

DESERTED from General WATERBURY's Brigade since the 17th of April last, Jabez Cook, New Milford, on the 18th of April, John Oaklin, Kent, 26th James Sprague, do. 6th May, William Hawley, Wethersfield, 29th April, Jonathan Graves, do. June 10th, Asahel Goodrich, do. 15th do. David Clark, Farmington, May 6th, Vest Eastman, Woodbury, June 12th, Ira Way, Litchfield, 7th do. William Winslow, Southington, July 5th, Thomas Brown, Colchester, 7th, William Hamilton, New-London, 7th, Daniel Reves, Derby 7th, Eliphalet Stevens, Isaac Basset, David Morris, and Thaddeus Beach, of Milford, 16th July, Stephen Burr, Haddam, Elihu Crane, Josiah

Hull, (22d) and John Norton, Durham, 26th, Daniel Vaughan, Lebanon, 26th, John Anthony, Aaron Ives, and Dan Carrington, Wallingford, 25th, Josiah Hull, Killingsworth, 26th, Edward Oris, Lyme, 9th, Grant Weckwin, East-Haddam, 27th, and Chapman St[ear]s, Torrington, 26th.

GENTLEMEN, By the above list you may see the number deserted in my brigade, which cannot be prevented without your assistance; and; and I most earnestly request you to detect all these that are to be found, and secure them in any of the gaol in this State, & acquaint me where, that I might send proper guards to conduct them back to their duty.

DAVID WATERBURY, Brig-Gen.

To the Authority and Selectmen, of the different towns in Connecticut.

N. B. All Officers & Soldiers belonging to my brigade are ordered to join immediately.

Camp, near White Plains, July 28, 1781.

The several printers of this state are requested to publish the above in their news papers.

The Connecticut Journal, August 2, 1781; August 9, 1781.

DESERTED from this rendezvous, John Harvey, an Irishman, 36 years old, 5 feet 7 inches high, fresh complexion, hazel eyes, dark hair, loves grog, and is pretty talkative. Richard Burk, (after mustering had liberty to go home and has not joined since) aged 25 years, 5 feet 7 inches high, fresh complexion, blue eyes, brown hair, an inhabitant of Chesterfield. Whoever secures said deserters, that they may be brought to justice, will be entitled to the reward given by this Commonwealth.   E. THORP, Capt. 7th M. R. M M.

Worcester, July 29th, 1782.

The Massachusetts Gazette Or The General Advertiser, August 6, 1782; August 13, 1782; August 20, 1782; *The Massachusetts Gazette Or The Springfield and Northampton Weekly Advertiser*, August 20, 1782.

DESERTED on the way from this Post, two Villains: Viz: John Brown, 27 years old, 5 feet high, grey eyes, black hair, light complexion, thin favoured, has a red humour in his face.

Daniel Brownson (as he calls himself) 16 years old, 5 feet 7 inches high, blue eyes, black hair, dark complexion, a slouching awkward boy. It is hoped no one will neglect detecting these and all deserters, as they wish to save their own interest, and their Country.

SETH BANISTER, Capt. 4th M. R. M. M.

The Massachusetts Or The Springfield and Northampton Weekly Advertiser, August 6, 1782; August 13, 1782; August 20, 1782; *The Massachusetts Gazette Or The General Advertiser*, August 13, 1782; August 20, 1782.

DESERTED *from this Post last evening a recruit for the Army, called his named Brean Annis, six feet high 35 years old, blue eyes, grey hair, light complexion, thin favoured, a long thin nose, a Scotch pedler, talks broad, has lived in Boston. Whoever will return the Villain to this post shall receive twenty Dollars on sight,*
     by SETH BANISTER Capt. M. M.
             Springfield September 2, 1782.
The Massachusetts Gazette Or The General Advertiser, September 10, 1782; October 1, 1782; *The Massachusetts Gazette Or The Springfield and Northampton Weekly Advertiser*, September 10, 1782; October 1, 1782.

       Ten Dollars Reward.
STOLEN out of the pasture of the subscriber, living in Princeton, county of Somerset, state of New-Jersey, A Brown HORSE, six years old, about 14 hands and a half high, has his mane plaitted and a small star; supposed to be taken by a DANIEL DALEY, an Irishman, about 5 feet 4 inches high, with short black hair, a deserter from the British army. Any person taking up said Horse and Thief, shall have the above Reward, or Six Dollars for the Horse and reasonable Charges
    paid, by JAMES ROCK,   Aug. 27.
The Pennsylvania Packet or the General Advertiser, September 2, 1782; September 19, 1782.

        TAKE NOTICE.
DESERTED *from his Most Christian Majesty's Fleet, under the Command of the Marquiss De Vaudreuil now in Boston Harbour, the following Sailors and Soldiers—Jean Adam Crow, Joseph Porvive, Jean Michael Zaber, Francois de Most, Jean Baptiste Vibal, Jean Portais, Blaise Francois Kallemand, Jean Joseph Voirambour Simon Viat, Laurens Boret, Antroine Rougon, Jacques Pecker, Pierre Alagie, Raimod LaFrise.*

 Whoever will secure and bring up the whole or any of the above Deserters to the Major's Office, opposite to Peck's-Wharf, shall receive TEN DOLLARS for each, and necessary Expences paid.
 The Boston Gazette, And The Country Journal, September 16, 1782; September 23, 1782.

BROKE out of the Goal in this town, on the night of the 10th instant a prisoner who called himself William Jones, committed for passing counterfeit state certificates; has lately frequented the town of Hensdale; said Jones was a recruit for the Continental Army, enlisted by the name of Joshua Bills; and deserted the service; is about 25 years old, 5 feet 9 inches high, dark eyes, black curled hair, light complexion: had on a blue great coat with a small black velvet cape: whoever will return the villain shall receive ten dollars, and expences paid by   JOHN MORGAN Goaler.

Springfield, September 16th, 1782.

The Massachusetts Gazette Or The General Advertiser, September 17, 1782; September 24, 1782; October 1, 1782; *The Massachusetts Gazette Or The Springfield and Northampton Weekly Advertiser*, November 24, 1782.

DESERTED on the way from this Post to Camp a recruit who called himself Ebenezer Nelson, it is supposed his name is Ebenezer Lewis, is 17 years old, 5 feet two inches and a half high, dark blue eyes, brown hair, dark complexion, a Cooper by trade, it is earnestly requested that the good people will exert themselves to detect such villains who change their names, rob a class of a large sum of money, take a sacred oath to be true to their ingagements and immediately desert. No crime is too bad for such perjured persons to commit. Neither the lives nor property of the Community can be safe while such knaves are at large.

SETH BANISTER, Capt. M. M.

Springfield, September 26, 1782.

The Massachusetts Or The Springfield and Northampton Weekly Advertiser, October 15, 1782; October 22, 1782, *The Massachusetts Gazette Or The General Advertiser*, October 22, 1782.

DESERTED *from his Majesty's ship Albacore, John Nucam, aged 22 years, about five feet six inches high, fresh complexion, light brown hair tied, had on when he left the ship, a light coloured coat with white metal buttons, black waistcoat and breeches.*

Whoever will bring the above Deserter on board the Ship, shall receive the usual reward for securing deserters.

The Royal Gazette, October 26, 1782.

DESERTED
From his Majesty's Ship PROTHEE,
ROBERT BLACK, Seaman,

FIVE feet three inches, and three quarters of an inch high, about thirty two years of age, swarthy complexion, stout made, long visaged, grey eyes, short black hair, pitted with the small pox. All masters of merchant ships are hereby warned not to receive him into employ, or entertain him, on pain of being prosecuted according to law. Any person or person upon taking him up and securing him in the main guard at New-York, will be paid Two Guineas, over and above the public reward for taking up Deserters.
The Royal Gazette, October 26, 1782.

NEWPORT, Nov. 30.

Last Wednesday Evening arrived here a small Schooner, Prize to the Privateer Schooner Rochambeau, Capt. Reed of this Port: And this morning arrived an armed Galley of 8 Carriage Guns, and 38 Men, captured by the above Privateer, off the Hook, after a close Engagement of the Glass, during which Capt. Reed lost a Prize Master (Mr. Benjamin Cornell of this Town.) The Galley had her Captain, and one other Officer killed, and several wounded.

The Captain of the aforesaid Galley is said to be the noted Deavenport, who has committed so many Depredations in the Jerseys; the other Person who was killed, is one Bentley, late of this State, who deserted from Col. Greene's Regiment, and gave the Enemy Intelligence of his Situation, by which that brave but unfortunate Officer, with Major Flag, were cruelly massacred.

The Connecticut Gazette; And The Universal Intelligencer, November 30, 1782; December 6, 1782.

WHEREAS Mary the wife of me the subscriber has for some time past behaved herself in a very unbecoming manner, in threatening the life of me and my child, and I am apprehensive that she will do all in her power to injure me. This is therefore to warn all persons from trusting her on my account, as I will pay no debt of her contracting
after this date. MARTIN WILLCOX.
New-Hartford, December 23, 1782.
The Connecticut Courant And Weekly Intelligencer, December 31, 1782. See *The Connecticut Courant And Weekly Intelligencer*, January 14, 1783.

1783

OBSERVING yesterdays paper, to my great surprize I found myself advertised by him who ought to have been my friend and husband; who forbids all persons trusting me on his account, which I can safely say they never did nor ever will, until he behaves better than he does at present—but he tells me what he is afraid of, &c. But one story is good till another is told; the truth of the matter is this: It was my misfortune to marry Martin Wilcocks, better than two years ago; for some time after we married he provided a place for us to live, and we lived comfortably together for a few months, although he was considerable in debt, yet I was willing to do every thing in my power to help him out; and for that reason I sold every thing I could possibly spare, and even rob'd myself of cloathing to pay his debts, in hopes to live always happy together.—But it was not long before he enlisted to go in the state service for the town, and took a considerable sum of money for bounty, which he was very careful not to let me have one farthing of. After spending considerable part of the money, he deserted and went into Massachusetts state, and has left me for this 18 months without providing bread, meat or cloathing, or any shelter to put my head in, with an infant child to take care of, and nothing to care of it with; without a friend, relation or acquaintance: As I was a stranger in these parts, I have endured hunger and cold and every thing that is possible for me to undergo, short of death, without any body to pity me or take my part. Finally he has rob'd me of my child, the only comfort of my life, after I have taken so much pains with it, and undergone every thing to support it; considering the matter, it appeared to me so cruel, that I talked unbecomingly and sinfully; for which I ask forgiveness of God and all christian people; and leave it to the world to judge betwixt us, as I was always willing to live with him and behave to him as well as I knew how.

        MARY WILCOCKS.

        New-Hartford, January 1st, 1783.

The Connecticut Courant And Weekly Intelligencer, January 14, 1783. See *The Connecticut Courant And Weekly Intelligencer*, December 31, 1782.

By His EXCELLENCY
BENJAMIN HARRISON, Esquire,
GOVERNOR *of the Commonwealth* of VIRGINIA.
A PROCLAMATION.

WHEREAS I have received information that the base and wicked practice of Desertion still continues among the New Levies, in defiance of the Law, and contrary to good faith and the duty they owe their Country; I HAVE therefore thought it proper, by and with the advice Council of State, to use this my Proclamation, offering a reward of TEN DOLLARS each, and Twelve-nineteiths of a Dollar per mile for traveling expences, for apprehending and delivering to a

Continental Officer, the following Soldiers, who have deserted from the barracks at Winchester, viz. John Botts, from the County of Halifax, about eighteen years old, five feet six inches high, has dark hair, black eyes, and a fair complexion. John Massey, eighteen years of age, five feet three inches high, has dark hair, grey eyes, fair complexion, and was born in Fluvanna County. John Spong, nineteen years of age, five feet four inches high, has brown hair, dark eyes, a swarthy complexion, marked with the small-pox, a taylor by trade, and from the County of Montgomery. Thomas Burton, twenty-five years of age, five feet six inches high, has brown hair, grey eyes, of a fair complexion, from the County of Albemarle, and a taylor by trade. William Howe, a native of Ireland, but inlisted in the County of Rockbridge; forty five years of age, five feet five inches high, has dark hair, grey eyes, and of a dark complexion. Griffith W. Bickham, about twenty years of age, five feet eight and three quarter inches high, has light hair, grey eyes, and of a fair complexion, marked with the small-pox, by trade a shoemaker, and from the County of Northumberland. Richard Thorns, about seventeen years of age, five feet seven inches high, has light hair, grey eyes, a fair complexion, and from Accomack County. Argyle Wilkins, about nineteen years of age, five feet four and a half inches high, light hair, grey eyes, and a fair complexion, from the County of Northampton. Thomas Crew, enlisted from Northampton, but a native of Hispaniola; about twenty four years of age, five feen seven inches high, has black eyes, black hair, of a tawny complexion, pitted with the small-pox, and brought up a sailor. Charles Dobbins, from the County of Dinwiddie; about twenty years old, five feet six and three-quarters inches high, has black hair and eyes, of a yellow complexion, and marked with the small-pox. Benjamin Payne, twenty years of age, five feet six and three quarter inches high, has black eyes and hair, of a yellow complexion, with a scar on his left cheek, and from the County of Buckingham. Fortunatus Sydnor, from the County of Hanover; about five feet eight inches high, marked with the small-pox; had on a blue coat with red facing, and a white cloth jacket and breeches. John Henry Beigting, a native of the United States of Holland; five feet six inches high, by trade a taylor, of a thin swarthy visage, dark short hair, light grey eyes, thin black beard, three small blue spots on his left ear, one of which is very discernable, the other two are not so plain, and which he says were occasioned by powder: He is fond of strong drink, and when enlivened thereby much inclined to sing. AND WHEREAS this growing evil calls in a most pointed manner for the attention and exertion of Government, and as it behoves every good citizen to use his utmost endeavours to suppress a practice so injurious to the interest of his Country, I DO farther enjoin all Captains of Officers commanding companies in the Militia, to make strict enquiry in their respective companies after the above Deserters, pursuant to an Act entitled, "An Act the more effectually to prevent and punish Desertion," and when apprehended to deliver them to the most convenient Continental Officer, or to secure them in gaol, and give the earlies notice thereof either to General MUHLENBURG, at Winchester barracks, or to me.

GIVEN under my hand and the seal of the Commonwealth, at Richmond, the thirteenth day of January, 1783.
BENJAMIN HARRISON.

The Virginia Gazette, or, The Weekly Advertiser, February 1, 1783.

DESERTED from this post the 13th instant, two recruits, viz. John Greenwall, 17 years old, five feet eight inches and a half high, blue eyes, brown hair, light complexion.

Also, David Moors, 20 years old, five feet nine inches and a half high, blue eyes, squints considerably, dark brown hair, darkish complexion.

Whoever will detect said deserters and return them to this post, shall receive ten dollars reward for each, and all necessary charges paid, by me

LUKE DAY, Capt. 7th Mass. Reg. M. M.

Springfield, Feb. 15, 1783.

The Massachusetts Gazette Or The General Advertiser, February 25, 1783; March 4, 1783.

DESERTED from the 7th Regiment of infantry, a certain BOSTON BLACK, about 20 Years old, very stout of his Age, 5 feet, 9 or 10 inches in Stature, walks heavy, his Knees interfering, speaks bad English. has an unpleasant Countenance, and is very Black;—has taken with him a new green Coat faced with red,—a blue Coat, not much worn, with green Cuffs and Collar, Button Holes white Tape;—one Pair new leather Breeches, & one Pair blue Cloth, old and patched. Whoever will apprehend said *Boston Black*, and deliver him at the Mustering-Office, Boston, will be entitled to the Reward given by this Commonwealth, for apprehending Deserters.

Boston, 24th March, 1783.

The Boston Gazette, and Country Journal, March 24, 1783; March 31, 1783; April 7, 1783.

DESERTED from the artillery company stationed at Groton, the last of October, 1782, THOMAS LAMBERT, of Preston, about 5 feet 8 inches high, light complexion, slender built.—Also JONATHAN DART, of Boston, a thick set fellow, dark complexion, he left the company some time in February last.—Also, CATO CUFF, a black fellow, belonging to Stonington, who run off some time last summer. Whoever will take up said deserters, and return them to Fort Griswold, shall receive twenty shillings in pay-table orders, and charges paid.
      WILLIAM LATHAM, Capt.
 The Connecticut Gazette; And The Universal Intelligencer, March 28, 1783; April 4, 1782; April 11, 1783.

       TEN DOLLARS REWARD.
STOLEN from the house of Capt. Ebenezer Fisk, of Southampton, on Sunday evening the 6th of April instant, a SILVER WATCH, No. 102, maker's name Thomas Robinson, of London; also a pair of square SILVER SHOE BUCKLES, with wide rims, curiously wrought, and a pair of MEN's PUMPS. They were stolen by a person who said his name was Henry Booth, or Monk; he is of a middling stature, well proportioned, of a sprightly behaviour, lightish complexion, round smooth face, lightish eyes, says he is an Englishman (though he appears to have something of the Irish brogue) and that he deserted from the British army about eight months since, has shortish brown hair, cut short on the top of his head, and the fore-top turn'd back, about twenty-three years old; had on a short brown coat, white vest and breeches, blue stockings, and a pair of boots.
 Whoever will take up the thief, and above articles, and secure them to the subscriber, shall have ten hard dollars reward, and all necessary charges paid; or if only the thief, or watch and buckles, shall be generously rewarded
    by me EBENEZER FISK,
           Southington, April 7, 1783.
 N. B. The thief says that he work'd with Joseph Pease, of Suffield, two months the beginning of last winter, and at General Wadsworth's, in Durham, the two last months.
 The Connecticut Journal, April 10, 1783; April 17, 1783; April 24, 1783.

THE Subscribers take this Method to inform the Publick, that whereas we have three Notes of Hand, to one JOSEPH MILLER, viz. one Note of *twenty Dollars,* upon demand, one other Note of *sixty-two Dollars and an half,* payable in one Years from Date of said Note; also, one other Note of *sixty-two Dollars and an half,* payable in two Years

from the Date of said Note; all bearing date 17th June 1782; which Notes were given to said MILLER, in Consideration that he should serve in the continental Army, three Years; and whereas said MILLER has deserted from said Army. and not fulfilled the Condition, on his Part, this is therefore to caution all Persons against purchasing said Notes, which were put into the Hands of one DANIEL JOHNSON, of SOUTH-BOROUGH, as a Trustee for said MILLER, as we are determined not to pay one Farthing of said Notes.
    BENJAMIN SAWIN, JONAS MORSE.
Marlborough, March 15, 1783.
Thomas's Massachusetts Spy Or, American Oracle of Liberty, April 10, 1783; April 17, 1783; April 24, 1783.

ONE GUINEA REWARD.
DESERTED, on the 10th or 11th instant, from the Hessian Hospital, William Samuel Clemens, born in the city of Hoff Geismar in Hesse, and a driver in the company of Colonel De Munchhausen, Hessian Regiment De Bose; he is about 31 years of age, 5 feet 2 inches high, slender, of a pale complexion, and black hair, speaks a little French, wears sometimes an ash coloured or green Coat. It is supposed he will engage as a cook or servant, by telling that he has been employed in that way.

 Whoever takes up the said William Samuel Clemens, and returns him to Colonel De Munchhausen, shall be entitled to the above reward, and all necessary expences. All Masters of vessels are warned and cautioned not to take him away.
The Royal American Gazette, April 16, 1783.

          CUMBERLAND, April 14, 1783.
RAN away from the subscriber a few days since, a tall slim mulatto man named <u>TOM</u>, about twenty years of age, five feet six and three quarters high, is much pitted with the small pox, has black eyes, and resembles an Indian from whom he is descended. He eloped about this time twelvemonth, was received as a substitute in the County of Dinwiddie, brought to Cumberland Old Court-house with the recruits of that County, re-inlisted for the war last fall, went with the troops to Winchester, from whence he deserted and appears in the Governor's proclamation relative to deserters, by the name of Charles Dobbins; since his desertion he has cut off the forefinger of his right hand, in order to marry a free woman near Fine creek mill, in Powhatan County, who had determined never to have a husband in the continental army, and supposed this mutilation would procure him a discharge. He was seen the day after his late departure in the upper

end of this County, moving southwardly, whither I suspect he means to make his escape. Whoever will secure said slave so that I get him again, or will deliver him to me, shall be handsomely rewarded.
                  HENRY SKIPWITH.
The Virginia Gazette, or, The American Advertiser (Hayes), April 19, 1783.

                  Thirty Guineas Reward

DESERTED on the 13th of April, from the 3d Battalion of the Royal Artillery, commanded by Lieutenant-Colonel *Peter Traille,* Corporal JOHN HORLER, aged thirty years, five feet ten inches high, born in England, in the county of Berkshire, by trade a wool comber; dark complection, black hair combed down on his fore-head, marked with the small pox, very corpulent; round shouldered, has a great volubility of tongue, very much in-kneed: He had on when he went away his regimental coat, with two epaulets, and was seen at East-Chester the 20th of April, and since at Philadelphia.—Whoever delivers said DESERTER to any of his Majesty's posts, shall receive the above reward, by applying to
                  Lieutenant-Colonel *Peter Traille*, at New-York.
The Royal American Gazette, May 27, 1783.

                  New-York, 27th May, 1783.
DESCRIPTION of *CHARLES BROESCKE*, Quarter-Master to Colonel de Linsing's battalion of Hessian Grenadiers, who absconded since yesterday afternoon, and took with him the sum of *Three hundred and forty pounds Sterling,* Subsistence Money belonging to the above-mentioned regiment.

    He is about 40 years old, under the middle size, rather fat, a round full and pale face, short neck, his head bending forwards, not much hair, which is of a brown colour, and which he used to tie in a queiu. Had on before he went away, a blue coat, with lappels, the button holes trimmed with a small silver lace, white under-cloaths, and boots.

    He had a connection with a young woman, named SALLY BUNN, from Perth-Amboy, who may now perhaps be with him; she went to the Jersies on Saturday the 24th instant, is a good looking woman, of the middle size, about 22 years old, her face and features rather large, dark hair, had on a yellow silk, when she went away.

    All persons, civil and military, are desired to assist in apprehending the above Deserter.
The Royal American Gazette, May 31, 1783.

SIX GUINEAS REWARD will be paid by the Printer to any person that will apprehend JOSEPH ROBERTSON, lately deserted from the 40th regiment, about 5 feet 8 inches high, 32 years of age, brown complection, dark brown hair, born in Raflisland in the County of Down, Ireland. The above Joseph Robertson is indebted to a Merchant in New-York 58l. 9s. Currency, who has authorised the printer to pay the above reward.

N. B. He the said Robertson intended to have gone to settle in Port-Roseway, which place its supposed he is gone to, or will endeavour to procure a passage; therefore, all Masters of vessels are forbid harbouring or carrying his away on any account, as they will be liable to be proceeded against according to law, on account of his being a deserter, as well as for the above debt.

New-York, October 7, 1783.
The Royal Gazette, October 8, 1783; October 11, 1783.

To the PUBLIC.

WHEREAS Gen. David Waterbury did in the month of May 1781, advertise me the subscriber, as a deserter from the State troops, under his command at Horseneck, promising rewards to any one who would apprehend me as such; and afterwards at sundry times sent out guards to pursue and take me, and subject me to military trial, or expose me, as he had done sundry others, to corporal punishment without trial by his own arbitrary command; whereby not daring to trust my person to the ungoverned fury of his passions, by which many others had severely suffered, I was necessitated to quit my habitation, my parents, my business, and the agreeable society of my friends and acquaintance, and to pass a long period in voluntary banishment, to the great damage of my private affairs, the loss of others with whom I had been connected in business, and the utmost injury to my feelings and reputation.—I beg the patience of the candid public, while I give a plain stating of the facts, which led to such an extraordinary piece of conduct in the General.

I enlisted in the State troops for a class in Stonington, about the 20th day of March 1781, in the company under the command of Capt. Smith, under this agreement, that I would serve myself or furnish an effective soldier to the Captain's Acceptance, by the time the troops were to meet. Accordingly by that time, I hired one Mr. Comstock, of New-Fairfield, to serve in my room. The Captain accepted him, and delivered up my enlistment on the 9th day of April following, and said Comstock faithfully served in my place and was honorably discharged at the end of the term. This was all the connection I ever had with the troops under the General's command, and he had full notice of my discharge from myself and Capt. Smith, and also from Col. Hayt, before he issued his advertisement. He had also received from gentlemen of the first reputation, ample recommendations of my character, as a good citizen, and faithful soldier, during more than three years, in which I had before served in the army. These he wholly disregarded, and treated all applications to him on the subject, either by myself or others, with the highest insult, and most outrageous threatnings. How he can justify his conduct to God, his conscience, or the person injured, I leave to his own feelings, and the judgment of the public.

Since my return, I have endeavoured to settle my accounts with all persons with whom I was concerned in any business contracts. But as I am about soon to leave this part of the country, and on account of the peculiar situation into which I have been driven, and the loss of many papers, sundry accounts may be yet unsettled, to my own loss or that of others, I desire all persons who have accounts open with him, to call upon me at New-Cambridge in Farmington, as soon as possible for an adjustment—and can asure them, however my character may have suffered by the unprovoked malice of an enemy, they will ever find me to the utmost of my ability, punctual and honest in my private dealings, and a faithful friend to my country.

JOSHUA SMITH. New-Cambridge,
(in Farmington) Oct. 13, 1783.

The Connecticut Courant, And Weekly Advertiser, November 4, 1783. No earlier ads could be found.

Fifty Dollars Reward.

LAST evening was stolen from the subscriber, by his servant, *John Bernard de Frank*, the following Articles, viz. A Silver Watch, English made, with a steel chain, a Purse, containing 16 ducats, and some silver, about 20 dollars (Spanish) loose, a pair of silver Shoe and Knee Buckles, together with a Quantity of Wearing Apparel, marked F. A. M. The said John Bernard de Frank is of a middling size, swarthy complexion, is a German, speaks Dutch and French with a little English; he was a serjeant or corporal in the Hessian Yagers, who deserted from, and joined the French army, and kept school in Lancaster: had on when he went away, a grey surtout coat, grey under ditto; but perhaps has put on some of my cloaths which he has stolen. Any person or persons who will discover or apprehend the said John Bernard de Frank, so that the subscriber may get his property again, shall be entitled to the above reward, or in proportion for any part, by applying to the subscriber, at Messers. *Clement Biddle & Co's,* Water-street.

F. ANTHONY METZGAR.   Dec. 27.
The Pennsylvania Packet, and General Advertiser, December 30, 1783; January 1, 1784; January 6, 1784; January 8, 1784.

Twenty Dollars Reward.

RAN-AWAY from the subscriber, living in New-Hanover township, Philadelphia county, a servant MAN, named JACOB RAUB, a deserter from the Hessian troops, about 30 years of age, about 5 feet high, squints a little, has black curled hair, has a hole under his chin and some other marks: had on when he went away and took with him, one white coat, a brown waistcoat with sleeves, a blue and white mixed ditto without sleeves, a new wool hat, new buckskin breeches, a pair of overalls, one fine shirt, and a coarse ditto, a pair of double soaled shoes. Whoever takes up said Servant, so that his master may have him again, shall have the above reward and reasonable charges paid, by me, FREDERICK VOGEL,
or GEORGE VOGEL, in Third-street, next door to the Golden Swan, Philadelphia.

New-Hanover, Dec. 29, 1783.

N. B. All masters of vessels are forbid to carry him off at their peril.

The Pennsylvania Packet, and General Advertiser, January 17, 1784.

INDEX

This is an index of complete names as well as those listed only by rank and last name, such as Captain Smith. In the relatively few cases that a Christian name is not given, they are listed by their last name alone. Where Native and African Americans are identified as such, they are listed both by their race and their given names.

Aaelsworth, James, 57
Abbot, Abiel, 231
Abby, Thomas, 99
Achison, Thomas, 231
Adams, Abijah, 104
Adams, Alexander, 145, 165
Adams, Edward, 201, 205
Adams, Jacob, 126
Adams, John, 58, 87, 232
Adams, Mr., 232
Adams, Thomas, Jr., 210
Adams, William, 60
Adams/Addams, Jonathan, Jr., 208, 210
Addams, Jonathan, 210
Ailes, James, 252
Airs, John, 90
Aitkin, James, 74
Akins, Moses, 124
Alagie, Pierre, 292
Alden, Ichabod, 52, 85, 95, 126, 206
Alden, John, 58
Aldrich, Nedebiah, 111
Alds, Benjamin, 245
Alexander, Captain, 53, 155
Alexander, Henry, 66
Alexander, John, 76
Alexander, Morgan, 61, 78
Alford, Drury, 32, 139
Allen, Capt., 119
Allen, Elisha, 35, 252
Allen, Eseck, 211, 213
Allen, Judah, 101

Allen, Right, 126
Allen, Thomas, 91, 241
Allen, William, 131, 196
Allensby, John, 222
Allin, Jonathan, 30
Allison, John, 13, 113
Alsop, William, 93
Altenbockum, de, 254
Alvis, Elijah, 186
Ames, Hugh, 125
Amonett, Daniel, 130
Amos, Isaac, 105
Amos, John, 176
Ams, George, 281
Ancram, Capt., 189, 211
Anderson, Bartlett, 62
Anderson, Capt., 79
Anderson, G., 211
Anderson, James, 43
Anderson, Matthew Lightfoot, 204
Anderson, Richard, 53, 54, 72
Anderson, Richard C., 108, 171
Anderson, Robert, 15
Anderson, Willam, 160
Anderson, William, 53, 54
Andrews, James, 200
Angel, Capt., 6
Angel, Joseph, 246
Angel, William, 95, 246
Angell, Israel, 73, 251
Angell, William, 115
Anglin, John V., 219
Annis, Brean, 292

Ansell, John, 254
Anthoney, John, 158
Anthony, John, 291
Antony, John, 7
Arbado, Francis, 102
Arbuckle, Capt., 32
Archer, Joseph, 50
Archer, William, 79, 171
Arell, Samuel, 47, 61
Armistead, Thomas, 57
Armond, John, 242
Armstrong, John, 126, 236
Armstrong, Richard, 234
Arnold, Benedict, 202
Arnold, James, 98
Arnold, James Hopkins, 108
Arnold, John, 152
Arnold, Robert, 41
Arnold, Thomas, 149
Arter, Joseph, 124
Arthur, John, 184
Askins, William, 160
Astins, Elisha, 138
Asuleck, Richard, 199
Atkins, Philip, 147, 184
Atkins, William, 196, 230
Atkinson, Philip, 9
Atwell, Mr., 120
Aubert, Jean Tousraiut, 283
Augustun, Peter, 30
Augustus, Caesar, 287
Austin, Israel, 211
Austin, Joshua, 245
Austin, Nathan, 255
Austin, Stephen, 262
Averill, Samuel, 65
Avery, Billey/Billy H., 10, 83
Avery, John, 283
Babb, James, 134
Bacon, Prince, 241
Bailey, Capt., 35
Bailey, Col., 279
Bailey, Daniel, 46

Bailey, David, 281
Bailey, Enoch, 243
Bailey, Stephen, 188
Bain, Daniel, 65
Bainbridge, Sergeant, 267
Baird, Capt., 117
Baird, John, 185
Baker, John, 146
Baker, Joseph, 263
Baker, Overton, 186
Balcom, Daniel, 245
Baldwin, Benjamin, 270
Baldwin, Brewen, 211, 213
Baldwin, Clark, 212
Baldwin, Jeduthan, 151
Baldwin, Nathan, 19
Baldwin, Pomp, 281
Baldwin. Jacob, 5
Baley, Lemuel, 24, 33
Baley, Nathan, Jr., 247
Ball, Capt., 77
Ball, Farling, 113
Ball, Mr., 23
Ballard, Capt., 58
Ballard, Col., 158
Ballard, Dudley, 58
Ballard, George, 179
Ballard, Robert, 66, 82
Ballew, David, 168
Ballou, Reuben, 55
Bancroft, James, 190
Bandy, George, 176
Banister, Seth, 287, 288, 289, 290, 291, 292, 293
Banks, Nehemiah, 212
Banks, Thomas, 121
Baour, Angelica Elizabeth, 217
Barber, Col.
Barber, Elihu, 208
Barber, Mr., 111
Barber, William, 121
Barclay, Alexander, 180
Bardine, James, 259

Barene/Barne, Frederick, 15, 16
Barene/Barne, Molly, 16
Barene/Barne, Nabby, 16
Barham, Peter, 92
Barker, James, 190
Barker, John, 232
Barker, Michael, 277
Barker, Mrs. Michael, 277
Barker, Thomas, 135, 138
Barnabas, Isaac, 22
Barnard, William, 272
Barnes, Daniel, 34, 138
Barnes, Stephen, 35
Barnett, David, 40
Barney, John, Jr., 201, 202
Barns, Daniel, 228
Barns, John, 244
Barns, Oliver, 210
Barron, William, 30
Barsley, John, Jr., 280
Barter, John, 124
Bartlet, Samuel, 36
Bartlett, Ichabot, 5
Bartlett, James, 13
Bartlett, William, 179, 189
Bartley, Alexander, 229
Bartley, William, 180, 229
Barton, William, 280
Baskerville, Ensign, 96
Baskerville, Samuel, 176
Baskerville, William, 183
Basnitt, Francis, 250
Bass, John, 143, 250
Bass, Samuel, 94
Basset, Isaac, 225, 290
Bates, Captain, 32
Bates, John, 200, 206, 230
Bates, Oliver, 34
Batley, Moses, 230
Batman, William, 159
Baton, Capt., 152
Batson, George, 163, 181
Battaly, Moses, 180

Batts, John, 196
Baudet, Pierre, 283
Baugh, Alex., 48, 61, 78
Bauman, Sebastian, 239
Baxter, Andrew, 31
Baylor, Colonel, George
Baytop, James, 53, 54
Beach, Thaddeus, 290
Beames, Benjamin, 173
Bear, Alexis, 244
Bear, Casper, 218
Beard, John, 243
Beasley, Samuel, 179
Beatty, Col., 62
Beckett, Philip, 215
Beckwith, Phinehas, 225
Beebe/Bebe,Bazelel/Bezaleel,
    203, 208, 210, 268
Beebe, Jabez, 71, 163
Beebe, Joseph, 44
Beebe, Ze., 44
Beebee, James, 119
Beigting, John Henry, 296
Belcher, Gill, 105
Belcher, Samuel, 126
Belcher, William, 27
Belding, Oliver, 278
Bell, Adam, 112
Bell, Capt., 146
Bell, Jesse, 268
Bell, John, 92
Bell, Thomas, 20
Belvin, Aaron, 53, 54
Belvin, George, 53, 54
Belvin, Lewis, 53, 54
Bence, Daniel, 179
Benham, Silas, 111
Benjamin, A., 229
Benjamin, Joseph, 78
Bennet, Amos, 279
Bennet, Joel, 25
Benson, Jacob, 35
Bent, Captain, 67

Bentley, Jesse, 230
Bentley, Samuel, 90
Bentley, W., 79
Bentley, William, 100
Bently, John, 83
Bently, Mr., 294
Bernard, Capt., 77
Bernard, John, 164
Bernard, Robert, 114
Berry, James, 20, 230
Berry, Nathaniel, 119
Bescott, John, 72
Bettesworth, William, 145
Betts, Eli, 3
Betts, Stephen, 109
Beyer, Jacob, 287
Bickerton, Brian, 250
Bickham, Griffith W., 296
Bickle, John, 42
Biddle, Clement, 302
Bigby, Elijah, 122
Bigelow, Timothy, 134, 138
Biggs, Randolph, 12
Bilbery, Nathaniel, 98
Bills, Joshua, 293
Bishop, John, 178
Bishop, Nath'l, 87
Bishop, Richard, 154
Bissel, John, 35
Blachford, John, 85
Black, Boston, 297
Black, Joseph, 220
Black, Robert, 293
Black, Samuel, 184
Black, Steward, 220
Black, William, 107, 260
Black, William, Jr., 107
Blackley, David, 208
Blackley, Jonathan, 208
Blackly, Ebenezer, Jr., 272
Blackman, Andrew, 119
Blackmar, Capt., 34
Blacknall, Thomas, 53, 54

Blackwell, Sam., 261
Blair, John, 135
Blair, Joseph Mitchell, 9
Blake, John, 166, 232
Blake, Martin, 176
Blakely, Merrit, 208
Blakeslee/Blackslee, Enos, 95, 116
Blakesley, Eno., 257
Blakman, Elijah, 141, 227
Blakslee, Isaiah, 221
Blamer, John, 222
Blanchard, Mr., 232
Blancher, Capt., 165
Bland, Theodorick, 57
Blandfield, Thomas, 8
Blaney, William, 151
Blankenship, Josiah, 83
Blare, Roswel, 169
Blasdel, Jacob, 6
Blick, James, 81
Bliss, Theodore, 6
Blood, Samuel, 126
Blush, Stacy, 8
Boar, Gideon, 186
Bohanan, Joseph, 23
Bohannan, Thomas, 196
Boice, Peter, 287
Boid, Jonathan, 3
Boing, Joshua, 129
Bolden, James, 51
Bolton, Nathaniel, 192
Bolton, William, 245
Bond, William, 5, 184
Bonnel, Benjamin, 273
Booker, Stephen, 102
Booth, Henry, 298
Borden, William, 31
Boret, Laurens, 292
Bortlett, Alexadder, 190
Boston, Gershom, 124
Bosworth, Joseph, 33
Bott, Jacob, 178

Bottom, Charles Hinging, 34
Botts, John, 296
Bottum, Joshua, 149
Bourdajau, Peter, 217
Bowens, John, 230
Bower, John, 237
Bowers, Joseph, 104
Bowie, John, 159, 233
Bowker, Lieut., 96
Bowler, Thomas, 204
Boyd, Augustine, 250
Boyd, James, 147
Boyd, John, 25
Boyden, John, 37
Bracey, Thomas, 171
Bradby, James, 98
Bradford, Gamaliel, 74
Bradley, Azariah, 210
Bradley, James W., 175
Bradley, Jesse, 176
Bradley, Philip Burr, 104, 105
Bradly, Joseph, 246
Bradshaw, Jeremiah, 57
Bradshaw, William, 45
Bragg, William, 14
Brakeen, James, 230
Branch, Aholiab, 159
Branch, Moses, 194, 196
Brasington, Samuel, 184
Brathwaite, Richard, 173
Brayman, John, 35
Breck, Robert, 9
Breeks, Charles, 187
Brent, William, 61
Bressie, Capt., 191
Bressie, Thomas, 102, 131
Brewer, David, 3, 6, 26, 86, 99, 115
Brewer, Elisha, 125
Brewer, Samuel, 123, 124, 127
Brewster, Elisha, 87
Brian, Patrick, 194
Briant, Hawkins, 187

Briant, Michael, 59
Brickett, James, 38
Bridges, James, 161
Briges, James, 220
Briggs, James, 244
Bright, Francis, 158
Brigs, Jeremiah, 134
Brim, Richard, 230
Brindle, Adam, 263
Brine, John, 259
Brinn, Richard, 160
Brinnon, Martin, 71
Brinston, John, 137
Brintnall, Abiel, 153
Britt, John, 46
Broadwater, Charles Lewis, 160
Brock, George, 179
Brock, John, 179
Brodhead, Daniel, 45
Broescke, Charles, 300
Brooks, Jacob, 62
Browder, Frederick, 178
Browder, Samuel, 178
Brown, Aaron, 80
Brown, Abel, 152
Brown, Andrew, 38
Brown, Capt., 45, 185
Brown, Daniel, 124
Brown, Eake, 96, 116
Brown, Edward, 184
Brown, Francis, 139
Brown, George, 88, 285
Brown, Gershom, Jr., 289
Brown, Henry, 281
Brown, James, 55, 133, 156, 174, 204
Brown, Jeremiah, 159
Brown, Jesse, 144
Brown, John, 48, 91, 112, 137, 204, 291
Brown, Jonathan, 105
Brown, Lewis, 135
Brown, Moses, 125

Brown, Mrs., 226
Brown, Richard, 230
Brown, Robert, 269, 282
Brown, Seth, 276
Brown, Solomon, 109
Brown, Thomas, 158, 278, 290
Brown, William, 137, 204
Brown, Windsor, 113
Brownson, Daniel, 291
Brune, Nicholas, 244
Brunsfield, James, 230
Brunson, Asa, 95
Brushwood, George, 196
Bryan, William, 25
Bryant, John, 245
Bryant, Jos., 81
Bryant, Joseph, 155
Buck, Thomas, 254
Buckard, Powell, 232
Buckland, Stephen, 116
Buckley, William, 212
Buckman, Edward, 17
Buckner, Mordecai, 27
Buell, John, 95
Buell, Lieut., 115
Buffen, John, 6
Bulkley, Abraham, 217
Bulkley, Edward, 170
Bullard, Capt., 106
Bullock, Jacob, 244
Bullock, James, 43
Bulman, John, 61, 94
Bunn, Sally, 300
Bunns, John, 231
Burbank, Silas, 123
Burcaw, Bursun, 30
Burchet, James, 178
Burges, Solomon, 232
Burgoyne, John, 206
Burk, Richard, 289, 291
Burke, William, 243
Burket, Arthur, 36
Burks, Philemon, 229

Burn, John, 59
Burnam, Elijah, 65
Burnet, Godfrey, 230
Burnet, Joseph, 230
Burnett, John, 273
Burnley, Col., 14
Burnley, Garland, 14
Burns, James, 230
Burr, Stephen, 290
Burrowes, John, 151
Burt, George, 118
Burtis, John, 259
Burtis, William, 261
Burton, Benja., 134
Burton, John, 160
Burton, Thomas, 296
Burwell, N./Nat., 166, 167
Bush, John, 133
Bush, Thomas, 184
Bushby, John, 224
Bushel, Thomas, 245
Bussel, James, 39
Bussol, Benjamin, 51
Butler, Aaron, 164
Butler, Christopher, 93
Butler, James, 23, 230
Butler, Joe, 184
Butler, John, 59, 232
Butler, Joseph, 186
Butler, Joshua, 179
Butler, R., 176
Butler, Thomas, 179
Butler, Walter, 128
Butler, William, 179, 277
Buzwell, Abraham, 126
Cabell, Samuel, 14, 15
Cabell, Samuel Jordan, 40
Cady, Palmer, 216
Cady, Stoddard, 152
Caher, Daniel, 206
Caine, John, 54
Caldwill/Calwill, William, 223
Calkings, Jonathan, 200

Calkins, Jonathan, 56
Call, Richard, 59
Callender, Eleazer, 174
Calmes, Marquis, 54
Calvert, Capt., 20, 182
Calvert, John, 34
Camby, James, 222
Camp, John, 76
Camp, Mrs., 15
Campbell, John, 89, 135
Campbell, Joshua, 191
Campbell, Patrick, 192
Campbell, Sergeant, 232
Campbell, William, 168
Candull, William, 94
Cane, Thomas, 31
Canfield, Abiel, 105
Canfield, Mr., 288
Canfield, Nathaniel, 211, 213
Canterbury, John, Jr., 230
Canterbury, Joseph, 40
Cantwell, Edward, 46
Carcass, Conrad, 277
Carew, James, 162
Carhell, Dugless, 97
Carlton, Christopher, 196
Carlton, Isaac, 189
Carlton, John, 280
Carmichael, Roderick, 131
Carney, John, 230, 277
Carpenter, Abel, 73
Carpenter, Edward, 197
Carr, Capt., 35
Carr, James, 108
Carr, Sam., 159
Carral, Thomas, 255
Carrigan, Barnaby, 146
Carrington, Dan, 291
Carrington, Edward, 196
Carrington, M., 77, 91
Carson, James, 91
Carter, John C., 137
Carter, Joseph, 240

Carter, Landon, 120
Cartwright, Judith, Jr., 271
Cary, Ephraim, 194
Cary, Patrick, 202
Cary, Sylvester, 97
Case, Fithian, 211, 213
Case, Josiah, 2d., 210
Case, Timothy, 145
Casey, John, 165
Cash, Archibald/Archbell, 122, 136
Cashedy, William, 277
Cashell, Samuel, 244
Casor, Daniel, 206
Cassedy, Hugh, 102
Caster, Henry, 249
Casuave, Salvat, 283
Caswell, Stephen, 67
Caswell/Caswel, Joseph, 228
Caswell, Thomas, 35
Catherwood, Patrick, 243
Catlett, Lieut., 150
Catton, William, 75
Cawdle, John, 178
Cawfield, Owen, 64
Cawley, Asa, 103
Caye, Samuel, 280
Cha, John, 287
Chace, Henry, 41
Chadwick, Capt., 99
Chadwick, John, 115, 124
Chamberlain, Ebenezer, 232
Chamberlain, Ephraim, 100
Chamberlain, Philip, 146, 156
Chambers, John, 133
Chamblis, John, 17
Champion, Henry, 74, 110, 130, 162
Chance, William, 135
Chandler, John, 95, 148, 178, 187
Chandler, Seal, 222
Chandler, Thomas, 80

Chaney, Nathaniel, 108
Channing, John, 38
Chaple, John, 122
Chapman, Isaac, 70
Chapman, John, 189, 239, 284
Chapman, Nathaniel, 263
Chapman, Richard, 88, 254
Chapman, Samuel, 267
Chappel, Comfort, 225
Charleonnier, Mr., 256
Charles, Lewis, 81, 121
Charles, Lewis, Jr., 144, 181
Chase, Joseph, 198
Cheathum/Cheatum, Josiah, 14, 15
Chester, Samuel, 255
Chestor, Christopher, 218
Chew, Samuel, 154
Chewning, John, 68
Chewning, Thomas, 68
Chilcott, John, 168
Child, Abijah, 124
Child, Henry, 276
Childers, John, 32
Childes, Isaac, 30
Childress, Abraham, 157, 170
Childress, John, 140
Chilman, Thomas, 73, 105
Chipman, John, 60
Choster, Levi, 242
Chriss/Criss, Jacob/Benjamin, 109
Christian, Daniel, 72
Christie, Jeremiah, 145
Christie, John, 179
Christin, Edward, 222
Church, Col., 5
Church, Nathaniel, 24
Church, Seth, 24
Church, Thomas, 185
Cillet, John, 222
Cilley, Joseph, 138, 147
Clap, Nathan, 278

Clark, Andrew, 185
Clark, David, 290
Clark, David, Jr., 115
Clark, Edward, 183
Clark, Jacob, 128
Clark, Jeremiah, 8
Clark, Jesse, 31
Clark, John, 134, 228, 232
Clark, Jonathan, 191
Clark, Joseph, 230
Clark, Josiah, 96, 116
Clark, Samuel, 211
Clark, William, 117
Clarke, Edward, 172
Clarke, James, 5
Clarke, John, 63
Clarke, Joseph, 132
Clarke, Josiah, 176
Clarke, William, 96, 102
Clay, John Moore, 190
Clayton, John, 82
Clayton, Lieutenant, 106, 163
Clayton, S. W., 230
Clemens, William Samuel, 299
Cleveland, Benjamin, 124
Clift, Lemuel, 134
Clift, Wills, 106
Cline, John, 250
Clopton, John, 92, 96, 186
Closs, John, 277
Clough, Zaccheus, 265
Cluverius, John, 114
Coate, John, 244
Coats, Edny, 246
Coats, Thomas, 246
Cobb, Thomas, 34
Cobbs, Ralph, 66
Cobbs, Samuel, 58
Cochran, Patrick, 230
Cock, Amos, 164
Cock, John, 187
Cocke, James, 21
Cocke, John C., 168, 189

Cocke, John Catesby, 137
Cocke, Nathaniel, 9, 72
Cockram, Charles, 80
Cocks, Capt., 32
Cocks, Mathew, 151
Coggins/Coggin/Goggin, John, 42
Cogswell, Samuel, 220
Colburn, Stephen, 281
Colby, James, 289
Cole, Col., 223
Cole, Ephraim, 110
Cole, Thomas, 67, 90, 122
Coleman, James, 264
Coleman, Whitehead, 204
Colley, William, 23
Collier, Alexander, 162
Collier, Charles, 108
Collier, James, 231
Collins, John, 67
Collins, Mitchell, 176
Collins, Robert Johnson, 147
Comes, Esdale, 168
Commins, Benjamin, 201
Commins, Joseph, 201
Comstock, Mr., 301
Cone, Capt., 252
Congdon, Joseph, 251
Conner, John, 139
Conneran, Thomas, 155
Converse, Paine, 226
Conway, Henry, 83
Conway, James, 277
Cook, Conrad, 248
Cook, Daniel, 66
Cook, Edward, 66
Cook, Governor, 194
Cook, Jabez, 290
Cook, James, 230
Cook, John, 125
Cook, Shem, 98, 185
Cook, Thaddeus, 44, 56
Cook, William, 42

Cooke, John, 90
Cooke, Mr., 290
Coolbuth, James, 126
Cooper, Isaac, 215
Cooper, Levi, 144
Cooper, William, 32
Corder, John, 139
Cordill, John, 83
Cornell, Benjamin, 294
Correll, William, 179
Cosgrieff, Dennis, 67
Cotley, Samuel, 130
Cotton, John, 112
Cottrell, John, 144
Cousins, Adam, 185
Cowan, Alexander, 256
Cowan, Duncan, 65
Cowen, William, 241
Cowley, Abraham, 15
Cowling, John, 65
Cowper, Willis, 179
Cox, Abraham, 91
Cox, George, 66
Cox, Reuben, 73, 117
Cox, Richard, 76
Cox, Thomas, 263
Coy, Toby, 90
Cradock, James, 189, 211
Craft, Abner, 22, 28
Craft, Thomas, 196
Crafts, Thomas, 220, 231
Craghorn, Capt., 107
Craig, John, 173
Crain, Philemon, 179
Cralle, Rodham Kenner, 33
Crandall, Joseph, 135, 138
Crandall, Peter, 279
Crane, Elihu, 290
Crane, John, 94, 95, 128, 133, 162, 198
Cranstoun, John, 282
Crary, Archibald, 67, 90, 207
Crawford, Hugh, 240

Crawford, Samuel, 230
Crawford, William, 119, 231
Crawley. Thomas, 179
Creasel, Andrew, 240
Creasel, Rudolph, 240
Crew, Josiah, 18
Crew, Thomas, 296
Critmore, Jesse, 177
Crittenden, John, 172
Crockett, Mr., 103
Croghan, Capt., 44
Crop, Richard, 160
Crosman, James, 138
Cross, Samuel, 68
Cross, Thomas, 68
Crossing, William, 228
Crow, Jean Adam, 292
Crow, William, 65
Croxton, William, 88
Crume, Philip, 139
Crump, Abner, 57, 65, 117
Crump, Goodrich, 27, 61, 88
Crump, Richard, 190
Cuff, Cato, 298
Cuff, James, 245
Culember, John, 230
Cullen, Bryan, 41
Culver, Joseph, 149
Culver, Samuel, 154
Cummings, Peter, 243
Cummins, Theophilus, 219
Cumstock, John, 65
Cunkery, Fortune, 150
Cunningham, James, 230
Cunningham, John, 120, 182
Cunningham, W., 5
Curle, John, 69
Curtis, W., 187
Curtis, William, 248
Cushing, Capt., 98
Cushing, James, 232
Cushing, Nathaniel, 58
Cutler, William, 58

Cutting, Benjamin, 34
Cutting, Zebulon, 34
Daby, John, 3
Dailey, Jadock, 102
Daily, John, 277
Dale, Richard, 56
Daley, Daniel, 292
Dalton, John, 180
Dam, Ebenezer, 141
Damore, John, 137
Dandridge, Alex. S., 58
Dandridge, John, 197
Danforth, Capt., 17
Danforth, Samuel, 52, 229
Daniel, Andrew, 150
Daniel, Henry, 176
Daniels, John, 90
Darby, Arnold, 58
Darby, William, 250
Dart, Jonathan, 298
Darton, William, 120
Dason, Coonrod, 3
Davenport,
    Barnet/Barnard/Nicholas, 257,
    258
Davenport, Thomas, 253
Davids, William, 189
Davidson, William, 77
Davies, Hugh, 226
Davies, John R., 53
Davis, Bartholomew, 187
Davis, Benjamin, 3
Davis, Capt., 4
Davis, Hugh, 270
Davis, James, 61, 88
Davis, John, 130
Davis, Joseph, 129
Davis, Thomas, 22
Davis, William, 10, 91, 176, 211
Dawley, Ephraim, 38
Dawson, Alexander, 19
Day, George, 250
Day, John, 97

Day, Luke, 85, 95, 297
Day, Nathaniel, 124
Day, Samuel, 190
Dayen, Joseph, 268
Dayton, Jonathan, 219
Deale, Thomas, 188
Dean, Benjamin, 73
Dean, Hugh, 188
Dean, Julias, 72
Dean, Richard, 176
Dean, William, 72
Deane, Benjamin, 118
Deane, Simon, 62
Deane, William, 237
Dearen/Dear, William, 107
Dearin, William, 230
Deavenport, Captain, 294
Deckar, Solomon, 289
deClovay, Captain, 112
Defoos, Micajah, 54
deFrank, John Bernard, 302
deGosen, Major General, 279
Degrout, Garret, 111
DeHuyn, General, 233
Dejarnett, Ren, 177
DeKlauman, Charles, 211
Delancey, Oliver, 147
Delany, John, 99
DeLaporte, Capt., 202
Delasie, Marshal, 236
deLinsing, Colonel, 300
Delk, Benjamin, 54
Deming, Lemuel, 208
Deming, Pownall, 136
deMost, Francois, 292
DeMunchhausen, Colonel, 299
Dennis, John, 30
Denny, William, 155
Denton, John, 46
Depak, Francis, 153
Dermen, Prince, 276
DeRoy, Coeur, 202
Deruce, John, 249

Deschoncle, John, 175
DeVaudreuil, Marquiss, 292
Deverix, James, 13
DeVoice, Abraham, 105
Dewees, Thomas, 50
Dewsey, John, 287
Dexter, Capt., 34
Dexter, John, 197
Diah, Bigford, 126
Dibley, William, 227
Dick, Alex., 23
Dickensen, Reuben, 41
Dickerson, David, 39
Dickerson, Henry, 79
Dickerson, William, 37, 39
Dickinson, Capt., 88
Dickinson, Edmund B., 21
Dickson, William, 186
Digges, E., 237
Digges, Edward, 153, 255
Dikes, Isham, 180
Dilley, Aaron, 119
Dillon, Jesse, 49
Dinkins, Theophilus, 97
Disko, John, 58
Dix, Thomas, 179, 182
Dixon, Capt., 26
Dobbins, Charles, 296, 299
Donnel, Capt., 86
Donnel, Henry, 230
Donnell, James, 125
Donoho, James, 13
Dooley, John, 170
Dooly, John, 158
Dority, William, 7
Dorton, George, 180
Dorton, John, 48
Dorton, William, 60
Dorum, James, 176
Doss, Joel, 118
Doty, John, 281
Doty, Samuel, 239
Douglas, Colonel, 116

Douglas, George, 1
Douglas, J., 233
Douglas, Richard, 139
Douglas, William, 111
Douglass, Thomas, 246, 247
Dow, Abner, 134
Dowe, Joseph, 152
Downe, James, 91
Downey, James, 222
Downman, Rawleigh, 229
Downs, John, 259
Dowyer, Philip, 193
Doyle, Alex., 172
Doyle, Matthew, 91
Doyle, William, 94
Drake, Simeon, 252
Draper, John, 179
Dresser, Richard, 243
Drew, Thomas H., 193
Dryskil, Francis, 155
Dudley, Ameroe, 184
Dudley, H., 196
Dudley, John, 154, 184
Duffy, Patrick, 43, 64
Duke, Cleviers, 107
Duke, Cluverious, 79
Dulaney, Thomas, 107
Dumont, Peter, 249
Dunbar, Joshua, 152
Duncan, James, 216, 271
Duning, Nathan, 218
Dunmore, Lord, 39
Dunn, Gersham, 30
Dunn, James, 146
Dunn, Joshua, 80
Dunn, Lieutenant, 18
Dunn, Peter, 83
Dunston, Wallace, 185
Dunton, James, 232
Durham, John, 94
Durham, Matthew, 66

Durkee, John, 58, 82, 87, 95, 134, 136, 162, 166, 200, 225, 267
duVerdier, Barnard, 215
Duzier, Simon, 151
Dychs, Isham, 229
Dyer, James Harden, 130
Dyke, Isham, 189
Dyre, Capt., 35
Eades, Peter, 168
Eagleston/Egelinstone, Benjamin, 16
Eames, Elijah, 7
Eames, Samuel, 281
Eanos/Enos, David, 193, 196
Earle, Baylis, 159, 233
Eastes, William, 230
Eastman, Vest, 290
Easton, James, 3
Easton, Stephen, 281
Eaton, Ezra, 152
Eaton, Timothy, 36
Eayres, Joseph, 263
Eclitee, John, 245
Edcon, Abijah, 115
Edes, Jonathan, 196
Edes, Jonathan W., 221
Edmondson, Benj./ Benjamin, 184, 230
Edmunds, Capt., 181
Edmunds, John, 81
Edmundson, Benjamin, 230
Edwards, Doctor, 231
Edwards, Edward, 125
Edwards, Ellis, 250
Edwards, William, 58, 246
Eggleston, Samuel, 242
Egmon, James, 236
Elam. W,lliam, 188
Elbert, Samuel, 185
Elder, Charles, 146

Elderkin, Vine, 112
Eldridge, James, 86
Eldridge, Jeremiah, 115
Eldridge, Joseph, 253
Eliot, Capt., 133
Elliot, George, 193
Elliot, Robert, 52
Elliott, Col., 242
Elliott, Geo., 146
Elliott, George, 211
Elliott, Robert, 36, 37, 51, 55
Elliott, Thomas, 33
Ellis, Elijah, 46
Ellis, Florra, 133
Ellis, John, 149, 223
Ellis, Paul, 134
Ellis, Thomas, 60
Ellison, James, 126
Ellison, Japher, 37
Elmes, Elkanah, 65
Ely, Capt., 60, 111, 266
Ely, John, 56, 57, 149, 159
Ely, Samuel, 173
Emmans, John, 34
Emmons, Daniel, 268
English, John, 125
Enos, David, 245
Erskine, Charls, 63
Erufridt, George, 248
Erving, Henry, 110, 128
Erwin, Willam, 219
Erwine, James, 249
Esdale, Thomas, 137
Eskridge, George, 129
Eton, William, 222
Eute, Capt., 95
Evans, Peter, 276
Evans, Phil., 184
Evens, Jacob, 198
Eversage, Michael, 113
Everton, Thomas, 279
Ewell, Thomas/Thomas W., 123, 136
Eymerie, John, 217
Fadro, Mrs., 190
Fahay, Michael, 259
Fair, Edmund, 118
Fairchild, Daniel, 272
Fall, Samuel, 85
Fanes, Isaac, 149
Fanning, Elisha, 150
Fanning, Mary, 254
Farinholtz, 196
Farley, John, 122
Farley, Michael, 129, 249
Farley, Solomon, 114
Farnum/Furnum, David, 203
Farrell, William, 146
Farringtom Reuben, 170
Fauns, Jacob, 25
Faxon, Richard, 264
Fay, Silas, 99, 124
Fear, Henry, 147
Fellow, John, 1, 2
Fellows, William, 152
Felton, Robert, 289
Fenner, Capt., 35
Fenner, Thomas, 35
Fentress, Nehemiah, 71
Ferguson, Edward, 180
Ferguson, Obadiah/Obediah, 180, 189, 229
Fernandes, James, 153
Ferr, John, 64
Ferris, Isaac, 83
Ferris, Joshua, 41
Fidler, William, 179
Fie, George, 232
Field, William, 139
Fields, Lieutenant, 163
Fish, Aaron, 212
Fish, Eliakim, 262

Fisher, Abraham, 35
Fisher, Eleazer, 152
Fisher, John, 196
Fisk, Ebenezer, 298
Fisk, Reuben, 55
Fisk, Squire, 84
Fitch, Andrew, 136
Fitch, Thomas, 190
Fitzgerald, Cornelius, 46
Fitzgerald, John, 216
Fitzpatrick, George, 260
Fitzpatrick, Philip, 71
Fitzpatrick, William, 91
Flagley, John, 239
Flanagan, Michael, 65
Fleet, William, 104
Fleming, Charles, 12, 76, 91
Fleming, James, 46
Fletcher, Carter, 73, 117
Florry, John Johnston, 230
Flower, Benjamin, 263
Flower, Samuel, 100, 115
Fog, William, 79
Folkes, Baxter, 172
Foot, Joseph, 127
Ford, Hezekiah, 186
Foreman, David, 203
Forfit, Edward, 253
Forman, David, 30, 151
Forshner, Andrew, 274
Fort, Jacob, 98
Fortune, Thomas, 222
Foster, Abraham, 158
Foster, James, 104
Foster, John, 87, 113
Foster, Joseph, 58
Foster, Samuel, 281
Foster, Thomas, 252
Foster, William, 281
Fostwick, Mr., 288
Fournier, John Francis, 287
Fowler, Jacob, 6

Fowles, John, 152
Fowles, John, Jr., 152
Fox, John, 90
Fox, Nathaniel, 57, 83
Foxwell, Richard, 108
France, Thomas, 129
Francis, Anthony, 240
Francis, Ebenezer, 90
Francis, William, Jr., 193
Franklin, James, 63
Franklin, John, 32
Franklin, Peter, 35
Franks, John, 232
Fraser/Frazer, William, 43, 88
Frazer, James, 94
Frazer, John, 186
Frazer, John G., 58
Freeland, John, 161
Freeman, Charles, 17
Freeman, David, 83
Freeman, William, 10, 35
Freetsell, Joseph, 108
French, Christopher, 42, 47
Freshwater, Thomas, 1
Fretter, John, 209
Frisbie, David, 269
Frisbie, Jonah, 85
Frost, George Pepperrel, 109
Frost, Joseph, 138
Frost, William, 123
Fry, Capt., 147
Fry, Henry, 88
Frye, Peter Pickman, 100
Fugate, Randolph, 119
Fugler, William, 96
Fuillade, La, 202
Fulcher, William, 179
Fuller, Edward, 125
Fuller, John, 232
Fuller, Nathan, 5, 6
Fuller, Thomas, 8
Fullerton, John, 125, 243

Furman, Nowel, 45
Futcher, Michael, 256
Gage, Thomas, 2
Gage, Tom, 228
Gaines, Francis, 180
Gaines, Thomas, 131
Gaines, William Fleming/ William F., 63, 63
Galden, Jesse, 96
Gams, Francis, 230
Gardiner, Calvan, 130
Gardner, Alexander, 19
Gardner, Bela, 232
Gardner, Jacob, 232
Gardner, John, 1, 24, 105
Gardner, Joseph, 133
Garland, Guthridge, 230
Garner, Presley, 182
Garnett, Henry, 68
Garret, Andrew, 150
Gary, Benjamin, 174
Garzia/Gazee, Capt., 55
Gaskins, Thomas, 102
Gaskins, Thomas, Jr., 33
Gatchel, Zachariah, 86
Gates, Horatio, 52, 177, 211, 213, 214, 217
Gates, Moses, 267
Gates, William, 34
Gauldin, William, 109
Gay, Fisher, 35
Gaylord, Elijah, 269
Gennet, Emon, 244
George, Jesse, 21
Gerard, Timothy, 119
Gerbaux, Pierre, 283
Gibbs, Herod, 172
Gibbs, John, 175
Gibson, George, 179
Gibson, Reuben, 157
Gilbert, Joseph, 218
Gilbert, Samuel, 218
Gilchrist, Mr., 192
Gile, Ezekiel, 209
Giles, Thomas, 232
Gilles, Robert, 193
Gillet, Nathan, 208
Gills, John, 82
Gilmore, Nathan, 241
Gilroy, John, 129
Gimbe, Thomas, 179
Gipson, Elisha, 179
Gipson, William, 54
Gist, Mordecai, 1
Givion, James, 93
Gleason, Thomas, 41, 259
Glen, Thomas, 137
Glover, John, 241
Glover, William, 98
Goalman, William, 96
Goggins/Coggons/Coggin, John, 42
Gold, John Whited, 208
Gold, Noah, 40
Golden, Peter, 195
Gooch, Joseph, 15
Good, Claiborne, 186
Goodale, John, 161
Goodhue, Hezekiah, 63
Goodman, William, 186
Goodrich, Asahel, 290
Goodrich, Timothy, 211, 213
Goodridge, Azel, 125
Goodwell, Nathan, 105
Goodwin, Capt., 111, 222
Goodwin, John, 113
Gordian, Albian, 196
Gordon, John, 124
Gorge, Samuel, 39
Gould, Abraham, 158
Gould, William, 1
Grace, James, 196, 231
Grady, William, 124
Graham, Alexander, 95
Graham, George, 214
Graham, John, 60

Graham/Grimes, John, 50
Granger, Capt., 119
Granger, Charles, 148
Grant, Daniel, 250
Grant, Thomas, 250
Grant, William, 46, 222, 289
Gratton, Thomas, 78
Graves, Abner, 165
Graves, Gideon, 4
Graves, Jonathan, 290
Graves, Robert, 53, 54
Graves/Greaves John, 12
Gray, James, 72
Gray, Robert, 133
Gray, Thomas, 222
Grayson, William, 102, 113, 157, 170, 193
Greaton, John, 22, 28, 59, 67, 100, 114, 124
Greaves, Lieut., 214
Green, Amos, 87
Green, Anderson, 116
Green, Anderson, 97
Green, Benjamin, 184
Green, Christopher, 149
Green, Ebenezer, 211, 213
Green, Garner, 167
Green, High, 44
Green, Hugh, 54
Green, James, 174
Green, Jedidiah, 106
Green, Simon, 53, 54
Green, Thomas, 91, 271
Green, William, 84
Greene, Christopher, 123, 271, 294
Greenup, Christ., 114
Greenwall, John, 297
Greenway, Thomas, 232
Greer, Abner, 212
Gregg, James, 260, 284
Gregory, George, 9
Gregory, John, 80

Gregory, William, 191
Grey, John, 244
Griffen, Abner, 208
Griffen, Mathew, 208
Griffith, John, 143
Griffith, William, 232
Griffiths, John, 222
Grigby, John, 139
Grigg, John, 87
Grigsby, James, 80
Grimes, William, 71, 121
Griswold, Adonijah, 280
Groome, John, 89
Grover, Ebenezer, 195
Grubbs, Heneley, 186
Grume, Thomas, 167
Grunsell, Thomas, 204
Guilson, John, 4
Gunter, William, 187
Habb, Joseph, 243
Hackett, Joseph, 34
Haddin, Capt., 30
Haden, John, 123
Haffa, Henry, 261
Haftman, John, 127
Hailey, John, 230
Hairlow, Joseph, 40
Halcomb, Capt., 144
Hale, Nathan, 108, 192
Hale, Simeon, 231
Haley, David, 179
Haley, Mr., 231
Hall, Asaph, 56
Hall, Capt., 99
Hall, Claiborne, 84
Hall, Edwin, 144
Hall, James, 198
Hall, Jedediah, 105
Hall, Nathaniel, 60
Hall, William, 119, 195
Hallaway, Aaron, 220
Halsey, Jeremiah, 57
Hambleton, Isaac, 154, 156

Hambleton, Robert, 133
Hamblin, Bryan, 56
Hamilton, Alexander, 246
Hamilton, James, 145, 154, 194
Hamilton, John, 41
Hamilton, Samuel, 96
Hamilton, Thomas, 94
Hamilton, William, 209, 290
Hamlet, William, 66
Hamlinton, James, 156
Hammond, Edward, 87
Hamond, Samuel, 236
Hancock, Belcher, 99
Hancock, George, 223
Hancock, John, 283
Hancock, Lieutenant, 46
Hand, Abraham, 208
Hand, Henry, 139
Hand, Thomas, 139
Handley, Samuel, 110
Handshaw, Capt., 119
Hanes, John, 65
Hanly, John, 275
Hansbrough, James, 93
Hansley, Charles, 83
Harbenson, Dominick, 222
Harden, Jesse, 40
Hardin, Captain, 283
Hardwick, John, 232
Hardy, Andrew, 62
Hardy, Curtis, 73, 118
Hardy, James, 273
Hardy, John, 137
Hardy, William, 53, 64
Harford, John, 168
Harley, Jeremiah, 63
Harness, William, 157, 170
Harper, Jesse, 57
Harrifield, James, 187
Harris, Aaron, 65
Harris, Capt., 40, 172
Harris, George, 259
Harris, Hugh, 49

Harris, Ishmael, 66
Harris, John, 167
Harris, Luke, 35
Harris, Nathaniel, 186
Harris, Rowland, 141
Harris, William, 167, 181
Harrison, Benjamin, 10, 295
Harrison, Charles, 65, 82, 140, 150, 161, 179, 196, 204
Harrison, Heatwell, 184
Harrison, Thomas, 68, 204, 205, 212
Harrison, William, 83
Hart, Levi, 211, 215
Hartley, Jonathan, 1
Hartly, Colonel, 127
Harvey, Captain, 3
Harvey, John, 189, 291
Harvey, Joseph, 67
Harvey, Matthew, 189, 211
Harvey, Moses, 4
Harwood, Nathaniel, 281
Haskall, Andrew, 109
Haskins, Joseph, 11
Hastings, Peter, 26
Hattan, Samuel, 137
Hattan, Solomon, 137
Haughton, Ebenezer, Jr., 218
Hawes, Samuel, 156
Hawk, Stephen, 235, 237
Hawkins, Capt., 56
Hawkins, James, 120
Hawkins, John, 64
Hawkins, Moses, 46
Hawkins, Mr., 63
Hawley, William, 290
Hawley, Wolcott, 16
Haws, Samuel, Jr., 68
Hay, Peter, 16
Hayden, Benjamin, 260
Haydon, Richard, 144
Hayes, Hugh, 232
Hayly, John, 160

Haynes, Peter, 281
Haynes, William, 204
Hays, Peter, 254
Hayt, Col., 302
Hazard, Stephen Fones, 123
Hazelwood, Luke, 78
Hazen, Moses, 128, 216
Hearsy, Peleg, 232
Heath, William, 123, 205
Heathcock, Elisha, 60
Hebbard, Jonathan, 282
Hebard, Nathaniel, 39
Hecock, James, 36
Hegeman, Mr., 279
Hellon, Alexander, 222
Hemingway, Rufus, 126
Hempsted, Joshua, Jr., 210, 214, 246
Henderson, Daniel, 32
Henderson, Zoath, 124
Hendrickson, James, 25
Hendry, John, 277
Henley, David, 224
Henley, Davis, 186
Henry, John, 220
Henry, Michael, 93
Hepper, William, 230
Herendeen, Barzilai, 35
Herron, Peter, 42
Hesley, John, 61
Hewett, John, 230
Hewit, James, 280
Hewlett, William, 137
Hiatt, George, 204
Hicks, Benjamin, 254
Hicks, Isaac, 117, 176
Hicock, Ezra, 26
Hicock, Reuben, 211, 213
Higens, Archibald, 272
Higgin, James, 44
Higgins, Peter, 7
Hill, Abraham, 121
Hill, Capt., 67

Hill, Elijah, 145
Hill, James, 134
Hill, Jere., 20
Hill, Nathaniel, 104
Hill, Richard, 87
Hill, Samuel, 135
Hill, Thomas, 20
Hill, William, 9, 139
Hillhouse, David, 266
Hilton, William, 58
Himes, John, 25
Hinckley, Ichabod, 242
Hinman, Amos, 208
Hisket/Hiskett, James, 90, 161
Hitchcock, Dan., 8
Hiwill, John, 128
Hix, Frederick, 66
Hix, John, 179
Hoadley, Ebenezer, 44
Hobson, Nicholas, 18
Hockaday, Philemon, 84
Hodgekins, Bennet, 232
Hodges, James, 189
Hodges, John, 183
Hodson, Nathaniel, 30
Hoffler, Capt., 137
Hogan, Michael, 91
Hogg, Gideon, 186
Holbrook, Elisha, 152
Holbrook, Ezra, 279
Holbrook, John, 207
Holcom, Joshua, Jr., 208
Holcomb, John, 108
Holden, Abel, 201, 205
Holland, Joel, 185
Holland, Joseph, 103
Holland, Thomas, 32
Hollingsworth, Henry, 278
Hollins, William, 92
Hollis, Ebenezer, 231
Holloway, George, 80
Holloway, William, 139
Holman, John, 34

Holmer, Christian, 150
Holmes, Ensign, 183
Holmes, Isaac, 167, 172
Holt, James, 266
Hood, William, 120
Hooghteling, William, 238
Hoomes, Ben, 81
Hooper, Anthony, 48
Hooper, Richard, 23, 81
Hopkin, Rees, 284
Hopkins, E., 278
Hopkins, Elisha, 90
Hopkins, Francis, 180, 230
Hopkins, James, 116
Hopkins, Jesse, 281
Hopkins, Patrick, 250
Hopkins, Samuel, 80, 83
Hopkins, Thomas, 58
Hopkins, William, 139
Hoppen, Capt., 35
Hopson, Ensign, 78
Horler, John, 300
Horn, David, 125
Horon, Patrick, 91
Horton, William, 90
Hosca, Samuel, 79
Hoskins, Eliphalet, 35
Hosmer, Prentice, 74
Hotchkiss, Samuel, 215
House, Jeremiah, 208
Houston, Stephen, 183
How, Bowers, 212
Howard, Caleb, 244
Howard, Corker, 72
Howard, James, 186
Howard, John, 72
Howard, Mr., 232
Howard, Samuel Harvey, 68
Howe, William, 296
Howell, Henry, 98
Howell, Richard, 10
Howerton, John, 145
Howes, Abner, 241

Hubbard, Benjamin, 40
Hubbell, William G., 3
Hubbert, Eli, 126
Hudgin, Isaac, 103
Hudson, Barz., 48
Hudson, Charles, 23
Hudson, James, 167
Hudson, John, 28, 132
Hudson, Stephen, 172
Hudson, Vincent, 118
Huet, John, 232
Huff, David, 287
Huffman, John, 125
Hughes, Henry, 188
Hughes, John, 72
Hull, Ezekiel, 212
Hull, Josiah, 290, 291
Hulm, Thomas, 204
Hundley, Matthew, 72
Hundley/Hunley, Matthew, 53, 54
Hunniford, John, 20
Hunt, A., 75
Hunt, Abraham, 73, 75
Hunt, Berry, 83
Hunt, Capt., 140
Hunt, Edward, 244
Hunt, James, 179, 220
Hunt, John, Jr., 208
Hunt, Joseph, 223
Hunt, Josiah, 245
Hunt, Thomas, 277
Hunter, Caleb, 189
Hunter, Calep, 229
Hunter, Capt., 179
Huntington, Colonel, 60, 86
Huntington, Jedediah, 242, 254
Hurbut, Adam, 208
Hurd, James, 68
Hurlbut, Gideon, Jr., 208
Hurlbut, Robert, 208
Hurley, Daniel, 241
Hurley, Jeremiah, 120

Huston, Thomas, 219
Hutcheson, Ambrose, 185
Hutchin, Nathaniel, 138
Hutchings, Capt., 35
Hutchings, Thomas, 10
Hutchinson, Jeremiah, 111
Hutchinson, Peter, 83
Hutchinson, Richard, 265
Hyde, Elijah, 174
Indians, Barnabas, Isaac, 22; Brown, Daniel, 124; Brown, Robert, 269; Clap, Nathan, 278; Coy, Toby, 90; Daniels, John, 90; Dobbins, Charles, 299; Hall, William, 195; Hubbard, Benjamin, 40; Pottage, Aanias, 219; Robbins, James, 124; Thompson, William, 124; Tom, 299; Wampey, Samuel, 200; Wire, Robert, 274; Wompey, John, 57; Yockae, James, 200; Wampee, Samuel, 124
Ingersoll, Benjamin, 151
Ingham, Jacob, 10
Ingot, Henry, 202
Ingram, Joseph, 187
Inman, Joseph, 35
Irby, Charles, 57, 70
Irvine, Capt., 32
Ives, Aaron, 291
Jackson, Col., 249
Jackson, Daniel, 272
Jackson, Henry, 151, 161, 171, 245
Jackson, John, 118
Jackson, Matthew, 160
Jackson, Michael, 190
Jackson, Robert, 113
Jackson, Thomas, 134
Jackson, William, 75
Jackson, Wilson, 236

Jacobs, Benjamin, 196
Jacobs, Mr., 232
James, Benjamin, 120
James, Edward, 187
James, John, 106, 253
James, Nathan, 125
James, Thomas, 236
Jannes, Francis, 266
Jarvis, N., 151
Jeffers, James, 164
Jeffery, Thomas, 158
Jefferys, James, 77
Jenings, James, 246
Jenkins, Josiah, 126
Jenkins, William, 119
Jennings, David, 185
Jennings, William, 188
Jepson, Wm., 269
Jeroldman, Capt., 282
Jerson, Michael, 280
Jew, Peter, 244
Jewell, Oliver, 62
Jinks, Loring, 3
Johens, William, 180
John, Edward, 264
Johns, Jesse, 63
Johnson, Alexander, 241
Johnson, Benjamin, 5, 124
Johnson, Col., 193, 196
Johnson, Daniel, 299
Johnson, David, 188, 230
Johnson, Enoch, 272
Johnson, Ezra, 152
Johnson, George, 160
Johnson, James, 17, 24, 81, 125
Johnson, James Alexander, 74
Johnson, Joel, 26, 76
Johnson, John, 41, 89, 113, 180, 189, 229, 260
Johnson, John B., 186, 187
Johnson, John-William, 275
Johnson, Mr., 232
Johnson, Thomas, 205, 236

Johnson, William, 122, 131
Johnson/Jonson, John, 74
Johnston, Benjamin, 81
Johnston, Gideon, 235, 261
Johnston, Isaac, 191
Johnston, James, 191
Johnston, Nathan, 125
Johnston, William, 147
Joiner, Matthew, 98
Jolley/Jolly, Joseph, 29
Jones, Abraham, 60
Jones, Adam, 58
Jones, Benjamin, 155
Jones, Benjmin, 103
Jones, Binns, 79
Jones, Bombardier, 72
Jones, Cadwallader, 130
Jones, Capt., 35
Jones, Charles, 230
Jones, David, 165
Jones, Ephraim, 270
Jones, Gib, 89
Jones, Henry, 159
Jones, James, 23, 143, 145
Jones, John, 52
Jones, Josiah, 40
Jones, Lewelling, 70
Jones, Lunsford, 131, 141
Jones, Major, 135
Jones, Mr., 232
Jones, Peter, 154, 178, 230
Jones, Reuben, 180
Jones, Richard, 97
Jones, Richard, Jr., 63
Jones, Robert, 81, 98
Jones, Solomon, 188
Jones, Thomas, 91, 179, 211, 213, 230
Jones, William, 35, 38, 118, 190, 229, 293
Jonesten, William, 184
Jonson, James, 56
Jordan, James, 147
Jordan, John, 60
Jordin, Charles, 144
Jordon, Solomon, 125
Jordon, Solomon/William, 86
Jordon, William, 125
Josea, William, 137
Jouett, M., 88
Judd, Wm., 206, 215
Judson, Chapman, 148
Judson, James, 211, 213, 214
Juke, James, 227
Jurden, James, 184
Kaeeve, Peter, 144
Kallemand, Blaise Francois, 292
Kearnes, James, 244
Keep, Capt., 130
Keith, Joseph, 22, 23
Kellam, Zorobabel, 49
Kelly, Edward, 241
Kelly, Emanuel, 43, 71
Kelly, John, 197
Kelly, Patrick, 202
Kelly, Thomas, 61, 78
Kelsey, Stephen, 166
Keltey, James, 263
Kelvin, Thomas, 269
Kemble, E., 71
Kemp, Frederick, 62
Kemp, James, 46
Kemp, Thomas, 204
Kempton, Thomas, 256
Kendel, Isaac, 66
Kenley, Francis, 87
Kennan, Lawrence, 102
Kennedy, John, 137
Kennett, Zachariah, 118
Kent, Phenias, 30
Kerber, John, 233
Kerr, Charles, 282
Kersey, John, 88
Ketchum, Hezekiah, 165
Ketchum, John, 275
Key, Charles, 144

Key, Robert, 100
Keyes, John, 152
Keys, Capt., 159
Kilby, David, 126
Killey, Samuel, 222
Kimball, Asa, 274
Kimball, Jesse, 178
King, Alexander, 23, 26
King, Andrew, 190
King, Benjamin, 191
King, Capt., 100
King, James, 175
King, Sergeant, 289
King, William, 6, 133
King, Zachariah, 58
Kingsberry, Sanford, 55
Kingsbury, Daniel, 56
Kinniston, Moses, 152
Kirkendall, Abraham, 139
Kline, John, 248
Knap, Moses, 13
Knap, Thomas, 257
Knight, Baptist, 240
Knowlton, Mr., 232
Knowlton, Robert, 243
Knox, Capt., 21
Knox, Henry, 33
Knox, Michael, 222
Kramer, Conrad, 232
Kyle, James, 157, 170
Laden, John, 65
Lafever, Luis, 263
LaFrise, Raimod, 292
Lagiroruete, Mr., 150
Lagirt, Peter, 232
Lahouw, Jeroma, 283
Lake, Thomas, 171
Lake, William, 179
Lakeman, Mr., 261
Lamb, Anthony, 4
Lamb, John, 4, 14, 74, 86, 105, 239
Lamb, Joshua, 237

Lamb, Robert, 112
Lambert, John, 177
Lambert, Thomas, 298
Lameson, William, 286
Lancaster, John, 29, 30
Lancaster, Samuel, 86, 125
Land, William, 107
Landolphe, Capt., 257
Lane, Capt., 46
Lane, Daniel, 127
Lane, Nathaniel, 11
Lane, William/Wm., 97, 242
Lane, William, Jr., 44, 50, 88
Lankester, Jacob, 85
Laren, Lewis, 172
Larkens, Covel, 251
Laskin, Stephen, 124
Latham, William, 255, 298
Lawell, Abraham, 219
Lawless, Austin, 49
Lawless, Benjamin, 179
Lawrel, Emanuel, 245
Lawrence, Ishmael, 78
Lawrence, John, 224, 237
Lawrence, Joseph, 185
Lawson, Edward, 232
Lawson, Mr., 232
Lawson, William, 83, 182
Lay, Asa, 111
Lay, Lee, 224
Lay, Capt, 266
Layland, Peter, 196
Layne, Julius, 186
le Marquis, Louis, 283
Leach, Benjamin, 198
Leach, Jonas, 269
Leadberry, William, 173
Lear, Abraham, 76, 91
Learned, Ebenezer, 178
Leary, Timothy, 262
Leavenworth, Eli, 209
Ledgard, John, 164
Ledger, Henry, 189

Lee, Capt., 82, 239
Lee, Col., 199
Lee, Edward, 46
Lee, Elisha, 166
Lee, Henry, 78, 230
Lee, James, 2, 168, 239
Lee, John, 48, 61, 78, 131
Lee, Levi, 242
Lee, Richard, 253
Lee, Timothy, 208
Lee, William R., 220
Lee. John, 93
Leed, Jacob, 277
Lefavour, John, 78
Leffingwell, Elisha, 279
Lehew, Jeridam, 139
LeJeunesse, Mr., 215
Lennis, Robert, 49
Lenox, John Rowland, 285, 286
Lester, Eben., 163
Lester, Stripling, 189, 211
LeTurk, Yone, 244
Levy, Mr., 214
Lewis, Andrew, 59, 69, 106, 118, 121, 156
Lewis, Athanasias, 152
Lewis, Bury, 177
Lewis, Capt., 95
Lewis, Charles, 133
Lewis, Ebenezer, 152, 293
Lewis, James, 164
Lewis, Jesse, 216
Lewis, John, 147, 177, 184, 260
Lewis, Mr., 42
Lewis, Richard, 155
Lewis, Robert, 96
Lewis, William, 243
Libby, Jothan, 244
Lichens, John, 53
Liddle, Adam, 34
Lilly, Thomas, 31
Lindley, Levi, 73
Lindsey, Nath., 51

Line, Enos, 116
Ling, William, 30
Linnen, John, 124
Linney, James, 87
Linton, William, 97, 251
Lippitt, Christopher, 33, 34
Lipscomb, Reuben, 53, 54, 72
Little, Moses, 152
Littlefield, David, 126
Lloyd, John, 85
Lock, Benjamin, 281
Lockett, Pleasant, 76
Lockhart, Patrick 15
Lockwood, Capt., 208
Lomiss, John, 273
Long, David, 7
Long, Robert, 263
Long, Thomas, 152
Longest, Thomas, 103
Lord, Lynde, 45, 257, 264
Loring, Mr., 151
Loring, Nathaniel, 281
Loring, Peter, 244
Losmer, Joseph, 130
Louther, James, 222
Love, Edmund, 191
Love, Thomas, 53
Lovell, George, 103
Lovell, Lieut., 113
Lovland, Epaphroditus, 268
Lowd, James, 13
Lowe, Jesse, 176
Lowel, Solomon, 152
Lowree, James, 208
Lowry, John, 22
Lozerat/Lazerat/, Jean, 235, 238
Lozerat/Lazeratt, Jean, 235
Lucas, Ambrose, 180, 229
Lucas, James, 81
Lucas, John, 160
Lucas, William, 72
Luce, Francis, 241
Lunsford, John, 168

Luthie, Peter, 260
Luvsey, Randol, 184
Lyal/Lyall, William, 75, 82
Lyman, Daniel, 205, 220
Lyon, Asa, 159
Lyon, Nathan, 30
Lyon, Tone, 116
Lyons, William, 193
Macbane, Archibald, 93
Mace, Henry, 155
Mack, Orlander, 95
Mackenzie, Collin, 129
MacMullen/McMullen, Patrick, 220, 221
Macneil, Daniel, 93
Maddox, James, 159
Madrey, Darling, 97
Madrey, William, 97
Magee, Christopher, 260
Maher, James, 91
Mains, Thomas, 250
Major, John, Jr., 184
Malady/Malony, John, 150
Malcolm, Charles, 277
Mallen, Robert, 165
Mallery, Caleb, 257, 258
Mallery, John, 186
Mallory, Philip, 81, 121, 143
Malone/Melone, John, 101
Manes, Thomas, 246
Mangum, William, 80
Manley, Michael, 206
Manning, John, 104
Manning, Thomas, 112
Mansfield, John, 1
Mansfield, Joseph, 221
Mansfield, Samuel, 74, 86
Mansfield, Theophilus, 99, 115
Manson, Capt., 181
March, John, 141
March, Samuel, 126
Marders. James, 168
Marie, Peter, 287

Markham, James, 174, 246
Marlin, Thomas, 118
Marril, Daniel, 125
Marshal, Edward, 21
Marshal, Robert, 108
Marshall, Capt., 151
Marshall, Christ'r, 71
Marshall, Col., 71, 100, 150, 164
Marshall, John, 250
Marshall, Preserved, 208
Marshall, Thomas, 153
Marshall, William, 277
Martin, James, 17
Martin, Job, 118
Martin, John, 91
Martin, Joseph, 143, 211, 213
Martin, Nathan, 194
Martin, Patrick, 277
Martin, Thomas, 32, 223
Marvill, Francis, 47
Mash, John, Jr., 196
Mason, David, 172, 177, 181, 201
Mason, Elnathan, 214
Mason, Gideon, 181
Mason, James, 79
Mason, James, 93
Mason, John, 193
Mason, Lieutenant, 61
Mason, S. Thomson, 192
Mason, Stuart, 199
Massey, Edmund, 103
Massey, John, 296
Massie, Capt., 163
Massie, Taomas, 135
Massie, Thomas, 11, 181
Masterman, James, 241
Mather, Zachariah, 169
Mathewson, Zebede, 34
Matteny, Hezekiah, 159
Matthews, John, 244
Matthews, Nehemiah, 167
Matthews, Richard, 260

Matthews, Sampson, 15
Matthews, Stephen, 16
Matthews, William, 162
Mattocks, Samuel, 187
Maxwell, Robert, 263
Maxwell, William, 249
May, John, 195
May, Lem., 268
May, Peter, 158
May, Thomas, 42
Mazaret, John, 189
Mazuzen, Mark, 128
McCallion, James, 59
McCalvey, Thomas, 275
McCann, William, 277
McCarter, John, 66
McClay, John, 180, 229
McClean, John, 216
McClellan, Samuel, 212, 224, 226, 282
McCloud, Alexander, 222
McCloud/McCleod, Roderic, 45
McClure, William, 46
McConnel, Hugh, 198
McConnell, John, 232
McConnelly, John, 46
McCord, William, 122
McCormick, Hugh, 193
McCormick, James, 183
McCoy, John, 263
McDaniel, Andrew, 147
McDaniel, Terry, 83
McDaniel, Thomas, 44
McDonald, Phillip, 132
McDonald, Sergeant, 265
McDowall, Alexander, 274, 275
McDuel, David, 139
McElheny, John, 184
McFarland, James, 183, 260
McFarland, Mr., 11, 12
McFession, Caleb, 121
McGehee, Christopher, 189
McGrooder, Elias, 176

McGuire, Allegana, 176
McGuire, Anderson, 176
McIntire, Col., 37
McKay, Samuel, 11, 12
McKever, William, 222
McKilsener, William, 265
McKinsey, James, 266
McLaine, Donnel, 169
McLane, Oliver, 245
McLau, David, 277
McLaughlin, John, 126
McLean, James, 47
McMichael, Captain, 283
McMicken, Joseph, 189
McMunnigan, James, 226
McNeal, Johm, 66
McNeil, Hector, 65
McPherson, Samuel, 152
Mead, G., 273
Mead, John, 273
Meade, Capt., 180
Meade, Richard K., 44, 61
Meaughir, Thomas, 26
Mecaffatee, James, 125
Mechuet, John, 125
Meeks, Edward, 160
Meeks, Jesse, 79, 107, 171
Meggerson, Benjamin, 185
Megriegier, Capt., 134
Meigs, Return Jonathan, 147, 221
Melion, William, 186
Melone/Malone, John, 80
Melton, Charles, 64
Melton, Joel, 87
Melton, Richard, 167
Men, unnamed, 102, 233, 235
Mennis, Francis, 175, 180, 186
Mercer, John, 93
Mercer, Samuel, 31
Meredith, William, 166
Meriman, Thomas, 40

Meriwether, James, 130, 131, 141
Meriwether, Thomas, 63, 114, 120
Merriman, Enoch, 174
Merryman, Thomas, 28
Merserau, Joshua, 222
Metzgar, F. Anthony, 303
Mewse, John, 128
Middleton, William, 44
Miles, James, 184
Miles, John, 3d., 86
Miles, William, 184
Mill, Capt., 7
Millbank, Ensign, 236
Miller, Adam, 133
Miller, Charles, 52, 77, 269
Miller, Elisha, 50, 97
Miller, James, 251
Miller, Jeremiah, 85
Miller, John, 97, 225, 270
Miller, Joseph, 298
Miller, Philip, 236
Miller, William, 156
Mills, Burditt, 168
Mills, Gideon, 36
Mills, Jesse, 185
Mills, John, 95
Mills, William, 8
Millward, George, 6
Minard, Philip, 224
Miner, Stephen, Jr., 266
Ming, Capt., 89
Mingovintjole, Mr., 112
Minnis, Ensign, 27
Minor, Lieutenant, 163
Miramblr, John, 273
Mitchel, John, 8
Mitchel, Richard, 127
Mitchell, James, 196
Mitchell/Mitchel, John, 8, 183, 189, 211, 224, 235, 238
Mitchell, Richard, 125

Mitchell, Thomas, 189
Mitchill, Thomas, 38
Moeballe, Nic. Geo., 204
Money, William, 223
Money/Mooney, Nicholas, 32
Monk, Henry, 298
Monro, Peter, 83
Montgomery, James, 7
Montgomery, John, 133
Montgomery, Nathaniel, 227
Moody, Edward, 21
Moody, James, 126
Moody, Thomas, 199
Mooney, William, 243
Moore, Cleon, 96
Moore, Francis, 49, 60
Moore, George, 196
Moore, John, 130
Moore, Robert, 196
Moore, Thomas, 187, 196, 223
Moore/Moors, Joseph, 109
Moors, David, 297
More, Samuel, 233
More, Sarhuel, 159
Morgan, David, 108
Morgan, Haynes, 139
Morgan, John, 13, 28, 254, 293
Morrel, Lewis, 84
Morris, David, 290
Morris, James, 105
Morris, Nath. G., 191
Morris, Thomas, 139
Morrison, Ensign, 46
Morrisson, James, 169
Morse, Jonas, 299
Morse, Joseph, 247
Morton, Eben'r, 195
Morton, Hezekiah, 177
Mory, Thomas, 86
Mosby, Lieutenant, 98
Moseley, David, 145
Mosely, John, 217
Moss, John, 50, 222

Moss, Robert, 222
Mott, Samuel, 23, 26, 36
Mott, Richard, 69
Mountjoy, J., 145
Mowet, David, 267
Mowet, James Ryder, 267
Moyland/Moland, Joseph, 42, 47
Mozner, Samuel, 149
Mr. DeLeTombe, 283
Muchmore, John, 152
Mucklehenny, J., 147
Muhlenberg, John Peter Gabriel, 297
Mullins, John, 91
Mullins, Richard, 107
Munro, John, 93
Munson, Capt. T. 229
Murphey, Andrew, 251
Murphy, Daniel, 179
Murray, Daniel, 230
Murray, Samuel, 86
Murray, William, 161
Murrey/Murry, Michael, 262
Murvey, Anthony, 250
Musick, Daniel, 20
Musteen, William, 230
Mustees, Thomson, Louden, 19; Toby, Letix, 18
Muter, George, 17, 29, 48, 69, 102
Nagle, Peter, 100
Nance, Thomas Vaughan, 140
Nash, John, 230
Nason, Stephen, 123
Navarre, James, 185
Nebon, Mr., 226
Negroes, Arbado, Francis, 102; Augustus, Caesar, 287; Berry, James, 20; Black, Boston, 297; Brown, Robert, 282; Butler, Joe, 184; Cambridge, 179; Cuff, Cato, 298; Cole, Thomas, 122;

Negroes, Cunkery, Fortune, 150; Dermen, Prince, 276; Dick, 4; Dobbins, Charles, 299; Dunston, Wallace, 185; Evans, Phil., 184; Gage, Tom, 228; Gillam, 266; Harris, Aaron, 65; Harris, William, 181; Harry, 182; Joe, 272; Lyon, Tone, 116; Newport, Israel, 124; Pass, 179; Payne, Evan, 168; Perkins, Joshua, 113; Potame, John, 17; Prince, 266; Senior, John, 276; Smith, Charles, 140; Smith, James, 185; Springs, Able, 246; Stuart, Jack, 184; Thompson, Will., 4; Tom, 299; Valentine, Charles, 231, 236; William, 223; Wood, Thomas, 246
Negus, Jesse, 208
Neil, James, 275
Nelson, Ebenezer, 293
Nelson, Hugh, 53
Nelson, John, 145
Nelson, Thomas, 50
Nelson, William, 272
Neville, John, 107
New, Jesse, 92
Newel, Norman, 95
Newell, John, 286
Newhall, James, 232
Newport, Israel, 124
Newsmith, John, 225
Newton, Thomas, 171
Nicholas, Capt., 58, 155
Nicholas, John, 88
Nicholls, Thomas, 232
Nichols, Samuel, 280
Nickerson, William, 121
Nicolls, Jesse, 281
Nightengale, John, 250
Nixon, John, 201, 205

Noble, Francis, 272
Noble, William, 222
Noonon, John, 245
Norcutt, Ephraim, 232
Norcutt, John, 231
Norcutt, Zenas, 232
Norman, John, 212
Norton, Capt., 36
Norton, Edward, 36
Norton, Jedediah, 240
Norton, John, 291
Norton, Prince, 232
Norwood, Joseph, 129
Nucam, John, 293
Nuttle, John, 167
O'Brian, Dennis, 250
O'Brian, John, 253
O'Dear, Majo, 196
O'Deer, John, 236
O'Narra, Francis, 277
O'Neal, John, 107
Oaklin, John, 290
Oldham, Edward, 263
Oldham, Isaac, 186
Oldham, John, 230
Olney, Jeremiah, 251
Olney, Nebediah, 15
Orange/Orangeman, James, 114, 120, 129
Oreen, Joel, 202
Orell, Samuel, 100
Oris, Edward, 291
Orton, Thomas, 235
Osborn, Abraham, 44
Osborne, Mr., 43
Oswald, Eleazer, 74
Otherlrbrow, Samuel, 222
Otis, Joseph, 223, 267
Otis, Joseph, Jr., 259
Overstreet, Henry, 146
Overton, J. jr., 82
Overton, Thomas, 135
Owen, Thomas, 223

Owens, Evan, 168
Owens, William, 53
Page, James, 230
Page, Lieut., 103
Page, Samuel, 91
Paine, Samuel, 141
Paine, Simeon, 35
Pakis, Edward, 126
Palmer, Charles, 57
Pangman, Stephen, 148
Pannill, Joseph, 46
Parday, David, 124
Parent, Assha, 284
Paris, Jean, 283
Parker, Alexander, 50
Parker, Benjamin, 34
Parker, David, 224
Parker, Edward, 18
Parker, James, 46, 66, 240
Parker, Moses, 287
Parker, Richard, 53
Parker, Thomas, 222
Parks, James, 22
Parks, William/Wm., 22, 28
Parmele, Jeremiah, 128
Parsons, David, 106, 110
Parsons, Samuel Holden, 95, 228
Patch, George, 245
Patten, John, 126
Patterson, Colonel, 67, 75, 85, 98
Patterson, Daniel, 75
Patterson, George, 22
Patterson, James, 135, 285
Patterson, John, 10
Patterson, Peter, 99
Patterson, Robert, 41, 86
Patteson, Capt., 140
Patteson, Gideon, 66
Paty, Bernard, 183
Payne, Anthony, 121
Payne, Benja./Benjamin, 105, 121
Payne, Evan, 168

Payne, John, 227
Payne, Jonathan, 199
Payne, Joseph, 32
Peabody, Francis, 232
Peabody, Stephen, 209
Peale, Robert, 79
Pearce, Benjamin, 131
Pearl, Richard, 12
Pearse, John, 56
Pease, Joseph, 298
Peay, Henry, 75
Peck, Darius, 195
Peck, Lee, 71, 163
Peck, Thomas, 36
Peck, William, 206, 228
Pecker, Jacques, 292
Peed, Thomas, 53, 54
Pelham, Capt., 27
Pelham, Charles, 88, 89
Pelham, Peter, 113
Pelton, Ebenezer, Jr., 254
Penn, Gabriel, 15
Perkins, Capt., 198
Perkins, Harden, 36
Perkins, Joshua, 113
Perkins, Mr., 108
Perry, Simon, 168
Peters, Ed., 189
Peters, George, 7
Peters, Mr., 102
Peters, Robert, 189
Peterson, Peter, 124
Pettengile, Major, 285
Pettit, Charles, 135
Pettit, William, 96, 102
Pettye, John, 162
Pew, Eli, 277
Peyton, John, 139
Phelps, David, 208
Phelps, Nathan, 212
Phelps, Reiben, 208
Phelps, Silas, 208
Philip, John, 230

Philips, Benjamin, 196
Philips, John, 34, 88
Philips, Joseph, 129, 145
Philips, Peter, 261
Phillips, Capt., 38
Phillips, John, 17, 120
Phillips, Levin, 181
Phillips, Richard, 71
Phillips, Samuel, 90
Phillips, William, 124, 126
Phillis, Charles, 64
Phiney, Edmund, 8, 67
Pickerin, Motto, 250
Pickett, John, 58
Pierce, Anthony, 15
Pierce, Capt., 143
Pierce, Thos., 15
Pierce, William, Jr., 49, 72, 114
Pierceall, Benjamin, 139
Pierpont, Rob., 182
Pinard, Louis, 217
Pinginton, Wilson, 121
Piquet, Nicholas Pierre, 283
Pitman, Isaac, 243
Pitt, James, 49
Pittee, Daniel, 38
Plaisted, Joseph, 67
Plant, Williamson, 132
Platt, Thomas, 197
Platts, Dan, 270
Pleasants, John, 29
Pollard, Ben./Benj., 23, 66, 180
Pollard, Thomas, 182
Pomeroy, Isaac, 273
Pomroy, Col, 281
Pomroy, Samuel, 244
Pool, Samuel, 125
Poore, James, 21
Pope, Capt., 130, 140
Pope, John, 102, 117, 163
Pope, Thomas, 246
Portais, Jean, 292
Porter, Asa, 101

Porter, Benjamin, 119
Porter, Capt., 75
Porter, Jacob, 231
Porter, John, 191
Porter, Samuel, 179
Porvive, Joseph, 292
Potame, John, 17
Pottage, Aanias, 219
Potter, Asael, 130
Potter, Capt., 73
Potter, Charles, 160
Potter, Thomas/Tho., Jr., 52, 271
Potts, Stacy, 46
Pounds, John, 179
Powell, Thomas, 171
Poythress, Robert, 43, 59
Poythress, William, 143
Pratt, Allen, 225
Pratt, James, 91
Pratt, Joel, 270
Pratt, Thomas, 230
Pratt, William, 103
Prentice, Jonas, 116
Prentice, Lieut. Colonel, 139
Prian, William, 222
Pribble, Daniel, 126
Price, Joseph, 119
Price, Ralph, 275
Price, Seward, 230
Price, Thomas, 127, 132, 133
Price, William, 133, 230
Priest, Elijah, 232
Prince, William, 180
Pritchett, Pater, 154
Prittraud, Mr,, 202
Privart, John, 125
Pryor, H., 140
Pryor, Zachariah, 53, 54
Pucket, Page, 167
Puckinghorn, William, 31
Puling, Augustus, 212
Purdie, David, 99
Putnam, Captain, 1

Putnam, Col., 247
Putnam, Israel, 227
Putnam, Rufus, 105
Pye, Walter, 239
Quarles, Henry, 77, 199, 234
Quarles, James, 84
Querry, Richard, 100
Quesenburg, John, 103
Quinn, John, 104
Radiger, William, 248
Ragan, Brice, 155
Ragan, Philip, 155
Ragland, John, 107
Ragland, Samuel, 69
Ragsdale, Drury, 82
Ragsdale, Edward, 78
Rain, Anthony, 177
Raines, Giles, 75, 82
Raines, Peter Green, 189, 211
Rainey, William, 196
Rakestraw, Ro., 158, 170
Ramay, John, 185
Ramor, Thomas, 126
Ramsay, Caleb, 139
Ramson, John, 218
Randal, James, 180
Randall, Ichabod, 193
Randall, Thomas, 284
Randol, John, 178
Randolph, Harwell, 236
Randolph, James, 230
Randon, Benajah, 35
Rankin, John, 55
Rano, John, 99
Ransone, Augustine, 53, 54
Ransone, Thomas, 53, 54
Ratcliff, Davis, 160
Ratcliff, George, 80
Rathbone, Gilbert, 52
Raub, Jacob, 303
Rawson, Mr., 290
Ray, John, 46
Raylay, Michael, 259

Raymend, William, 123
Raymond, Joshua, 266
Read, Benjamin, 95
Read, John, 107
Read, Joseph, 7
Ready, John, 209
Reason, Reuben, 163
Redford, Edward, 244
Reding, Henry, 263
Redman, Martin, 79
Reed, Captain, 67, 294
Reed, Col., 52
Reed, Enoch, 60
Reed, Joseph, 39
Reed, Lieut., 115
Reed, Samuel, 126
Reemer, John, 138
Rees, David, 22
Reeves, Charles, 168
Reid, Nathan, 132, 133
Reinwald, Wm., 232
Relph, David, 18
Remick, Lieut., 123
Rennolds, J., Jr., 146
Revere, Paul, 232
Reves, Daniel, 290
Rice, James, 139
Rice, Seth, 138
Rice, Stephen, 97
Richards, Samuel, 110, 145
Richardson, Jacob, 281
Richardson, William, 188
Richey, James, 78
Richmond, William, 16, 18, 19, 24, 31, 37, 38
Ridgway, Edward, 30
Ridley, John, 256
Riel, Conrad, 279
Rigauden, Francis, 287
Rigdel, C., 197
Riggs, Abimeleck, 55, 59
Riggs, Capt., 84
Rigs, John, 171

Riley, Edward, 23
Rine, Barnet, 36
Ring, Nathaniel, 124
Rise, Alexander, 230
Rittor, John, 245
Rivington, Mr., 215
Roach, Thomas, 92
Robarts, Ezekiel, 210
Robbins, James, 124
Roberts, Dudley, 208
Roberts, Griffeth, 222
Roberts, Hezekiah, 139
Roberts, John, 165
Roberts, Matthew, 189
Roberts, Nehemiah, 139
Roberts, William, 160
Robertson, John, 129
Robertson, Joseph, 301
Robertson, Moses, 176
Robertson, Thomas, 120, 234
Robinson, Abiathar, 165
Robinson, Benja., 125
Robinson, Capt., 23, 26, 36, 89
Robinson, James, 23, 284
Robinson, John, 29, 51, 242, 273, 284
Robinson, T., 285
Robinson, Thomas, 29, 298
Robinson, William, 179, 239
Roche, E., 158
Rock, James, 292
Rodgers, Arthur, 55
Rodmore, John, 261
Roe, Abijah, 165
Rogers, Larking, 129
Rogers, Major, 288
Rogers, Robert, 67
Rogers, Thomas, 32
Rogers, William, 144, 241
Rogers, Zabdiel, 279
Roose, Anthony, 222
Root, James, 211
Root, Moses, 47

Roper, William, 244
Rose, Benjamin, 7
Rose, Gideon, 130
Rose, Nathaniel, 106, 110
Roseberry, James, 222
Ross, David, 117
Ross, John, 219
Ross, Samford, 35
Rostin, Jacques, 283
Rotham, William, 208
Rotier, Jean, 158
Rougon, Antroine, 292
Rounds, George, 33
Rounds, Isaac, 37
Rouse, Thomas, 198
Rowden, Abraham, 32
Rowland, John, 176
Rowland, Uriah, 74
Royce, Matthew, 208
Rucker, Lieut., 119
Rudder, Epaphroditus, 78
Rudiner, Epaph., 108
Ruffin, Capt., 10
Rush, Henry, 233
Rush, James, 160
Russel, John, 42
Russel, Nathan, 167
Russel, William, 161
Russell, Col., 64, 269
Russell, George, 157, 170
Russell, James, 139
Russell, John, 157, 170
Russell, William, 281
Rustin, Joseph, 222
Rutherford, James, 256
Ryan, John, 91
Ryan, Thomas, 91
Rynes, John, 207
Sack, John, 98
Sack, Thomas, 98
Sadler, John, 230
Sage, Comfort, 26
Sage, Edward, 161

Sager, Joshua, 52
Samator, Anthony, 84
Sammis, Jarvis, 152
Sammons, Samuel, 181
Sampson, Aaron, 140
Sampson, Joseph, 46
Sampson, William, 267
Samuel, Mr., 214
Sandal, Osmond, 158
Sanders, Benjamin, 186
Sanders, Ephras, 208
Sanders, Jesse, 199
Sanders, Mr., 232
Sandford, William, 141
Sandford/Sanford, Thomas, 270
Sandler, James, 222
Sanford, Ezekiel, 104, 105
Sanford, Peleg, 240
Sanford, Philemon, 203
Sanford, William, 50
Sangster, John, 178
Sargent, Capt., 198
Sargent, W., 275
Sarls, Thomas, 251
Sartwell, Simon, 138
Saullard, John, 25
Saunders, Captain, 1
Saunders, Celey, 146
Saunders, John, 65, 144, 155
Saunders, Ro. Hyde, 130
Saunders, Robert, 93
Saunders, Robert H., 179
Saunders, Samuel, 118
Saunders, William, 103, 137, 168, 179, 189
Savage, Abijah, 149, 191
Savage, J., 164
Savage, Simon, 46
Savale, Charles, 283
Sawin, Benjamin, 299
Sawtill, Thomas, 220
Sayer/Sawyer, Jotham, 209
Sayles, John, 44

Scates, John, 179
Schenk, John I., 234
Scolfield, James, 127
Scott, Amasa, 105
Scott, Captain, 43, 59, 227
Scott, Ebenezer, 44
Scott, Joseph, 89
Scott, Samuel, 32, 129, 179
Scott, Thomas, 190
Scott, William, 224
Scovel, John, 262
Scribner, Herekiah, 272
Scribner, Stephen, 208
Scruggs, Gross, 32
Seagrave, Edward, 7
Seale, Lewis, 180
Sealeck, Darling, 272
Sealeck, Nathan, 272
Sears, Joseph, 18
Seaward, Benjamin, 117
Seeley, Abner, 199
Seger, Mr., 232
Selah, John, 278
Selden, Joseph, 135
Selden, Samuel, 27
Self, James, 33
Self, William, 33
Senior, John, 276
Sergeant, Capt., 94
Serjeant/Sergeant, Paul Dudley, 1
Sewall, Henry, 86
Seward, Benjamin, 79
Seward, Thomas, 133
Seymour, Thomas Y., 67
Seymour, Uriah, 211, 213
Shackelford, William, 131
Shade, George, 151
Shapley, Adam, 254, 269, 271, 282
Sharaway, Capt., 195
Sharpe, John, 140
Shaw, Nath'l, 240

Shaw, Thomas, 222
Shearman, John, 118
Sheffield, Ichabod, 124
Sheldon, Elisha, 67, 257
Shelton, Beverley, 60
Shepard, Abraham, 26
Shepard/Sheppard/Shepherd, William, 13, 73, 77, 130, 228, 242, 276
Sherburne, Henry, 110, 134, 141, 149, 191, 194, 227
Sherder, Henry, 232
Sherman, Samuel, 27
Sherman, William, 27
Sherwood, Amos, 212
Sherwood, John, 212
Sherwood, Richard, 204
Shey, Richard, 226
Shield, John, 63, 93
Shields/Sheilds, William, 5, 288
Shiels, William, 65
Shipman, John, 282
Shippen, William, 268
Shippey, Abraham, 244
Shippey, Nicholas, 84
Shoemaker, John, 277
Shore, Thomas, 204
Shores, Richard, 230
Short, Thomas, 157
Showels, Nathaniel, 104
Shreve, Israel, 10
Silk, Thomas, 182
Silly, Jonathan, 6
Silvey, Archibald, 179
Simmons, William, 257
Simpson, Robert, 74
Simpson, Thomas, 253
Sinclair, Charles, 133
Singleton, Robert, 196
Sire, Antoine-Thomas, 283
Skeen, Philip Wharton, 177
Skelton, James, 186

Skinner, John, 211, 212, 213. 214
Skinner, Roswel, 211, 213
Skipwith, Henry, 300
Skipwith, Peyton, 176
Slate, Thomas, 246
Slaughter, John, 117
Slayton, Reuben, 228
Slight, Mr., 272
Slocum, Edward, 124
Smart, Alexander, 127, 161
Smith, Alexander, 115
Smith, Andrew, 65
Smith, Archibald/Arthur, 1, 29, 31
Smith, Captain, 46, 60, 78, 301
Smith, Charles, 140, 191
Smith, Col., 84
Smith, Ezra, 268
Smith, Francis, 157
Smith, Frederick, 38
Smith, Granville, 83, 199
Smith, Gregory, 42
Smith, Jacob, 42, 232
Smith, James, 149, 164, 185, 230, 240
Smith, John, 58, 60, 89, 113, 125, 126, 136, 160, 161, 162, 184, 222, 227, 277
Smith, John Gilbert, 73
Smith, Joseph, 83, 212, 230
Smith, Joshua, 302
Smith, Josiah, 153
Smith, Jury, 84
Smith, Levin, 135
Smith, Lewis, 27
Smith, Martin, 77
Smith, Matthew, 27, 107
Smith, Matthias, 3
Smith, Moses, 149
Smith, Nathaniel, 25, 119
Smith, Peter, 277
Smith, Reuben, 45
Smith, Robert, 145
Smith, Roswel, 51
Smith, Rozzel, 16, 18
Smith, Sam./Samuel, 192, 215
Smith, Simeon, 3, 215, 219
Smith, Solomon, 121
Smith, Thomas, 84, 93, 220
Smith, William, 43, 64, 85, 230
Smock, Abraham, 30
Snapley, Adam, 197
Snevd, Edward, 42
Snoke, Thomas, 51
Snow, James, 130
Snow, John, 91
Snyder, George, 201, 202
Snydor, Fortunatus, 296
Soleham, John, 230
Soper, Allen, 41
Soper, Amasa, 150
Sorel/Sorrel/Sorrell, John, 82, 108, 132
Soul, Moses, 1, 2
Southall, Mr., 182
Spear, Henry, 98
Spencer, John, 211, 213
Spencer, Joseph, 14, 20
Spendergress, Thomas, 241
Spiller, B. C., 188
Spinkhouse, Anthony, 277
Spinney, Daniel, 161
Spong, John, 296
Spotswood, Alexander, 141, 155
Sprague, James, 290
Springer, Joseph, 44
Springs, Able, 246
Sprouse, Charles, 117
St. John, John, 105
Stacnon, George, 249
Stacy, Joseph, 230
Stacy, Lt. Col., 248
Stacy, Wm., 52
Stafford, Thomas, 137
Stalker, Andrew, 197

Stanback, Francis, 144
Stanhope, Henry E., 41
Stanhope, Henry Edwin, 8
Stanley, George Newmash, 51
Stanley, John, 186
Stanley, Thomas, 186
Stanley, Thomas, Jr., 186
Stanly, Nathaniel, 67
Stanton, Col., 56
Stapler, William, 244
Star, David, 7
Stark, Col., 67
Stark, W., 144
Starkey, Noah, 208
Starr, Col., 254
Starr, David, 73
Starr, Joshua, 148
Starr, Moses, 125
Steal, Seth, 211
Stearns, Col., 207
Stearns, Jonathan, 65
Stearns, Josiah, 281
Stears, Chapman, 291
Stebbins, Seth, 153
Stebbins, Thomas, 41
Steel, Seth, 213
Steel, Thomas, 205, 212
Steele, John, 139
Steele, Robert, 241
Stephens, Benjamin, 85
Stephens, James, 54
Stephens, John, 131
Stephens, Peter, 287
Stevens, Capt., 219
Stevens, Ebenezer, 169
Stevens, Edward, 159
Stevens, Eliphalet, 290
Stevens, Jeremy, 107
Stevens, Richard, 80, 101
Stevens, Smith, 160
Stevens, William, 80, 95
Stevenson, Capt., 146, 156
Steward, Benjamin, 230

Steward/Stewart, Captain, 6, 267
Steward, Maximillian, 137
Steward, William, 115
Stewart, James, 26
Stewart, Lemuel, 3
Stewart, William, 179, 245
Stiff, John, 78
Still, Henry, 140
Still, John, 186, 276
Still, Samuel, 208
Still, William, 83
Stith, J., 272
Stith, John, 48, 61
Stith, Joseph, 118, 122
Stith, Richard, 118, 122
Stoddard, Capt., 164
Stoddard, Nath./Nathan, 149, 150
Stokes, John, 140, 155
Stokes, Young, 23
Stone, Enos, 125, 127
Stone, John H., 152
Stone, Moses, 290
Stone, Noah, 112
Stone, Pritchard, 133
Stone, William, 212, 235, 238
Stoner, John, 62
Stores, Printice, 278
Story, Wm., 190
Stouton, Joseph, 160
Stover, John, 73
Stow, John Johnson, 178
Stow, Timothy, 38
Strange, William, 48, 61
Stratton, Henry, 69
Straw, William, 186
Strawther, Mr., 155
Strickland, Ichabod, 208
Strong, Asa, 27
Strong, John, 58
Strother, Lieut., 120
Stuart, Jack, 184
Stubblefield, Peter, 76

Stubbs, Samuel, 65
Studavant, Eliphalet, 3
Stupart, George, 216
Stuston, Levi, 231
Sufield, James, 125
Sulfa, Francis, 125
Sullivan, Conor, 183
Sullivan, James, 265
Sullivan, John, 191, 228
Sullivan, Patrick, 91
Summer, John, 133
Sutherland, Lancelot, 139
Sutherland, Thomas, 139
Sutton, Nathan, 30
Sutton, Thomas, 167
Swan, Edward, 246
Swan, Elias, 289
Swaney, John, 210
Sweet, Azariah, 77
Sweet, Samuel, 138
Sweetland, Richard, 65
Swepson, John, 176
Swift, Heman, 99, 112, 274
Syllia, Lewis, 73
Symonds, Capt., 8
Syze, James, 221
Tabb, Augustine, 193
Taber, Samuel, Jr., 200
Taft, Isaac, 249
Talbert, Capt., 123
Talbot, Charles, 122
Taliaferro, Peter, 88
Taliaferro, William Harris, 88
Taller, William, 118
Talley, Micajah, 186
Talley, Nathan, 186
Tallman, James, 30
Talman, Colonel, 55, 59, 66
Talman, Giles, 36
Tamborough, John, 83
Tandy, Roger, 229
Tankersley, John, 69, 168, 171
Tappan, Isaac, 216

Targee, Philip, 245
Tarrant, Manlove, 171
Tart, John, 137
Tate, George, 231
Tate, Robert, 62, 255
Taylor, Benoni, 123
Taylor, Daniel, 241
Taylor, Deborah, 85
Taylor, Francis, 26, 68, 156
Taylor, George, 260
Taylor, J. S., 279
Taylor, James, 21, 85, 163, 181
Taylor, John, 66, 77, 80, 189
Taylor, Richard, 19, 143, 171, 204
Taylor, Samuel, 271
Taylor, Thomas, 137, 211
Taylor, William, 222
Teamey, Matthews, 67
Tearry, Champness, 230
Temple, Benjamin, 58
Terrel/Terrell, Jonathan, 66, 106
Terrell, Harry, 32, 118, 121
Terry, James, 145
Tetherly, Samuel, 284
Tew, John, 193
Thacker, William, 69
Tharp, Jesse, 221
Thayer, Capt., 151
Thayer, Jedediah, 152
Thomas, Arthur, 232
Thomas, Henry, 222
Thomas, John, 73, 103, 167, 230
Thomas, Nehemiah, 231
Thomas, Samuel, 145, 172
Thomas, William, 129
Thompson, Capt., 84
Thompson, Cornelius, 174
Thompson, David, 232
Thompson, John, 66, 230
Thompson, John D., 278
Thompson, Matthew, 32
Thompson, Robert, 170

Thompson, William/Will., 4, 94, 124, 235, 236, 238, 257
Thomson, Drury, 175
Thomson, Edward, Jr., 208
Thomson, Farley, 175
Thomson, George, 69
Thomson, Joshua, 147
Thomson, Louden, 19
Thomson, Perkins, 154
Thomson, Perkins, Jr., 183
Thomson, William, 159, 233
Thomson/Thompson, George, 185
Thorington, Thomas, 137
Thornhill, John, 19
Thorns, Richard, 296
Thornton, Peter Presly, 21
Thornton, Randolph, 78
Thorp, E., 290, 291
Thorp, Eliphalet, 217
Thorp, Solomon, 30
Thrasher, Samuel, 240
Thrift, John Graves, 178
Thweatt, Thomas, 107, 131
Tidd, Samuel, 281
Tier, James, 222
Tillage, Richard, 38
Tillard, Captain, 64
Tilleson, Benjamin, 179
Tillet, Pierre, 283
Timberlake, John, 284
Timberlake, Richard, 250
Tinker, Nehemiah, 267
Tinsley, Richard, 243
Tisdale, Thomas, 231, 236
Tivy, Thomas, 31
Toby, Letix, 18
Toley, Daniel, 230
Tolley, Richard, 207
Tom, John, 207
Tomkies, Charles, 37, 39, 52, 54
Tomlin, John, 83
Tompkins, Daniel, 80
Tompkins, Robert, 114, 178
Tooley, Ennell, 131
Tooley, Jesse, 121
Touper, Thomas, 290
Tourtelot, Abraham, 207
Towley, Phero, 212
Towns, John, 78
Townsing, George, 137
Townsing, John, 137
Tracy, Isaac, 279
Traiger, Paul, 240
Traille, Peter, 300
Trap, Mrs. Thomas, 155
Trap, Thomas, 155
Travis, Andrew, 277
Travis, Edward, 93
Treadwell, M., 126
Trescott, Experance, 199
Tresscott, Lemuel, 186
Triplett, George, 64
Tronzo, Jacob, 277
Troop, James, 9
Troubridge, John, 125
Truffin, Joshua, 194
Tucker, James, 189, 211
Tucker, Lemuel, 244
Tuckerman, Abraham, 67
Tuckerman, John, 232
Tulley, Daniel, 180
Tumberlen, James, 137
Tunison, Cornelius, 3
Tupper, Benjamin, 204
Turberville, Geo., 79
Turberville, George Lee, 160
Turley, John, 230
Turner, Benjamin, 131, 179
Turner, Capt., 97
Turner, David, 152
Turner, James, 91, 139
Turner, John, 95, 96
Turner, Kinchen/Kenchen, 29, 30
Turner, Thomas, 74
Turner, William, 50

Turpin, Ephraim, 12
Turrel, Josiah, 44
Tutt, Thomas, 139
Tyler, Ambrose, 105
Tyler, Col., 82
Tyler, Francis, 186
Ulmer, Philip, 73
Underhill, Isham, 181
Usrey, Richard, 186
Valentine, Charles, 231, 236
Valentine, Edward, 49, 150
Valentine, Jacob, 14, 28, 40
Valentine, Lieut., 78
Valnais, Mr., 226
Van Rosen, Ryner, 41
Van Schaick, Goose, 7
Vandike, Charles, 30
Vansant, Capt, 49
Vassel, Benjamin, 152
Vaughan, Daniel, 291
Vaughan, James, 14, 15, 93
Vaughan, John, 230, 232
Vauner, John, 224
Vauters, David, 76
Vawter, Samuel, 97
Venjoul, John Lewis, 67
Vential, Dominick, 211
Verdier, Stephen, 226
Verry, Benjamin, 66
Vest, John, 48, 61, 78
Viat, John, 197
Viat, Simon, 292
Vibal, Jean Baptiste, 292
Vilgouain, Jean Bapteste, 283
Vinceson, Henry, 179
Vivion, Charles, 101
Vogel, Frederick, 303
Vogel, George, 303
Voirambour, Jean Joseph, 292
von Heer, Bartholomew, 234
Vose, Joseph, 140, 164, 224
Vose, Spencer, 231

Wadden, Thomas, 243
Waddy, Francis, 33
Wade, Moses, 179
Wadhams, Jonathan, 203
Wadsworth, General, 298
Wadsworth, Samuel, 166, 218
Wagstaff, John, 50
Wait, Daniel, 82, 166
Wakefield, William, 133
Wakeman, Stephen, 217
Waker, Randolph, 168
Walch, Thomas, 56
Walcom, Markalm, 222
Walcott, Capt., 164
Wales, John, 180
Walker, David, 176, 178
Walker, George, 98
Walker, John, 246
Walker, Mr., 232
Walker, Omes, 230
Walker, Robert, 253
Walker, Samuel, 277
Walker, William, 151
Wallace, James, 24
Wallen, Jonathan, 31, 51
Waller, Edward, 69, 75, 231, 237
Waller, William, 256
Walsh, Elemuel, 126
Walter, John, 219
Walters, Walter, 10, 83
Walton, George, 32
Walton, Jesse H., 187
Walton, John, 35
Walton, Robert, 32
Wampee, Samuel, 124
Wampey, Samuel, 200
Ward, Artemas, 28
Ward, Capt., 104
Ward, Col., 6
Ward, Lieutenant, 46
Ward, Robert, 54
Ward, Thomas, 246

Ward, William, 222
Warden, Jesse, 27
Wardrop, David, 38
Ware, Nicholas, 49
Warner, Benjamin, 232
Warner, Daniel, 139
Warner, John, 51
Warner, Samuel, 94
Warner, Seth, 199, 218, 219
Warren, John, 161
Warren, Timothy, 179
Warren, William, 107, 179
Warwick, Joseph, 76
Wash, John, 255
Washburn, Gideon, 65
Washburn, Seth, 275
Washington, George, 41, 106, 181, 185, 274
Waterbury, David, 290, 301
Waterman, Capt., 279
Waters, James, 235, 238
Waters, Thomas, 62
Waters, William, 137
Watkins, Nathan, 126
Watkins, Thomas, 97
Watkins, William, 179
Watson, James, 133
Watson, Johannes, 207
Watson, John, 169, 178
Watson, Mr., 45
Watson, William, 230
Watt, Benjamin, 83
Watt, James, 83
Watts, Arthur, 196
Watts, John, 144
Way, Abner, 265
Way, Ira, 290
Way, Samuel, 208
Wayles, John, 191
Wayne, Anthony, 288
Weathers, Zebulon, 47
Weaver, James, 121, 122

Weaver, Samuel, 35
Webb, Captain, 73
Webb, Charles, 2, 95, 106, 109, 110, 111, 119, 174, 200
Webb, James, 110
Webb, John, 73, 117
Webb, Joseph, 285, 286
Webb, Lt. Col., 281
Webb, Samuel, 218
Webb, Samuel B., 90, 169, 218, 278
Webster, Henry, 80
Webster, John, 30, 57, 65, 117, 185, 241
Webster, Levi, 152
Weckwin, Grant, 291
Welch, John, 264
Welch, Nathaniel, 167
Welch, Patrick, 178
Welch, Thomas, 166
Weld, Benjamin, 232
Weld, John, 232
Weld, Mr., 232
Wellman, Edward, 94
Wells, Colonel, 266
Wells, John, 143, 170, 230, 253
Wells, Levi, 266, 274, 275
Wells/Welles, Jonathan, 252
Welsh, James, 91
Welsh, John, 75
Welsh, John Lewis, 59
Welsh, Michael, 168
Wescot, Ebenezer, 112
Wescott, Zorobabel, 18
Wesson, James, 159, 165
West, George, 59
West, John, 112
West, Thomas, 159
West, William, 47
Westcott, Capt., 16
Westcott, Gid., 51, 242
Westcott, Wright, 22, 34, 182

Westcott/Westcot, Zorobabel, 18, 19
Westfall, Capt., 44
Weston, Col., 104
Weston, George, 53, 54
Weston, James, 180
Wharton, Samuel, 146
Wheatly, John, Jr., 196
Wheaton, Charles, 199
Wheaton, John, 162
Wheelar, Edward, 152
Wheeler, John, 197
Wheeler, Samuel, 248
Wheelock, Moses, 38
Wherton, Jacob, 58
Whigh, Edward, 124
Whipple, Abraham, 38
Whipple, Capt., 123
Whipple, Thomas, 207
Whitcom, Ezra, 244
White, Charles, 7
White, Daniel, 227
White, David, 72
White, Ebenezer, 232
White, Edward, 99
White, George, 162
White, Henry, 177
White, Jacob, 226
White, James, 53, 54
White, John, 58, 144, 222
White, Morris, 133
White, N., 250
White, Robert Tate, 72, 114
White, Samuel, 64
White, Tarpley, 72
Whitehurst, Levi, 71
Whitlow, John, 107
Whitmore, Jabez, 208
Whitmore/Whitmore, Gurdon, 47
Whitney, William, 212
Whittam, James, 126
Whittelsey, Nathan, 251

Wiempey, Charles, 110
Wigger, Ely, 225
Wiggon, Francis, 232
Wight, John, 247
Wikoff, Peter, 30
Wilcocks/Willcox, Martin, 294, 295
Wilcocks/Willcox, Mary, 294, 295
Wilcox, Daniel, 211, 213
Wilde, John, 193
Wilkins, Argyle, 296
Wilkins, Robert, 48, 61, 78
Wilkins, William, 168
Wilkinson, Christopher, 277
Wilkinson, Gabriel, 119
Wilkinson, John, 102
Wilkinson, Joseph, 244
Willard, Colonel, 22
Willard, John, 107
Willbery, Capt., 5
Willcocks, James, 229
Williams Ezekiel, 148
Williams, Anthony, 230
Williams, Archibald, 83
Williams, David, 125, 127
Williams, Ebenezer, 99, 165
Williams, Ezekiel, 42, 148, 166, 195, 200, 206, 208, 247, 269
Williams, Hart, 8
Williams, Henry, 2, 104
Williams, Jesse, 184
Williams, John, 2, 19, 48, 61, 72, 78, 114, 140, 141, 255, 266
Williams, Joseph, 59
Williams, Lazarus, 129
Williams, Mr., 273
Williams, Thomas, 117, 205, 212, 230
Williams, William, 173
Williams, Zadock, 159
Williamson, John, 160

Williamson, Littleton, 60
Williamson, Thomas, 255
Williamson, William, 65, 178
Willie, Thomas, 137
Willis, Abel, 49
Willis, John, 52, 53, 54, 78, 81
Willis, Zachariah, 58
Willman, William, 214
Wills, Elleck, 178
Wills, John, 230
Willson, Alexander, 231
Willson, Daniel, 152
Wilmore, Henry, 196
Wilson, Charles, 32
Wilson, Andrew, 236, 255
Wilson, David, 166
Wilson, George, 204
Wilson, James, 198, 272
Wilson, John, 54, 161, 224
Wilson, Joseph, 83, 224
Wilson, Munford, 230
Wilson, Samuel, 41
Wilson, William, 7
Winchester, James, 128
Winfrey, Lieutenant, 62
Winn, Henry, 249
Winn, James, 23
Winn, John, 70
Winslove, William, 268
Winslow, John, 169
Winslow, William, 254, 290
Winstin, Capt., 82
Winston, Capt., 58
Winston, John, 132, 187
Winston, William, 58
Wire, Robert, 274
Witechurch, Nath., 232
Withers, James, 119
Witman, William, 232
Witt, Benjamin, 243
Wolcott, Simon, 35
Wolfkill, John, 261

Womack, David, 229
Womath, David, 189
Womock, David, 180
Wompey, John, 57
Wonycott, Edward, 131
Wood, Benjamain, 55
Wood, Charles, 136
Wood, Jacob, 30
Wood, James, 112, 125
Wood, John, 252
Wood, M., 265
Wood, Nathan, 281
Wood, Thomas, 35, 246
Wood, William, 13, 20, 89, 232
Woodbridge, Ruggles, 40
Wooderfield, Robert, 251
Wooderosse, William, 229
Woodford, William, 192
Woodhouse, William, 46
Woodkough, William, 180
Woodmansee, Squire, 35
Woodruff, Charles, 211, 213
Woodruff, David, 36
Woodruff, William, 190
Woods, Richard, 15
Woodson, Hughes, 97, 116
Woodward, Caleb, 121
Woodward, Charles, 137
Woodworth, Simeon, 6, 56, 57
Woolley, Abraham, 30
Workman, John, 274
Worsham, Richard, 66, 83
Worthington, Nathaniel, 124
Worthington, William, 208
Wright, Aaron, 41, 125
Wright, Dudley, 119
Wright, Francis, 139
Wright, John, 96, 192
Wright, Richard, 132
Wright, Solomon, 152
Wright, Sugar, 24
Wright, William, 139, 141

Wyatt, William, 13
Wyckoff, Peter, 262
Wyer, John, 243
Wyllys, Samuel, 74, 77, 99, 106, 110, 119, 130, 145, 162, 164, 206, 215
Wyman, Jeduthen, 231
Wyman, John, 259
Wyman, Jonas, 109
Yarborough, Cha., 129
Yeomans, Daniel, 265
Yherts, John, 273
Yocake, James, 200
Young, Daniel, 132
Young, Henry, 118
Young, Ralph, 192
Younger, Joseph, 157, 170
Younghusband, Isaac, 13, 27
Yours, Thomas, 192
Zaber, Jean Michael, 292
Zackley, William, 180
Zidilidge, William, 230

www.ingramcontent.com/pod-product-compliance
Lightning Source LLC
Chambersburg PA
CBHW071758300426
44116CB00009B/1127